TECHNIQUES IN ADLERIAN PSYCHOLOGY

TECHNIQUES IN ADLERIAN PSYCHOLOGY

Edited by
Jon Carlson, Psy.D., Ed.D., and Steven Slavik, M.A.

ACCELERATED DEVELOPMENT
A member of the Taylor & Francis Group

USA	Publishing Office:	ACCELERATED DEVELOPMENT *A member of the Taylor & Francis Group* 1101 Vermont Avenue, NW, Suite 200 Washington, DC 2000-53521 Tel: (202) 289-2174 Fax: (202) 289-3665
	Distribution Center:	ACCELERATED DEVELOPMENT *A member of the Taylor & Francis Group* 1900 Frost Road, Suite 101 Bristol, PA 19007-1598 Tel: (215) 785-5800 Fax: (215) 785-5515
UK		Taylor & Francis Ltd. 1 Gunpowder Square London EC4A 3DE

TECHNIQUES IN ADLERIAN PSYCHOLOGY

1 2 3 4 5 6 7 8 9 0 EBEB 9 8 7

This book was set in Times Roman. Technical development by Cynthia Long. Cover design by Michelle Fleitz.

A CIP catalog record for this book is available from the British Library.
∞ The paper in this publication meets the requirements of the ANSI Standard Z39.48-1984 (Permanence of Paper)

Library of Congress Cataloging-in-Publication Data

Techniques in Adlerian psychology / edited by Jon Carlson and Steven
Slavik.
p. cm.
Collection of classic and recent papers published between 1964 and
1994.
Includes bibliographical references and index.
ISBN 1-56032-555-0 (pbk. : alk. paper)
1. Psychotherapy. 2. Adlerian psychology. I. Carlson, Jon.
II. Slavik, Steven.
RC480.5.T39 1997
616.89'14—dc21 97-8530
CIP

ISBN 1-56032-555-0 (paper)

To the past editors of the *Journal of Individual Psychology:* Alfred Adler, Rudolf Dreikurs, Heinz Ansbacher, Ray Corsini, Guy Manaster, and Jon Carlson.

CONTENTS

PREFACE xi

Section I.
INTRODUCTION

EDITORS' COMMENTS 1

Section II.
GENERAL TECHNIQUES

EDITORS' COMMENTS 3

I-Thou Relationship Versus Manipulation in Counseling and Psychotherapy 7
Sidney M. Jourard

Interpretation of Patient Behavior Through Goals, Feelings, and Context 13
Alvin R. Mahrer

Encouraging Client Responsibility 24
Thomas J. Murphy

Section III.
INDIVIDUAL ADULT COUNSELING AND THERAPY TECHNIQUES

EDITORS' COMMENTS 35

Life Style Assessment: A Demonstration Focused on Family Constellation 39
Harold H. Mosak

The Family Constellation in Personality Diagnosis 56
Bernard H. Shulman
The Use of Birth Order Information in Psychotherapy 69
Lucille K. Forer

Part A. *Early Recollection Analysis* 79

The Use of Early Recollections in Psychotherapy 81
Helene Papanek
Changing Mistaken Beliefs Through Visualization of Early Recollections 89
MaryAnn Lingg and Terry Kottman
A Practical Use of Dreams 95
Steven Slavik

Part B. *Questioning and Confrontation Techniques* 105

The "Rediscovery" of Interventive Interviewing 107
Len Sperry
Confrontation Techniques in Adlerian Psychotherapy 111
Bernard H. Shulman
Confrontation Techniques 121
Bernard H. Shulman

Part C. *Use of Stories, Fables, Aphorisms* 129

The Use of Parables and Fables in Adlerian Psychotherapy 131
Kristin R. Pancner
Religious Allusions in Psychotherapy 143
Harold H. Mosak

Part D. *Acting "Af If"* 151

Variations of the "As If" Technique 153
Mark S. Carich

Part E. *Humor* 161

Laughing Together: Humor as Encouragement in Couples Counseling 163
Robert J. McBrien

Part F. *Paradox and "Spitting in the Soup"* 173

The Relapse Technique in Counseling and Psychotherapy 175
Raymond J. Corsini
The Paradoxical Prescription in Individual Psychology 182
John D. West, Frank O. Main, and John J. Zarski

Traps and Escapes: An Adlerian Approach to Understanding Resistance and Resolving Impasses in Psychotherapy 193
Richard Royal Kopp and Carol Kivel

Part G. *Hypnosis* 203

Incorporating Hypnotherapeutic Methods into Ongoing Psychotherapy 205
Len Sperry
Reorientation: The Use of Hypnosis for Life-Style Change 213
Barbara Fairfield
Hypnosis, Tailoring, and Multimodal Treatment 221
Len Sperry and Jon Carlson

Part H. *Substance Abuse* 229

Alcoholics and Their Treatment: Current Adlerian Thinking 231
Joseph (Yosi) Prinz
Alcoholism and Drug Dependency: Some Mistakes We Can Avoid 244
Helen K. Cooley
Marital Therapy with Alcohol-Affected Couples: Treatment Strategies 256
Sharon Arkin, Judith A. Lewis, and Jon Carlson

Part I. *Miscellaneous* 265

Interrupting a Depression: The Pushbutton Technique 267
Harold H. Mosak

Section IV.
CHILD COUNSELING

EDITORS' COMMENTS 273
Counseling a Boy: A Demonstration 275
Rudolf Dreikurs
Adlerian Usage of Children's Play 285
Michael T. Yura and Merna D. Galassi
The Loyalty Dilemma 293
Marie Hartwell-Walker and P. Lawrence Belove
Early Recollections as a Diagnostic Technique with Primary Age Children 305
Barbara L. Borden

Children's Stories for Psychological Self-Understanding 312
John D. West and Linda K. Dann
Adlerian Play Therapy: Practical Considerations 323
Terry Kottman and Jayne Warlick
The Mutual Storytelling Technique:
An Adlerian Application in Child Therapy 338
Terry Kottman and Kathy Stiles

Section V.

COUPLE AND FAMILY COUNSELING AND THERAPY TECHNIQUES

EDITORS' COMMENTS 347
Adlerian Marriage Counseling 350
Miriam L. Pew and W. L. Pew
First Encounters of the Close Kind (FECK):
The Use of the Story of the First Interaction as an
Early Recollection of a Marriage 362
P. Lawrence Belove
Adlerian Marriage Therapy 380
Don Dinkmeyer and James Dinkmeyer
Equality in Male/Female Relationships 389
Ann H. Tuites and Donald E. Tuites
Marital Issues of Intimacy and Techniques for Change:
An Adlerian Systems Perspective 400
Robert Sherman
Helping Adults Change Disjunctive Emotional Responses
to Children's Misbehavior 413
Gary D. McKay and Oscar C. Christensen
Consequences: An Alternative to Punishment 429
Floy C. Pepper and Mildred Roberson
Family Lifestyle Assessment: The Role of Family Myths
and Values in the Client's Presenting Issues 441
William G. Nicoll and E. Clair Hawes
Adlerian Family Therapy: An Integrative Therapy 456
Don Dinkmeyer
Family Counseling: A Demonstration 466
Rudolf Dreikurs

INDEX 485

LIST OF CONTRIBUTORS 497

ABOUT THE EDITORS 501

PREFACE

If you have chosen this book to read, it is likely that you have some understanding of Adler and the Adlerian approach to psychology. You undoubtedly know that Adler was clearly ahead of his time as a psychotherapist. According to Prochaska and Norcross (1994),

> his social recasting of Freudian theory predated the evolution of psychodynamic therapy; his task assignments foreshadowed the development of behavioral and other directive therapy; his specific techniques involving imagery and "as if" anticipated the cognitive therapy; and his community outreach and psychoeducational programs foreshadowed contemporary community mental health. (p. 89)

A cornerstone of Adlerian psychology is the belief that people are indivisible, social, creative, decision-making beings whose beliefs and behavior have a purpose. Therefore, the individual is best understood holistically as a total being whose thoughts, feelings, and beliefs are present in a consistent and unified pattern of actions. The major principles of this theory thus can be identified separately for the purposes of understanding, but as the reader quickly will see in the articles in this book, they function together as an intimate whole, each carefully being interrelated and integrated with the others. The principles are as follows:

- *All behavior has social meaning.* Each individual is socially embedded in his/her social system. Humans are social beings, and their behaviors are best understood within the social context. Each individual is attempting to belong in the larger society.

- *All behavior has purpose.* Perhaps the basic tenet of Adlerian psychology is the purposiveness of all behavior. Behavior is goal-directed. It is movement toward a goal. This movement, action, and direction of the individual reveals his/her purpose and intentions. Once a therapist understands the goals, he/she can modify behavior effectively.
- *Holism.* Adler viewed people holistically, believing that all components (i.e., conscious, unconscious, physical, mental, and emotional) were all part of a unified system moving toward the same psychological goal. Individuals cannot be understood by an analysis of the elements but instead must be understood as a unified whole. Individual or isolated events are understood in relationship to the total pattern and are seen as a component of movement toward a goal.
- *Striving for significance.* Another of Adler's major principles is that of an individual's overcoming feelings of inferiority in order to attain feelings of superiority. Adler believed that all humans have inferiority feelings that emerge in childhood and serve as catalysts to the individual to help achieve his/her goals.
- *Behavior is a function of one's subjective perceptions.* It is important for the therapist to understand the perception of each individual. Each person develops and is responsible for his/her own subjective view of life. Individuals give all of their experiences meaning.
- *Psychology of use rather than psychology of possession.* Adlerians are more concerned with how an individual uses his/her capacities than with what his/her potential is. The focus is on motivation, not just possibilities. Therefore, assessment is directed toward what an individual is doing currently rather than on what he/she could be doing potentially.
- *Family atmosphere and values.* The Adlerian approach is a social approach and places a great deal of importance on family process. An individual learns through observing and interacting within his/her family how to interpret life.
- *The family constellation.* The family constellation is another term for birth order. The child's position in the family constellation provides his/her perspective on social relationships and ability. Adlerians believe that it is the psychological position rather than the ordinal position that is most important. In other words, it is the meaning a person gives to his/her position and the positions of his/her siblings that has more importance than the actual ordinal or chronological age.
- *Lifestyle.* Lifestyle refers to the person's basic orientation to life, a set of patterns or themes that runs through the person's existence, or what other theories call "personality."
- *Social interest.* Adlerians place great value on the social context of behavior, and all behavior is understood within the social context. Adle-

> rians believe that people are continuously striving to belong, and many of their problems occur when they fail to achieve belonging. Adler believed that social interest was the measure of one's mental health. It reflects the individual's capacity to give and take and the willingness to participate and cooperate for the common benefit of the group. Social interest often is a measure of an individual's sense of belonging as a person with social interest works with people, agrees to participate, shows caring concern for others, and shows a larger concern for the community as a whole.

These principles provide an overview of Adlerian psychology. It is easy to see from these principles that this is a pragmatic theory. Many of Adler's ideas and techniques have been involved in modern psychological thinking without proper credit. As Ellenberger (1970) concluded, "it would not be easy to find another author from which so much has been borrowed from all sides without acknowledgement than Adler" (p. 645). Therefore, it is only fitting that a book on Adlerian techniques be developed.

Individual or Adlerian psychology is a well-established mode of therapy and counseling, with a strong following in North America and western Europe. There are over 2,000 members of the major professional organization for this group, the North American Society of Adlerian Psychology. Numerous schools and training centers exist in the United States and Canada that are dedicated to teaching graduate level and professional level courses in Adlerian psychology. Other universities have programs that to a greater or lesser degree emphasize or teach this approach to helping. The theory and methods of Adler still flourish.

Adlerian psychology is a "blue-collar" pragmatic approach to helping. Adler and his followers are more concerned with practice and application than with research and theory. Since 1964, almost 200 technique-oriented articles have been published in the *Journal of Individual Psychology, The Individual Psychologist,* and *Individual Psychology.* Nonetheless, no single volume exists that presents an active compilation of the techniques.

This volume presents a collection of classic and recent papers published between 1964 and 1994 and not previously reprinted. The intention of this volume is not to overemphasize technique. We are well aware that it is the process, not the techniques, that produces the change. We also realize, however, that techniques are an important part of the helping process.

Jon Carlson
Steven Slavik

REFERENCES

Ellenberger, H. (1970). *The discovery of the unconscious: The history and evolution of dynamic psychiatry*. New York: Basic Books.

Prochaska, J. O., & Norcross, J. C. (1994). *Systems of psychotherapy: A transtheoretical analysis* (3rd ed.). Pacific Grove, CA: Brooks/Cole.

SECTION I
INTRODUCTION

EDITORS' COMMENTS

So, we are offering yet another book on technique, on how "to do it right" for the therapist and counselor. We run the risk of being put on the shelf with all the other "cookbooks" in therapy and counseling.

In fact, we agree with Mozdzierz and Greenblatt (1994), who suggested in a paper that we recommend wholeheartedly to the reader, that there are many pitfalls in thinking about and using techniques. The first, and largest, pitfall on our list is that in considering technique, our thinking and practice run the risk of reifying technique, that is, of assuming that a technique has a use independent of a client, his/her difficulty in life, the situation in which an individual finds himself/herself, and the client-counselor relationship. How do we justify offering another "how to" text?

As we emphasize throughout the section introductions in this text, and in agreement with Mozdzierz and Greenblatt (1994), we believe therapy is a task in which a therapist encourages a situation-orientation in life, an orientation in which there may not be clearcut answers. Therapists encourage individuals to consider what is best for everyone under the circumstances. In this context, a therapist is not an expert whose job is to "fix" or advise a client. He/she more often acts as a catalyst for change, as a facilitator in the consideration of options, and may take on the role of a leader to do so. In order to do this, a therapist needs a well-defined philosophy or theory about human nature and about what enables change. A therapist also needs the ability to create and maintain an egalitarian relationship. This ability includes having a clear conception of the role of a therapist as leader and of a client as "doer" (although this distinction is not hard and fast by any means). Thus, as Hervat (1932) simplistically stated, "To the patient's stereotyped question, 'Shall I get better?' we give the stereotyped answer, 'That depends on you' " (p. 21). If at times a specific activity or "technique" can be used to improve the relationship or to enhance results of therapy, it comes forth in an egalitarian relationship as something a therapist knows how to do and can propose for therapeutic effectiveness. Use of the activity then becomes part of moving forward in life, not a way to get to a specific place or to attain a specific result.

A colleague of ours, Len Sperry, told a story that he attributed to General Patton. As the story went, General Patton was driving one day on a very important mission and his car stalled. No one could make the car move. The military mechanics tried, and the convoy was going nowhere until Patton's vehicle could be fixed. Someone mentioned that there was a local mechanic who could fix anything. This man was summoned and was asked whether or not he could fix Patton's car. The mechanic looked closely at the stalled car and said, yes, he could, but his fee would be $100. General Patton was more than willing to pay this fee. The man went over to his truck, reached in, took out a hammer, walked up to the engine, and banged the hammer right on the side of the engine. Then he said, "Start the engine." The driver reached in for the keys, turned the ignition switch, and the engine started right up. The man said, "Now can I be paid?" Patton looked and said, "Am I supposed to give you $100 for hitting my engine with a hammer?" The mechanic said, "No. Hitting your engine with the hammer was free. Knowing where to hit was what the $100 was for."

So it is with technique. It is not so much the technique that is important. It is knowing how to use it, when to use it, and where.

We believe most techniques discussed in the articles reprinted in this book are activities that aid the therapist as much as the client in the assignment of self-responsibility and that encourage awareness of choice. They all assume the establishment of an appropriate, cooperative, client-therapist relationship.

REFERENCES

Hervat, A. (1932). The technique of treatment. *Individual Psychology Medical Pamphlet, 3*, 21–28.

Mozdzierz, G. J., & Greenblatt, R. L. (1994). Technique in psychotherapy. *Individual Psychology, 50*(2), 232–249.

SECTION II
GENERAL TECHNIQUES

EDITORS' COMMENTS

Mozdzierz and Greenblatt (1986) "describe the misunderstandings, pitfalls, and potential problems associated with an overemphasis on and misunderstanding of technique and treatment." The use of technique without a theoretical framework is the problem and the central tenet of this paper. Adler and others talked about the importance of the client and the need to tailor treatment and technique to each unique client. The therapist needs to be flexible in interacting to the demands of the clinical situation, and to the client's condition and complaint. Clinical technique is an outgrowth of clinical assessment and is used to assist the client in reaching a goal.

A number of articles describe techniques that are direct and literal applications of Adlerian theory. Those in this section exemplify such direct application.

A fundamental assumption of Adlerian theory is that individuals are involved thoroughly in ongoing, future-oriented activity within a social field (Adler, 1956). This activity has an integrated cognitive-behavioral-affective orientation known as a goal. In one's orientation, one acts *as if* one has certain stable convictions regarding oneself, others, and the world in general. This set of convictions is known as one's private logic. One's orientation is particularly dependent upon the assessment of one's own abilities and of obstacles or resources that others and the world offer. Given these appraisals, one orients activity towards whatever success or satisfaction in life represents or maintains self-esteem. One may use many methods in attaining such satisfaction or success. Methods may range from rigid, repeated ways to promote individual self-aggrandizement to those that flexibly promote socially interested objectives.

Good adult therapy and involved technique become a way of aiding people in understanding their goal, their private logic, their methods of achieving the goal, and possible adverse consequences of their goal or methods. They may come to see that inflexible application of certain methods is detrimental to cooperative living. Presumably individuals, with sufficient encouragement, then can change their goal or methods to become more situation oriented.

One consequence of Adlerian theory is that a technique used in the service of attaining some guaranteed *result*, even if it looks prosocial to a therapist, is artificial in a therapeutic relationship. Therapy too must be situation oriented. The essential goal of therapy is to demonstrate, teach, or allow a client to discover that any method in his/her life that requires specific results from others is self-aggrandizing. The same applies to therapy. Rather than to obtain specific results, the intention of therapy is to point out how an individual tends to restrict his/her choices in life and to aid an individual in examining other possibilities of behavior, thinking, and feeling.

For example, Jourard (1959) took the stance that manipulation through technique is harmful to a therapeutic relationship. Only therapists who strive to know a client without formulaic or compulsive reliance on technique to gain certain results can aid a client in his/her difficulties. "Change . . . in patients is fostered when the therapist is a rather free individual functioning as a person with all of his feelings, fantasies, as well as his wits" (1959, p. 177).

It is only fitting that a book on techniques begin with the single most important aspect—creating the relationship. Jourard was clearly one of the leading writers and thinkers in this area. In this essay, he described the importance of Buber's "I-Thou" relationship, or the ability to *be* yourself. He cautioned therapists to avoid manipulation, as if they know what is best for someone else. Adler would echo this concern, as he spent his life in opposition to tyrannical behavior.

We can distinguish techniques that aid one to know a client, or that can be used to aid a client to recognize new choices, from those used to maneuver a client in a specific direction. The former offer a client greater choice in his/her life, whereas the latter attempt to restrict a client's choices. Perhaps it is better said that this distinction depends on a therapist's intention in using a technique rather than on a technique itself. We can distinguish therapists who use techniques to better know a client and to help a client know himself/herself from therapists who aim for specific results with clients.

In this light, Mahrer (1970) offered a direct method or technique for knowing a client and for aiding a client in knowing himself/herself. Mahrer suggested understanding client behavior, client feelings, and the situations within which clients place themselves in terms of their goal. Behavior, feelings, and situations can be placed in relationship to a client's goal. The questions Mahrer suggested therapists ask are direct and obviously intended to explore a client's unity of personality. A client's behavior is interpreted in terms of the goals toward which it is directed; in terms of immediate, predominant feelings; and in terms of a defined situational context.

The general topic of self-responsibility is reviewed by Murphy (1984) who also outlined a number of techniques for teaching self-responsibility. Because without care, use of some techniques can approach therapeutic insistence that the client "get it right," Murphy warned the reader that "techniques or methods for encouraging client responsibility are likely to prove ineffective or perhaps even deteriorate into gimmicks unless a relationship of trust, respect, and cooperation between client and therapist has been established" (p. 130). Thus, for example, "placing responsibility" without trust can be tantamount to saying, "don't ask me." When both therapist and client are cooperative, issues of who is responsible for what in life and therapy can be discussed more openly.

Most techniques that encourage self-responsibility are, however, likely to involve attitudes of an experienced therapist and are not called upon in abrupt fashions. One can begin to set tasks, to encourage, to confront attitudes and timing, to present alternatives, and to assign responsibility for change and for responsibility in general in gentle and comfortable ways within a first session. In later sessions, with more trust and friendliness, many techniques can become jokes between client and therapist that are nonetheless effective: "I see you're procrastinating again. Let's pretend this is our first session and start all over, shall we?" Used appropriately, these techniques encourage client awareness of self and of choice rather than obtain specific results.

Mozdzierz, Murphy, and Greenblatt (1986) discussed the advantages of understanding private logic in psychotherapy. Understanding client private logic aids in avoiding resistance and builds cooperation, builds rapport, and helps therapy in general become more efficient. Used at appropriate or teachable moments, understanding private logic can facilitate change in a number of ways: in communicating basic mistakes, in disclosing hidden reasons, and in enabling a therapist to use paradox, redefinition, and building self-esteem and social interest. Again, used as methods of promoting self-knowledge and choice, these techniques do not demand specific results from clients.

REFERENCES

Adler, A. (1956). In H. L. Ansbacher & R. R. Ansbacher (Eds.), *The individual psychology of Alfred Adler.* New York: Basic Books.

Mozdzierz, G. J., Murphy, T. J., & Greenblatt, R. L. (1986). Private logic and the strategy of psychotherapy. *Individual Psychology*, *42*(3), 339–349.

I-THOU RELATIONSHIP VERSUS MANIPULATION IN COUNSELING AND PSYCHOTHERAPY

Sidney M. Jourard
University of Florida

There is ample evidence that man can mould and structure the behavior of his fellowman according to some predetermined scheme; we need point only to such phenomena as "teaching meachines" (9), Chinese "thought reform," Dale Carnegie's ways of "making" friends, "hidden persuaders," political propaganda, "subliminal advertisements" on TV screens, and, of course, the centuries-old techniques employed by women to make men see, feel, believe, and do what they want them to. The question is, "Can techniques for the manipulation of behavior, of demonstrated effectiveness in the rat laboratory, the market place, and the boudoir, be deliberately employed in the arts of counseling and psychotherapy?" It is my contention in the present paper that "behavioristic" approaches to counseling and psychotherapy, while rightly acknowledging a man's susceptibility to manipulation by another, ignore the possibly deletrious impact of such manipulation on the whole man and, moreover, on the would-be manipulator himself—whereas the essential factor in the psychotherapeutic situation is a loving, honest and spontaneous relationship between the therapist and the patient.

Adapted from a paper presented at a symposium on "Behavioristic Approaches to Counseling and Psychotherapy," Southeastern Psychological Association, St. Augustine, Florida, April 25, 1959.

NATURE AND EFFECTS OF MANIPULATION

We are beginning to get some notions of what healthy personality looks like (5, 6) and what health-yielding behavior might be. In the light of this it is tempting to imagine some such situation as a therapist flashing a light, or a smile, or a glance at the patient whenever the latter emits behavior thought to be health-promoting. If these stimuli have become reinforcing, the therapist thus will increase the rate of wellness-yielding behavior in his presence, and weaken those responses which produced and perpetuated symptoms. In fact, if such a procedure were desirable, one might construct a therapy-machine, somewhat as follows: Whenever the patient talks about subject-matter which leaves him "cold" and unemotional, a light remains off. The patient's job is to get the light on and keep it on. As soon as he discusses emotionally meaningful material, his autonomic responses will close switches that turn on the light. Shades of 1984! Then, the therapist can go fishing, and the patient will subsequently display healthy behavior whenever he encounters a machine. Monstrous though these ideas sound, they are not implausible. Greenspoon (3) and numerous workers (7) following his lead have demonstrated the power of a well-placed verbal reinforcer to increase the rate at which selected verbal operants are emitted. What is wrong with aiming toward the eventual control of patients' behavior in situ by means of reinforcements deliberately administered by the therapist?

I believe that a program of psychotherapy undertaken with such an aim is a contradiction in terms. It cannot achieve the aim of fostering a patient's growth toward healthier personality, one aspect of which, I believe, is healthy interpersonal behavior (6, p. 150). It cannot achieve such therapeutic aims purely because it constitutes deliberate manipulation of man by man. Such is not a healthy interpersonal transaction by criteria of which I have written elsewhere (6, pp. 180–226). The aim of rational psychotherapy is not so much that of remitting salient symptoms, as it is to alter interpersonal behavior from the range which generates the symptoms (manipulating self and others) to a pattern which generates and maintains healthy personality.

My patients have been vociferous in deploring those times when I have experimented with manipulation. I have tried delimiting my behavior to the dispensing of reflections of feelings. I did a pretty good job of it, too. I have tried imposing the fundamental rule on patients, remaining silent except for well-timed utterance of ex cathedra interpretations. I have, I confess, even tried deliberately to shape my patient's behavior in the therapy hour with some rather ingeniously discovered reinforcers which varied from patient to patient, e.g., the head-bob when the output was "right," looking away from the patient's face whenever he was uttering what I thought would be most helpful, and so on. The only trouble with these devices was that in time the patients would "see through them," and become quite angered at being manipulated in these ways. I am beginning to think that people, even patients, resent being manipulated. I know I do. I become furious when, for example, a salesman gives me a canned pitch which his supervisor told him "worked" in some percentage of cases. I can't stand a Dale-Carnegie smile, or any of the other departures from simple, spontaneous honesty in a relationship between man and man. There is something downright degrading in being treted like a ninny, as something less than human.

What is the impact of therapy on the therapist? In our concern with what we do to clients and patients we have never asked what we do to ourselves. The "technical" therapist is striving to manipulate himself and his patient rather than respond to him. He does this by striving to be a good disciple of his master or practitioner of his technique. I have come to recognize that those who habitually strive to manipulate others in one way or another, do violence to their own integrity as well as to that of their victim. Surely behavior that does not do a bit of good for the therapist, cannot do much good for his patient. We need data on this point.

THE I-THOU NATURE OF THE PSYCHOTHERAPEUTIC SITUATION

If we look naively at the psychotherapeutic situation, we observe a patient talking about himself to his therapist. At first, the patient is trying to manipulate the therapist's perceptions of him. But the latter listens, seems to avoid conventional responses to what is told him, such as scolding, shock, scorn and moral indignation, and so on. Encouraged by the lack of expected censure, the patient may go on spontaneously to reveal all manner of things about himself. One gathers he had never before in his life told these things, or expressed these feelings to anyone. In fact, in the therapy situation, the patient remembers things which surprise him; he experiences feelings that never before had he even envisioned. As time goes on, he becomes remarkably free in expressing what is passing through his mind, and if you asked him to describe himself late in therapy, he would give a much more comprehensive picture of his wishes, feelings, motives, etc. than he might have earlier in the game. Outside the therapy room, people who have known him notice he has changed, in that he seems less tense, more able to acknowledge a broader range of motives, and often much more spontaneous in his behavior with others. Moreover, he seems to be much more "genuine" in his dealings with others. The absence of his symptoms becomes almost incidental in the face of the more basic changes that seem to have gone on.

What has been responsible for these changes? The man has gone through a unique experience which evidently has changed his behavior from responses that generated and perpetuated "symptoms" to responses which yield more valued outcomes.

This seems to be the experience of being permitted to be—to be himself. It is the experience of being utterly attended to by a professional man who is of good will, who seeks to understand the patient utterly, and to communicate both his good will and his understanding as these grow. It is the experience of feeling free to be and to disclose oneself in the presence of another person whose good will is assured but whose responses are unpredictable. Recent studies, summarized by Carl Rogers (8), have shown that it is not the technique or the theoretical orientation of the therapist which fosters growth of the sort I have been describing. Rather it is the manner of the therapist's being when in the presence of the patient. Effective therapists seem to follow this implicit hypothesis: If they are themselves in the presence of the patient, avoiding compulsions to silence, to reflection, to interpretation, to impersonal technique, and kindred character disorders, but instead striving to know their patient, involving themselves in his situation, and then responding to his utterances spontaneously—this fosters growth. In short, they love their patients. They employ their powers in the service of their patient's well-being and growth, not inflict them on him. Somehow there is a difference (2).

This loving relationship is a far cry from the impersonal administration of reflections, interpretations, or the equivalent of pellets. The loving therapist is quite free and spontaneous in his relationship: his responses are bound only by his ethics and his judgment. He may laugh, scold, become angry, give advice, in short break most of the rules laid down in psychotherapy training manuals. This differs sharply from the deliberate restriction of therapist behavior to some range thought to be health-fostering. Such restriction of behavior by therapists makes them the legitimate butt of jokes and caricatures—they become so predictable. Evidently it is only the therapist's good will which needs to be predictable, not his specific responses to a patient's disclosures. In this connection I should like to mention the beautifully written satire by Jay Haley which portrays psychoanalysis as a special case of the game of one-up-manship (4).

It is my growing opinion, somewhat buttressed by accumulating experience in my own therapeutic work, that valued change—growth—in patients is fostered when the therapist is a rather free individual functioning as a person with all of his feelings, fantasies, as well as his wits, and that the therapist who strives to remain a thinking, and only thinking creature in the therapeutic situation is a failure at promoting growth.

Martin Buber has succinctly summed up these observations with his concepts of the I-Thou relationship, and of the dialogue (1). When a therapist is committed to the task of helping a patient grow, he functions as a whole person, and not as a disembodied intellect, computer, or reinforcement programmer. He strives to know his patient by hearing him out. He does not limit his behavior to some range prescribed by theory or cook book. He does, however, retain his separate identity, and is thus able to see and understand things which the patient cannot. If he spontaneously and honestly conveys his thoughts and reactions, I believe he is not only communicating his concern, but is in effect both eliciting and reinforcing kindred uncontrived behavior in his patient. To a shocking extent, behavior begets its own kind. Manipulation begets counter-manipulation. A therapist who is concerned about his patient's lot eventually will be perceived as a man of good will by his patient. Any man will hide from those thought to be not of good will, just as a power-player hides his hand from the other players who are not of good will, insofar as the player's money is concerned (10). In the presence of a man who is of good will, even the most defensive will strip themselves, so that the other will know their lot and be able to help them.

CONCLUSION

No patient can be expected to drop all his defenses and reveal himself except in the presence of someone whom he believes is for him, and not for a theory, dogma, or technique. I believe that if the therapist abandons all attempts to shape his patient's behavior according to some predetermined scheme, and instead strives to know and to respond honestly to what he has learned, and to establish a relationship of I and Thou, then he is doing his job as well as it can be done—that is, if spontaneous honesty between man and man, and between a man and himself are worthwhile therapeutic goals. Somehow, I feel that orthodox therapists—we might call them Rogerian, Freudian, or even Skinnerian technicians—are more concerned to verify their respective dogmas than to know and respond to their patients as individual persons. Techniques treat with categories and fictions. Therapy proceeds through honest responses to this very person by this very person.

REFERENCES

1. Buber, M. *I and thou.* New York: Scribner, 1937.

2. Fromm, E. *The art of loving.* New York: Harper, 1957.

3. Greenspoon, J. The reinforcing effect of two spoken sounds on the frequency of two responses. *Amer. J. Psychol.,* 1955, 68, 409–416.

4. Haley, J. The art of psychoanalysis. *Etc. Rev. gen. Semant.,* 1958, 15, 190–200.

5. Jahoda, Marie. *Current concepts of positive mental health.* New York: Basic Books, 1958.

6. Jourard, S. M. *Personal adjustment.* New York: Macmillan, 1958.

7. Krasner, L. Studies of the conditioning of verbal behavior. *Psychol. Bull.,* 1958, 55, 148–170.

8. Rogers, C. R. The characteristics of a helping relationship. *Personnel Guid. J.,* 1958, 37, 6–16.

9. Skinner, B. F. Teaching machines. *Science,* 1958, 128, 969–977.

10. Stewart, D. A. *A preface to empathy.* New York: Phil. Library, 1956.

INTERPRETATION OF PATIENT BEHAVIOR THROUGH GOALS, FEELINGS, AND CONTEXT[1]

Alvin R. Mahrer
Professor of psychology and director of the clinical psychology program at Miami University, Oxford, Ohio. He is a clinical psychologist dedicated to the theory, research, and practice of personality change. He is editor of *The Goals of Psychotherapy* (1967) with contributions by van Kaam, E. T. Gendlin, Albert Ellis, Rudolf Dreikurs, and G. A. Kelly, among others.

Every response by the therapist requires some way of making sense of the patient's behavior. With a plethora of conceptual nets, the clinician typically has a bewildering bag of descriptive constructs but no effective working guidelines for making practical sense of what is going on with the patient. The thesis of this paper is that three working guidelines enable the therapist to interpret and make sense of patient behavior: (*a*) the goal-directed component of the patient's behavior, (*b*) the accompanying feelings, and (*c*) the situational context.

GOAL-DIRECTIONALITY

With the paradoxical exception of psychotherapy, it is axiomatic that psychological behavior is goal-directed. Psychotherapy stands almost by itself in

---

[1]The author is most grateful for the constructive criticisms and editorial suggestions of Dr. Kjell Erik Rudestam and Phillip Grover.

Journal of Individual Psychology, 26(2), November, 1970, **pp. 186–195**

jettisoning goal-directionality, and, instead, understanding patient behavior in terms of the interplay of pathological processes, disease-ridden dynamics, or psychoanalytic mental forces (17). Much of the appeal of motivational analysts such as Kanfer and Saslow (15), social learning theorists such as Rotter (28), and motivational interactionists such as Haley (13) and Szasz (30) lies in the simple elegance of rediscovering the Adlerian (1, 2, 3, 4) conception of behavior, including patient behavior, as goal-directed. They have helped remove the mystique of mental pathology from patient behavior.

In the analysis of patient behavior, the pertinent questions are: What is the patient doing? What could be the goals of this behavior? What behavior is accompanied with hidden inner feelings of pleasure and satisfaction? What kind of relationship is he constructing or maintaining? What is he avoiding, denying, pushing away? To obtain the answer to this last very important question Adler (4, p. 332) would ask the patient, "What would you do if you were completely well?"

Four refinements assist the answering of these questions: focusing on (*a*) presently ongoing motivation, (*b*) behavior rather than denoted content, (*c*) goal-directionality of all behavior, (*d*) extraction of ultimate goals.

1. *Presently ongoing motivation* (8, 18, 20). As Adler (4, p. 89) asserts, this is more important than motivations not in operation at the moment, or deep-seated personality processes unrelated to the patient's current behavior (9). Although dependency may be among a patient's deep-seated personality processes, and passive-aggressive motivations may characterize other segments of his behavior, at the present ongoing moment his behavior may be most aptly described, for example, as directed toward the goal of avoiding a threatened rejection.

"Causal" explanations may be accurate but are unprofitable in telling us what is happening right now. It becomes irrelevant to describe a patient as psychopathic, of low ego strength, of dull normal intelligence, being brain damaged, being schizophrenic, being a delinquent (19). Instead, the focus should be on the goals which account for the behaviors to which these descriptions refer.

2. *Behavior rather than denoted content* (27), i.e., what the patient is doing rather than what he says. For example, when the patient's talk is of a depressed suicidal nature, his ongoing behavior may warrant the inference that his motive is to hurt and trouble others (3, 16), or to appeal for help in alleviating self-rejection (16). When another patient talks about a series of childhood events, his ongoing motivation may be carefully to organize the world into systematic compartments, or to open himself to the therapist, or to fend off compassion (24, p. 38). A patient may *talk* about his aggressive outbursts, replete with recounted examples of his

impulsive temper, whereas his immediate goal may be to convince the therapist that he is not the scared, impotent person he suspects the therapist believes him to be. He may *describe* himself as being loving and compassionate toward his wife and children, although the more accurate ongoing motivation is to convey how unappreciated he really is. She may *refer* to a life of loneliness, but, rather than being lonely right now, she is inviting the therapist's compassion and nurturant understanding.

I term the misidentification of the denoted content with the immediately ongoing motivation the *content error*. The current apotheosis of behavior in contemporary learning-approaches to psychotherapy runs the danger of incurring the content error. While the patient tells about his fear of open spaces, facial tic, compulsive handwashing, enuresis, or school phobia, and this is all the therapist is concerned with, the patient's ongoing motivations are missed.

3. *Goal-directionality of all behavior*, verbal and nonverbal, "normal" and "pathological" (2, 13, 17, 19). The therapist must attend to the rich source of motivational cues provided by postures, body movements, gestures and expressions. The cues may refer to oneself (e.g., to praise, protect, show, or hide aspects of oneself) or to others (e.g., to elicit concern from them, dominate them, be sexually involved with them). Motivational analysis applies to the entire realm of behavior, from "normal" to "pathological," from bits of behavior to sweeping behavioral units, including what other viewpoints conceptualize as severe psychotic behavior or behavioral symptoms of brain damage. Behind the scrambled and bizarre incoherences of such persons is a mode of communication (13, 26) guided by motivations such as fending off understanding, blocking closeness, gaining superiority, or expressing resentment (19).

4. *Extraction of ultimate goals*. Every behavior is directed toward some ultimate goal the approaching of which is accompanied with positive, constructive feelings of pleasure, excitement, satisfaction, and happiness (19, 20, 21). The therapist may extract these goals by asking himself what is the hidden satisfaction, the pleasurable excitement, that the patient could possibly experience by carrying out this behavior? The patient who talks in a confusing, communication-blocking, incoherent way may be interpreted as directed toward the goal of preventing the therapist from reaching him, or of gaining a sense of superiority over the therapist, or of working the therapist into a state of frustration.

The therapist has three positions from which he can identify the motivational component of the patient's behavior: (*a*) as sensitive clinical observer of the patient's behavior directed toward the therapist and others; (*b*) as the patient's inner voice, if the therapist can free himself sufficiently to get inside the patient's motivational skin; and (*c*) as the direct object of the patient's motivations, in accord with the thesis that certain patient motivations will be reflected in their effects on the therapist (5; 14, p. 49; 25, p. 28; 29). How is the patient treating me? What are my reactions to him? How am I being affected? Although the therapist's feelings and reactions typically have been considered as confounding intrusions, when properly understood they constitute a rich source of cues to the patient's immediate motivations. This is pointed out by Dreikurs particularly with regard to children's misbehavior. "What the teacher feels inclined to do . . . provides an indication of the child's intentions . . . It is [therefore] of great importance that the teacher learn to observe her own emotional response to the child's disturbing behavior" (7, p. 45).

FEELING

Feelings as clinical data have been substantially acknowledged by Adler, Jung, Sullivan, Fromm-Reichmann, Federn, and Rank, and, more recently, in the experiental approaches of Rogers, Whitaker, Malone, May, Maslow, and Gendlin. Whereas one component of patient behavior is its goal-directedness, these writers recognize the accompanying feelings as a second component. As working guidelines for the clinician, the following four characteristics of feelings may be understood:

1. Feelings refer to inwardly felt bodily events and sensations (10, 11, 12). These may be described in terms of their nature and bodily locus, for example, a dizziness in the head, a heaviness in the legs, throbbing in the genitals, tight aching band around the head, etc. Or, feelings may be described as internal behavioral states such as terror, helplessness, feeling calm and peaceful, feeling strange and unreal, alone and separated, frozen and tight, a sense of relief, etc.

2. Feelings may consist of inner respondings to ongoing behaviors, e.g. "I'm scared to death" (as the person is beginning to confess a secret sexual ritual); "This is marvelous" (as he finally is decisive about what he is going to do); "I shouldn't have said that" (as he sarcastically inquires whether the therapist has been listening); "I hate being like this" (as he is uninvolved); "All this is too much for me; I'm falling apart" (as he is about to express violence and rage).

3. It is important that the therapist note the immediately ongoing feelings (11, 21, 23, 31). Feelings are relatively open to identification and description. Even bizarrely behaving, or withdrawn, or scrambled and incoherent patients pro-

vide cues to their ongoing immediate feelings. They still can, with relative facility, locate and identify the feeling which is occurring in them right now. A little training and practice is all that is required.

4. The person can have only a single predominant feeling at the current moment, pleasant or unpleasant. The clinician tracks the concatenation of predominant feelings.

The patient has a given feeling in relation to a given motivation. He is scared (feeling) in relation to reaching out for affection (motivation); he is excited in relation to open expression of independence; she is feeling a peaceful sense of relief in relation to sharing her deepest thoughts.

The clinician can identify the predominant ongoing feelings from the following sources: (*a*) Both the patient's verbal and nonverbal behavior provide cues. (*b*) The patient may himself describe his feelings as a participant-observer rather than a subject. (*c*) The ongoing feelings of the therapist, when he is in close alignment with the patient, indicate the patient's feelings (22).

SITUATIONAL CONTEXT

Outside of psychotherapy, a full psychological understanding of human behavior typically includes a description of the situation in which the behavior occurs. Any goal directionality involves specific others in defined relationships within particular settings. With regard to the interpretation of patient behavior, a goal to experience love may gear the female patient toward seeking an older, fatherly male therapist; or toward situations where an accepting male offers special favors and indications of extra concern. Pertinent questions include: What kind of situation is the patient seeking to establish? What kinds of roles is the patient assigning to specific others? With what kind of encompassing situation is the patient surrounding himself? What are the targets, objects or instruments of the patient's motivation? What is the nature of the situational context in which the patient is living at this current moment?

Two refinements guide the therapist's answer to these questions, (*a*) Situational context relates to the ongoing present (6), with the addition of components from the recent and distant past. The situation encompassing a female patient's motivation for complete sexual submission may include a powerfully sadistic male figure relating to the ongoing present (e.g. the husband's firm and tough boss), with components from the recent past (e.g. a near-rape experience while the patient was travelling in Europe), and the distant past (e.g. sexual play during childhood with her mother's second husband). The patient may be described as living in a present situational context with added components from recent and distant past situations.

(*b*) The patient lives in a situational context which bears some relationship to the immediate therapeutic situation. Thus, the female patient may relate to the therapist as a powerfully sadistic male figure, but her behavior is directed beyond the therapist to her older brother. In some instances the patient is living fully in the immediate therapeutic situation, with the critical situational context at some distance; in other instances the therapeutic situation and the critical situational context are intimately fused. There are times when the role of the therapeutic situation is negligible, and the patient is interacting directly within the critical situational context.

Less commonly, the therapeutic situation serves as the instrumental pathway toward an external goal. By being in treatment, the patient avoids a jail sentence; being in therapy serves to warn the spouse that the patient must be given more concern and attention; therapy is a means of maintaining or increasing compensation or welfare aid; or of forcing a family to reduce its pressures.

CLINICAL APPLICATION

The following examples illustrate how the therapist may apply the above three guidelines of goal, feelings, and context to the interpretation of patient behavior:

1. A young, heavy-set, swarthy high-school teacher who had recently been asked to resign his position, in the 6th session expostulated his social philosophy with regard to the "Establishment," United States foreign policy, and the ghetto communities.

Goal: The therapist inferred that the goal is to attack critically, and thus to convey and to experience a pleasurable intellectual superiority.

Context: The cues suggest the therapist as the target of the patient's intellectual attacks. The situation permits the patient to demonstrate and experience his intellectual capability and superiority over the therapist. Information about the patient's present, recent and past life suggests that the critical situational context includes a compound of authority figures (school administrators, supervisors, family, etc.) against whom the patient is warring and over whom the patient is seeking to gain intellectual superiority.

Feelings: Visible cues permit the inference of an inner sensation of bodily shaking, verging on fear and fright.

We conclude that the patient's overall present behavior is to be interpreted as critically attacking and gaining intellectual superiority (goal-directionality), directed toward the therapist and critical authority figures (situational context), with internal shaking, fear and fright (feeling) in relation to this motivation.

2. A young woman began therapy because of a gradual depression which she dated from the death of her mother two years ago, exacerbating with her subsequent marriage a year ago. At the present moment she is giving the story of her life, almost reliving each episode, without interruption from the therapist. Each episode is remembered lovingly and described as if it were charmingly revisited.

Goal: She seemed to be giving the therapist her personal life story as if it were a specially treasured gift which the therapist was to receive. The motivation seemed to be that of giving something special (herself), something very prized and highly personal.

Context: She assigned to the therapist the role of a listener, receiver, to whom a special and prized gift is to be awarded. This was the role of the deceased mother, and the patient's striving to give herself as a specially prized gift is occurring within a context which includes mother, husband, and therapist in the role of wholly accepting receivers.

Feelings: These included warmth, softness, a sense of peace and inner tranquility.

The patient's immediate behavior may be described as strivings toward a highly personal giving of herself (goal-directionality) to the therapist, husband and mother as specially valued figures in an intimately receiving, accepting situation (situational context), with feelings of warmth, softness, peace and tranquility.

3. A man in his late forties initially focused on his teen-aged daughter's escapades and his angry feelings about her and her acquaintances. The focus then shifted to his sexual arousal by the activities of his daughter and her female friends, including growing tendencies toward adulterous behavior. In the present session the patient finally spoke of his wife, describing her as the essence of almost childlike goodness and sweetness, lovingly protected by her husband. He sobbed continually and inquired whether the therapist considered him a bad, evil person.

Goal: The patient had been struggling to deny his sexual thoughts and tendencies throughout his adult life. Recently he has been increasingly confronted by his sexuality through his daughter's activities. During the present session he sought loving acceptance and forgiveness for his exposed, secretly thrilling sexuality.

Context: The therapist is to serve as the accepting and forgiving judge to whom the patient confesses his evil inclinations.

Feelings: Sobbing openness, a letting down of barriers, a sense of raw exposure, good feeling of "this is what I am like."

The patient's present behavior may be described as a seeking of forgiveness and acceptance of his own thrilling wicked sexuality (goal-directionality), before a lovingly understanding, empathic judge to whom he confesses his sexual sins (situational context), with accompanying feelings of raw, open relief (feeling) with regard to this motivation.

4. A twenty-two year old girl living at home with her parents, was completely dominated by the family. Depression and suicidal thoughts followed the parents' thorough squashing of her abortive overtures to leave the family. During the present session, after her depression was reduced, she cited her parents' oppressive demands and pressures. Then she lapsed into a silent period of ten minutes. Cues arising from both the patient and the therapist suggested that the silence was her way of standing up, declaring her goal of independence, stoutly resisting. The message was that, for the first time in her life, she was going to do what she wanted; to become a person in her own right.

Context: The patient seemed to go beyond the immediate therapeutic situation, and appeared to be living in a protest scene with her parents, a situation which had begun to occur first with her overtures to leave the family and again through the onset of the depression and the suicidal thoughts.

Feelings: She seemed comfortable, almost pleasantly excited and satisfied during the silence. Following the silence, she confirmed this impression with further reportings of a lightness and tingling throughout the chest and head, and rising bodily sensations of aliveness.

In sum, the patient's behavior during the silent period seemed to indicate a protesting, a declaring of independence, a becoming a person in her own right (goal-directionality), directed toward her parents, especially in a scene in which they are domineering figures (situational context), with accompanying feelings of internal excitement, pleasureful tingling and aliveness (feelings) in relation to the motivation.

SUMMARY

In order to understand and respond to a patient, the clinician requires guidelines to interpret and make sense out of the complex of cues comprising the patient's behavior. Three conjoint guidelines are proposed:

1. The patient's behavior is interpreted in terms of the goals toward which it is directed. These are identified by focusing upon what the patient is immediately striving to achieve, the underlying motivation guiding his behavior, the nature of the relationship he is establishing, and the source of the internal, hidden, secret feelings of pleasure and satisfaction.

2. The patient's behavior is interpreted in terms of the immediately ongoing, predominant feelings. Inwardly felt bodily events and sensations occur in relation to the goal.

3. The patient's behavior is interpreted as occurring within a defined situational context, including relationships to others within particular settings. The total context includes components from the recent and distant past, as well as the situation occurring in the ongoing present.

Four cases are briefly described, illustrating the use of these three guidelines.

REFERENCES

1. Adler, A. *The science of living* (1929). Garden City, N.Y.: Doubleday Anchor Books, 1969.

2. Ansbacher, H. L. The structure of Individual Psychology. In B. B. Wolman (Ed.) *Scientific psychology*. New York: Basic Books, 1965. Pp. 340–364.

3. Ansbacher, H. L. Suicide as communication: Adler's concept and current application. *J. Indiv. Psychol.*, 1969, 25, 174–180.

4. Ansbacher, H. L., & Ansbacher, Rowena R. (Eds.) *The Individual Psychology of Alfred Adler*. New York: Basic Books, 1956.

5. Bachrach, H. Adaptive regression, empathy and psychotherapy. *Psychotherapy*, 1968, 5, 203–209.

6. Binswanger, L. The existential analysis school of thought. In R. May, E. Angel, & H. F. Ellenberger (Eds.) *Existence: a new dimension in psychiatry and psychology*. New York: Basic Books, 1958. Pp. 191–213.

7. Dreikurs, R. *Psychology in the classroom*. 2nd ed. New York: Harper & Row, 1968.

8. Eldred, S. H., Hamburg, D. A., Inwood, E. R., Salzman, L., Meyersburg, H. A., & Goodrich, G. A procedure for the systematic analysis of psychotherapeutic interviews. *Psychiatry*, 1954, 17, 337–345.

9. Freud, S. Analysis terminable and interminable. *Int. J. Psychoanal.*, 1937, 18, 373–405.

10. Gendlin, E. T. *Experiencing and the creation of meaning*. New York: Glencoe Free Press, 1962.

11. Gendlin, E. T. A theory of personality change. In P. Worchel & D. Byrne (Eds.) *Personality change*. New York: Wiley, 1964. Pp. 100–148.

12. Gendlin, E. T. Existentialism and experiential psychotherapy. In C. Moustakas (Ed.) *Existential child therapy*. New York: Basic Books, 1966. Pp. 206–246.

13. Haley, J. *Strategies of psychotherapy*. New York: Grune & Stratton, 1963.

14. Jung, C. G. *Modern man in search of a soul*. New York: Harcourt & Brace, 1933.

15. Kanfer, F. H., & Saslow, G. Behavior analysis: an alternative to diagnostic classification. *Arch. gen. Psychiat.*, 1965, 12, 529–538.

16. Kangas, P., & Mahrer, A. R. Suicide attempts and threats as goal-directed communications in psychotic males. *Psychol. Rep.*, in press.

17. Leary, T. & Gill, M. The dimensions and a measure of the process of psychotherapy: a system for the analysis of content of clinical evaluations and patient-therapist interactions. In E. A. Rubenstein & M. B. Parloff (Eds.) *Research in psychotherapy, Vol. 1*. Washington, D.C.: Amer. Psychol. Ass., 1959. Pp. 62–95.

18. Mahrer, A. R. The goals of intensive psychotherapy. In A. R. Mahrer (Ed.) *The goals of psychotherapy*. New York: Appleton-Century-Crofts, 1967. Pp. 162–179.

19. Mahrer, A. R. Motivational theory: foundations for personality classification. In A. R. Mahrer (Ed.) *New approaches to personality classification.* New York: Columbia Univer. Press, 1970. Pp. 239–276.

20. Mahrer, A. R., & Pearson, L. The directions of psychotherapeutic change. In A. R. Mahrer & L. Pearson (Eds.) *Creative developments in psychotherapy.* Vol. 1. Cleveland: Case Western Res. Univ. Press, in press.

21. Mahrer, A. R., & Pearson, L. The working processes of psychotherapy: creative developments. In A. R. Mahrer & L. Pearson (Eds.) *Creative developments in psychotherapy.* Vol. 1. Cleveland: Case Western Res. Univ. Press, in press.

22. May, R., Angel, E., & Ellenberger, H. F. (Eds.) *Existence: a new dimension in psychiatry and psychology.* New York: Basic Books, 1958.

23. May, R. Existential bases of psychotherapy. In R. May (Ed.) *Existential psychology.* New York: Random House, 1969. Pp. 1–48.

24. Mullan, H., & Sangiuliano I. *The therapist's contribution to the treatment process.* Springfield, Ill.: C. C. Thomas, 1964.

25. Reik, T. *Listening with the third ear.* New York: Grove Press, 1948.

26. Rogers, C. R. Some learnings from a study of psychotherapy with schizophrenics. In A. Goldstein & S. Dean (Eds.) *The investigation of psychotherapy.* New York: Wiley, 1966. Pp. 5–13.

27. Rogers, C. R. The process of the basic encounter group. In J. F. T. Bugental (Ed.) *Challenges of humanistic psychology.* New York: McGraw-Hill, 1967. Pp. 261–276.

28. Rotter, J. B. *Social learning and clinical psychology.* Englewood Cliffs, N.J.: Prentice-Hall, 1954.

29. Schafer, R. Regression in the service of the ego. In G. Lindzey (Ed.) *Assessment of human motives.* New York: Rinehart, 1958.

30. Szasz, T. S. *The myth of mental illness.* New York: Hoeber-Harper, 1961.

31. Truax, C. B., & Carkhuff, R. R. New directions in clinical research. In B. G. Berenson & R. R. Carkhuff (Eds.) *Sources of gain in counseling and psychotherapy.* New York: Holt, Rinehart & Winston, 1967. Pp. 358–391.

ENCOURAGING CLIENT RESPONSIBILITY

Thomas J. Murphy
A clinical psychologist at Veterans Administration Edward Hines, Jr. Hospital, Hines, Illinois. He is Adjunct Assistant Professor of Psychiatry at Loyola University of Chicago, Stritch School of Medicine.

Alfred Adler (1973a, 1973b) seems to have been among the first of the modern theorists/clinicians to emphasize personal responsibility for one's behavior. Viewing neurotic symptoms as a means of avoiding responsibility, Adler wrote: "The life plan of the neurotic demands categorically that if he fails, it should be through someone else's fault and that he should be freed from personal responsibility. . . . Every therapeutic cure . . . tears him from the cradle of his freedom from responsibility" (Ansbacher & Ansbacher, 1956, pp. 270–271).

Adler (1973a) stressed the patient's active, responsible role in psychotherapy when he stated, "The actual change in the nature of the patient can only be his own doing" (p. 336). According to Adler, "From the very beginning the consultant must try to make it clear that the responsibility for his cure is the patient's business" (p. 336).

Today many schools of psychotherapy emphasize that an individual is responsible for his or her behavior. Stressing the importance of client responsibility in psychotherapy, Yalom (1980) indicated: "The assumption of responsibility is a

---

This article is based on a paper submitted to the faculty of the Alfred Adler Institute of Chicago in partial fulfillment of the requirements for the certificate in psychotherapy. The author wishes to express his appreciation to Dr. Harold H. Mosak, his advisor, for his assistance and encouragement. Appreciation is also expressed to Dr. Gerald J. Mozdzierz for reading the original paper and for his helpful comments on a draft of this article. The author also wishes to thank Mr. Howard Pollock for reading the original paper.

Individual Psychology, 40(2), June, 1984, **pp. 122–132**

precondition of therapeutic change" (p. 226). He added: "Once having reached this point, a patient has entered the vestibule of change" (p. 240).

Since Adler's emphasis on personal responsibility is shared by many current schools of psychotherapy, it seems worthwhile and timely to examine how the Adlerian therapist encourages client responsibility and to describe techniques or methods used by other schools of psychotherapy to encourage client responsibility.

THE ADLERIAN THERAPIST'S ATTITUDE

The initial step that the therapist takes to encourage client responsibility involves his or her attitude toward clients (Yalom, 1980). For the Adlerian, mutual trust and respect are important qualities of the effective psychotherapeutic relationship (Dreikurs, 1956). Other important characteristics are cooperation between therapist and client and attitudes of equality and friendliness (Adler, 1958; Mosak, 1979).

Viewing Adlerian psychotherapy as "a cooperative educational enterprise," Mosak stressed the client's responsibility and active role:

> Therapy is structured to inform the patient that a creative human being plays a role in creating one's problems, that one is responsible (not in the sense of blame) for one's actions, and that one's problems are based upon faulty perceptions, and inadequate or faulty learnings, especially of faulty values. If this is so, one can assume responsibility for change. . . . From the initiation of treatment, the patient's efforts to remain passive are discouraged. (1979, p. 65)

Often the Adlerian will assess the client's life-style, which is made up of the convictions the individual has about himself or herself and about the world (Mosak, 1979). The life-style assessment includes investigation of the client's family constellation, "a grouping of members playing various social roles in relation to each other" (Shulman, 1973, p. 30). Examining the family constellation helps the Adlerian understand how the client found significance in his or her family and how convictions and values developed. The life-style investigation also includes analyzing the client's early recollections, which is considered a projective technique (Mosak, 1958). Early recollections "are reminders he carries about with him of his own limits and of the meaning of circumstances"

(Adler, 1958, p. 73). From the summary of the individual's early recollections, his or her "basic mistakes" are identified (Mosak, 1979). Among the types of "basic mistakes" that Mosak (1979) identifies are overgeneralizations and faulty values. An example of an overgeneralization is: "Men cannot be trusted." A faulty value would be: "The most important thing in life is to be liked by everybody." While identifying a client's weaknesses, the Adlerian can encourage by listing his or her assets.

During the life-style assessment, the client also plays an active role. He or she is asked what in the assessment has special significance, what he or she agrees and/or disagrees with, and what needs to be modified. Frequently the client is given a copy of the life-style summary. By sharing the completed life-style with the client, the therapist fosters cooperation and responsibility, which are vital for future progress.

ADLERIAN TECHNIQUES

In addition to adopting an attitude that the client is responsible for his or her own therapy and for making changes, the Adlerian therapist may use a wide range of methods or techniques that encourage the client to assume responsibility for himself or herself. However, unless a relationship of trust, respect, and cooperation between client and therapist has been established, these methods are likely to be ineffective.

Task-Setting

One method Adlerians use to encourage clients to assume responsibility for their lives is task-setting. "The prototype for task-setting" is seen in Adler's therapy of depressed individuals (Mosak, 1979, p. 71). In dealing with depressed patients, Adler (1958) advised, "You can be cured in fourteen days if you follow this prescription. Try to think every day how you can please someone" (p. 259). "All my efforts are devoted toward increasing the social interest of the patient. . . . As soon as he can connect himself with his fellow men on an equal and cooperative footing, he is cured" (Adler, 1958, p. 260).

Another example of task-setting would be suggesting that a shy college freshman have a conversation each day with a student he or she does not know. A student who comes to therapy because he or she is procrastinating in writing his or her master's thesis could be given the task of writing two hundred words each day.

The Pushbutton Technique

A method Mosak (1979) uses to encourage client responsibility is the pushbutton technique. This method teaches clients that they are responsible for both their good feelings as well as their bad feelings—that they create their own moods.

In the pushbutton technique, clients are asked to close their eyes and visualize an event in their life that made them very happy (e.g., graduation, wedding day). They are asked to re-experience the good feelings they had on this occasion. Next, clients are requested to visualize an unpleasant event such as when they felt humiliated and like a failure and to experience those feelings. Then they are asked again to visualize and re-experience the happy incident and the associated positive feelings. What the Adlerian therapist wants his or her clients to learn is they can create their feelings by the thoughts they choose to have (Mosak, 1979).

Encouragement Techniques

Encouragement techniques are also used by Adlerian therapists to foster client responsibility. Stressing the importance of encouragement in psychotherapy, Adler stated, "Altogether, in every step of the treatment, we must not deviate from the path of encouragement" (Ansbacher & Ansbacher, 1956, p. 342). Demonstrating concern for the patient, instilling hope, showing the patient that there are answers to problems, and emphasizing the positive are encouragement techniques (Mosak & Shulman, 1974). Helping the client to redefine goals in order to lessen overambition and decrease fear of failing is another encouragement method. Use of these methods often results in the client actively accepting responsibility for himself or herself.

In his article entitled "Encouragement Techniques," Perman (1975) indicated that having the client actively participate in treatment decisions helps the individual to view himself or herself as able to assume responsibility for his or her behavior and decisions. Perman told of treating an eleven-year-old boy who was extremely shy and had difficulty in being assertive and in making decisions. A condition of treatment was that the boy would decide what would be discussed in the sessions as well as the time and frequency of their meetings. Perman stated that this approach resulted in the boy taking responsibility for himself.

Confrontation Techniques

Adlerian therapists also encourage client responsibility by using confrontation techniques of which Shulman (1972) described various categories. Statements that specifically encourage client responsibility are described here.

Responsibility for Responses of Others. In this confrontation technique, the therapist points out to the client that he or she is responsible for the way that others respond to him or her. In other words, the client learns that his or her behavior encourages a type of response from others. Shulman (1972) gave the following example:

> When a patient asks, "Why do people walk over me? I'm only trying to be a good guy," the therapist answers, "Because you want them to walk over you. After all, it is a lot easier to be a good guy if you let other people walk over you than if you don't let them walk over you. You are the one who is causing it." (p. 180)

Presenting Existing Alternatives. Another confrontation technique for enhancing client responsibility is to present him or her with alternatives (Mosak & Shulman, 1974). Shulman (1972) gave the following example: "You don't have to spend your life complaining about how little money your husband makes, you can get a job and help out. What do you want to do about it?" (p. 182). Shulman then commented: "One of the things you are in this way telling the patient is, 'Look at the choice you are making' ".

Responsibility for change. Another technique directly confronts the client by stating that he or she is responsible for making changes in his or her life (Mosak & Shulman, 1974). Shulman (1972) suggests: "And we will say, 'Do you want to change or do you want to just sit and talk about it for a while?' " (p. 182).

Time Factor. Following naturally from the above-mentioned confrontation of responsibility for change is focusing on what the client will do and when. Shulman (1972) indicated that the Adlerian therapist often will ask: "You now have insight, what are you going to do about it?" He will follow that question with: "How long do you plan to wait before you do it? Ten years?" Shulman remarked: "This is a nonsense statement calculated to provoke the patient into recognizing that nothing will change until he takes the first step to change".

Placing Responsibility

Dinkmeyer, Pew, and Dinkmeyer (1979) described a technique they used in marital counseling called "placing responsibility." They put responsibility on the husband and wife at the beginning of the session by asking what they would like to work on. If the clients decide to tell about a suggestion given previously by the therapists, they will ask the couple to state what it was. They will then ask: "What did you do?" and "What did you learn?" (p. 261). These two questions were frequently asked by Dreikurs (1972a, 1972b) in his counseling sessions.

TECHNIQUES USED BY OTHER SCHOOLS OF PSYCHOTHERAPY

Other schools of psychotherapy also use techniques to encourage client responsibility. Some of these methods they share with Adlerians, others can be incorporated into Adlerian psychotherapy.

Transactional Analysis

One contemporary school of psychotherapy that encourages client responsibility is Transactional Analysis. As Yalom (1980) pointed out, transactional analysts encourage clients to assume responsibility for themselves by requesting that they make a contract. Steiner (1974) indicated that the contract puts responsibility on both the client and the therapist. In making the contract, clients specify what they want to change about themselves in order to attain the goals they have chosen (Goulding & Goulding, 1979).

Another method that encourages client responsibility is focusing on words that Goulding and Goulding stated "deny autonomy." Among the words that they listed are "can't," "try," and "make feel."

Goulding and Goulding suggested that therapists pay more attention to the word "can't," which usually translates as "won't." The response to clients' statements such as "I can't stop smoking," "I can't stay on a diet," or "I can't write my master's thesis" is: "You mean you won't." Goulding and Goulding wrote,

> A client said, "I can't talk about myself or write about myself. I have a very important letter to write and I have to write it to get a promotion. But I just can't." Obviously, she can and she won't. As long as she believes her "can't," she remains a victim. Her work in therapy begins with the statement, "I won't write about me." (p. 86)

Goulding and Goulding further indicated: "When a client says, 'I will try to . . . ,' we suspect that she is willing to put forth effort in such a way as to fail to accomplish" (p. 85). They wrote: "We ask the client to be in touch with how she plans to sabotage herself when she says 'try' rather than 'do' " (p. 86).

Clients do not accept their autonomy and responsibility when they make statements such as "He makes me feel angry" or "The weather makes me feel depressed." Goulding and Goulding recommended that therapists be aware of "make feel" statements. By confronting clients when they use these statements, therapists teach them that they choose and are therefore responsible for their feelings.

Focusing on words that "deny autonomy" resembles Adlerian confrontation and encouragement methods of enhancing client responsibility. In addition, Mosak and Gushurst (1971), Adlerian therapists, have indicated that patients' statements (e.g., "I'll try" and "I just can't help it; it's a habit with me") reflect their movement and can help the therapist understand "both immediate goals and underlying personality."

Gestalt Therapy

Gestalt therapists also emphasize personal responsibility. Perls (1970) stated, "Full identification with yourself can take place if you are willing to take full responsibility—*response-ability*—for yourself, for your actions, feelings, thoughts; and if you stop mixing up responsibility with obligation" (pp. 29–30).

As Yalom (1980) has pointed out, Perls encouraged clients to assume responsibility for themselves by asking them to make "I statements" and by using the "I take responsibility" exercise (Levitsky & Perls, 1970). Perls (1969) described a participant in his dreamwork seminar:

> She told me that she has a wall between herself and the world. Of course here we have an *it* to work with. She says she has got a *thing*: something outside, something May is not responsible for. It just happens that she's a victim of circumstances. (p. 100)

In working with Perls, this client made the statement: "I'm closing myself up and not talking" (p. 106). Perls commented that she "got quite a little bit of integration by identifying with her wall" (ibid.). He advised her "to listen to whenever you use the *it* . . . and just reformulate your sentence. Start on the pure verbal level until the experience comes: It's not an *it*, there, but *I* ".

In the "I take responsibility" exercise, when a client makes a statement, he or she is asked to add "and I take responsibility for it" (Levitsky & Perls, 1970, p. 146). For example, if a client said, "I'm scared," he or she would add "and I take responsibility for it." If the individual said, "I am aware that my hand is quivering," he or she would again add "and I take responsibility for it." If the client remarked, "I am feeling more comfortable and relaxed," again he or she would say "and I take responsibility for it."

Another method that Gestalt therapists use to encourage responsibility is to ask clients to change their questions into statements. Often questions are not essential and may reflect the client's passive style and laziness. Enright (1970) pointed out that asking questions in group therapy may be a way of avoiding participation.

Yalom's Existential Approach

In his book entitled *Existential Psychotherapy*, Yalom (1980) devoted a whole chapter to the idea of responsibility.

> To assist the patient in assuming responsibility, the therapist's first step is not a technique but the adoption of an attitude upon which subsequent technique will rest. The therapist must continually operate within the frame of reference that a patient has created his or her own distress. . . . The therapist must determine what role a particular patient plays in his or her own dilemma, and find ways to communicate this insight to the patient. (p. 231)

Yalom recommended that the therapist be alert to situations and ways in which a client avoids responsibility and communicate these to him or her. The therapist can examine instances of "responsibility avoidance" that occur in therapy and help the client realize that these are similar to his or her life situation.

According to Yalom, therapists who feel that they alone must make things happen in the therapy session have allowed clients to place responsibility for change onto them. Yalom pointed out that therapists may express their feeling of bearing the entire responsibility for therapy. Therapists may also indicate that they do "not experience the patient as actively collaborating in therapy" (p. 236). Yalom also indicated: "Or the therapist may find that there is no more potent mode of galvanizing a sluggish patient into action than by simply asking, 'Why do you come?' " (p. 236).

Malamud's Laughing Game

Malamud (1980) developed an exercise known as the Laughing Game to enhance awareness of responsibility. In this technique, participants are directed to make their partner smile or laugh and are told that they will receive a paper token when they do. Malamud indicated that participants give very different meanings to the purpose of this procedure. Some assume it is to compete with their partner and collect as many tokens as they can, while others believe they should comply with their partner and not offend or frustrate him or her. For other participants, the exercise is a chance to relate with others and have some fun. Malamud states that toward the end of the Laughing Game "you decided what this game was 'really' all about, and then you reacted to the requirements, pressures, and demands of this 'reality' as if it were the only reality, a given imposed upon you from the outside rather than a 'reality' you yourself invented or projected" (p. 71).

Malamud indicated that as the players of the Laughing Game achieve greater insight into their role as creators of their life-scripts, they have a greater need to take responsibility for their lives.

SUMMARY AND CONCLUSION

Viewing psychotherapy as "an exercise in cooperation" (Adler, 1958) and as "a cooperative educational enterprise" (Mosak, 1979), the Adlerian therapist encourages client responsibility. In addition to adopting the attitude that the client is responsible for his or her therapy and for making changes, the Adlerian psychotherapist may use several methods or techniques that encourage the client to assume responsibility for himself or herself. These methods include task-setting, the pushbutton technique, encouragement techniques, confrontation techniques, and "placing responsibility."

Other schools of psychotherapy also use techniques of encouraging client responsibility. Some of these methods they share with Adlerians, others can be incorporated into Adlerian psychotherapy. Methods used by transactional analysts include making a therapeutic contract, and focusing on words such as "can't," "try," and "make feel" that "deny autonomy." Gestalt therapists also foster client responsibility by asking clients to make "I-statements," to participate in the "I take responsibility" exercise, and to change questions into statements. Yalom suggested encouraging client responsibility by examining instances of "responsibility avoidance" that occur in therapy and helping the client realize that these are similar to his or her life situation. Malamud developed the Laughing Game to show clients how they give meaning to their experiences and thereby enhance their awareness of their responsibility.

The techniques or methods for encouraging client responsibility are likely to prove ineffective or perhaps even deteriorate into gimmicks unless a relationship of trust, respect, and cooperation between client and therapist has been established.

Finally, the creative efforts of therapists are needed to develop new methods of encouraging clients to assume responsibility for themselves. The importance of client responsibility is highlighted in Yalom's (1980) statement:

> To be aware of responsibility is to be aware of creating one's own self, destiny, life predicament, feelings and, if such be the case, one's own suffering. For the patient who will not accept such responsibility, who persists in blaming others—either other individuals or other forces—for his or her dysphoria, no real therapy is possible. (1980, p. 218)

REFERENCES

Adler, A. (1958). *What life should mean to you.* Ed. A. Porter. New York: Capricorn Books. (Originally published 1931)

Adler, A. (1973a). Life-lie and responsibility in neurosis and psychosis; a contribution to melancholia. In P. Radin (trans.), *The practice and theory of Individual Psychology.* Totowa, N.J.: Littlefield, Adams & Co. (Originally published 1914)

Adler, A. (1973b). Melancholia and paranoia. In P. Radin (trans.), *The practice and theory of Individual Psychology.* Totowa, N.J.: Littlefield, Adams & Co. (Originally published 1924)

Ansbacher, H. L., & Ansbacher, R. (eds.) (1956). *The Individual Psychology of Alfred Adler.* New York: Basic Books.

Dinkmeyer, D. C., Pew, W. L., & Dinkmeyer, D. C., Jr. (1979). *Adlerian counseling and psychotherapy.* Monterey, Calif.: Brooks/Cole.

Dreikurs, R. (1956). Adlerian psychotherapy. In F. Fromm-Reichmann & J. L. Moreno (eds.), *Progress in psychotherapy.* New York: Grune & Stratton.

Dreikurs, R. (1972a). Counseling a boy: A demonstration. *Journal of Individual Psychology, 28,* 223–231.

Dreikurs, R. (1972b). Family counseling: A demonstration. *Journal of Individual Psychology, 28,* 207–222.

Enright, J. B. (1970). An introduction to Gestalt techniques. In J. Fagen & I. L. Shepherd (eds.), *Gestalt therapy now.* Palo Alto, Calif.: Science and Behavior Books.

Goulding, M. M., & Goulding, R. L. (1979). *Changing lives through redecision therapy.* New York: Brunner/Mazel.

Levitsky, A., & Perls, F. (1970). The rules and games of Gestalt therapy. In J. Fagen & I. L. Shepherd (eds.), *Gestalt therapy now*. Palo Alto, Calif.: Science and Behavior Books.

Malamud, D. I. (1980). The Laughing Game: An exercise for sharpening awareness of self-responsibility. *Psychotherapy: Theory, Research and Practice, 17*, 69–73.

Mosak, H. (1958). Early recollections as a projective technique. *Journal of Projective Techniques, 22*, 302–311.

Mosak, H. (1979). Adlerian psychotherapy. In R. Corsini (ed.), *Current psychotherapies*. 2nd ed. Itasca, Ill.: F. E. Peacock.

Mosak, H., & Gushurst, R. (1971). What patients say and what they mean. *American Journal of Psychotherapy, 25*, 428–436.

Mosak, H., & Shulman, B. H. (1974). *Individual psychotherapy: A syllabus*. 2nd ed. Chicago: Alfred Adler Institute.

Perls, F. S. (1969). *Gestalt therapy verbatim*. Moab, Utah: Real People Press.

Perls, F. S. (1970). Four lectures. In J. Fagen & I. L. Shepherd (eds.), *Gestalt therapy now*. Palo Alto, Calif.: Science and Behavior Books.

Perman, S. (1975). Encouragement techniques. *Individual Psychologist, 11*(2), 13–18.

Shulman, B. H. (1972). Confrontation techniques. *Journal of Individual Psychology, 28*, 177–183.

Shulman, B. H. (1973). Life style. In *Contributions to Individual Psychology*. Chicago: Alfred Adler Institute.

Steiner, C. (1974). *Scripts people live*. New York: Grove Press.

Yalom, I. D. (1980). *Existential psychotherapy*. New York: Basic Books.

SECTION III
INDIVIDUAL ADULT COUNSELING AND THERAPY TECHNIQUES

EDITORS' COMMENTS

Adlerian psychology is based on the principle that all behavior has a goal or purpose. This fundamental tenet is rooted in the early learning experiences and social context of the individual. Adler believed that each individual develops a "lifestyle" or characteristic/unique way of living based upon these experiences. The lifestyle promotes a goal or purpose of life. The format is

I am . . .
Life is . . .
Others are . . .
Therefore . . .

For example,

I am weak.
Life is scary.
Others are there to take care of me.
Therefore, I must live very carefully.

Adlerians assess recollections, early experiences, birth orders, and dreams to understand the individual's cognitive explanations about life.

The master psychotherapist, Harold Mosak, discussed a meeting he had with a woman named Ann. The lifestyle assessment is described. This technique helps Ann learn her beliefs about herself, the world, and how she must live her life. Mosak makes the process look deceptively simple. The simplicity is the result of his clear principles about human behavior.

One important component of the lifestyle or personality assessment is the family constellation. Mosak showed how important this was to how Ann lived her life. Shulman provided a more in-depth look at Adler's ideas about the family constellation. The family constellation interview guide provides a good outline of the important ingredients for personality diagnosis. In the case example, Pearl described her "subjectively perceived early environment" and her choice of reaction to it.

Forer described how birth order affects life, both in and out of the therapy session. This knowledge clearly affects an individual's personality structure, as Shulman discussed. Additionally, it provides important information for the therapeutic process. With this knowledge, the therapist can reduce therapeutic resistance and increase cooperation and collaboration with the client.

Mosak highlighted the unity or consistency of the personality. He showed how our early memories reflect our lifestyle. The content and the pattern of the memories are important. The therapist can learn to predict quickly the client's response generally to therapy and specifically to the therapist.

Papanek's classic paper clearly shows how early recollections (ERs) are collected and interpreted. Two cases are presented to show the process in action. Papanek believed that ERs help both the therapist and client understand the client's lifestyle in order to make healthier behavior possible.

ERs contain faults or mistaken beliefs that limit an individual's potential. After the mistaken beliefs are identified, how can they be changed? Sometimes insight or awareness is all that is needed. In other cases, the pattern is too ingrained and not readily accessible to change. Lingg and Kottman described the creative use of visualization to help individuals examine their basic convictions. Lew and Bettner described how ERs can be used as a basis for problem-directed therapy. Their eight-step process, called Connexions Focusing Technique, is presented and enhanced through case study examples.

Dream analysis is another important skill used for both assessment and intervention. Slavik showed how dreams can serve as the basis in short-term solution-focused treatment. In Adlerian analysis, dreams are seen as purposeful rehearsals for future situations. The symbols are not universal, as Freud suggested, but are chosen directly to fit the individual's private logic.

Adlerians use a variety of techniques in the counseling and therapy process. The Adlerian interview has been viewed as both diagnostic and therapeutic, or what Sperry called "interventive interviewing." In this brief paper, Sperry described the basic interviewing questions and their purposes.

Shulman's two papers describe the active movement by the therapist leading to confrontation. This technique forces the client to provide an immediate response, make an immediate change, or do immediate examination of a social issue. Confrontation techniques are therapeutic challenges designed to force the client to face and change troublesome goals and beliefs. Shulman described 11 categories where confrontation can be used: moods and feelings, hidden reasons, biased apperceptions and private logic, private goals, mottos, responsibility for the responses of others, self-defeating behavior, existing alternatives, responsibility for change, and time factor.

Metaphors, fables, and parables are useful techniques in therapy, as they allow clients to grasp personally difficult concepts. These procedures offer both implicit and explicit pathways to teach lessons. Pancner showed how parables and fables can be used to create meaningful change. Mosak used religious allusions to help clients with spiritual, existential, and religious problems. He believed that these procedures have messages and usefulness with all clients, not just those presenting with "religious issues."

The "as if" technique was created by Adler as an intervention in which the client anticipates, pretends, and/or enacts a future event, belief, or desired behavior. Carich presented several variations of this technique including role-play, imagery, fantasy/daydreaming, implosion, metaphors, paradoxical prescription, reframe, and non-strategic task assignments.

Many therapists believe that humor as a therapeutic technique has great value; however, proving this has been elusive. There does not appear to be any exact "technique." Humor can assist the client/therapist relationship, however, as well as assist in the client's diagnosis, interpretation, and reorientation. Rutherford (1984) provided an overview of the use of humor in therapy as well as several examples. McBrien extended the use of humor as an explicit encouragement technique in couples counseling.

The use of paradox in therapy has been a hallmark of the Adlerian approach. This idea seems almost absurd—prescribing the very symptom the client is hoping to have disappear! This procedure however, is therapeutically solid in that the therapist does not oppose his/her client but rather joins him/her while exhibiting a warm, accepting relationship.

The creative therapeutic genius, Ray Corsini, took paradoxical techniques a step further with the relapse technique. This procedure prevents behavioral relapse by prescribing the relapse. West, Main, and Zarski built on the work of Jay Haley and offered an eight-step model for implementing paradoxical prescriptions. Kopp and Kivel showed that paradoxes can be used as a means of understanding therapeutic resistance and resolving impasses. A case example highlights a four-phase process of "traps and escapes."

Sperry offered five hypnotherapy methods. These techniques do not require the induction of a formal trance. The five techniques have been found very useful in insight-oriented therapy. Fairfield showed how hypnosis techniques can be used to reorient the individual and create lifestyle change, while Sperry and Carlson described a multi-modal treatment program including hypnosis to create habit change. In this paper, the procedure is applied to smoking cessation.

Prinz encouraged Adlerians to work with substance abusers. He believed that the Alderian approach and techniques are particularly well-adapted to this population. Cooley described techniques for overcoming resistance in working with substance abuse clients, while Arkin, Lewis, and Carlson described treatment strategies for use with couples with alcohol problems. They categorized treatment into three general types: alcohol intervention, general marital improvement strategies, and relapse prevention.

In the final part of this section, Mosak used the "pushbutton" technique to disrupt depressive thinking. Once this occurs, the goal of depression can be assessed and a treatment plan formulated.

REFERENCE

Rutherford, R. (1984). Humor in psychotherapy. *Individual Psychology, 50*(2), 207–222.

LIFE STYLE ASSESSMENT: A DEMONSTRATION FOCUSED ON FAMILY CONSTELLATION[1,2]

Harold H. Mosak
A clinical psychologist in private practice in Chicago.
He is currently president of the Alfred Adler Institute there,
and is also engaged in writing, teaching, and consulting.

The phrase, life style, is currently used in many ways which Adler never intended. As Adler used it, life style refers to the "unity in each individual—in his thinking, feeling, acting; in his so-called conscious and unconscious, in every expression of his personality. This unity we call the style of life of the individual" (3, p. 175). While we agree with this definition of life style, we prefer one somewhat more limited, namely, a person's central convictions which, to oversimplify, describe how he views himself in relation to his view of life.

We formally assess a life style by interviewing the person regarding his family constellation and his early recollections, as Adler had emphasized the importance of birth order position and early recollections (3, p. 328). The family constellation part was described first by Dreikurs (4) and then by Shulman (7); the early recollections part has been described by this author (5). In an actual case we give equal importance to the two parts. In the present demonstration

[1]The tape of the demonstration at the Fourth Brief Psychotherapy Conference, Chicago, March 25, 1972, was not available to the author. The demonstration reported here instead, was conducted the following day before the audience at a workshop of the Alfred Adler Institute, Chicago.

[2]Introductory statement and comments addressed to the audience are in roman type; the interview proper is in italic type.

Journal of Individual Psychology, 28(2), November, 1972, **pp. 232–247**

early recollections are merely touched upon during the last few minutes, while the emphasis is on the investigation of the family constellation. Dreikurs outlines the significance of this procedure in the following:

> The family constellation is a sociogram of the group at home during the person's formative years. This investigation reveals his field of early experiences, the circumstances under which he developed his personal perspectives and biases, his concepts and convictions about himself and others, his fundamental attitudes, and his own approaches to life, which are the basis for his character, his personality (4, p. 109).

Some comments are in order regarding variations from our usual clinical procedure. At a demonstration such as the present, time is limited. Therefore, (*a*) we could not complete the assessment nor write the summary we ordinarily undertake in clinical practice, (*b*) we interpreted for the client as we proceeded whereas in actual practice the interpretive summary is postponed until data collection is complete, (*c*) the result is not necessarily a model of good interviewing. We also wish to mention that at a demonstration we use a blackboard to enter the main facts obtained through the interview as we go along, so that the audience may keep these before their eyes.

At the present session the client was a high school student, Ann, whom I had never met before, and about whom I did not have any information. Her high school counselor, who attended the workshop, had invited her to serve as a subject for this demonstration before an audience, and she had agreed.

At the beginning of the interview we established that Ann was 17 years old, one of five children, with an older sister, Debbie, age 19; a younger brother, Sam, age 13; and a pair of twins, Marty and Mary, age 10. One can start formulating hypotheses immediately. Thus I said, looking at this information, my best guess at this point is that Debbie, Ann and Sam form one subgroup and the twins, a second subgroup.

> **Dr. M.:** *How do you feel about this, Ann?*
> **Ann:** *It's right.*
> **Dr. M.:** *To confirm this, let me ask, who played with whom?*
> **Ann:** *I played with Debbie. Sam usually played by himself, and Marty and Mary played together.*

Here Ann may be suggesting that my guess of a two-group family was wrong, that it was actually a three-group family, 2-1-2. We shall keep this in mind and see which it might be. To help ascertain I shall ask:

Dr. M.: *Who fought with each other?*
Ann: *Debbie and I fought constantly, and Sam and Debbie fought constantly.*
Dr. M.: *And who else fought?*
Ann: *The twins fought.*

"Sam and Debbie fought constantly" would suggest that they are in the same subgroup. At this point I could ascertain more information about the subgroups, but I shall not go into that. These questions, and most of those which I shall ask can be found in the Dreikurs paper to which I have referred (4).

Regarding subgroups, psychologists have a difficult time with families beyond three children. They can more or less accurately describe an oldest, a middle, or a youngest child; but the fourth child is not described and the fifth certainly not. However, by dividing families into subgroups of children, it is possible to determine the psychological position of each child within the family. Sometimes, just on the basis of what we have so far here on the blackboard we can already begin to formulate some hypotheses, some alternatives.

Dr. M.: *What kind of child was Debbie when you were growing up?*
Ann: *She was* very *studious all the time. . . . Well, from my point of view, she was a goody-goody. . . . . It's hard to talk about your own sister.*
Dr. M.: *Especially if you have to say such nice things about her.*
Ann: *No, she was* very *reliable and* very *responsible. . . . and* very *talkative.*
Dr. M.: *Did she get into trouble at school for that?*
Ann: *Occasionally.*
Dr. M.: *So, while she was a goody-goody, she still got into trouble occasionally. She wasn't quite perfect. What else was she like?*
Ann: *Well, she* always *tried to please my parents. And she was* very *sensitive. You know like she cried very easily. . . . that's about all.*
Dr. M.: *I'm going to invite you, Ann, to look at all of this on the blackboard. If you had one word to describe your sister, what word would you use? Let me give you an incomplete sentence. She was . . .*
Ann: *Responsible, I guess.*
Dr. M.: *That's a good word.*
Ann: *I can't do it in* one *word.*
Dr. M.: *I can. Would you like to hear my one word?*
Ann: *Yes.*
Dr. M.: *She was very . . .* (Audience laughter.) *How does that sound?*
Ann: *Very good.* (Ann and audience laughter.)

She was not just *very* studious, but *very* studious *all* the time. She *always* tried to please the parents. Even though Ann does not use the word "very" each time, she uses it quite consistently. Even when she doesn't use it, she still describes her sister as a "very," and a "very" is *always* something positive. *Very* responsible, good-goody, *very* studious, *always* wanting to please, and so forth. It must have been a hard act to follow.

Now, one thing Adlerians observe is that when you have two children in competition (and when two children are this close in age, they generally are in competition), they operate as "teeter-totter twins." Where one succeeds, the other fails or does not even get into that area. He just decides, "The heck with it; its really not worth it. I'm going to do something else." They carve up the territory because every child in every family, you (*to audience*), Ann, and I, is striving for significance. We want to count; we want to belong; we want to have the feeling that people take notice of us, that we are part of it. We don't always use the best methods for gaining significance, but even sometimes with the poorest methods, people do take notice of us, as any teacher will testify. If that is the case, we can already begin to make some predictions in terms of probabilities with respect to Ann.

> **Dr. M.:** *Since Debbie was "very," and "hardly ever." Let's find out, Ann, what kind of kid you were.*
> **Ann:** *"Hardly ever" and not "very."* (Ann and audience laughter.) *I wasn't studious, and I wasn't a goody-goody. Well I was actually . . .*
> **Dr. M.:** *Very reliable?* (Traits with which she described Debbie.)
> **Ann:** *No, I wasn't.*
> **Dr. M.:** *Very responsible?*
> **Ann:** *No.*
> **Dr. M.:** *Very talkative?*
> **Ann:** *No.*
> **Dr. M.:** *Always tried to please parents?*

If you could see Ann as I can see her from this position, you would have seen the glimmer of a recognition reflex when I mentioned "always tried to please parents." And you are going to discover that she does not try to please them very much—although she wants to.

> **Dr. M.:** *Right?*
> **Ann:** *Right!*
> **Dr. M.:** *Very sensitive? Cry easily?*
> **Ann:** *Yeah!*

Sibling competition is one of the major factors leading to differences between children. Similarities occur in the area of the family values. A family value is one which *both* parents hold in common, and every child must take a stand, positive or negative, with respect to that particular value or behavior. You can well imagine because of the potency of the parents that most of the children will adopt positive attitudes to the parental values. If it's a family where both parents stress being good in school, all the children will do *something* about being good in school. They'll either be very good or very poor. Where the family values are not involved, the child may not take a stand at all. Consequently, one can suspect that both parents have some kind of stand in common on sensitivity, and Ann is now nodding her head, and consequently each child has to make up his mind whether he is going to be sensitive or not. It is not determined by the competition, because in terms of the competition, whatever Debbie does, Ann does the opposite.

Dr. M.: *Anything you want to add to just the "minuses"?*
Ann: *I was athletic, whereas Debbie didn't even bother with sports.*
Dr. M.: *You were athletic and therefore Debbie was minus.*
Ann: *I think I was more interested—well maybe I was more generally creative than she was as a child.*

You notice here the intensity of the competition. She does not merely say, I was athletic or I was creative. I was *more* creative, I was *more* athletic, which means that she grew up with one eye on her sister, watched how well her sister was doing and then compared herself to that. Since her sister was so "very," she had to feel inferior in most respects. Ann lives life *comparatively*.

Dr. M.: *What was Sam like?*
Ann: *If you want to compare him between Debbie and me, he was more like Debbie. He was a good student, but at the same time he was athletic and enjoyed sports like my parents did.*
Dr. M.: *Both parents did? So you see we have another family value. Both parents enjoyed sports and every child is going to take a positive or negative stand on it.*
Ann: *He's athletic,* very *responsible for a kid his age, too, and likeable. That's about all.*

That makes a good start. If you look at Sam, you will notice that he has many of the same characteristics that Debbie had, with one major exception. He's not "very." He's likeable, he's athletic, and he's a good student, but he's not "very." Only one time does she use the word "very" with respect to him. One reason that Sam could become these things is that Ann had already become discouraged and had defaulted. Therefore, he could become those things which she was not. Since Ann was a poor student, it was easy for him to become a good student, but, of course, as he became a good student, Ann found herself in the middle of a pincers movement—the two "good" ones, and herself in the middle. Not "very" good, not "very" accomplished, between two good kids! The squeeze was on. Now she said previously that Sam and Debbie fought, not Sam and she, but Sam and Debbie. And you can see the competition there, too, because Sam wanted to do the same things Debbie was doing, except she had a six-year head start. She could even like her six-year younger brother as long as he knew his place. If he occasionally decided to compete, she shoved him down.

Dr. M.: *What kind of boy was Sam?*
Ann: *Well, he was the kind of boy that I suppose any father would like.*

"The kind of boy any father would like." You see that Sam had a place merely by being a boy, so that while he competed, he didn't *have* to compete. But he wasn't merely content to take the place he could have had easily. He figured that you can't have enough of a good thing, so he would see if he could also intrude on Ann's territory a bit. She has not told us this yet, but she will (*Ann nods and bursts out laughing in confirmation.*) I sometimes tell my interns that someday I hope to get good enough at this so that I won't even need the subject. (*Audience laughter.*)

If *any* father would like a boy like this, then her father would like a boy like this. So, Sam must have been his favorite, at least his favorite in the older group. Perhaps when Marty arrived her father transferred his preference to the younger boy; but at least in the older group, we would guess that Sam was father's favorite.

Now, you have Debbie who was "very," and she must have been everybody's favorite—teacher's, parents'. I suspect when teachers got Ann after Debbie, the first day they said, "Gee, I hope you're like your sister."

Dr. M.: *Did they?*
Ann: *Occasionally.*

Teachers, incidentally, think that this is an encouraging remark (*audience laughter*) and they probably said to Sam, "I hope you're not like your sister, Ann." You can imagine what Ann must have felt like, growing up. Unless she had grandparents or an uncle or aunt or a favorite teacher, it must have been, "Why does everyone love everyone else but me?" (*Ann nods.*)

Dr. M.: *Tell me a little bit about Marty.*
Ann: *He's very likeable.*
Dr. M.: *Does anybody know what the next word is going to be?*
Ann: *It's not going to be "very."* (Audience laughter.)
Dr. M.: *Don't let us intimidate you, please, Ann. If you want to use it, okay.*

Ann: *He's amusing.*
Dr. M.: *To whom?*
Ann: *To me, I like him. I think he's just a typical little kid with a big imagination.*
Dr. M.: *He's something like you?*
Ann: *Yes, he is in a way.*
Dr. M.: *And what about Mary?*
Ann: *Mary is a replica of my mother, sort of.*

Now, without asking a question about her mother, you're going to find out what her mother was like.

Dr. M.: *What was Mary like?*
Ann: *She's very domestic, but she's intelligent.* (Audience laughter.)
Dr. M.: *And your mother is not?*
Ann: *Well, I don't want to go . . . well, they're both domestic, yet they're both intelligent at the same time.*
Dr. M.: *Are you trying to say or indicate that these two don't ordinarily go together?*
Ann: *Not ordinarily. I was just . . . you know, you asked me what Mary was like and she's . . .*
Dr. M.: *Are you a candidate for Women's Lib?*
Ann: *Yes!*
Dr. M.: *I thought so.*
Ann: *Well, I was just trying to straighten you out that Mary . . . she tries to act like a mother. Like any ten-year-old girl, she tries to assume the tasks that my mother assumes. It's obvious to me.*
Dr. M.: *Is there much competition between her and Marty?*
Ann: *No, not really.*
Dr. M.: *Yet you said they fight.*
Ann: *Yes, they do fight, but . . .*
Dr. M.: *Go on, tell us how it is.*
Ann: *Well, I don't know. It seems like Mary has her own . . . well my parents expect one thing of Mary and one thing of Marty. I think the twins realize this and they don't cross in each other's territory, so to speak.*
Dr. M.: *Except, apparently when they do, and then they fight.*
Ann: *Then they fight.*

If you look at the blackboard, you will see something interesting. You might not catch it if you did not write it down. Every person but one is "very" in something. Some more than others. If you look at the positive traits that Ann has described—studious, responsible, reliable, etc.—everybody has at least one "very," except Ann. She's the only "un-very" child in this family, except that she is not, because her parents probably regard her as "very" much of a problem.

> **Ann:** *Very true.* (Ann and audience laughter.)

That is apparently the only way in which Ann makes sure that the family or school community take notice of her. She can't be "very" studious "all" the time; she can't please "all" the time; she's had "very" little training in responsibility. She figures that at least through—and I will use the word broadly because I have no more knowledge than you—some kind of "misbehavior," they take notice of her. They know she's there. I would also suspect that through her own "very," she keeps her parents and teachers busier than the other four kids together. Now, her hairdo is hiding her recognition reflex. (*Audience laughter.*)

> **Dr. M.:** *I know you have given us these descriptions as best you could, but let's round out the picture a bit. Who was the most intelligent, and who the least intelligent?*[3]
> **Ann:** *Sam, I think, was most intelligent, and Mary, the least.*
> **Dr. M.:** *I'll tell you what I'm going to do. Ordinarily I would ask you to rate all five of you. But because of the limited blackboard space, and since the twins are not in your group, I am going to restrict the rating to the older three who make up one group. Now then, the most intelligent is Sam, and the least intelligent is?*
> **Ann:** *Well, me.*
> **Dr. M.:** *You say that almost proudly.*
> **Ann:** *Well, no.*
> **Dr. M.:** *Who got the best grades in grade school, and who the poorest?*
> **Ann:** *Debbie got the best grades. Yours truly got the poorest.*
> **Dr. M.:** *What were your favorite subjects in grade school?*
> **Ann:** *Art, gym, and English.*
> **Dr. M.:** *And you didn't like?*
> **Ann:** *Math, science, and social studies.*

Yesterday, at the Brief Psychotherapy Conference, I discussed with some of you the meaning of achievement or underachievement in school subjects. Unfortunately I don't have time to go through all subjects today, but let me take math as an example. Math is a problem-solving activity. To do math or arithmetic isn't, like spelling, a matter of just putting it in your head and when the teacher says,

[3]All the "most" and "least" questions, as well as other pairwise questions, were asked separately, but we combined them here for more compact presentation.—Ed. note.

"Okay, spell 'dog,' " grinding it out for the teacher. You must be able to use past experience to solve the current problem. You have to use your brain as a filter. You have to know what solutions seem to be on the right track (even if eventually they are not) and to discard immediately those which you know aren't going to work at all.

Adler had noted, "Arithmetic demands the greatest degree of independence. In arithmetic, apart from the multiplication table, there is no security: everything depends on free and independent combinations" (2, p. 10). The child who does poorly in math, assuming he's had reasonably good instruction is not self-reliant. Faced with a problem, he says, "I'll never figure that out. Gee, I hope someone will help me. Maybe somebody will get me out of this jam, or maybe fate will do it, but I don't trust my own abilities to do it." So, apparently Ann had already made up her mind very early that all the capability in the family lay with her siblings and there was none left over for her.

Dr. M.: *Who's the most industrious, and who the least?*
Ann: *Debbie, the most; me, the least.*
Dr. M.: *Who's the "goodest", and who rebelled openly?*
Ann: *Debbie was the "goodest," and I was the rebel.*
Dr. M.: *Proudly?*
Ann: *Yep!*
Dr. M.: *Who was the covert rebel, never fought openly, just did what he wanted?*
Ann: *Sam.*
Dr. M.: *Who demanded his own way, and who got it?*
Ann: *I demanded it, and Debbie got it.*
Dr. M.: *And Sam?*
Ann: *Sam got his way also.*

After all, if you're the kind of boy that any father would like, you get your way. Besides which he was the baby of the older group. And that isn't going to hurt your chances of getting your own way. If you look at these two things in combination—who demanded and who got his way—you know the answer to the next question. Who felt sorry for himself? And the answer, of course, has to be Ann. She demanded most and got least. Or perhaps, she felt she got nothing. (*Ann nods.*)

Dr. M.: *Who has a temper?*
Ann: *I do.*

There are only two major reasons for temper. One reason is to announce to the world, "I want to have my own way. You better do it or I'm going to intimidate you." In the words of Adler, "Children make use of outbursts of temper to conquer by terrifying" (1, p. 59). Such a child throws himself on the floor, bangs and kicks, turns purple, hoping that you'll come across. The other reason is righteous indignation. "I'm the custodian of the right, and how dare you do something as wrong as that?" From Ann's answers it would seem that her temper was in the service of enforcing her own way. "I'm going to do what I want; I'm going to get what I want, and nobody's going to tell me how to do, what to do, when to do, and if they don't like it, too bad."

Ann: *Exactly!*

Even though she says, "Exactly," I should like to take a stab also at the second reason for temper. "This family may have its set of values, but I have my set of values, and my ethic is higher than theirs. Therefore, if they don't come across, they are wrong. Those old fogies over thirty don't understand, etc." She already told you she is a candidate for Women's Lib so she has her own ethic there, and I am quite sure that what started out as "I want my own way," as she got older, was tied in with "and I'm right, besides." And because she is right, nobody can tell her anything. Is that the problem?

Ann: *It seems to be.*
Dr. M.: *Who's considerate of others, and who's inconsiderate?*
Ann: *Debbie is considerate, and I guess I am inconsiderate.*
Dr. M.: *Who is most sensitive, and who is least sensitive?*
Ann: *I'm probably the most sensitive, and Sam the least sensitive.*
Dr. M.: *I think we have forgotten to tell them something. Were you a tomboy?*
Ann: *Yes.*

Ann was the tomboy. She was the tomboy for several reasons. One is, it was the opposite of what her folks wanted. Ann is what I call a "reverse puppet." With a regular puppet, if you pull the right string, the right hand goes up; but with a reverse puppet, the left hand goes up. It doesn't stop you from being a puppet. Yet many kids think, "Look how free I am when I am defiant." But actually they are still puppets. The person who is free decides for himself; he does not just do the opposite. If he does, he is still a puppet; he is merely wired wrong, i.e., his left hand goes up instead of his right. You can well imagine that at one level Ann was a tomboy because this is what she should not have been according to her parents. For another reason, it was easier to compete with Sam than with Debbie. At least in competing with Sam she had a chance. With Debbie, there was no chance. So she tried to tackle him on his home grounds, and of course this was reinforced by the fact that the parents were athletic and fostered or encouraged athletic behavior. So it was not a total disaster. She was doing something her parents wanted, and maybe, just maybe, her parents would be pleased with her if she were athletic. She almost *had* to be a tomboy. Let's get back to the ratings.

> **Dr. M.:** *Who had the most friends and who the fewest?*
> **Ann:** *Sam probably had the most friends, Debbie the fewest.*
> **Dr. M.:** *This is the first area we find where you did better than Debbie. Except for one thing. Do you want to tell the audience? According to your family, you didn't have the right friends?*
> **Ann:** *Exactly, exactly.* (Audience laughter.)

Even where she did find some significance, where she did outdistance her sister, it still did not gain her what she really wanted, namely the feeling of belonging. Even though she had more friends and outdid her sister, they really were not the friends a girl like her ought to have, as far as her parents thought.

> **Dr. M.:** *Who was the most shy, and who the least shy?*
> **Ann:** *Maybe Sam was most shy. I was least shy.*
> **Dr. M.:** *Who was most neat and who was least neat?*
> **Ann:** *Debbie was the neatest, and I was least neat.*

There are many more of these ratings but time will not permit me to continue with them; yet each one we have so far, seems to follow in the same pattern. You can almost predict the sequence. As you have seen, as I say these things, Ann says, "exactly." I am going to have to, at this time, move on to her parents.

> **Dr. M.:** *How old is your father, and your mother?*
> **Ann:** *My Dad is 46; my mother is 42.*
> **Dr. M.:** *So you had relatively young parents. Now, when you were growing up, let's say during your grade school period, what was your father like?*
> **Ann:** *Well, my Dad was the type of person that expected a great deal from everyone, including all of his children.*

She tells us here that her father was a discouraging individual in the guise of an encouraging individual. He was the type of man who had such high standards that people had to push and push to achieve them, and probably feeling that they could not achieve them, they became more or less discouraged.

> **Ann:** *He is a business man,* very *industrious,* very *responsible.* (Audience laughter.) *He tried to be understanding.*

"He tried to be . . ." Ann just said about her father. Now, in therapy, in counseling, you hear people say, "I tried," "I'm gonna try," "I will try," etc., especially when you ask them to do something. "I try" or "I will try" has an implicit ending to that sentence. The ending is, "but I don't have the feeling that I will succeed." And when a person starts trying without expecting any success, he usually makes his anticipations come true. He does not succeed. So Ann feels that her father did not succeed in understanding. He merely "tried" to be understanding. Perhaps, father himself, despite his tremendous ambition and varied successes, was discouraged like the rest.

> **Dr. M.:** *Did your father have many friends? Was he respected in the community?*
> **Ann:** *Yes, both.*
> **Dr. M.:** *We know he favored Sam, but was Sam his* very *favorite?*
> **Ann:** *I don't think he made it that obvious. I don't think he did that to the rest of us kids. He's* very *fair.* (Ann and audience laughter.)
> **Dr. M.:** *Yes, he had to be* very *fair.*
> **Ann:** *He* tried *to be fair.* (Audience laughter.)
> **Dr. M.:** *And he didn't succeed at that, either.*

In a recent paper, Dr. Gushurst and myself (6) described these phrases that patients use, and what they really mean. Most of us are not tuned in. I would suspect that most people in this room if they heard "he tried," would write it down on their sheet dutifully without realizing what it really means. He did not expect to succeed, and probably did not succeed.

> **Dr. M.:** *Okay, he tried to be fair and therefore, he never expressed favoritism.*
> **Ann:** *He seemed to . . . Well, he was a strong person. At least he wanted to live up to the reputation that he was strong, so he concealed any emotion that he might have. He did not allow things to faze him, because he had to be the strong individual. By the same token he also believed that his was the role of the father of the house. His authority should not be questioned.*

Here you see a strong masculine value. This is not a family value unless shared by mother. I don't know yet. With such a strong, masculine value, you can imagine the pressure on Sam and Marty. The girls, at least, to some extent, escaped this. However, now Ann is ready to give father his comeuppance.

> **Dr. M.:** *Women are just as strong as men, aren't they?* (Ann nods.) *What was mother like?*

Ann: *Mother* tries *to be understanding.* (Audience laughter.) *Okay, she isn't either. She's pretty weak, weaker than my father. In fact, she's everything that he is not. They fit together perfectly for that reason.*
Dr. M.: *A sort of master-slave, superior-inferior relationship?*
Ann: *No, I don't want to get that across.*
Dr. M.: *A dominant-submissive kind of relationship?*
Ann: *No, I think it's more of a what she doesn't have, he fills in, and what he doesn't have, she fills in. I think she fills in for the emotional part of the relationship.*
Dr. M.: *Yes, I buy that, but what about the strong-weak bit? You know if father married a strong woman, they would "kill each other."*
Ann: *No, she's* not *strong.*
Dr. M.: *So, on that basis, they have a sort of covenant—he's the head of the house, and she knows the proper responses to make so they don't run into trouble.*
Ann: *Probably.*
Dr. M.: *But other than that you see them as rather complementary? What he has, fills in for what she doesn't have; and what she has, fills in for what he doesn't have?*
Ann: *If she's a slave, I think she enjoys being one. She's happy.*
Dr. M.: *Tell me some of the things that she is.*
Ann: *She's creative.*
Dr. M.: *That sounds like somebody else in the family.*
Ann: *She's very emotional.*
Dr. M.: *Like somebody else in the family. And it isn't Mary. You mean you grew up weak like mother? Is that what you've been thinking the whole time? That you're creative and sensitive and in other ways like mother, instead of the strong, "I can do anything I want and people better listen to me," father? I am going to ask you to look out into the audience a minute, Ann, because I'm going to ask them a question. I don't know the answer but we're going to have to take our chances. Willing to risk it?*
Ann: *Sure!*
Dr. M.: (To audience.) *I want you to give an honest answer. I don't want you to please me nor Ann. How many of you feel that creativity and sensitivity are negative traits? Not one. How many think that they are positive traits? All. Well, they are neither intrinsically positive nor negative. Either can be* used *negatively. Of course, one can use, as many delinquents do, his creativity to make all kinds of mischief. As Dr. Dreikurs has said, "Neurosis is a testimony to man's ingenuity."* (Audience laughter.) *What do you think?*
Ann: *I think I realize that creativity and sensitivity aren't bad things to have; it's probably just my way of looking at it. It's the thing I associate*

with my mother's weakness and inability to cope with my father, or my inability to adjust in school.

Dr. M.: *You know, Ann, those people in the audience are creative and sensitive, but since they don't know your mother, they don't worry about it. They just enjoy being creative and sensitive. But you associate it with your mother's weakness and don't want any part of it. May I suggest what you might do with that vote you got out there? How you might interpret it? There's an old Hungarian proverb: If one person tells you you are drunk, laugh it off. If two people tell you, give it some serious thought. But if three people tell you, you better go home.* (Audience laughter.) *Now there are at least three people out there who say that your creativity and your sensitivity can be used as* positive *traits. You might want to think about it.* (Ann smiles and nods.) *What's the nature of the relationship between your parents? I know we discussed that just a little while ago in terms of complementarity.*

Ann: *Well, basically they both have great ambitions, materialistic ambitions. They want to make money. They* are *making money. They enjoy eating out. They enjoy playing golf.*

Ann is now telling the family values. *They* enjoy. Not *he* enjoys, but *she* does not; not that *he* would prefer, but *she* would not prefer. *They* are materialistic, etc. These are the family values.

Ann: *They are united in what they are supposed to accomplish. I don't know, I guess their relationship is . . . it's mutual what they want, and I think money is a big factor, even bigger than happiness, sometimes.*

Dr. M.: *Who's mother's favorite?*

Ann: *I think I am.*

Dr. M.: *Why?*

Ann: *Maybe it's because she recognizes that I have some of the same traits that she has. Creativity and sensitivity.*

Dr. M.: *In other words, we two people who have nothing going for us have to stick together.*

Ann: (Reflectively.) *Maybe. I never thought of it that way.*

Dr. M.: *I hope you will because it's a myth. It's just as much a myth as the belief that Zeus is sitting atop Mt. Olympus. It's something you believe but it just isn't so. We'll have to stop here with respect to your family. I would like to use my last few minutes getting your early recollections.*

From all the things which a person can remember from his early childhood, each of us remembers about a half dozen incidents. It is not important whether these things actually happened or happened the way the person says they happened. What is important is that the individual says and feels that he remembers them. A person engages in this selective process and believes that these things are so because they describe how the individual right now views himself in relationship to life.

> **Dr. M.:** *I want you to think back as far as you can. What is the first incident you remember? Something about which you can say, "One thing I remember . . ."*
> **Ann:** *I remember my First Communion.*
> **Dr. M.:** *Okay, please tell us about your First Communion.*
> **Ann:** *It was about 7 o'clock in the morning and we all had to get up real early to get down to the church on time.*
> **Dr. M.:** *And, what's going on? Supposing you are making a motion picture right now of what's going on at 7:30 in the morning on the day of your First Communion.*
> **Ann:** *I remember I was half asleep and my mother was pulling curlers out of my hair, telling me what I had to do and what I had to say, and all that kind of stuff.*
> **Dr. M.:** *And you were feeling . . .*
> **Ann:** *I was feeling tired and I was scared, too.*
> **Dr. M.:** *Scared of what?*
> **Ann:** *Of walking down the aisle in front of all those people.*
> **Dr. M.:** *And . . . and you were just lying in bed and mother was pulling curlers out of your hair?*
> **Ann:** *It was like everyone was making a big fuss over me and I was supposed to feel something and I didn't feel anything.*

Here you see, first of all, her role in life. She is the person they do it to. Secondly, she tells you their standards are quite different from her standards. They are making a big fuss, and she feels, "I'll be darned, I don't know what everybody is excited about, because I sure am not." Third, you see her own reflection of her own lack of self-reliance. "I'll have to walk down that aisle, and I'm scared."

> **Dr. M.:** *What is the next thing you remember?*
> **Ann:** *I don't remember anything specifically, but I just remember soon after I made my communion, I joined a speed skating club. One day I cracked my head open, because I slid into the wall.*
> **Dr. M.:** *How did that happen?*
> **Ann:** *I was racing. I was about ten years old, and it was up in Minneapolis. Somehow I just cracked my head open, and I remember that my Dad was real upset about it, and I probably felt sort of guilty, you know, for him for letting this happen to me.*

Dr. M.: *How did he let it? I'm not quite clear. How did he let it happen to you?*
Ann: *I was going to get into that. When I got home, my mother was aghast that my father had . . . She blamed the fact that I cracked my head open on him.*
Dr. M.: *But how was he responsible for it?*
Ann: *Because he had encouraged me to go out for speed skating. He had taken me up there against my mother's wishes.*
Dr. M.: *In the first part of the recollection what are you trying to do? What do you do on a speed-skating team? What's the whole goal?*
Ann: *To get there first.*

To get there first, to get ahead, to win. Even when she tries, it does not happen. I can't go into any more recollections with her, but you see, she sees herself as a victim of life. She is also a victim, as is mother, of father's encouragement or neglect, or something or another. She is the victim; whether she tries to get ahead, or to be first, or to succeed, all she is going to get for her troubles is a split head. Actually, what she is saying is she is discouraged. Why try if you can't win? Since she is working with a counselor now, her counselor will have to encourage her. At this moment she does not believe in herself.

Dr. M.: *We can see, Ann, why you would not believe in yourself, growing up the way you did. I guess if I grew up in that spot, I would feel pretty much the way you feel. The question is, is it necessary* now*? Or do you want to stop being a "reverse puppet" and decide what* you *want to do in life? Not, "what* they *want me to do which I will not do." That's the issue you and your counselor will have to work out together. Is there anything you would like to add, ask, or comment out?*
Ann: *I think you are just remarkable, I mean the way you can . . .* (Audience laughter and applause.)
Dr. M.: *Thank you, you are very kind. Other than that . . .*
Ann: *I guess I didn't realize that I was the victim of, what I was suffering from. I think I can accept myself a lot easier now.*
Dr. M.: *You are suffering from the ignorance that you are a good, competent person. You are competent, you* are *good, but you are too busy looking at Debbie and your mother, and judging yourself negatively, instead of deciding what* you *want to do. Did you feel comfortable up here, Ann?*
Ann: *Well, no, to be perfectly honest, I didn't.*
Dr. M.: *Why?*
Ann: *I just feel self-conscious in front of all these people.*
Dr. M.: *But this thing itself did not make you uncomfortable or nervous or anything like that?*

Ann: *No, I enjoyed it.*
Dr. M.: *We didn't step on your toes in any way?*
Ann: *No!*
Dr. M.: *Thank you very much for coming.*

REFERENCES

1. Adler, A. *Problems of neurosis* (1929). New York: Harper Torchbooks, 1964.

2. Adler, A. *The problem child* (1930). New York: Putnam Capricorn Books, 1963.

3. Adler, A. *The Individual Psychology of Alfred Adler*. Ed. by H. L. & Rowena R. Ansbacher. New York: Basic Books, 1956.

4. Dreikurs, R. The psychological interview in medicine. *Amer. J. Indiv. Psychol.*, 1952–53, 10, 99–122. Also in *Psychodynamics, psychotherapy, and counseling*. Chicago, Ill.: Alfred Adler Inst. Chicago, 1967. Pp. 125–152.

5. Mosak, H. H. Early recollections as a projective technique. *J. proj. Tech.*, 1958, 22, 302–311. Also in G. Lindzey & C. S. Hall (Eds.), *Theories of personality: primary sources and research*. New York: Wiley, 1965. Pp. 105–113.

6. Mosak, H. H., & Gushurst, R. S. What patients say and what they mean. *Amer. J. Psychother.*, 1971, 25, 428–436.

7. Shulman, B. H. The family constellation in personality diagnosis. *J. Indiv. Psychol.*, 1962, 18, 35–47.

THE FAMILY CONSTELLATION IN PERSONALITY DIAGNOSIS

Bernard H. Shulman

President of the American Society of Adlerian Psychology and a faculty member of the Alfred Adler Institute, Chicago. He is an associate in neurology and psychiatry at Northwestern University School of Medicine, and training consultant at Galesburg State Research Hospital, Illinois State Psychiatric Institute, and Downey Veterans Administration Hospital.

While the family constellation is generally recognized as important in personality development, in personality diagnosis it has been stressed mostly by Adlerians. Dreikurs has described it as

> a sociogram of the group at home during (the individual's) formative years. (It) reveals his field of early experiences, the circumstances under which he developed his personal perspectives and biases, his concepts and convictions about himself and others, his fundamental attitudes, and his own approaches to life, which are the basis for his personality (4, p. 109).

The writer has been using in practice and teaching a list of questions by Dreikurs (4, pp. 110–112), an interview guide which provides a bird's-eye view of the personality in its nascent state, permitting still to see "the child in the man." Since students have frequently asked for elaboration regarding what one looks for in taking a family constellation and why, such elaboration is attempted in this present paper.

Journal of Individual Psychology, 18(1), May, 1962, **pp. 35–47**

UNDERLYING ASSUMPTIONS

Several important assumptions regarding the dynamics of the formative years are made in Adlerian theory.

1. Personality is the result of *purposiveness*, of an active training on the part of the child—self-training—in traits he considers will be most useful to him. Without being aware of this, he will train "those qualities by which he hopes to achieve significance or even a degree of power and superiority in the family constellation" (3). Not that he necessarily considers these traits ideal, but he must come to terms with his limitations. For example, a girl may most desire to be strong and masculine, but may recognize the impossibility of achieving such a goal. She may then decide to train herself in certain traits of submission because these would serve her best, although they may still be contemptible in her private value system.

2. Personality is formed in *social relatedness*, the family being the first social group of the child. "In his efforts to play a part in group life (within his first group, his family), the child is guided by the example of and his experiences with other members of the family . . . The influence is dynamic and not mechanistic" (5, p. 5).

3. Personality is *phenomenologically determined*, that is, by the child's own perception of what he needs. In deciding what is needed, the child influences his future pattern of living, and may make the crucial mistakes that may later cripple his endeavors.

In summary, the purposive, socially related personality development depends on the child's perception of himself and others. His subsequent training takes place in line with the basic dynamic principle, namely, that man strives to move upward from a minus to a plus position.

ORDINAL POSITION

Adler seems to have been the first psychologist to point to the ordinal position in the family as a personality determinant (1). Here it must be emphasized: (*a*) Like all determinants in Adler's view, it provides only probabilities since the individual's response is always a creative act of self-determination. (*b*) Ordinal position is not to be taken literally, but in its context. "It is not the child's number in the order of successive births which influences his character, but the *situation* into which he is born and the way in which he interprets it" (2, p. 377). If the eldest is feeble-minded, the second may acquire the life style of an eldest child. If two children are born much later than the rest, the elder of these may develop like an eldest child.

Briefly, the various family positions have been described as follows. The *only child* is unique, he is weaker and smaller than his family, and need not share his prerogatives. The *eldest child* has been dethroned by a competitor but retains his position of being first. He thus will make an effort to remain first, unless he is surpassed and becomes discouraged, then giving up the struggle and accepting a role secondary to his rival. The *second child* (and each succeeding child) finds himself in the position of starting a race with a handicap. Characteristically he will feel the necessity to catch up to the rival who is ahead of him—again, unless he becomes discouraged. The *middle child* has neither the superior position of the eldest nor of the youngest. Characteristically, he feels squeezed, and either elbows his way to a more favorable spot, or is in danger of being squeezed out of competition. The *youngest child*, being last, may feel "not least" and try to overtake all the others. Or, if he is pampered, he may decide to remain a baby.

These are the five basic positions, and all others are variations, combinations, or permutations of these five. For example, a family of nine children may be divided into three groups of three. In a case where this actually occurred each child showed traits of his group and his position in the group; the patient was the 5th, or the middle child of the middle group and showed exaggerated middle-child characteristics.

The *favorite* has an undisputed place of prestige; he need struggle less to make his mark. He therefore conforms more easily and expects to be more acceptable than the other siblings. On the other hand, he may never learn to fight for his position, and he may become unable to face a situation in which he is not the favorite. The *non-favored* sibling may learn early to accept "second-best," or to depend on himself, without feeling discouraged by lack of deference of others.

PARENTAL INFLUENCES

It is a truism that parents exert a great influence on the child. They are his earliest and often his only models, from whom he chooses values, attitudes, and techniques. Parents are forces to be obeyed or defied, and models to be imitated or from which to turn away. Much of this takes place before the development of speech, without the child's awareness.

The parents' behavior generally sets the atmosphere of the home, i.e., whether it is peaceful or warlike; cheerful or depressing; marked by warmth, closeness and mutual involvement; or cold, distant and detached. Parents also encourage certain directions of behavior by allowing some of the children's techniques to be successful and others not. Some family values are common to the culture and can be found throughout the community, others vary from family to family.

Like ordinal position, parental influences by no means inevitably determine the child's behavior. "Nevertheless, children of the same family . . . show an inclination to similar behavior, developing characteristic values and moral concepts, especially when these are clearly defined and accepted by both parents" (5, p. 9). When the parents provide separate, or confused and contradictory examples, it is not easy for the child to decide what he is supposed to be. When there is marked conflict between the parents, the child may view this as a natural state of existence. He may take sides against one of the parents, or may decide to remove himself as much as possible from the conflict and withdraw or disown the family.

The behavior of the child always reflects some facet of the parents' attitudes and values, just as it reflects the child's own. One can assume that a power-drunk child has at least one parent to whom force and forcefulness have a high positive, or negative value. The child who fights his mother, has a mother who fights him. The child can be said to have "caught" from his mother the interest in opposing and in power.

If the grandparents were important, the child may choose to imitate one of them rather than a parent. If other persons live with the family "some of them may play a more important role for the patient's development than the parents" (4, p. 114). An extremely discouraged child may feel that he belongs only to his pet and companion, usually a dog.

FAMILY DYNAMICS

Infinite patterning between siblings and parents is possible. A first-born may pattern himself after the parent perceived as having the more desirable position (when there is a sharp enough division between the positions of the parents); he may become convinced that he cannot match the attainments of the desirable parent, and yet fruitlessly continue his attempts to do so; or he may give up and switch to another form of behavior. The second child may choose to imitate the other parent or those aspects of the dominant parent that the first-born has overlooked. Divergence in behavior between siblings is partly due to competition between them for a place in the sun; the second avoids the territory of the first and goes elsewhere to seek his fortune.

According to Dreikurs, personality traits are the children's responses to the power politics within the family group. "Similarities and differences . . . indicate alliance and competition" (5, p. 11). "The siblings who are most alike are the allies" (4, p. 113). Conversely, the siblings most different from each other are the main competitors, even though there may have been no open rivalry.

Dreikurs distinguishes between rivalry and competition, describing the first as an open contest, the second as having "a much deeper impact on each child leading to the development of opposite character traits . . . as each child seeks success where the other one fails" (5, p. 10). Competition develops mainly with the proximal sibling, the one who always had to be taken into account during the formative years.

> Siblings who died very young may have had considerable influence on the patient's life; they may be responsible for parental anxiety about patient's health and survival, or they may represent an unbeatable rival, since nobody can compete successfully with a dead brother or sister. Sometimes a patient may have felt accused or responsible for a sibling's death, so that his whole childhood life was affected (4, p. 112).

Sometimes a child will carry his opposition to another family member so far that he cannot freely choose what he wants, but must wait until he knows what the other wants, so that he can oppose him. Opposition may be in the form of overt defiance, negativism, passivity, or overt attempts to please the opponent while secretly arranging to disappoint him.

However, differences need not indicate competition. It may be that the parents encouraged different traits in the different children. Or, in a family with one boy and one girl, differences may reflect how each accepts his sex role.

FAMILY CONSTELLATION INTERVIEW

To elicit information pertinent to the family constellation, Dreikurs, as mentioned initially, has devised an interview guide, following Adler's pattern. This is shown in essence in Table 1.

Not all items of this guide are pertinent in any one case. They need not be followed in any special order, nor should they be asked mechanically. Indeed, the patient's answers will often suggest other, further questions. Although all the information can be gathered in one interview, if needed, it is usually advisable to go more slowly so that the patient may think about the family constellation. The total time required is at the most two hours.

TABLE 1
Family Constellation Interview Guide

Sibling sequence: List all siblings in descending order, including the patient in his position. Give patient's age, and note for each sibling the plus or minus difference in years between him and patient. Include siblings now dead.

A. *Description of siblings*:
  1. Who is most different from you In what respect?
  2. Who is most like you? In what respect?
  3. What kind of child were you?
  4. Describe the other siblings.

B. *Ratings of personality attributes*: Obtain a rating for each sibling, including the patient, for each of 21 attributes. Ask first for the extremes of each attribute and then where the other sibs fit in. The 21 attributes are given, in essence, in the left-hand column of Table 2, where they are shown with answers from an illustrative case.

C. *Sibling interrelationships*:
  1. Who took care of whom?
  2. Who played with whom?
  3. Who got along best with whom?
  4. Which two fought and argued the most?
  5. Who was Father's favorite?
  6. Who was Mother's favorite?

D. *Description of parents*:
  1–2. How old is your Father? Mother?
  3–4. What kind of person is your Father? Mother?
  5–6. Which of the children is most like Father, and in what way? Mother?
  7. What kind of relationship existed between your Father and Mother?
     (*a*) Who was dominant, made decisions, etc.?
     (*b*) Did they agree or disagree on methods of raising children?
     (*c*) Did they quarrel openly? About what? How did these quarrels end?
     (*d*) How did you feel about these quarrels? Whose side did you take?
  8. Which of the parents was more ambitious for the children, and in what way?
  9. Did any other persons (grandparent, uncle, aunt, roomer, etc.) live with the family? Describe them and your relationship to them.

An important advantage of this technique is that it is conducive to objectivity on the part of the patient, and a good way to get him to talk about significant people in his life. If he tends to guard himself, he may do so less with these specific questions which require specific answers, especially since he seldom knows what they might signify in the total personality picture. Furthermore, defensive covering up is brought to light if the answers are inconsistent. Even if the patient cannot answer all questions, he can, if he tries, answer enough of them to permit the formulation of his family constellation. Some patients become more cooperative when told that the questions, concerned with childhood behavior as they are, have no current "moral" value.

The ratings (see Table 2) are not all to be taken at face value. The sibling who tries to please, for example, may alienate, because he tries to please in order to exploit. The rebellious child may use overt or covert techniques; if the patient

TABLE 2
Pearl's Ratings of Herself and Her Three Siblings Regarding the 21 Attributes of Section B of the Family Constellation Interview Guide (Table 1)

	Siblings in sequence, and their ages relative to patient's age			
Attributes	**Mary +5 yrs.**	**Jack +3 yrs.**	**Pearl**	**Richard –1 yr.**
1. Intelligence	All seemed equally intelligent			
2. Work attitude	Hard worker	Preferred to take it easy	Hard worker	Can work hard when he wants to
3. School grades	Best grades	Poor grades	Good grades	Fair grades
4. Helping around house	Helped	Tried to avoid chores	Most helpful	Least helpful
5, 6. Conformity, rebellion	Generally conforming	Most rebellious toward Father, ran away from home several times	Most conforming	Did what he wanted and got away with it through his charm
7. Trying to please and its effectiveness	Pleased, because knew how to do what parents wanted	Only tried to please his friends	Tried to please the hardest but was less successful than Mary & Richard	Pleased the most because of charm
8. Criticism, judgmental attitudes	Openly critical of other siblings	Rebelled, but did not openly criticize	Often felt critical but did not voice this	Not critical
9, 10. Considerateness, selfishness		Selfish at home, not with friends	Most considerate	Most selfish
11. Having own way	Parents let her have her way, respecting her ability and judgment	Tried, but did not get his way because he antagonized Father	Tried to obey rather than have own way	Had his way the most, could get away with things

12. Sensitivity, easily hurt	Not sensitive, the most persuasive arguer, would try to prove she was right	Belligerent and defensive, would argue he was unfairly treated	Most sensitive and easily hurt, would sulk and cry when she felt unappreciated	Happy-go-lucky
13. Temper tantrums		The only one with tantrums		
14. Sense of humor	A serious person	Good sense of humor	Always unhappy and tense, but covered it up	Good sense of humor
15, 16. Idealism, materialism	Practical, yet idealistic	Materialistic	Most idealistic	Materialistic, always wanted more
17. Standards, aspirations (for achievement, behavior, morals, etc.)	Highest intellectual achievement and ambitions	Seemed unambitious and with lowest standards	Highest moral standards, most interested in "proper" behavior	Low morals, but could get things done
18. Physical and sex-linked attributes	Not athletic, not so interested in her appearance, most assertive verbally	Best athlete, good at mechanical activities, strongest, good fighter, most masculine	Not athletic, not pretty, best dresser, most feminine, most shy	Best looking, good athlete
19. Maintaining friendships	Few but close friends	Many friends, but Father did not like them	Some friends, tried to like everybody	Most friends, most popular, a leader and organizer, socially aggressive
20, 21. Being parental favorite, reject	Father's favorite	Most punished by Father	Favorite of neither, felt closer to Mother	Most spoiled by Mother, Mother's favorite

cannot say who was most rebellious, ask, who got into most mischief. The most intelligent may not have gotten the best grades in school since good grades also imply willingness to work and cooperate. The hardest worker may not be the most helpful; he may work hard only on his own personal interests. The person whose behavior seems contradictory—conforming and rebellious, considerate and selfish—is a person of extremes, capable of using positive and negative, pro-social and antisocial ways of behaving according to whatever his perceptual system requires. He may conform if life pleases him, and rebel if it does not. It is not generally known that certain traits which are not in themselves inferior can still function as organ inferiorities. Extreme good looks and superior intelligence, for example, may cause disturbances in the child's social adjustment and call forth compensatory tendencies. A similar problem may be found in a wealthy child among poor children.

The ratings are intended to show how the siblings found their areas of success and failure. The ratings also give a profile of the patient's position on each of these continua. This helps to give an idea of his status evaluation of himself in relation to the other siblings, and to show how consciously he feels inferior.

The present author has found the following additional questions useful: What is the father's occupation, the extent of his friendships and social participation, the time spent at home, his worldly success? A woman should always be asked if she ever wanted to be a boy, and about her reactions to the menarche and puberty. A man should be asked about doubts of his masculinity. One might ask about significant childhood illnesses, whether one sibling was excessively frail or sickly. Were there other stress situations such as death of a parent or sibling, birth of a sibling, any drastic change in familial environment? It is pertinent to know the family's economic situation and whether the family was a member of a minority group in the neighborhood.

A CASE

This case description follows the order of the Family Constellation Interview Guide (Table 1). The patient, Pearl, is a woman of 35 years. Her sibling sequence was: Mary (+5 years), Jack (+3 years), the patient, Richard (–1 year).

A. Description of siblings. Most different from Pearl was Richard, her chief competitor. He was active, aggressive, charming, wanted his own way. Pearl was more bashful and quiet. She was a good child and a good student, getting into little mischief. Mary, the eldest, was the bossiest, a forceful person who was also a good student. Jack was rebellious, fought with his father, and was not good in school. Note that Pearl's description, in answer to these open-ended questions, stresses the values of goodness, being good in school, and agressiveness.

B. Ratings of personality attributes. Shown in Table 2.

C. Sibling interrelationships. No one took care of any other. They all played together. Pearl got along the best with Jack though she disapproved of his behavior. She could not feel close to Mary who was so critical. Neither did she feel close to Richard; perhaps she resented that Mother spoiled him.

D. Description of parents. Father had an explosive temper, but has now become more mellow. He wants his own way and has strong ideas about how children should behave. He is a hard worker who tried to provide well for his children. Mary knew how to please him; they shared some intellectual interests. Pearl tried to please Father, but was afraid of him and could not feel close to him.

Mother was warm, could not hold a grudge, got stepped on by her friends, tried to please, was never strict, and seldom punished. Pearl was most like Mother. While Jack was like Father in temper, Mary was like him in seriousness and intellectual interests. Richard wanted his own way like Father.

Father was dominant, though he shared decisions with Mother. Mother thought Father was too hard on Jack, but Father couldn't stand being talked back to. They seldom quarreled, Mother usually tried to please Father. Father seemed more ambitious for the children.

INTERPRETATION

Personality Development

The answers to the above questions give us the following picture: Pearl is the third of four children with an older sister and brother and a younger brother. The eldest, Mary, achieved a dominant role in the family and retained it through her assertiveness, conformity, intellectual achievements, and ability to please and persuade the parents, especially the dominant father. Jack, the second, apparently felt unable to compete with Mary on her chosen ground, and tried to assert himself in more forceful and negative ways. These tactics did not work, and Jack became increasingly discouraged, probably feeling he had no place at home and was more accepted among his friends. Whereas Mary was either willing to please the parents or win them over with persuasion, Jack only complained about them and opposed them. He, however, could feel successful outside the house by reason of his physical and mechanical prowess.

Pearl was impressed by Mary's success and Jack's failure. Therefore she tended to imitate Mary and avoid displaying behavior that got Jack into trouble. However, not feeling able to achieve Mary's success, she stressed conforming and submissive traits, becoming the most obedient, most helpful, and most proper. This is a direction frequently chosen by the person who hopes that his "goodness" will win him a favored position. Pearl's choice of this direction was also influenced by the apparently unpleasant consequences of "badness" as seen in Jack.

Richard and his success as a carefree, selfish favorite discouraged Pearl. In spite of her virtue, she was not as successful as either Mary or Richard; she was "squeezed" between them and felt like a loser. Dreading the consequences of open rebellion and committed to "proper" behavior, she maintained an outer conformity while training herself to be sensitive to unfairness. In her pessimism, her sensitivity became her chief tool of rebellion, and by her suffering and her virtue she felt elevated into the role of a martyr.

Richard, as the youngest and mother's favorite, probably never felt the obligation to be virtuous as Pearl did. He used charm, sociability, and assertiveness to find his place, and seemed confident that he had a right to do as he pleased. He was successful where Jack had failed.

Thus, each child excelled in a different area: Mary in the intellectual area and in her ability to win respect; Jack in the so-called masculine area of physical prowess; Pearl in the area of idealism and virtuous behavior; and Richard in social leadership and doing as he pleased.

The guiding lines suggested to the children by the example of the parents were that women are expected to be good and helpful, while men are expected to want their own way. Mary somewhat imitated the dominant father; Jack used the father's own weapons of force and temper and got into a contest with him; Pearl avoided Jack's problem by becoming obedient; while Richard avoided it with charm. Both middle children were "squeezed" by the oldest and youngest who found more successful techniques.

The patient imitated the good, sweet mother, and equated femininity with goodness and submissiveness. She felt, however, that all her efforts got her nowhere, and she rebelled inwardly, through unhappiness and sensitivity.

Current Situation

The patient is married, a housewife, and the mother of an 11-year old son. The husband is a hard-working businessman, moderately successful. She feels that the marital relationship is good, but wishes that her husband would give her more sympathy and support in her endeavors to influence the son. While her husband is protective of her, he is also critical of her attitude toward the son, saying, "boys will be boys." The son is a weak student, not helpful around the house, wants his own way and, though he can be charming, is often rude to his mother. She wants him to behave better, be a better sudent, and "love his mother more."

What light does the analysis of the family constellation throw on the patient's present situation? She came for treatment because she was suffering from a depressive reaction precipitated by difficulty in controlling her son. In an attempt to help her son more, she had consulted several child-guidance agencies. There her own role in her son's misbehavior was pointed out to her. Her sacrificing nature and desire to be good, which had previously given her self-esteem, now became faults. Instead of a good mother, she now felt herself a bad mother. Thus she became severely depressed and sought psychiatric help for herself.

She had always felt that it was a difficult job to raise her son because he was so demanding. But partly, she expected trouble anyway, because she had acquired the belief that it was the lot of a woman to suffer and to sacrifice. Partly, she found her own sense of importance through being a sacrificer, and thus was not able to stop indulging the child. Furthermore, her son reminded her of her younger brother, Richard, who had generally done what he wanted and gotten his own way. Through being defiant, demanding, abusive and critical of her, her son reminded her also of her older brother, Jack.

The perfectionistic moral standards that she developed during childhood were still with her. She still felt she had to be "good," although she really did not expect her virtue to bring any reward other than that of martyrdom. However, she had thought of herself as a person who suffered in a good cause. Now, her role as a good person was threatened by the difficulties in her relationship with her son, and this threat was too much for her to bear. She could not face the idea that her son's difficulties might be caused by her failure. She responded by suffering from herself, becoming the chief victim of her own defect. As in her childhood, the patient saw no choice but to be virtuous and sit in judgment on the unfairness of life through her sensitivity and silent criticism. By being depressed and unhappy she was now atoning for her "badness" as a mother.

Psychotherapy with Pearl would include teaching her to see her mistaken use of sensitivity as a device for finding fault with life, and her mistaken idea that nothing she can do will offer her a chance to find a place. She needs to see that her over-concern with goodness has probably aggravated her son's provocation and defiant behavior; he "shows her up as a bad mother" perhaps in rebellion against her excessively high standards of propriety. She also needs to see that all her outward conformity conceals an inner rebellion and antagonism and that she too (like most depressed patients) wants her own way and silently loses her temper and sulks when her idealistic standards are not met.

SUMMARY

Individual Psychologists see personality development as a purposive, socially related, phenomenologically determined process. They see the individual's family constellation as a most important environmental influence. A Family Constellation Interview Guide, questioning the subject about his parents and siblings, and calling for his rating of himself and his siblings in essential respects, is presented, discussed, and illustrated by a case. It reveals the subjectively perceived early environment and the individual's choice of reactions to it. It gives an historical illumination of the patient's present values and techniques, opinion of himself and others—in short, of his style of life—in less time and more easily than any other diagnostic tool with which the writer is acquainted.

REFERENCES

1. Adler, A. Individual-psychological education (1918). In *Practice and theory of Individual Psychology*. Paterson, N.J.: Littlefield, Adams, 1959. Pp. 317–326.

2. Adler, A. *The Individual Psychology of Alfred Adler*. New York: Basic Books, 1956.

3. Dreikurs, R. *Fundamentals of Adlerian psychology*. New York: Greenberg, 1950.

4. Dreikurs, R. The psychological interview in medicine. *Amer. J. Indiv. Psychol.*, 1952–53, 10, 99–122.

5. Dreikurs, R. *Psychology in the classroom*. New York: Harper, 1957.

THE USE OF BIRTH ORDER INFORMATION IN PSYCHOTHERAPY

Lucille K. Forer
In private practice in Los Angeles, California.
Former National Executive Secretary of Psi Chi and Assistant Professor at California State University of Los Angeles, she is now on the Board of Directors of Psychologists in Clinical and Independent Practice, Division 1 of California State Psychological Association.

Alfred Adler considered the position of the individual in the childhood family to be one of the developmental conditions which afford the therapist the "most trustworthy approaches to the exploration of the personality" (Ansbacher & Ansbacher, 1956). The reader of Adler's case studies will observe that he used information about birth order effects in winning the patient's confidence, in developing understanding of the patient, and in interpreting the patient's dreams and early behavior (Adler, 1954, 1964).

Psychotherapists are enriched in their understanding of patients and in their therapeutic efforts by information presented by Adler and other writers concerning birth order effects. However, despite such evidence which can be gleaned from more than a thousand birth order research studies made in the United States alone during the past forty years, few guidelines can be found in current literature for the practical use of this information in psychotherapy and counseling.

Kurt A. Adler (1972) briefly describes the use of the birth order position for "quickly arriving at a thumbnail sketch of the total personality" (p. 156). Dreikurs (1972), in an exposition of a counseling session with a 12-year old boy, shows a

Journal of Individual Psychology, 33(1), May, 1977, **pp. 105–113**

sensitive appreciation of the conditions under which an only child develops. M. L. Pew and W. L. Pew (1972) utilized diagrams and interpretations of the childhood family constellation in marriage counseling. Mosak (1972) demonstrated life style assessment focused on family constellation with a 17-year old girl.

These published accounts of the use of the family constellation in therapy and counseling reflect the value to the therapist of knowledge of birth order effects, and suggest the need for therapists of any theoretical orientation to utilize, in their training and practical application of therapeutic skills, the vast amount of information about birth order effects now available.

This is the attempt of one psychotherapist to provide a general description of the use of information concerning birth order effects during the psychotherapeutic process, with emphasis on information derived from research studies.

AREAS OF UTILIZATION OF BIRTH ORDER EFFECTS

Enriching the Therapist's Understanding of Human Development and Personality

There seems to be little disagreement among psychotherapists of any theoretical orientation that it is important for the therapist to bring to the patient as much understanding of the development of human personality and its mature characteristics as it is possible for the therapist to acquire. Adler put it more sensitively, writing that the therapist working with a patient needs "to see with his eyes and to hear with his ears" (1958, p. 71).

Knowing experiences of an individual growing up in a specific place in the family and the usual effects of those experiences enables the therapist to internalize the patient's phenomenological field, to utilize the patient's frame of reference, and also to describe the patient's childhood environment in a way that the client may not have directly recognized. The reason for this is that the therapist can associate along with the patient as the patient talks, hearing the meaning of the current symptoms in terms of the past experiences which the therapist suspects the patient may have had in his childhood place in the family.

Adler predicted that the "outlines of patterns of behavior" (1964, p. 117) described by him for each birth order position would be found generally correct with further study, and further research has vindicated his prediction. We are, however, able to go beyond his summaries as more recent research has uncovered new findings concerning birth order effects. One of the best supported findings in studies of birth order effects is that firstborns tend to achieve at a higher level than laterborns, particularly in intellectual pursuits (Altus, 1966; Zajonc & Markus, 1975). When we also discover research evidence that mothers relate differently to their firstborns than to their laterborns, even during the first weeks of the infants' lives (Thoman, Turner, Leiderman, & Barnett, 1970; Tulkin & Kagan, 1970), we wonder if the difference in the behavior of mothers is related to the greater intellectual achievement of firstborns. We then find evidence that mothers are shown to give more conditional acceptance to firstborns than to laterborns, the acceptance being conditional on achievement of firstborns according to the mothers' values (Hilton, 1967).

As we then listen to a firstborn tell of his or her tension and emotional discomfort, we have a basis for the hypothesis that a problem about achievement as well as a problem about feeling appreciated or loved "for himself or herself" may be the basis for the firstborn's symptoms.

Another well-established difference between firstborns and laterborns is in "affiliative behavior," or the way persons behave as the result of what they need from other people (Adams, 1972). Firstborns exhibit high need for affiliation, laterborns less. Firstborns exhibit dependence on approval of others, while laterborns tend to be less concerned with the approval of others and more concerned with establishing relationships for their own sake. For the therapist, these differences have many implications. They suggest differences in the way firstborns and laterborns may relate in therapy. Firstborns stay longer in therapy. They tend to develop a dependent stance on the authority, the therapist, while laterborns prefer the therapist to relate to them more or less as comrade and friend. Firstborns will often respond quickly to encouragement from the therapist; laterborns tend to want practical advice and to withdraw from therapy when the therapist has no more advice to give. The differences in ways of relating to other people also suggest the kinds of problems firstborns and laterborns may bring to therapy: firstborns, problems of dependency and need for approval; laterborns, too great an emphasis on relationships and too little on achievement.

Other relatively well-established differences in birth order effects indicate that laterborns have more empathy with others than firstborns do (Stotland, Sherman, & Shaver, 1971); and that there is a difference in cognitive functioning: firstborns tend to generalize while laterborns tend to be more specific (Harris, 1964). Among the many other differences suggested by research findings are greater fearfulness in new situations on the part of firstborns (Collard, 1968; Longstreth, 1970); and more tendency on the part of firstborns than laterborns to be swayed by popular opinion and to be influenced by authority (Becker, Lerner, & Carroll, 1966). On the other hand, earlier and less conventional sexuality seems to be the case with firstborns (Touhey, 1971). There are a few recent works integrating and summarizing many of these differences (Forer, 1969; Forer, 1976; Sutton-Smith & Rosenberg, 1970).

It is the role of the clinician to apply these findings, which often seem cold and sterile in their research garb, to the behavior of their patients. Each finding suggesting or affirming differences among persons according to birth order gives the clinician additional information to guide him in understanding the patient.

Enlisting the Cooperation of the Patient in the Therapeutic Process

No psychotherapist has developed more clearly than Adler the need to draw the client into cooperating with the therapist in the therapeutic experience. As he stated: "The patient must be appealed to in a friendly way, coaxed into a receptive frame of mind" (1964, p. XXI). The need to win the confidence of the patient by exhibiting correct recognition of his difficulties, his deep feelings, in order to avoid prompt resistance and withdrawal from therapy, is emphasized by Adler.

This therapist, and others who have reported to her, observe that brief interpretations of behavior and feelings in terms of family position indicate to the patient that the therapist understands the difficulties the patient had in relating to others in the childhood family. The patient comes to us with feelings of resentment from childhood experiences with parents and siblings. While these may be dealt with generally, it is far more effective to exhibit greater understanding by being able to discuss with the patient the more specific aspects of birth order. If the psychotherapist has knowledge of the possible sources of disturbance for a younger brother with an older sister, or for an oldest girl in a large family, or for a youngest girl with several older brothers, or for any other specific situation that an individual may occupy in a family, that psychotherapist can listen to the client with deep empathy and indicate through appropriate responses that he does understand. The therapist's tentative interpretations will meet often with almost delighted response from the patient: "You've hit the nail on the head!" Such accurate reflections of what the patient must have experienced and the nature of family pressures upon him or her bring the patient to the "receptive frame of mind." Attempts to interpret based on incomplete knowledge of birth order effects, however, often lead to hostile rejection by the patient because it sounds to him or her as though the therapist is attempting to place the patient in a rigid pattern that the patient does not recognize because it is not specific enough. Such statements as "You were the oldest, so you must be an achiever," do not reveal the same level of knowledge of birth order effects as "You were the oldest in a large family and were made responsible for the younger children; perhaps that's why you feel taken advantage of."

With accurate descriptions and interpretations, the patient develops confidence in the therapist, and his cooperation is enlisted in the therapeutic process. Children, who are immediately involved in the complicated relationships of the birth order position, respond quickly to recognition that the therapist understands their problems. For parents, information concerning the way children relate in terms of their birth orders lessens their self-blame and hence their resistance to therapy or counseling. Similar lessening of guilt and resistance occurs for couples who learn that some of their problems may grow out of their relationship in terms of their birth orders rather than out of some basic inability to relate intimately to another person.

Developing Hypotheses Concerning the Patient's Life Style

It is within the early family situation that the patient developed his goal-directed behavior and thus his self-consistent style of life. If the therapist has knowledge of the struggles the only child must undergo in achieving status with two adults as competitors, or of the environment that surrounds the child within the small or large family, or of the effects of having siblings of the same or opposite sex, or the effect of having a much older or a much younger sibling, the therapist has a basis for developing hypotheses about the patient's lifestyle.

The matter is more complicated, for instance, with the only child than simply the problem of an improperly resolved Oedipal conflict.

A young woman, an only child, refused to speak of sexual feelings or behavior. She had never asked questions of her parents, but had simply accepted their dicta that she must not have sexual intercourse until she married and that, in the interests of such a goal, she should not even think about such matters, if she could avoid it. Further, sexual behavior was linked in their minds, as in hers, with the precepts of their religion, about which no questioning was permitted. Her immediate complaint was that she felt unable to grasp some of the material with which she was being presented in her graduate courses although she had made excellent grades as an undergraduate. 'I think I have some kind of cognitive limitation,' she said.

It became apparent that she was repressing curiosity in any area connected with either sex or religion. Curiosity seems to be repressed by only children to a greater extent than by a child with a sibling of the opposite sex whose presence is a stimulant to curiosity (Smelser, 1968). For this particular only child there was the factor that both her parents were successful professional people and she had never been able to consider herself being other than a small, ignorant child in relation to them. Her inability to assume some aspect of power in relation to her parents caused her to limit interest in any aspect of adult behavior, much as they had directed her.

Enabling the Patient to Understand His or Her Life Style

Accurate knowledge of birth order effects enables the therapist to be convincing. As Adler said (Ansbacher & Ansbacher, 1956, p. 2), the therapist must be able "to explain in the light of the patient's self-consistent, goal-directed style of life all the patient's actions, even to the point of predicting them correctly."

When it is explained to the patient that he or she was attempting in childhood to meet parental goals of achieving status or affection or power among siblings, the patient no longer feels somehow especially "bad." The patient can see that he or she was reacting to the circumstances of the childhood position. For instance, many people raised as only children complain that they cannot feel comfortable with other people. When the therapist explains that the only child has no sibling(s) to bring additional information about the outside world into the home and that the only child acquires his first knowledge about human behavior and relationships from parents who may be uncomfortable or disinterested in talking with a child about such matters, the patient begins to understand why he does not feel comfortable with other people and that he has only to find a way to improve his relationships. He no longer feels that he was, somehow, born without the capacity to form them. Recognition of family influences on his life style can lessen self-blame, and lessen resistance. Thus the therapist can maintain the cooperation of the patient even though the therapist must confront him or her with evidence that a life style is being followed that can only result in failure in achieving constructive goals.

Encouraging and Aiding the Patient to Adopt New Behavior

Of all approaches that the therapist can take to interpreting the patient's behavior to the patient, information involving birth order effects seems most easily accepted by the patient and most quickly motivates the patient to change behavior. This kind of information does not challenge the patient but rather provides a way of reflecting the life style of the patient in an ego-syntonic way. The information usually leads to the rapid "cognitive reorganization" that Adler stipulates (1964, p. xix) as a prelude to changed behavior.

Whenever a patient attempts to develop new patterns of behavior, there will be frequent regressions, and the experienced therapist is aware of the resistance that can be encountered when these regressions must be repeatedly brought to the attention of the patient. The ego-syntonic quality of birth order information, however, permits the therapist to remind the patient that he is once again carrying into the present situation roles learned in the family position of the past, so that the patient can slowly evolve a new life style.

CASE STUDY ILLUSTRATING USE OF BIRTH ORDER EFFECTS

A young male presented numerous problems relating to his performance as a salesman. He had never been interested in studying; hence he rejected training in any specific area and had taken a position as a salesman in a general store. Even there, however, he met with difficulty because his supervisor complained that he was not sufficiently aggressive. He also was criticized for doing no more than he had to, for not seeing new work to be done.

The patient was the younger brother of a brother. He described a childhood with an older brother who achieved well in school. However, the older brother was much in conflict with their mother because he was aggressive and demanding. This younger brother was the favorite of the mother, who saw him as much less difficult than his older brother. It was important to be nonassertive to maintain the mother's affections, and the younger brother learned to be that. He also then ensured that he would not be able to pursue a career aggressively in young adulthood.

Knowing that this is a frequent pattern of a younger brother with an older brother allowed the therapist to develop hypotheses quickly and to help the patient re-evaluate his childhood and the means he had adopted to compete with his brother. With the therapist's assistance, the patient was able to reorganize perception of his potentialities and he came to value his intelligence which, as for most siblings, was relatively similar in level to that of his brother. He struggled to be more assertive, not only in relationship to customers, but also in establishing his place in the firm. As would be expected, he often found reasons for returning to behavior in accordance with the original role he had taken in the childhood family; but with continued encouragement, he developed new patterns of asserting himself. The accuracy with which the therapist evaluated his original situation and the empathy he recognized in the therapist for his past and present feelings enabled him to accept the therapist as a collaborator in the work he had to do to develop a new life style.

SUMMARY

This has been an attempt to show how the psychotherapist can utilize the detailed information about birth order effects now available as the result of numerous research studies in the following areas of the psychotherapeutic process:

1. Developing understanding of human personality.
2. Enlisting the cooperation of the patient in the therapeutic process.
3. Developing hypotheses concerning the patient's life style.
4. Enabling the patient himself to understand his life style.
5. Describing the external situational determinants of his way of life.
6. Reducing self-blame.
7. Reducing resistance.
8. Helping the patient adopt a more constructive life style.

REFERENCES

Adams, B. N. Birth order: A critical review. *Sociometry*, 1972, *35*, 411–439.

Adler, A. *Understanding human nature*. Greenwich, Conn.: Fawcett Publications, 1954.

Adler, A. *What life should mean to you*. New York: Capricorn Books, 1958.

Adler, A. *Problems of neurosis: A book of case histories*. New York: Harper Torchbooks, 1964.

Adler, K. A. Techniques that shorten psychotherapy: Illustrated with five cases. *Journal of Individual Psychology*, 1972, *28*(2), 155–168.

Altus, W. D. Birth order and its sequelae. *Science*, 1966, *151*, 44–49.

Ansbacher, H. L., & Ansbacher, R. (Eds.). *The individual psychology of Alfred Adler: A systematic presentation in selections from his writings.* New York: Basic Books, 1956.

Becker, S. W., Lerner, M. J., & Carroll, J. Conformity as a function of birth order and type of group pressure: A verification. *Journal of Personality and Social Psychology*, 1966, *3*, 242–244.

Collard, R. Social and play responses of first born and later born infants in an unfamiliar situation. *Child Development*, 1968, *39*, 325–334.

Dreikurs, R. Counseling a boy: A demonstration. *Journal of Individual Psychotherapy*, 1972, *28*, 223–231.

Forer, L. K. *Birth order and life roles.* Springfield, Ill.: Charles C Thomas, 1969.

Forer, L. K. *The birth order factor.* New York: David McKay Co., 1976.

Harris, I. D. *The promised seed: A comparative study of eminent first and later sons.* London: Free Press of Glencoe, 1964.

Hilton, I. Differences in the behavior of mothers toward first- and later-born children. *Journal of Personality and Social Psychology*, 1967, *7*, 282–290.

Longstreth, L. E. Birth order and avoidance of dangerous activities. *Developmental Psychology*, 1970, *2*, 154.

Mosak, H. H. Life style assessment: A demonstration focused on family constellation. *Journal of Individual Psychology*, 1972, *28*(2), 232–247.

Pew, M. L., & Pew, W. L. Adlerian marriage counseling. *Journal of Individual Psychology*, 1972, *28*(2), 192–196.

Stotland, E., Sherman, S. E., & Shaver, K. G. *Empathy and birth order: Some experimental explorations.* Lincoln: University of Nebraska Press, 1971.

Sutton-Smith, B., & Rosenberg, B. G. *The sibling.* New York: Holt, Rinehart & Winston, Inc., 1970.

Thoman, E. B., Turner, A. M., Leiderman, P. H., & Barnett, C. R. Neonate-mother interaction: Effects of parity on feeding behavior. *Child Development*, 1970, *41*, 1103–1111.

Touhey, J. C. Birth order and virginity. *Psychological Reports*, 1971, *28*, 894.

Tulkin, S. R., & Kagan, J. Mother-child interaction: Social class differences in the first year of life. *Proceedings of the Annual Convention of the American Psychological Association*, 1970, *5*, 261–262.

Zajonc, R. B., & Markus, G. B. Birth order and intellectual development. *Psychological Review*, 1975, *82*, 74–88.

Part A
EARLY RECOLLECTION ANALYSIS

THE USE OF EARLY RECOLLECTIONS IN PSYCHOTHERAPY[1]

Helene Papanek

My paper deals with only one technique of Adlerian psychotherapy. But it is an important one. The preceding speaker, Dr. Kurt Adler (2), has referred to it in each of his cases. It is the use of early recollections (ERs). I want to clarify this technique because sometimes there is some difficulty in understanding it. How is it that the Adlerian approach which, in contrast to Freud, emphasizes the present purposes of symptoms and present relationships of the grown-up, and tends not to talk much about the past, does stress ERs? The answer is, as I am sure you have gathered from Dr. Adler's presentation, that our use of ERs differs from that of other schools of thought. I shall deal here with the Adlerian theoretical basis for the ER technique and some psychotherapeutic applications of it.

An individual's life style includes most importantly a cognitive framework which enables him to understand the world, and to select behavior which will advance him toward his goals of safety, security, self-esteem, and success; and will protect him from insecurity, danger, and frustration. All this is more or less "erroneous," depending on whether the individual is more neurotic or more healthy. Each child selects from his many experiences some which impress him deeply and which he makes the landmarks of his cognitive map. We are not interested in the forgotten, but in what is remembered in this way. It is as if the individual would say to himself, "Because this or that happened to me, I should never again behave in a certain way," or, "This or that brought such desirable results that I will behave again in a similar way and thereby reap the same reward."

---

[1]Paper read at the Fourth Brief Psychotherapy Conference, Chicago Medical School, Chicago, March 24–25, 1972.

Journal of Individual Psychology, 28(2), November, 1972, **pp. 169–176**

The ERs reflect the person's guidelines for his behavior. An incident may really have happened as it is remembered, or the individual's assumptions and explanations about it may have been added, or it may never have happened. The result is the same. The ER will reflect the individual's opinion of the world and himself and the path of behavior he has selected for himself to cope with a complicated world.

ERs understood in this way are of the greatest help in psychotherapy. Instead of meandering in the patient's so-called unconscious and hoping that so-called free association will bring valuable material to light, the therapist is enabled by the ERs to follow an active course, focused on important material, to understand the life style. Such material also includes dreams, and observations of the patient's relationships to the therapist and others in his life, and the like. But ERs in particular help to focus quickly on crucial problems, the nature of the patient's or client's mistake about himself, his aspirations, and the world around him.

The first stage in establishing the therapeutic relationship and atmosphere should be given to questions about the patient's complaints and what brings him to therapy. At the same time there is opportunity to observe the patient's face, figure, the way he talks, thinks, and relates to us. As the next step the therapist shows his interest in ERs, and the patient is asked, "Think back as far as you can, and tell me your earliest memory from your childhood years." We differentiate between early memories and reports. We do not want a report, a generalization of the person's life as a child, such as, "I had a happy childhood," or "My parents rejected me and I was always lonely." ERs are vivid concrete incidents with all the details and emotions attached to them. To quote Adler:

> His memories are the reminders [the person] carries about with him of his own limits and of the meaning of circumstances. There are no "chance memories": out of the incalculable number of impressions which meet an individual, he chooses to remember only those which he feels, however darkly, to have a bearing on his situation. Thus his memories represent his "Story of My Life"; a story he repeats to himself to warn him or comfort him. . . . A depressed individual could not remain depressed if he remembered his good moments and his successes. He must say to himself, "All my life I was unfortunate," and select only those events which he can interpret as instances of his unhappy fate. Memories can never run counter to the style of life. If an individual's goal of superiority demands that he should feel, "Other people always humiliate me," he will choose for remembrance incidents which he can interpret as humiliations . . . The first memory will show his fundamental view of life, his first satisfactory crystallization of his attitude (1, p. 351).

These old memories are not reasons for present behavior. They are not causes; they do not determine present behavior. They are hints; they help to understand the guiding fiction; they indicate the movement towards a goal and what obstacles have to be overcome. Because we can use them sooner or later, I write them down, so as to be sure to remember them for later use.

But first a therapeutic atmosphere of mutual involvement must be established. The patient must be brought into a state where he likes to listen, where he wants to understand. Only then can he be influenced to live what he has understood. Insight is only useful in an atmosphere of trust and courage. After such an atmosphere has been established, the therapist must evaluate the next therapeutic steps: how to use his knowledge about the patient's difficulties, and how and when to confront him with the errors in his life style based on childish apprehension and misunderstanding. The timing of these interpretations and confrontations differs from case to case.

Some therapists differentiate between emotional and intellectual insight. This seems to me a mistaken dichotomy. Insight becomes meaningful to the patient if it is accompanied by two discoveries: first, that his neurotic suffering has been unnecessary; ERs are chosen, voluntary landmarks in an environment obtruding itself and influencing his developing cognitive structuring; and second, that a more realistic, adequate understanding of his present-day environment gives him the opportunity for socially directed, rewarding, coping behavior.

The whole idea is that we can explain to the patient that even if all the past happened as he remembers it, he can still shape the present and the future, and he is not just a victim of his past. This view makes the patient much more hopeful, and optimistic about therapy.

Usually I ask a patient to recollect a series of from five to ten incidents, in one or two therapeutic sessions, although this many may not be necessary. Often a single ER can illustrate a life style and bring therapeutic gain.

My first example will be one of a patient in whose case the interpretation of one ER brought immediate relief. Yet I do not think it easy to change a person's life style and life goal by a very short course of therapy. But I do think that even a patient who has had a long previous therapy can gain new hope and a new outlook on his symptoms if he sees the connection between his early recollections and present-day sufferings. It seems that in my practice patients have frequently been in therapy previously, often for years, without any change for the better. Time and money run out and they want a more active approach, a new, so-called new therapy, although we consider our method quite an old one.

SICKNESS, THE PRICE FOR ATTENTION

This is the case of a 30-year-old divorcee who had been in treatment, elsewhere, for years, because of headaches. She is a very gifted person who publishes and illustrates children's books, has a good job, and is also a free-lance writer. Her headaches are so severe that she is sometimes unable to work, either for herself or where she is employed.

She told me the following in the second session. Her father had been a very busy general practitioner who spent most of his time in his office which was not in the home. The mother felt always very neglected and angry at the father's absences, and the mother, the patient, already when she was ten years old, and her younger brother, suspected that the father used his office to have an affair. So his neglect of the children was an important factor. Even when the children were sick he frequently said, "Ah, it's nothing serious," and didn't come home any earlier from his office.

But once when the patient was six years old she had a stomach ache, and the mother called the father up, and he came home and suspected appendicitis. He got upset and took her to the hospital himself. It turned out not to be appendicitis and the patient was not operated on; so she did not have that satisfaction in the hospital. But she did have the satisfaction of seeing her father upset and caring for her. When I asked her to describe the feeling of the memory, she said it was "exquisite." I found this very striking, because, you know, she vomited, had a stomach ache, and all the symptoms of a severe disease. But the care and the concern of her father made it an exquisite memory.

Now that was so striking that I told her right then, in the second session, that perhaps she feels being sick is the only way to get attention. Thereupon she reported in the next session that her headaches had diminished to a very great extent, and that she now understands the difference between me and her previous therapist. During the several years that she had worked with him, he had always explained her headaches as repressed anger and had suggested that each time she had a headache, she should find out at whom she was angry. It hadn't worked, she said. Though she believed in this interpretation, it seemed six-times-removed because it was so hard to find anybody at whom she really was angry. But my interpretation, that she wanted somebody to be nice to her, to show her concern or attention, seemed to be only once removed. It still didn't strike her as the only true explanation, but it was somehow easier to accept that she really wanted somebody to be nice to her and that the disappointment brought on the headaches. She was in a very good mood because she hadn't had any headaches during this week, whereas she used to have headaches at least three days a week, and she could work so much better now.

This of course does not mean that her life style changed, which is still in many ways one of dependency, but it certainly gave her more hope to straighten out her other problems which she has with men and girl friends, and to feel in general, which I think is very important, that relying on others is not a very safe attitude. Though as a child she had to rely on others, now she could try to be self-reliant with her girl friends and with her boy friend, to be more outspoken in her relationships, and not hope others would give her care and attention just because she is she.

LACK OF COURAGE TO FIGHT OPENLY

The second case, Ann, is a 36-year-old, very attractive woman who seemed extremely successful in her private and her professional life. With a master's degree in school psychology she had a very good position as an instructor at a college, and she is married to a man who is a professor of physiology at a medical school.

She had become terribly dissatisfied with her life, with her marriage, and with her situation at work. She found her husband dull, uninterested in her and much more involved in his work. She was afraid of groups.

What bothered her most was an older woman at the college who had been her friend and helpful in getting Ann her present job three years ago. Today this woman still had a fantastic hold over her, as she said, putting her in a very difficult position because the woman was very unpopular. Still, Ann felt she had to be grateful to her sponsor, take her side, and protect her, even when Ann did not like her at all, for which she was really angry at herself.

Besides these complaints Ann had started an affair at the college with a man whom in a way she did not respect. She felt he was proud of his affair with her and wanted to let people know about it. She became especially upset when he arranged to meet her with two other men in a coffee house with a large window where all four of them sat, so that everybody passing by could see them. When she became pregnant she did not know whether it was by her husband or this man, and had an abortion. So she went through a very terrible time and was extremely upset when she came to me. She had not been in therapy before and came to me now because she was, as she felt, in a crisis situation.

Ann recalled that when she was three years old she was afraid to talk to her parents. From there she went on to say that her father was shallow and empty and she did not respect him. Her mother was always angry at her father, delivering violent tirades. Once she threatened him with a knife and threw a cup at him. When the parents fought, Ann always felt guilty.

Her brother who is six years older was out of the house at that time, and she has not much contact with him now.

She felt at the mercy of her parents. At ten or eleven years of age she always had to be home after school, and could have no friends. She developed suicidal ideas at that age, wanting to drown herself; but she did not make any actual attempt. When she tried to rebel against her parents, she would feel guilty and apologized. Maybe it was to get away from home that she got married when she was 20, although she had not really been in love with her husband.

According to Ann, her parents' oppression went so far as not to permit her to attend her own high school graduation although she had been nominated to be the valedictorian. Instead, she had to stay home to help her mother with her housework. When I expressed doubt that she had been to such an extent at the mercy of her parents, she said, "Yes, you are right. You know, I was always called very sneaky." I replied that in this case she must have done many things behind her parents' back to justify this description.

Indeed, it seems she never had the courage for open rebellion. At the age of 15, when she was already very pretty and had many dates, she used to lie to her mother, telling her she was studying with a girl friend instead of admitting that she was with a date. When she was not permitted to read at night, she switched out the light and read with a flashlight.

It is the same pretense and lack of courage that becomes again evident in her relationships to the woman who had given her her job, whom she detested yet with whom she did not break relations; to her husband who she felt was cold and whom she only had the courage to deceive; and to the other man who she felt actually despised her yet with whom she continued her relationship.

Even in her relationship to me, she also had this pretense. For example, in the beginning of her treatment when she told me all the sad stories of her life, she cried profusely using up many paper tissues. Yet at the same time she insisted that she was not at all involved in the treatment.

I put it to her this way, after about 4 to 6 weeks: I told her that she considered herself a second-rate person who at best fights only in a sneaky way. She never feels entitled to a first-rate position. Rather she shapes her life to feel second-rate—in her marriage, at her work, and in the affair that she had. At no point does she fight openly for the position of a really first-rate person, nor does she fight like such a person.

This is quite incongruous with the fact that she was, after all, an extremely attractive woman, with dark curls and very good color; had a very good job, prestige, and many friends. Why should such a woman make herself so miserable?

This interpretation apparently opened new alternatives to her and offered her real encouragement. It made her very happy. She saw its relevance to her problems, past and present. Ann was now able to resolve in one day the relationship to the older woman by talking to her openly, telling her that she really does not want to be her friend any more and wants to make her own way, in another department. She put her affair with the other man on a new basis by telling him how much she had resented to be, as she felt, exhibited. Only with her husband does she still not know what to do: Should she be more open with him and dissolve the marriage? But this will also depend on whether he might change his job, and so on.

CONCLUDING COMMENTS

The ER technique has the special advantage that the data can be gathered in a group situation. The teacher, e.g., can ask a class of school children to write down their ERs and then read them. This will give her, with very little training, a very valuable insight into the children of her class.

ERs, both written and verbal, can also be used in group therapy. For instance I asked a group of women of very low education, with psychosomatic symptoms, to write down their ERs. Not all of them could do this, but they could think about it; and some gave ERs verbally, which then prompted others who did not remember anything at first, to relate their ERs.

I have used ERs furthermore to demonstrate Adlerian methods in a training institute which was not Adlerian. The trainees were psychologists, psychiatrists, and social workers who all had had so called teaching analyses. I was supposed to demonstrate Adlerian techniques. So we started with ERs. The first one who remembered was a trainee physician. His ER was that his mother was sick. The doctor and his father were in her room with her. The door to this room was closed, so that the children including the speaker had to wait outside, anxious for the outcome of the mysterious happening inside. When telling his memory he suddenly exclaimed, "All my life I never wanted to feel excluded like that, to be kept in the dark when important things were happening. That's why I wanted to study medicine myself so that I would not be excluded, but know what is going on." This, then, was a recollection which had never come up in his many years of "classical" Freudian analysis, and which gave him now such an interesting insight into what motivated him, at least in part, in his choice of profession. Through this he also became aware of how angry and resentful he was because of being excluded, and he realized his whole ambitious attitude.

Returning in conclusion to psychotherapy, we may summarize: The uses of early recollections are (*a*) to help the therapist understand the patient's life style, (*b*) to help the patient understand his own life style, and thereby (*c*) to open for the patient the possibility of choosing more healthy behavior and gaining the courage to try out new, socially and individually more useful attitudes.

REFERENCES

1. Adler, A. *The Individual Psychology of Alfred Adler*. Ed. by H. L. & Rowena R. Ansbacher. New York: Basic Books, 1956.

2. Adler, K. A. Techniques that shorten psychotherapy. *J. Indiv. Psychol.*, 1972, 28, 155–168.

CHANGING MISTAKEN BELIEFS THROUGH VISUALIZATION OF EARLY RECOLLECTIONS

MaryAnn Lingg
An assistant professor in the Department of Behavioral Studies at the University of Missouri-St. Louis. She teaches personality development, professional issues, and school counseling classes.

Terry Kottman
An assistant professor at the University of North Texas. She teaches school counseling classes, doctoral internship, and human relations. Kottman is the director of the Child and Family Resource Clinic at the University of North Texas.

> There are no chance memories: out of the incalculable number of impressions which meet an individual he chooses to remember only those which he feels, however darkly, to have bearing on his situation. Thus his memories represent his "Story of My Life"; a story he repeats to himself to warm him or comfort him, to keep him concentrated on his goal and to prepare him by means of past experiences so that he will meet the future with an already tested style of action (Adler, 1958, p. 73).

Early recollections are traditionally used in Individual Psychology to facilitate the investigation into a client's life-style. While early memories do not determine behavior, they do reflect the client's current self-image, views of the world, and style of interaction with others. When asked to describe specific incidents that

Individual Psychology, 47(2), June, 1991, **pp. 255–260**

took place during the early years of life, the client selects, alters, or imagines events that express the central issues and interests of his or her life (Ackerknecht, 1976; Bruhn & Last, 1982). Gathering early recollections can help the counselor begin to understand the client's struggles, attitudes, hopes, and behaviors (Papanek, 1972). They give the counselor clues about the direction of the client's strivings and the ways the client gains significance. Early recollections indicate the values to which the client ascribes and the dangers the client wishes to avoid (Adler, 1937). Basic mistakes, illuminated by the early recollections, represent the client's basic convictions about self, the world, and others. These ideas, which govern behavior, may or may not be within the client's awareness (Manaster & Corsini, 1982).

Basic mistakes are *basic* because they are the original ideas a child develops to fulfill the needs of belonging and significance. They are considered *mistakes* because they are faulty conclusions drawn from a child's perspective while the child is engaged in the struggle to establish a place in the world. As Dreikurs and Soltz (1964) indicated, "Children are expert observers but make many mistakes in interpreting what they observe. They often draw wrong conclusions and choose mistaken ways in which to find their place" (p. 15).

One of the goals of counseling is to identify basic mistakes and bring them to the client's awareness. It is the counselor's responsibility to discover those early, erroneously developed convictions and to help the client see how those ideas are false and how they can interfere with effective social and personal functioning. Manaster and Corsini (1982) refer to the process of psychotherapy as uncovering the basic mistakes and correcting them.

Sometimes simply talking to the client about mistaken beliefs and bringing them to the client's awareness is enough to bring about changes in the client's self-perception. However, at other times, mistaken beliefs and private logic are so ingrained in the client's way of looking at life and self that talking about them does not bring about a change. When this happens the counselor must introduce creative ways of helping the client reexamine basic convictions in order to bring about changes. Early recollections have been used to help the client gain insight into his or her life-style. By interpreting an early recollection or series of early recollections to the client, the counselor can hold up a "mirror reflecting the patient's present attitudes and intentions" (Ackerknecht, 1976, p. 54). Since early recollections represent a microcosm of the client's mistaken beliefs and private logic, active interpretation and visualization of early recollections may be an excellent tool for helping the client reconsider mistaken beliefs. It may then be possible for the client to substitute positive convictions for negative beliefs.

THE TECHNIQUE

Before initiating the visualization process, the counselor reviews any previously presented early recollections and asks for any others the client may remember. The counselor is then free to choose the early recollection which best typifies the basic mistake currently under examination.

The counselor begins the visualization process with some basic relaxation techniques such as asking the client to close his or her eyes, take a few deep breaths, and get as comfortable as possible. The counselor then asks the client to visualize the specific incident chosen to represent the particular mistaken belief. It may facilitate the process if the counselor suggests to the client to think of the early recollections as a scene in a play or television show to be watched from the perspective of an audience. The counselor then asks the client to describe the scene as it is unfolding. With eyes still shut, the client is asked to describe the feelings experienced during the interaction. In order to begin to change the mistaken belief, the counselor asks the client to visualize himself or herself as an adult actually entering the scene. The client is asked to visualize the adult self comforting the child self, telling the child self how valuable, important, and lovable he or she is. Then the counselor suggests that the visualized adult begin to help reconsider any mistaken beliefs about what is necessary to achieve significance and belonging.

For instance, in one early recollection, a client was frightened for appropriate reasons, but her father pushed her aside and called her a baby for being fearful. By interpreting this to mean that her father would not accept her feelings, she formulated a mistaken belief which stated that in order to be loved and belong in her family she needed to deny her feelings and be someone other than who she really was. The visualized adult version of her self comforted her child self and reassured her of the appropriateness of her feelings and encouraged her to express those feelings. The adult self also expressed a willingness to accept her as she was, without a need for pretense.

The counselor then asks the client if there is anything else in the visualized interaction that needs to be changed or if there is anything else the child self needs. If the client answers affirmatively, the counselor guides the client through the process of visualizing the adult self making those changes, doing whatever needs to be done in order to help the child self feel comfortable and safe. After bringing the client back to the present, the counselor asks the client to reexamine mistaken beliefs and to consider other more useful ways of gaining a sense of significance and belonging. At this time, the counselor also helps the client change the wording of selected negative self statements.

A CASE STUDY

A 32-year-old female entered counseling after the breakup of a love relationship. The client was experiencing extreme sadness at the disintegration of the relationship and was having difficulty letting go of her investment in the relationship. After establishing rapport with the client, the counselor began to explore her mistaken beliefs. They identified these mistaken beliefs: (a) "it is my responsibility to make and keep others happy"; (b) "I must control others' behavior to feel important"; and (c) "I must hold things together in the family."

For several sessions the client repeatedly stated that she wanted to change her mistaken beliefs, but that she could not change the way she interacted with others. The counselor decided to employ the technique of early recollection visualization as a possible method of helping her get past this impasse. The counselor asked the client to close her eyes, sit comfortably in the chair, take several deep breaths, then recount one of her early recollections and she related this memory:

> I remember one day my mother was supposed to visit an old friend who happened to live on the other side of the city, near an amusement park. My father was going to drop my mother off at her friend's house and take my younger brother and I to the amusement park while my mother visited her friend. Some time before we were getting ready to go, my father was nagging my mother about something and before you knew it, it was a huge argument with my father nitpicking at my mother over anything. This happened quite often. Finally, my mother was so upset that she decided not to visit her friend. My mother was standing at the front door looking out the window crying. My father was standing in the dining room telling my mother there was no reason to be upset and she should get ready to go out. I was running back and forth between the two of them trying to interpret what the other was saying and trying to smooth things over. I was trying to get my father to stop harassing my mother and trying to get my mother to feel better. I wanted them to stop so things could go as planned.

When the counselor asked about feelings the client replied:

> I remember feeling helpless and pulled in two directions. I wanted them to stop arguing because I didn't like my mother to be upset or my father to be angry. I felt responsible for making things better between them and making everyone happy. I wanted things to be OK so we could still go to the park and I felt selfish about that.

The counselor guided the client through the early recollection visualization process described above. The counselor asked the client to visualize herself entering the scene as an adult and encouraged her to hug and comfort her child self. The counselor coached her through a process in which her adult self told the child self that she did not need to always take care of other people nor did she have the power to control others' behavior. The counselor prompted the adult self to tell the child self that she was not responsible for resolving the parental conflict. The counselor also prompted the adult self to hold the child self and reassure her that she was lovable and significant even when she was not taking care of others. When the counselor asked the client if there was anything else she wanted to change in the visualization she replied "I want her to know (child self) that she is really loved." After the adult self told the child self how much she loved her, the counselor brought her out of the visualization.

The counselor and the client processed the early recollection visualization and discussed changes she wished to make in her basic convictions. They talked about how this early recollection illustrated all three of the basic mistakes they had identified. They discussed the client's feelings of sadness and hopelessness in trying to live her life in accordance with these mistaken beliefs. The client said she would like to change her erroneous convictions to the following: (a) "although I can contribute to others' happiness, I do not have the power to make or keep them happy"; (b) "I do not have the power to control others' behavior"; and (c) "it is not my responsibility to hold things together in my family."

After this session, the client reported a release of responsibility from a job that was not hers in the first place: taking care of her parents' relationship and happiness. The client continued to examine her basic mistakes and to look at how these ideas interfered with her present functioning. With the help of the counselor she was also able to relate the basic mistakes highlighted in this early recollection to her continuing investment in the recently ended love relationship. She had experienced difficulty in letting go of the relationship because she believed she was solely responsible for its continuance. She replaced this belief with one that allowed her to stop being responsible for the happiness of others. Thus, she could let go of the illusion that she must control all of her relationships.

A one-month follow-up found the client still experiencing the same release of responsibility and emotional disengagement from the defunct relationship. She reported an increase in her ability to concentrate on other matters and was no longer obsessing about the relationship. She was continuing to redefine her priorities for future relationships and her beliefs about how she could gain a sense of belonging and significance.

CONCLUSION

Counselors can assist clients in belief reorientation through the use of early recollection visualization. This technique helps clients gain a clearer understanding of their mistaken beliefs and facilitates changes in the ways they gain significance. Early recollection visualization is an action-oriented method which is helpful with clients who have difficulty making a connection between their early decisions and their present behavior. Counselors may recognize this type of client as the one who frequently asks, "Why do I continue to do this?" or who says, "I do not understand why I do the things I do." This technique is also effective with clients who resist examining their mistaken beliefs or persist in negative self-talk. Visualization may also help clients who have a cognitive understanding of their problem but seem to have difficulty changing their feelings and behaviors.

However, counselors should be aware that this technique is not a magical cure. Early recollection visualization is simply one of many therapeutic tools to be used in conjunction with other strategies. It should never be used without a strong counselor-client relationship and an understanding of the client's life-style. Following a visualization, it is imperative that counselors process clients' experiences with them to insure client understanding and well-being.

REFERENCES

Ackerknecht, L. (1976). New aspects of early recollections (ER) as a diagnostic and therapeutic device. *Individual Psychologist, 13*, 44–54.

Adler, A. (1937). Significance of early recollections. *International Journal of Individual Psychology, 3*, 283–287.

Adler, A. (1958). *What life should mean to you*. New York: Capricorn Books.

Bruhn, A. R., & Last, J. (1982). Earliest childhood memories: Four theoretical perspectives. *Journal of Personality Assessment, 46*, 119–127.

Dreikurs, R., & Soltz, V. (1964). *Children: The challenge*. New York: Hawthorn/Dutton.

Manaster, G., & Corsini, R. (1982). *Individual psychology: Theory and practice*. Itasca, IL: F. E. Peacock.

Papanek, H. (1972). The use of early recollections in psychotherapy. *Individual Psychology, 28*, 169–176.

A PRACTICAL USE OF DREAMS

Steven Slavik
A graduate of the Adler School of Professional Psychology. Currently he is director of the Family Counseling Service in Trail, British Columbia.

INTRODUCTION

Dream interpretation is an important skill for therapists. The Adlerian style of dream interpretation is direct and practical. Indeed, Dreikurs (1973, p. 226) states that "it is generally satisfactory and sufficient to know the general direction of the dream without wasting too much time and effort to discover from where the details of the dream-material come." In Adlerian therapy, to be practical entails determination of main outlines or general direction of a coping style without worrying over the details. This practical attitude has benefits in therapy, encouraging direct solutions to problems. The aim of this article is to outline Adlerian theory and use of dreams in short-term, solution-focused therapy, and, through an example, to contrast the aims of short-term Adlerian therapy with those of a longer-term Adlerian therapy.

In short-term, solution-focused therapy, therapists try to use clients' attitudes and beliefs to find solutions to presenting issues, rather than to try to modify or replace those attitudes and beliefs (Dreikurs, 1973; O'Hanlon & Weiner-Davis, 1989). Essentially, through dreams the behavior of the dreamer is interpreted. Using dreams in such therapy can shorten the time spent in therapy. A therapist can frequently get to the crux of issues quickly (Weiss, 1986) and promote behavioral change by extracting the dream message or by using the dream language itself to promote movement (Gold, 1979; Rosen, 1990; Weiss, 1986).

Individual Psychology, 50(3), September, 1994, **pp. 279–287**

THEORY

Symbolism

All symbols have sociocultural origins (Gold, 1979; Shulman, 1969). Verbal uses, images, and symbols in general found in individual language, thinking, fantasy, or dreams originate in actual conventions of culture. One learns to use symbols in a specific culture which provides a common range of meanings for the symbol. It is only because a common range of meanings exists that a contrasting, idiosyncratic use of a symbol by an individual is understood (Gold, 1979). For example, consider the sentence offered from a dream: "I'm too busy at a track meet selling pencils." The dreamer understood this to mean "I'm busy with people, but I never see them." To him, "selling pencils" meant "blind." The theory of symbolism is an example of Adler's "psychology of use" in which the use that individuals make of resources available to them dominates hereditary or environmental givens (Adler, 1964).

Function

In Adlerian theory, the purpose of symbolism is to orient oneself and one's activity in an uncertain, ever-changing social and physical environment (Adler, 1926). Thus, symbol usage is adaptive. More specifically, it is integral to and implements the orientation of the human being toward future, task-oriented activity (Adler, 1929, 1946; Gold, 1978).

The function of thinking is to orient oneself toward and to plan action. Thinking ranges between deliberate planning to overcome obstacles on one extreme and provoking attitudes and emotions regarding difficulties on the other (Dreikurs, 1973). It ranges from a definite, organized activity to a free-flowing look toward the future. In the latter, thinking easily merges into provoking attitudes and emotions preparatory to action. Nonetheless, thinking does not have to conform to rules based on the need to communicate with others (Gold, 1978).

Dreaming is a part of the process of forward-looking, solution-oriented thinking. The "*anticipatory, prescient function of the dream* is always clearly discernable; it foreshadows the *preparations developed in connection with actual difficulties encountered by the dreamer's life-line*" (Adler, 1929, p. 217). The activity of dreaming is identical to that of thinking in general: one looks forward in one's usual manner to solutions of actual problems in living (Adler, 1931,

1979; Beck, 1971). In contrast to thinking, however, dreaming is not to be taken as a means for the attainment of a goal. It is, rather, a sign or proof that one is groping with a problem (Adler, 1926). The purpose of dreams is to create feelings, preparatory to action.

Dreaming, like all one's thinking, conforms to one's private logic or idiosyncratic way of thinking of self, others, and the world. However, in dreaming, how one perceives the here-and-now and the anticipations one makes about oneself, others, or the world become more apparent (Beck, 1971). "Demands of society are not so urgently present with us. In our dream thought we are not stimulated to reckon so honestly with the situation around us" (Adler, 1931, p. 99).

Dreaming offers solutions to unfinished problems of the day, unfettered by felt social demands or constraints and in line with one's usual coping style and mode of activity. Dreams create solutions to problems without demanding anything new from the individual, and in this sense are self-deceptive. In Adler's frank statement, dreams "are an attempt to reach an easy solution for problems, and they reveal the individual's failure of courage" (Adler, 1931, p. 96).

Mechanisms

There are several mechanisms typically used throughout thinking and dreaming. The use of these mechanisms is as idiosyncratic as the use of symbols. First, an individual chooses certain pictures, incidents, and occurrences as symbols which, in themselves, offer justification for a preferred coping style. Second, dreams are metaphorical, allegorical, or analogical. Dreams would not serve to generate emotions and to motivate oneself if they were too literal and could be examined in terms of common sense. They present a solution to a problem in the form, "How would it be if . . . ?" Perhaps we can say that the degree of mystery in a dream reflects the degree to which the dreamer does not want to solve a problem in a common-sense fashion (Gold, 1979). Third, dreams simplify. In dreaming, one can curtail a problem, boil it down, express it in a metaphor, and treat it as if it were the same as the original problem. How one simplifies depends on one's usual way of treating problems (Adler, 1931, 1979; Wexberg, 1970).

In summary, an Adlerian therapist assumes that idiosyncratic uses are tied together. The choice of symbols, the metaphors used, the simplifications, the elements of a personality style, the presentation and use of a dream, the very choice of issues themselves, and the message of the dream regarding issues are holographically tied into a consistent and cohesive style of coping with the challenge of living.

PRACTICE

There are several ways in which dreams or the use of dreams reveal one's idiosyncratic logic. The dream itself, both its content and process, shows what one does in life. The attitudes and patterns shown in the dream are those of waking life. In addition, how one uses the dream in waking life as an excuse to justify one's goal or as material in one's goal shows how one is inclined to justify one's movement in life (Dreikurs, 1973; Shulman, 1969). One's style of relating a dream will, like all nonverbal communication, reveal one's attitude and orientation in life. In short-term therapy, a therapist is primarily concerned with the content and process of the dream and will consider the client's use of the dream to confirm hypotheses about the client's movement.

Procedure and Interpretation

As the dream is related, the therapist transcribes it verbatim or has the client write it. The therapist observes in detail whether the dream is delivered shyly, aggressively, with reluctance, with pleasure, slyly, or whatever. In this sample of the client's typical behavior, nuances of presentation can be important. The therapist notices whether the dream is long and complicated, confused, dramatic, or short and direct. He or she formulates a way in which the content and process of the dream are consistent with the dreamer's presentation. The therapist asks what might have been on the dreamer's mind before sleeping. He or she inquires to what problem the dream may be a solution.

In the content of the dream itself, the therapist notices the position and the presentation of self, and asks, "Is the self in the dream or an external observer?" He or she notes the activity of the self on others and how others act upon the self. An important movement to observe is whether the self is acted against, or whether the self acts with or against others. The therapist notices the presentation of others, of the context of the action, and of other nonpersonal images such as houses, buildings, vehicles, and animals. He or she uses whatever he or she already knows about the dreamer to look for patterns and meaning in the dream (Beck, 1971). The therapist observes the presentation of objects with possible unusual and symbolic uses, and looks for idiosyncratic uses (Gold, 1979; Weiss, 1986). He or she inquires regarding feelings which were aroused in the dream and regarding feelings with which the dreamer woke.

To obtain the "message" there are many interpretive techniques. Works by Bonime (1982) and Weiss (1986) are particularly useful in regard to technique. In general, one might start with what seems to be most obvious, offer an interpretation for confirmation and modification, and work into the remainder. It is important that any interpretation be acceptable to the client (Gold, 1979). Dream interpretation is a cooperative process, and if the interpretation does not accord with the client, it is not correct.

An Example

A 31-year-old, somewhat dramatic, registered nurse came to therapy to clarify issues in her life. She was considering leaving her full-time nursing job to follow a partner who was moving elsewhere for employment. This was her first relationship in approximately four years. She was also considering leaving nursing permanently. She offered the following dream in a written version, but a great many details had to be clarified and filled in before presenting it in the form given here. In discussing the dream, she was somewhat suspicious, as if I might use the information against her. It was noticeably difficult to involve her in curious discussion and verification of meanings.

> In the opening scene I could see the hospital Emergency Room and two nurses there. (I know them.) They were preparing for a code [Emergency]. (At this time I am able to see this yet I am not there.) I am to be the code so I come on a stretcher. They work on me and realize that all I need is a splint to my left hand. We all thought it was a relief and hilarious. (I knew it all the time.) This whole scene is only a test for them.
>
> Next we are in a hall and I was getting an award from the two nurses for the performance/test. Then someone else was talking about friendship and respect that can grow. One nurse turned and we hugged; the other glared and walked away. So it was over and I went out to my white 4 × 4 truck. I had a parking ticket for being there too long.
>
> Next I am driving along (home) and noticed a street I have not driven down for a long time. I decide to take it. This street is long and narrow—surrounded by barren, broken concrete. The time is dusk. Vehicles are driving with no lights on. These people are driving against me all over the road and sidewalk. These people are vacant-looking or like zombies. I was trying to dodge these vehicles and flickering my lights. Eventually I decided to turn around and go home my usual way. I went up on the sidewalk and onto the rocky open area. There were pieces of concrete there too. Thank God I had a 4 × 4. When I got turned around back to the road the traffic was so heavy that I could not get back on the road. Then two people (men?) walked by talking. They were talking about all the

> murders that had happened here. Then an ominous, slender, tallish guy in a trench coat with high leather boots, hat, and gloves, face wrapped like a ninja's, with grey/brown sunglasses on, with a medium-size dog, same color, appeared. The guy was carrying a flash light and he walked up to the point where I was, stopped, and turned toward me. I wondered if this was the person killing people. Yet I was not sure how to get away for I knew he felt and knew everything I did. I felt doomed.
>
> I woke up and I knew the zombie people were his victims.

After approximately an hour of discussion she agreed on the following summary of the dream's content.

> I'm a nurse and I do it well. I take nursing (and the medical profession) as a bit of a joke, and it's only a performance for me, but others may make a big deal of it. I cope well with acceptance and rejection by women there. But I've been there too long, and I've paid for it—in terms of health and mood.
>
> I've chosen a road I haven't been down for awhile—having a relationship. I try to keep on the straight and narrow but zombie-like people are against me and don't approve of what I need to be—alive! They're not alive and I signal to awaken them to their predicament, but I give up in disgust and disheartenment. I try to turn around and I get stuck in loosened-up feelings. It's hard to get back in control. When I'm stuck and don't do the usual thing, every which way I turn is difficult. Then men are ominous and threatening, and I feel vulnerable.

And even more briefly:

> With women I get along well, in give-and-take relationships. With men I can feel stuck, trapped, and vulnerable. I want to be in control.

These summaries present the client's private analysis of issues before her. The dream presents both a "go" and a "stop" (Mosak, 1992). It seems clear that she has made up her mind to leave nursing. In regard to relationships, she does well with women, but she feels apprehension with men under some circumstances. When she perceives herself as not doing the "usual thing," she feels vulnerable to men. This issue is currently related to leaving nursing, which sets the stage: Leaving her usual nursing profession, she feels more at risk in following a man. The primary issue presented in this dream is one of needing to know where and how she belongs—her place in life. When she does not know, she feels vulnerable to men.

Clarifying this dream aided in reducing her uneasiness. It led to three ways to reduce her sense of risk: by understanding that some men are less risky than others, by clarifying her place in this relationship, and by finding concrete ways within the relationship (and in other relationships) to deal with her sense of risk when it hinders the primary relationship. The former is called "spitting in her soup" by Adler, since it encourages her to maintain her movement, but not without examination. The latter two increase her ability to cooperate since they encourage her to deal with her expectation of defeat by men usefully within the relationship (Adler, 1931).

We did not delve deeply into origins and meanings of possible symbols in the dream. We discussed three. When asked how the dream would be different if the splint were not on her left hand, but on her right foot, she said it would make it more difficult to work. The splint on the left hand did not immobilize her much. It was a token disability. The difference a blue Mazda would make was more significant. In a blue Mazda she would not be able to negotiate over the broken concrete with the stability she wanted in relationships. And the broken concrete itself represented her new-found ability to uncover herself in a relationship. What had been cemented up was loosened. Of course there are many other symbols: the dog, the lights, the vehicles, and so forth. These were not discussed because of the difficulty in engaging her in such discussion and because we had achieved the short-term goals of clarifying and reducing her apprehension, and of finding ways for her to reduce or manage her sense of risk within the relationship.

The way she understood this dream initially was somewhat as an omen (dramatically), and she presented the dream with some suspicion. Since she knew she wanted to leave nursing and had conflicts with physicians, she initially interpreted the ominous man as the "medical profession," and the feeling of doom helped justify her leaving. This is in line with her sense of vulnerability when she is not "doing the usual thing" and in line with an exaggerated way of presenting herself as vulnerable. However, in further discussion, the second part of the dream was found to be more about her relationship than work. Her presenting suspicion is consistent with being at risk to men (possibly myself, a male therapist).

This dream uses the three mechanisms described earlier. The images chosen help to justify the conclusion. The ominous man helps justify dread. Zombie-like people help justify aversion. Clearly the dream is metaphorical. She could not merely dream "I am done with nursing." Instead, she dreamed "It's all a performance and I can leave easily—especially since I've paid too much already." These are two reasons to move on her way without regret. Finally, this dream simplifies. Not all men are ominous, nor do they know everything about her. The dream omits certain considerations about men to justify the point of view.

In conclusion, this is a dream which offers answers to two questions: "Shall I leave nursing?" and "Shall I follow this relationship?" It appears to offer a clear-cut answer to the former: "It has already cost me too much." To the latter, it offers the warning, "When I do not do the usual thing, men are dangerous. Think it over carefully."

A number of other elements of personality style seem to be indicated in the dream. Short-term, solution-focused therapy did not address them, but longer-term Adlerian therapy might. *First*, she seeks to be in control of how and where she moves. She feels good when in control, such as in nursing, and she feels very much at risk when she cannot move to her choice. Short-term therapy *used* but did not *address* this. *Second*, she signals to awaken others to their deadness. She wants to "save" people. But she gives up in discouragement when they do not respond. This might be a martyred style (Mosak, 1977), emphasized by people being against her. *Third*, she states issues in dramatic, complicated, and exaggerated images. She has a dramatic style that is her way of contrasting herself to others. Relationships are life-and-death matters, whereas nursing is not; it is only performance. *Fourth*, when she feels vulnerable, she perceives men as threatening. Her delivery of the dream might have shown this. *Fifth*, relationships with men are a source of some anxiety. She might be saying something like, "Men know everything about me. I don't trust them. To preserve some privacy and safety, I act dramatically and I present myself in a complicated way."

The premise of short-term therapy is to use current attitudes and beliefs as a lever to change behavior, rather than to change those attitudes and beliefs. This short-term therapy used the belief that she needs control to prevent defeat by men, to increase her sense of control in useful ways. However, since this is a holistic theory, Adlerians believe that change in one's behavior may precipitate change in other aspects of functioning. For example, to maintain her sense of control in useful ways may diminish her need to retain privacy through drama.

SUMMARY

According to Adlerian theory, dreams both show the unity of the personality and are problem-solving, forward-looking experiences that produce emotions for the next day's waking life. Dreams are purposeful rehearsals for future situations. Adler did not believe in the idea of universal symbols in dreams. The content of a dream is a reflection of the private logic of the dreamer, based on symbols that are culturally available but which may be turned to private and idiosyncratic use.

Dreams can be useful in a short-term, solution-focused therapy. They can provide a summary of client's thinking concerning current issues of life. Through symbols, metaphor, and simplification, they incorporate the individual's style of thinking which may aid or hinder common-sense solutions to problems. Given an understanding of the client's imagery and thinking, solutions are found which use the client's style of thinking to aid the client's movement.

REFERENCES

Adler, A. (1926). *The neurotic constitution.* Salem, NH: Ayer.

Adler, A. (1929). Dreams and dream-interpretation. In *The practice and theory of Individual Psychology* (pp. 214–226). London: Kegan Paul.

Adler, A. (1931). *What life should mean to you.* New York: Blue Ribbon Books.

Adler, A. (1946). *Understanding human nature.* New York: Greenberg.

Ansbacher, H. L., & Ansbacher, R. R. (Eds.). (1956). *The individual psychology of Alfred Adler: A systematic presentation in selections from his writings.* New York: Basic Books.

Ansbacher, H. L., & Ansbacher, R. R. (Eds.). (1979). *Superiority and social interest: A collection of later writings.* New York: Norton.

Beck, A. T. (1971). Cognitive patterns in dreams and daydreams. In J. H. Masserman (Ed.), *Science and psychoanalysis. Volume XIX. Dream dynamics* (pp. 2–7). New York: Grune & Stratton.

Bonime, W. (1982). *The clinical use of dreams.* New York: Da Capo.

Dreikurs, R. (1973). *Psychodynamics, psychotherapy, and counseling.* Chicago: Alfred Adler Institute.

Gold, L. (1978). Life style and dreams. In L. Baruth & D. Eckstein (Eds.), *Life style: Theory, practice, and research* (pp. 24–30). Dubuque: Kendall & Hunt.

Gold, L. (1979). Adler's theory of dreams: An holistic approach to interpretation. In B. B. Wolman (Ed.), *Handbook of dreams: Research, theories and applications* (pp. 319–341). New York: Van Nostrand.

Mosak, H. H. (1977). *On purpose.* Chicago: Alfred Adler Institute.

Mosak, H. H. (1992). The "traffic cop" function of dreams and early recollections. *Individual Psychology, 48*(3), 319–323.

O'Hanlon, W. H., & Weiner-Davis, M. (1989). *In search of solutions: A new direction in psychotherapy*. New York: Norton.

Rosen, S. (1990). Concretizing of symptoms and their manipulation. In J. K. Zeig & S. G. Gilligan (Eds.), *Brief therapy: Myths, methods, and metaphors* (pp. 258–272). New York: Brunner/Mazel.

Shulman, B. H. (1969). An Adlerian theory of dreams. In M. Kramer (Ed.), *Dream psychology and the new biology of dreaming* (pp. 118–137). Springfield, IL: Thomas.

Weiss, L. (1986). *Dream analysis in psychotherapy*. New York: Pergamon.

Wexberg, E. (1970). *Individual psychological treatment*. Chicago: Alfred Adler Institute.

Part B
QUESTIONING AND CONFRONTATION TECHNIQUES

THE "REDISCOVERY" OF INTERVENTIVE INTERVIEWING

Len Sperry
A faculty member of the Adler School of Professional Psychology, Chicago.

Interviewing has traditionally been described as either diagnostic or therapeutic. Whereas diagnostic interviewing elicits data about symptoms and early life determinants, therapeutic interviewing follows it by one or more intake and evaluation sessions and focuses on insight and change. Today, the trend toward more time-limited and cost-effective treatment has seen the blurring of diagnostic and therapeutic interviewing into what is called "interventive interviewing".

In 1987, Karl Tomm, M.D. proposed the concept "interventive interviewing" to describe questioning that sought not only information from the individual, but also a change in how the patient processed information. In other words, the intent of the clinician's questioning is to impact the individual's cognitive processing of the questions themselves which will facilitate therapeutic change, aside from the content of my specific answer to the questions (Tomm, 1987). White and Epston (1990) have also described interventive interviewing.

For Adler, diagnosis and treatment were so closely related he discussed diagnostic interviewing strategies in his 1932 paper "Technique of Treatment" (Adler, 1964). In 1933 Adler detailed an interview schedule which included both diagnostic and therapeutic queries which appears remarkably similar to the interventive interviewing strategies (Adler, 1956 p. 408–9).

Interestingly, Adler believed that an experienced clinician could gain considerable insight into the life style of the individual within about half an hour. The

NASAP Newsletter, 25(5), June, 1992, **pp. 3–4**

rest of this paper described three common types of questioning strategies utilized in interventive interviewing. The reader will note the similarity in these questioning strategies to the type of queries in Adler's interview schedule for adults. These similarities reflect the current "rediscovery"—without apparent recognition or citation—of Adler's genius as a clinician.

CIRCULAR QUESTIONS

Circular questions are extremely valuable in mapping an individual's or family's relational world. Circular questions are based on circular rather than linear causality, i.e., that A effects B and B, in turn, effects A. Circular questions elicit the patterns that connect individuals and are thus a mainstay of systemic therapy approaches. They are questions about comparisons and differences, and form the basis for reframing life events. Some examples of circular questions are: Besides you, who else worries about your wife's depression? Who worries more, you or your daughter? When you wife is depressed, how do you respond? How do you respond to her response? How does your daughter react to this? How do you respond to your daughter's reaction?"

Adler suggests a similar type of question in his 1933 interview schedule. One of his questioning sequences is: "How many brothers and sisters have you? What is their attitude toward you? How do they get along in life? Do they also have any illness?" Another questioning sequence is: "What sort of persons are around you at present? Are they impatient, bad-tempered or affectionate?" (Adler, 1956, p. 409).

REFLEXIVE QUESTIONS

Reflexive questions are also based on circular assumptions and are intended to influence the patient or family in an indirect or general manner. They help individuals generate new perspective or contexts. Reflexive questions prompt patients to reconstruct meaning or shift contexts. Their intent is to facilitate and mobilize the individual's or family members' own problem-solving resources. Such questions can facilitate an individual or family member to think about the implications of their current perceptions or behavior and consider alternatives. Some examples of reflexive questions are: "If you were to share with her how worried you are about her depression, what do you suppose she might think or do? Let's suppose she was resentful about something but feared bringing it to your attention, how could you convince her it was safe to tell you? If her depression miraculously cleared up, how would your lives be different?"

This last question is reminiscent of "The Question" (Adler, 1964): "If I had a magic wand or magic pill that would eliminate your symptom immediately, what would be different in your life?" Actually, several other authors also take credit for "The Questions" besides Thom (1984). Insoo Berg (in press) and Steve De Shazer report that in 1984 they developed "The Miracle Question". It is basically restatement of Adler's Questions published in the 1929 edition of Problems of Neurosis (1964a). In his interview schedule Adler also proposes a reflexive question: "What occupation would have interested you the most, and if you did not adopt it, why not?"

STRATEGIC QUESTIONS

Strategic questions are the mainstay of strategic therapy approaches. Their purpose is to alter the individual's behavior in a therapeutic direction. While based on linear assumptions of causality, this type of question assumes that when the clinician discovers dysfunctionality, he or she can proceed to correct or change it. Strategic questions are a powerful mode of influencing individuals, couples or families, either overtly or covertly. Some examples of strategic questions are: "Why don't you talk to her about your worries instead of you daughters? What would happen if for the next week you would suggest she make breakfast every morning instead of staying in bed until noon? How come you're not willing to try harder to get her up and around? Would you prefer making sure she gets up every morning or confronting her with your fears that she might overdose?"

Adler's use of paradox in his stories and in paradoxical injunctions, such as prescribing the symptom, reflect strategic questions. For example, when an individual complains of inability to fall asleep within a reasonable time interval, the clinician might prescribe the symptom by requiring the patient to remain awake for as long as possible. The patient will faithfully follow the directive, or become perplexed or even angry at the clinician and refuse to comply with it. In either case the patient falls asleep and the problem is solved.

CONCLUDING NOTE

Fifty years after Adler proposed some radically unique strategies for questioning and interviewing individuals, "interventive interviewing" has been touted as a distinctly new method. This unwitting "rediscovery" of one of Adler's unique contributions suggests how little most clinicians know about the actual contribution of Alfred Adler and Individual Psychology.

Many who consider themselves well-educated only associate concepts such as inferiority complex and birth order with Adler, convinced that he made no other contributions. Here is an instance where "a little knowledge is dangerous" and paves the way for the contributions of Adler to be invented anew by subsequent generations. This phenomenon could prompt NASAP leadership to examine how effective and faithful they have been to NASAP's mission of promulgating the principles of Individual Psychology.

REFERENCES

Adler, A. (1956) *The individual psychology of Alfred Adler.* H. L. Ansbacher & R. R. Ansbacher (Eds.) New York: Harper & Row.

Adler, A. (1964) *Superiority and social interest.* H. L. Ansbacher & R. R. Ansbacher (Eds.) Evanston, IL: Northwestern University Press.

Adler, A. (1964b) *Problems of neurosis.* New York: Harper & Row.

Berg, I. (in press) You can't see the forest for the trees. *Topics in Family Psychology and Counseling. 1,* 3.

Tomm, K. (1988) Interventive interviewing: Part III. Intending to ask lineal, circular, strategic, or reflexive questions? *Family Process, 22:* 1–16.

White, M. & Epston, D. (1990) *Narrative means to therapeutic ends.* New York: W. W. Norton.

CONFRONTATION TECHNIQUES IN ADLERIAN PSYCHOTHERAPY

Bernard H. Shulman
Assistant professor of psychiatry, Northwestern University, and chairman of the department of psychiatry, St. Joseph Hospital, Chicago. He is president of the International Association of Individual Psychology.

The characteristics and purposes of confrontation techniques have been variously described by different authors. Devereux (5), a psychoanalyst, perhaps the first to write on the subject, defines confrontation as "a device whereby the patient's attention is directed to the bare factual content of his actions or statements, or to a coincidence which he has perceived but has not, or professes to have not, registered." The purpose, says Devereux, is to "induce or force the patient to pay attention to something he has just said or done" in order to open up new avenues for examination and to increase awareness. Wolberg (17, p. 429) points out contradictions to the patient and asks him why he so behaved. He then examines the patient's response to the confrontation. Ruesch also uses confrontation to "confront the patient with the facts" and describes it as containing "an element of aggressiveness, and . . . designed to produce shock . . . usually demonstrates discrepancies between intent and effect, between word and action" (14, p. 194). Berne likewise defines confrontation as "pointing out an inconsistency" and suggests its use in three specific situations: when the patient tries to deceive the therapist, when the patient "plays stupid," or when he does not perceive the inconsistency himself (3, pp. 235–236).

Dreyfus and Nikelly describe the technique in existential language: "Two of the most important kinds of human relatedness which frequently occur during psychotherapy are encounter and confrontation . . . Confrontation involves being

Journal of Individual Psychology, 27(2), November, 1971, **pp. 167–175**

faced with a choice regarding one's own existence. The therapist confronts the client with an aspect of the latter's world, and the client must choose whether or not he will respond and what the response must be" (7, pp. 18–19).

Garner (9, 10) more than anyone has described the various kinds of patient material on which confrontation may be focused. One may choose one of many "conflicts" as object of a direct, authoritarian statement, sometimes a command. No matter what the focus of the statement, Garner then adds, "What do you think or feel about what I told you?" (10, p. 24). The command is a message to the patient that the therapist is intervening and is therefore supportive. The question which follows "enables the therapist, by following the responses and behavior of the patient, to evaluate the degree to which doctrinal compliance or problem solving is developing in the patient" (10, p. 93).

All these authors tend to see confrontation as a direct challenge requiring an immediate response. Some use confrontation mostly to elicit new material, others, to increase awareness. Wolberg, and Dreyfus and Nikelly warn against making confrontations in such a way that the patient will perceive them as a hostile attack or a disregard of his feelings.

We understand by confrontation any reasonable therapeutic technique which brings the client face to face with an issue in a manner calculated to provoke an immediate response.

While Devereux carefully distinguishes between confrontation and interpretation, it is obvious from our definition that the two need not be mutually exclusive. Some confrontations are interpretations as well, but not all interpretations are confrontations. Thus, the statement, "Perhaps you arrange to suffer, so you can feel righteous," is an interpretation, not a confrontation, which the client may or may not accept. Even if it brings closure to him and satisfies his sense of fit, he is not required to do anything other than *consider* the therapist's comment. On the other hand, comments such as, "Why didn't you do it the way we had planned?" or "Why did you decide to stay and feel bad when you could have gone home?" are questions which request an immediate response, and thus are confrontations. Such questions can be made even more challenging by attacking the client's position, belief, or behavior, e.g.,"Since you admitted that you provoked the argument, by what right do you still remain angry?"

The main characteristic of the confrontation is its *challenge*, and it is the combination of challenge and question which evokes the feeling that immediate response is required. "You behave with him the same way you behaved with your father," is an interpretation. But if one then adds, "Don't you?", the statement becomes an interpretation plus confrontation. The patient's response may be an explanation or a defensive maneuver, such as confusing the issues, changing the subject, or rationalizing (which maneuvers themselves become material for confrontation); or the response may be a positive therapeutic one in which the patient gains an insight, experiences a cognitive dissonance and changes a belief, or acts in a new way.

Confrontation is used to provoke therapeutic movement. As an active, directive technique it is less likely to be used by therapists who spend most of their time listening to free associations, being a "neutral screen," giving unconditional positive regard, permitting ventilation, or just offering emotional support. Action-oriented therapists, on the other hand, tend to use confrontation because it places the client constantly into new roles and situations to which he is asked to respond. Thus, Gestalt, experiential, sensitivity, and psychodrama therapists tend to move from one emotionally intense situation to another, with many confrontations (4, p. 16; 16, p. 92).

Group therapies by their nature contain numerous confrontations, because typically the members often confront each other (2, 11, 12, 13). Marriage and family counseling or therapy also lends itself to confrontations, as the family members are brought face to face with the dynamics of their relationships (14, 15).

A number of confrontation techniques have been used particularly in Adlerian psychotherapy. While Adlerian theory does not insist that the therapist be directive, it does say that the aim of therapy is to help the client recognize and change his mistaken goals and beliefs and their associated moods and actions. Such an understanding of therapy (which is very different from one of "working through" of inner conflicts) favors confrontation techniques since these are so effective in holding up before the client, as if in a mirror, his mistaken goals.

Of the following techniques some seem to be commonly used by Adlerians, while others have grown out of years of mutual endeavor of my more close Adlerian colleagues and myself. They are presented in terms of the object of the confrontation—the client's inner or overt behavior.

CONFRONTING THE CLIENT WITH HIS SUBJECTIVE VIEWS

Subjective Feeling

> An agitated, distressed, unhappy young woman came into my office for her initial visit. Her description of her symptoms was not very clear, except that she feared having a "breakdown." But she made enough disparaging references to what her husband did or said that it was easy to guess that she was angry at him.

> When she asked, "How sick do you think I am, doctor?", I responded with a statement intended to confront her with her emotions. "I'm not sure how sick you are," I said, "but one thing impresses me: you are very angry." The remark surprised her and she asked, "About what?" "From what I hear you saying, you seem to be angry at your husband. Am I right?" She immediately agreed, which allowed me to make an encouraging interpretive comment. "When people are very angry, they are also upset and they can even feel sick. So let us find out why you are angry at your husband and how much that anger may be upsetting you."
>
> The patient later recalled this statement that she was angry, saying it gave her the feeling I was able to teach her something about herself.

Rudolf Dreikurs (personal communication) gives the name, "revealing the hidden reason," to a confronting technique described in the following:

> The counselor had been discussing with a couple in marital counseling how each was out to "get" the other; he, by accusing her of fiscal recklessness; she, by excessive spending and complaints that his income was inadequate. At one session they each seemed to agree with the counselor's interpretations.
>
> When they left his office, they passed a jewelry store, and the wife stopped to look in the window. Whereupon the husband said, "We were just talking about this in Dr. Dreikurs' office and here you go looking again at things to buy. Now, remember, you agreed to stop buying things." She immediately went in the store and bought a ring while he stood by protesting.
>
> At the next session she was contrite, and he was triumphant. He offered the incident as evidence of her deficiencies. She admitted that she had transgressed, and "could not understand" why she had done it.
>
> The counselor asked, "What were you thinking at the moment you went in to buy the ring, just after your husband warned you?" At first she did not understand what the counselor was after, and said she did not recall. When asked, "What reason did you give yourself for going into the store?" she said, "I just wanted to go in and look at things. I had no idea of buying until I saw the ring, and it was so beautiful I just had to have it."
>
> "What did you say to yourself then?" "I thought, now he was going to be angry with me again, but it was all his fault anyway. I had no intention of going into the store when I stopped to look in the window, but what he said made me so mad, I just said to myself that it was all his fault for always criticizing me even when I don't do anything, and that I was going to show him."

> This was what the counselor was looking for, and he then said, "So you quietly wait until he says something that you consider provocative and then you use it to justify retaliation. In this way you can get him and make believe he deserved it."

"Hidden reason" describes the private justification and rationalization a person gives himself to make his behavior immediately acceptable to himself. Thus, "I'm only acting this way because I'm drunk," "I had so little sleep I couldn't get anything done if I went to work anyway," "I'm too nervous," are all examples of such private self-justifications. They give the person freedom from responsibility as Adler had observed. "Every therapeutic cure . . . tears the patient from the cradle of his freedom from responsibility" (1, p. 271).

Since this technique pinpoints a specific rationalization, it is not surprising that Albert Ellis also describes the same kind of pinpointing in his rational therapy (8, p. 126).

Mistaken Belief or Attitude

Since, for Adlerians, a person acts according to his convictions, it becomes important to discover what are the convictions that have lead to troublesome and distressing behavior. All material brought by the client is available for examination and for inferences regarding mistaken beliefs. But we are particularly interested in "basic convictions"; i.e., beliefs about one's own nature, the nature of the world in which one lives, and the nature of life, its meaning and requirements. These basic convictions fill in the following blanks: "I am. . . . Life is. . . . Therefore. . . ."

In Adler's words, a person's actions depend on the way he "looks upon himself and the world . . . Behavior springs from his opinion" (1, p. 182). "Each one organizes himself according to his personal view of things, and some views are more sound, some less sound" (p. 183). Those that are more sound, are in accordance with "common sense," those less sound, represent what Adler called at first "private man . . . for making one's way through life," the "private intelligence" (pp. 253–254), and sometimes also "private logic" (p. 143). Actually the last term is not quite correct, because even in patients the logic, the "therefore," is sound enough as a rule. It is their presuppositions, their opinions about themselves and life, which are not sound. Yet "private logic" has become the term preferred by Dreikurs (6, pp. 69, 96, 194, 271). But regardless of the term, the revelation of the patient's private beliefs is considered an important part of psychotherapy.

Showing the Private Logic. If the client who suffers from tension symptoms says, "Why am I so tense?" or, "How can I stop being so tense?" or, "I never could relax, I'm the nervous type" or, "Wouldn't you be disturbed also?" or some similar form of verbal garbage that every therapist hears, the therapist can counter with an interpretation plus confrontation: "Since you see the world as inimical (hostile, dangerous, threatening), you must always be on the alert (keep your guard up, stay poised for action, keep your armies mobilized). Why should you expect to change the tension as long as you feel so surrounded by danger?"

Tua Culpa. "Why do people walk over me?" asked another patient. "I'm only trying to be a good guy." The therapist's answer was, "Because you let them. You look, act and talk like a doormat, and you invite people to walk on you. Don't blame people, they're only giving you what you asked for. Since you invite them, you have to suffer the consequences. Isn't that right?"

The Private Goal

The private goal of the patient's behavior is often interpreted to him without confrontation, but there are common confronting techniques in this connection. One of these is the confronting interpretation which often elicits a "recognition reflex" (6, p. 261). Thus, when a patient tries to deny a feeling that the therapist suspects is present, the latter may say:

> "Didn't you feel a little bit that you were glad he got upset?"
> "Didn't you feel powerful, getting your mother to spend all that time with you?"
> "Didn't you like all the fuss that was made over you?"
> "Could it be you wanted to get your wife upset?"
> "Didn't you think just a little that now you would have an excuse for staying home a little longer and not go to work yet?"

These types of confronting statements produce the recognition reflex more readily in children then adults, but adults will also often respond with an indication that the remark hit home.

CONFRONTING THE CLIENT WITH HIS DESTRUCTIVE BEHAVIOR

What Did You Just Do?

"Here and now" confrontations are considered by several writers (4, p. 16; 8, p. 126; 10) to be therapeutically the most active. While all confrontations mentioned have a quality of contemporaneity, those that deal with the immediate behavior of the client precisely at the moment of discussion are the most contemporaneous and simultaneous. They deal with his thoughts, feelings, and actions at the moment of questioning, often with his at-that-moment behavior in the therapeutic relationship, with his reactions to the therapy, especially his resistance, his repeated "game-playing," and his private logic.

For example, it is a common manifestation of resistance in intellectualizing, compulsive patients to respond to an interpretation by arguing about one word instead of dealing with the whole statement. One confronts this by simply saying, "I notice that you are arguing about one word. Why are you ignoring the rest of what I said?" Other manifestations of resistance can be confronted the same way Some examples are:

> "When I asked you about your parents you stopped talking. How come?"
>
> "You just started to hallucinate. You decided to pay attention to the voices instead of to me. I wonder why?"
>
> "You just changed the subject. Were we getting too close to something?"
>
> "Whenever we talk about something important you belch. I wonder why?"
>
> "Your face just turned red. What's up?"

Not only resistances, but other aspects of behavior can be noted:

> "I notice you keep swinging your leg. What do you suppose it means?"
>
> "A look passed over your face. What thought went through your mind?"
>
> "How do you feel right now as we are talking?"
>
> "The headache you are getting, started just a few minutes ago. What were we discussing then?"
>
> "You just changed the subject again. Let's see if you can recall what the subject was when you chose to change it."
>
> "Do you remember what I just said?"
>
> "You just contradicted yourself. What are you trying to do?"
>
> "You just made a slip of the tongue. Did you catch it?"

Especially useful are confronting statements which call attention to repeated patterns of self-defeating behavior.

> "Now that you have told me your plans, I can see that you are planning to be a victim again. You still seem to insist on playing that role. Don't you?"

> "You just berated yourself again. Keep it up and in five minutes you will really be depressed. Is that what you want?"
>
> "You've spent the whole session complaining about your mother. I wonder when we can start talking about you?"
>
> "Another married man? I think you are devoted to avoiding eligible men. And how do you expect this one to turn out?"

Presenting Alternatives

Confrontation is sometimes a dramatic way of presenting alternatives. This can be most clearly seen in role-playing where role reversal and auxiliary ego techniques provide immediate alternatives. In the dialogue situation one can confront with alternatives by statements like:

> "You can study and try to pass the exam or you can goof off and pretend you don't care. Which will it be?"
>
> "You don't have to spend your life complaining about how much your husband makes. You can get a job and help out. The choice is yours. Which will it be?"
>
> "I know you don't want your in-laws to visit. You have three choices. You can tell them not to come; you can let them come and be gracious about it; or you can do what you did last time, let them come and spend the whole time being irritated and feeling abused. Which will it be?"

Examining the Future

Confrontation can also be used to present the future and its requirements to the client so that again, it is an immediate challenge, an attempt to evoke an immediate response.

Immediate Future. Sometimes in the therapeutic dialogue a client recognizes the illogic of his behavior or a mistake in the way he thinks and feels. Sometimes he sees clearly the purpose of his symptoms and his behavior. At these moments the therapist may use confrontation: "O.K., you see it. What are you going to do about it?" "How long do you plan to wait before you change it? Six months? A year?"

Distant Future. Sometimes it is appropriate to confront the patient with a picture of the future in general and his life in it. For this purpose the following confronting statements can be used: "What do you plan to be doing five years from now?" "What do you intend to do with your life?" "What do you really expect to get out of all this therapy?"

SUMMARY

Confrontation techniques are intended to challenge the client to give an immediate response, make an immediate change or an immediate examination of some issue. When appropriately timed they are effective additions to the therapist's armamentarium of techniques. They are *active* movements by the therapist, directing and guiding the attention of the client. Adlerian confronting techniques are intended to help the client become immediately and more intensively aware of his private logic, his goals, his behavior and his responsibilities for all these as well as his ability to change. Examples of the various confrontation techniques are given.

REFERENCES

1. Adler, A. *The Individual Psychology of Alfred Adler.* Ed. by H. L. & Rowena R. Ansbacher. New York: Basic Books, 1956.

2. Anderson, S. C. Effects of confrontation by high and low-functioning therapists on high and low-feeling clients. *J. counsel. Psychol.*, 1969, 16, 299–302.

3. Berne, E. *Principles of group treatment.* New York: Grove Press, 1966.

4. Corsini, R. J. *Roleplaying in psychotherapy.* Chicago, Ill.: Aldine, 1966.

5. Devereux, G. Some criteria for the timing of confrontations and interpretations. *Int. J. Psychoanal.*, 1951, 32, 19–24.

6. Dreikurs, R. *Psychodynamics, psychotherapy, and counseling.* Chicago, Ill.: Alfred Adler Institute, 1967.

7. Dreyfus, E. A., & Nikelly, A. G. Existential humanism in Adlerian psychotherapy. In A. G. Nikelly (Ed.), *Techniques for behavior change.* Springfield, Ill.: C. C. Thomas, 1971. Pp. 13–20.

8. Ellis, A. *Reason and emotion in psychotherapy.* New York: Lyle Stuart, 1962.

9. Garner, H. H. The confrontation problem-solving technique: developing a psychotherapeutic focus. *Amer. J. Psychother.*, 1970, 24, 27–48.

10. Garner, H. H. *Psychotherapy: confrontation problem-solving technique.* St. Louis, Mo.: W. H. Green, 1970.

11. Kaswan, J., & Love, L. R. Confrontation as a method of psychological intervention. *J. nerv. ment. Dis.*, 1969, 148, 224–237.

12. Lifton, W. M. Group centered counseling. In G. M. Gazda (Ed.), *Basic approaches to group psychotherapy and group counseling*. Springfield, Ill.: C. C. Thomas, 1968.

13. Mainard, W. A., et al. Confrontation vs. diversion in group therapy with chronic schizophrenics as measured by a "positive incident" criterion. *J. clin. Psychol.*, 1956, 21, 222–225.

14. Ruesch, J. *Therapeutic communication.* New York: Norton, 1961.

15. Satir, V. *Conjoint family therapy.* Palo Alto, Calif.: Science & Behavior Books, 1967.

16. Shulman, B. H. The use of dramatic confrontation in group psychotherapy. *Psychiat. Quart.*, 1962, 36 (Suppl. Part I).

17. Wolberg, L. R. *The technique of psychotherapy.* 2nd ed. New York: Grune & Stratton, 1967.

CONFRONTATION TECHNIQUES

Bernard H. Shulman

Chairman, department of psychiatry, St. Joseph Hospital, Chicago, and medical director of its community mental health program. He is also assistant professor of psychiatry, Northwestern University Medical School, training consultant, VA Hospital, Downey, Illinois, and an instructor at the Alfred Adler Institute, Chicago. He is currently president of the International Association of Individual Psychology. He is author of *Essays in Schizophrenia*, book chapters and journal articles.

One of the people who has done much work with confrontation techniques, possibly the most, is Dr. Garner, who is right here in the audience. It was he who started me thinking in terms of confrontation techniques, to try to figure out what he was doing (4). And I asked myself, "Just what is it that Adlerians do that can be considered confrontation techniques, and when and why do we use them?"

Dr. Dreikurs has given us examples of some confrontation techniques, and Dr. Kurt Adler and Dr. Helene Papanek earlier this morning mentioned certain kinds of confrontation. I should like to take up very briefly the whole issue of confrontation.

The first person to have written about confrontation seems to be a psychoanalyst named Devereux (1) who defined confrontation as a device which directs the patient's attention to the bare factual content of his actions and of his statements, or shows him a coincidence which he professes not to have perceived or is not aware of. The purpose of confrontation is to force the patient to

---

The paper as read, while largely based on an earlier one (6), does contain some new aspects and different examples. The present version omits the earlier material as much as possible and attempts to bring out the latter, so that it may be considered a supplement to the earlier publication.

Journal of Individual Psychology, 28(2), November, 1972, **pp. 177–183**

pay attention to something he has just said or done. In other words it has a here-and-now quality.

The difference between confrontation and interpretation is that the confrontation forces the patient to pay attention to, and to respond to something right here and now. Dr. Garner especially uses confrontation to focus on what goes on during the interview. It is a direct approach to a problem or an issue, a way of getting to the heart of something right away. To the extent that an interpretation accomplishes this by itself or by an additional response-demanding statement or question, it becomes a confrontation. Otherwise the interpretation may leave the patient just listening, in the mood of "thinking it over," or silently rejecting the proposition—without being forced to take a frank stand now.

An example of an interpretation might be, "Alright, so you thought your mother wouldn't love you if you hated your little brother." This is an explanatory, clarifying statement that can be made to a patient in a certain therapeutic situation. An Adlerian might turn this into a confrontation by adding the question, "How much longer do you intend to feel that way? How much longer are you going to believe that your mother will stop loving you if you hate your little brother?"

Especially therapists who are action-oriented and group-oriented will tend to use confrontation techniques. Among these especially role playing is designed to create a here-and-now situation to which the patient must respond on the spot.

A number of confrontation techniques have been used particularly in Adlerian psychotherapy. While the Adlerian therapist is not necessarily directive, his aim is to help the client recognize the mistaken goals which Dr. Dreikurs was talking about, and the associated beliefs, moods, and actions. We do not use the concept of "working through" a conflict, nor the concept of an "inner conflict" as being responsible for the problem. Instead, we are trying to help the patient see what his mistaken way of dealing with the world, of living with the world, is at any given moment. And since we like to use mirror techniques—showing the patient what he is doing, right on the spot—these often become confrontations.

What exactly does the therapist confront the patient with? Without claiming to be exhaustive, I shall briefly describe eleven categories: moods and feelings, hidden reasons, biased apperception and private logic, private goals, mottos, responsibility for the responses of others, self-defeating behavior, existing alternatives, responsibility for change, and time factor. These categories are not necessarily mutually exclusive.

MOOD STATES, FEELINGS

We confront the patient with his subjective mood states, with his feelings, as these appear to us. For example, I might say, "From the way you wear your hair, not one hair out of place, I can see that you are afraid of falling apart." Or, "From the look on your face, I can see that you don't believe a word I am saying." Or, "From the way you talk about your husband, you must be very angry at him." These are statements that deal with something that the patient is demonstrating at the moment.

HIDDEN REASONS

Another matter with which we confront the patient is what Dr. Dreikurs calls the "hidden reason" (2, p. 108) for the patient's behavior, his private justification, his private rationalization, or the reason he gives to himself—in distinction from the reason or rationalization he gives publicly to others and often to himself. Usually he is somewhat aware of his hidden reason, but he has not brought it to the front of his awareness, has not looked at it, or examined it. We bring it to his awareness by asking, "What did you say to yourself when you did this?"

For example, a man insists on staying at home while his wife would have wanted him to go out with her that evening. He may tell her, "Well, I'm too tired," his public reason, while he may have said to himself, "She doesn't really deserve that I should take her out," the hidden reason.

BIASED APPERCEPTION AND PRIVATE LOGIC

The third matter with which we confront the patient is his biased apperception, from which follow his ways of thinking about the world (private logic) and of dealing with it. For example, you may ask the patient, "If you put on dark glasses, how do you expect the world to look?" Or, "If you have already decided that you have no chance in life, how do you expect to make it any better?" Or, "If you already felt that you can't be helped, then why are you here anyway? Just to prove that you are right and that you can't be helped?"

PRIVATE GOALS

Another kind of confrontation is regarding the patient's private goal. This was the case in Dr. Dreikurs' interview with Mike and his parents. Dr. D.: "Why do you do this?" Mike: "I don't know." Dr. D.: "Shall I tell you? Could it be?" So, the Adlerian asks questions like, "Do you know why you did that?" Or, "If you don't know, do you want me to tell you why I think you did it?" And then it is a "Could it be?" or a "Didn't you?" kind of statement. "Didn't you feel a little bit powerful when you were able to get your mother all upset like that? Didn't you enjoy it a little bit when all these people were making a fuss over you?"

One of the early recollections that Dr. Papanek described was about the patient who was sick and whose father showed a tremendous concern over her. The confronting question would be, "Didn't you feel glad that you were able to get your father this concerned with you?"

MOTTOS

Sometimes, instead of confronting the patient with a goal or reason, we say, he acts as if according to a certain motto, and then confront him with this motto. For example, "I must never let anyone catch me making a mistake. I must always be right." Or, "Above all, if anybody gets ahead of me, I must get even." Sometimes we'll stress this by giving the patient a sort of certificate. You can write it out for him and say, "Here, you can take this and frame it and hang it on your wall, next to your bathroom mirror, and you can look at it every morning to remind yourself, because this is the motto by which you are trying to live."

IMMEDIATE BEHAVIOR

Sometimes we confront the patient with his immediate behavior in the therapy session. This is the "What did you just do?" question. "When I asked you about your parents. you stopped talking. How come?" Or, "You just made a slip of the tongue, did you catch it? I wonder what it means?" Or, "How do you feel right now when I'm talking to you?" Or, "A look just passed over your face, what just went through your mind?" Or, "I notice you keep swinging your leg when you talk. What does it mean?" Or, "Your face just turned red, what's up?" That is, you are asking the patient to deal with his immediate behavior in the situation. You are asking him first of all to look at it. This is part of the mirror technique, holding his behavior up for him to see what he is doing.

RESPONSIBILITY FOR RESPONSES OF OTHERS

Another point with which we confront the patient at times is his own responsibility for the responses of others to him. When a patient asks, "Why do people walk over me? I'm only trying to be a good guy," the therapist answers, "Because you want them to walk over you. After all, it is a lot easier to be a good guy if you let other people walk over you than if you don't let them walk over you. You are the one who is causing it."

SELF-DEFEATING BEHAVIOR

Especially useful are confronting statements which call attention to repeated patterns of self-defeating behavior. "Look how you are bringing on the symptom." We show the depressed patient how he depresses himself every day. You can sometimes teach the patient this. The following sequence with a depressed patient who was telling how badly she felt and how all of her thoughts were unpleasant, will illustrate this.

> **Dr. S.:** *What do you like to do most of all? If you felt completely well, what would you like to be doing?*
> **Patient:** *I would like to be in Florida bone fishing.*
> **Dr. S.:** *Well, tell me about bone fishing.*
> **Patient:** *(Telling me for about two minutes about bone fishing.)*
> **Dr. S.:** *Now how do you feel?*
> **Patient:** *I feel better.*
> **Dr. S.:** *Why do you think you feel better?*
> **Patient:** *Well, I was talking about something I liked.*
> **Dr. S.:** *All right, now tell me about your depression.*
> **Patient:** *(Spends about two minutes talking about her depression.)*
> **Dr. S.:** *How do you feel now?*
> **Patient:** *Now I feel bad.*
> **Dr. S.:** *Why do you think that a few minutes ago you felt good and now you feel bad?*

Patient: *Well, it was what I was talking about.*
Dr. S.: *Do you think that you can make yourself feel better or make yourself feel worse by what you talk about?*
Patient: *Well, maybe I can.*
Dr. S.: *Well, all right, then all you have to do is spend the day talking to yourself about bone fishing and you will feel better.*

Now one does not expect the patient to give up her depression immediately so easily. After all people work pretty hard to get depressed. The purpose is to show the patient that he has some immediate control over the way he feels by what he chooses to think about. This particular technique is very close to what is described by Ellis and Harper (3, pp. 14–18) under "Feeling well by thinking straight."

One may also say to the depressed patient, "Well, you have just berated yourself again. Keep it up and in five minutes you will really be depressed. Is that what you want? Or, do you think that you could stop berating yourself?" Or, "You just spent two-thirds of your session complaining about your mother. What do you want, to spend the rest of the session tattling on your mother, or do you want psychotherapy? Do you want to help yourself, or do you just want to complain about what a victim you are? Unless you start talking to me about yourself, I can't help you." Do you see what a strong confrontation that is, asking the patient to do something immediately?

EXISTING ALTERNATIVES

Confrontation is also a dramatic way of presenting alternatives: This is certainly seen clearly in role playing where you give the patient an alternative role to play. But you can confront him with an alternative merely by saying, "You're going to take an examination. You are worried about the examination. Now you have a choice. You can study and try to pass the exam or you can goof off and pretend that you don't care. Which will it be? You make the choice." Or, "You don't have to spend your life complaining about how little money your husband makes, you can get a job and help out. What do you want to do about it?" One of the things you are in this way telling the patient is, "Look at the choice you are making."

RESPONSIBILITY FOR CHANGE

We also try to confront the patient with the fact that he has the responsibility for changing. And we will say, "Do you want to change or do you want to just sit and talk about it for a while?" The patient often says, "What should I do?" One of the statements that Adler used to make with irony in it was "Above all, don't do anything yet. After all you've been this way for many years, another few months won't hurt" (7, p. 101). The object is again, to help the patient see as clearly as possible that the responsibility for change is his.

TIME FACTOR

Now since, when we get to the question of choices, you've heard that Adlerians are future oriented and use interpretations that deal with the here and now, the Adlerian therapist often asks questions like, "Okay, do you see what is going on? You now have the insight, what are you going to do about it?" And the patient will say something like, "Well I have to do such and such." The next confronting question is, "How long do you plan to wait before you do it? Ten years?" This is a nonsense statement calculated to provoke the patient into recognizing that nothing will change until he takes the first step to change.

THREE MAIN ISSUES

The confrontation techniques that Adlerians use are then intended to create an atmosphere of an immediate challenge. They are examples of direct focusing. It is a way of stirring things up, but doing so in connection with an important therapeutic issue. There are three such main issues according to which the confrontation techniques can be divided.

First is the issue of insight—confronting the patient in order to help him become aware of something. The first six categories would belong here.

Second is the issue of helping the patient to recognize where he is running away from his responsibilities. Adlerians talk about the life tasks, but we could also use Heidegger's concept of being or *Dasein* (5, p. 136). For Heidegger the task of living is to give a meaning to life. The Adlerian therapist recognizes that the patient gives his own private meaning to his life, which is a mistaken meaning, and that he is going after the wrong things. Why wrong? Because they violate "common sense" and have accordingly gotten him into trouble. Adler, as a clinician, from the start was concerned with a meaning that one can give to life which is not neurotic, not psychotic, nor a predatory or criminal meaning, but a meaning which is ethical, moral, and respectful of humanness. Thus Adlerians to this day end up with *social interest* as being the mentally healthiest meaning that one can give to life. It is the meaning that permits the most satisfying fulfillment of life. The seventh to tenth confrontation categories would belong here.

The third issue for the Adlerian therapist is that the patient recognize where the power to change lies and that the moment of change is decided by the patient. And thus the confrontation he uses, the eleventh category, is the one that was used by the ancient Rabbi Hillel who said, "If you are not going to do it now, then when?"

REFERENCES

1. Devereux, G. Some criteria for the timing of confrontations and interpretations. *Int. J. Psychoanal.*, 1951, 32, 19–24.

2. Dreikurs, R. *Understanding your children.* Chicago: Alfred Adler Institute, 1969.

3. Ellis, A., & Harper, R. A. *A guide to rational living*. 2nd ed. North Hollywood Calif.: Wilshire Book Co., 1970.

4. Garner, H. H. The confrontation problem-solving technique: developing a psychotherapeutic focus. *Amer. J. Psychother.*, 1970, 24, 27–48.

5. Reinhardt, K. F. *The existential revolt.* New York: Frederick Ungar, 1960.

6. Shulman, B. H. Confrontation techniques in Adlerian psychology. *J. Indiv. Psychol.*, 1971, 27, 167–175.

7. Wexberg, E. *Individual Psychological treatment.* 2nd ed. Chicago: Alfred Adler Institute, 1970.

Part C
USE OF STORIES, FABLES, APHORISMS

THE USE OF PARABLES AND FABLES IN ADLERIAN PSYCHOTHERAPY

Kristin R. Pancner
A psychiatric nurse in a group private practice in Fort Wayne, Indiana. She is on the faculty of the Alfred Adler Institute, Fort Wayne, Indiana.

The purpose of this paper is to record some parables and fables and discuss their implication and application to various problems encountered in psychotherapy. The use of a parable to illustrate one concept does not necessarily exempt or limit it from being used to illustrate other concepts the psychotherapist may wish to convey to the patient. The therapist will also observe that patients may interpret and retain parts of the story according to their bias and lifestyle goals, over and above the point intended by the therapist.

A parable is a simple story that sets the familiar in an unfamiliar context, where the meaning is found only within the story itself (Morris, 1969). Because the stories are always about people in relationship to their world, they help to keep our beliefs and philosophies more "down to earth" and, therefore, are easier to understand and apply in everyday life. Our philosophy and theology can become more believable, less abstract, and more applicable to the here and now (Heffner, 1974).

The parable, unlike the fable, does not directly teach a lesson. A fable must have a moral teaching, either explicit or implicit (Noel, 1975). As the secure, familiar everydayness of a parable unfolds, it suddenly catches the listener offbalance; and the "mundaneness" is transformed into a different logic. The listener,

The Individual Psychologist, 15(4), December, 1978, **pp. 19–29**

then, may glimpse the possibility and begin to understand that there might be another way of believing, living, and thinking.

With the use of the parable and fable in psychotherapy, no new world is created. Rather, the old way of looking at things is transformed, the old information is changed and challenged by new insight, and one's individual ways of viewing life may be broadened. Parables do not have a message; they are a message! Fables give a message that the individual can apply to his or her situation.

In psychotherapy, patients find it easier to grasp concepts, rules for living, and new ways of looking at life through the medium of stories. Stories are easier to remember and less threatening than direct confrontation and can be shelved and later reexamined as the patients deal with all aspects of their therapy.

A feeling and sense of equality can be established as the therapist shares a story with the patient. In exploring a truth or concept together, the therapist can be partially removed from the "authority-with-all-the-answers" role; and mutual respect and rapport can be developed.

Humor is a vital ingredient of successful psychotherapy. It is important to "lighten" patients' self-imposed burdens. Parables and fables allow the touch of humor, transforming what appears to be a tremendous burden into something less weighty. Humor also redirects patients' focus off themselves and toward the characters in the story. In seeing the characters' situations as humorous, having a way out, or having a variety of solutions, patients may be able to relax and view their "burdens" with some humor and lightness. As some of the intensity decreases, it may be easier to problem-solve and gain objectivity.

Parables and fables offer therapists an opportunity to present insightful interpretations and a way of viewing things on a "silver platter" (Mosak & Shulman, 1974). They are an indirect way to present a message or psychological point in more acceptable, less accusatory form, thus reducing patients' tendencies to be defensive.

The use of stories to illustrate a point or capsulize a concept is not new to modern psychotherapy. Much of the teaching of Jesus is set forth in parable form, and his rules for living a happy, successful life are delineated throughout the Scriptures (Smith, 1948). His parables dealt with the familiar, and the characters and scenes were taken from ordinary life experience. Similarly, as in modern psychotherapy, some of his parables were understood; some had several meanings; and some were not understood because the listener was not ready to hear. The fact that the stories were handed down by the spoken word, later recorded, and continue to have tremendous impact on modern man and society illustrates their value as teaching devices.

The Stubborn Mule

> There is an old parable about a man who wanted to move his very obdurate, defiant mule. The more he pulled and tugged, the deeper the hooves of the mule dug into the dirt road. A traveler came ambling along this road, saw the old man's predicament, and offered to help. He picked up a huge log and clobbered the stubborn mule between the eyes. The old man became very angry with the traveler and demanded to know the reason for such action. Replied the traveler, "Before I can get him to move, I have to get his attention!"

Before patients decide to "move" in therapy, therapists have to get their attention. A parable or fable can do just that. In seeing others on their life journeys, patients can begin to identify and believe in themselves and glimpse another way of looking at things.

SOCIAL ISOLATION

One of our basic goals, according to Individual Psychology, is our need for people and the development of our place and sense of belonging (Adler, 1967). One of the common reasons that prompts a person to seek psychotherapy is an inability to get along and cooperate with people. Various coping devices are used to solve these conflicts: from complete withdrawal and noninvolvement to aggressively being on the alert and defensive. It becomes the task of the therapist to encourage and guide the patient into reforming and establishing meaningful, cooperative relationships.

The following parable illustrates how all humans engage in social behavior, even those who are isolates, and shows all behavior as having social implications. It can be used in individual as well as in group therapy to demonstrate our need for people.

The Hermit

> Once long ago there lived outside a village in a cave an old man, the Hermit. One day the village and its inhabitants were totally destroyed by an erupting volcano. Sadly, the

> Hermit tied his belongings on his back and set out to find another cave outside another village.

As in the hermit story, one cannot even be a hermit without people!

EXCESSIVE PLEASING

While some people avoid contact with other people or deny their need for them, others train themselves early in life to depend too heavily on other people and their actions. The latter are the "people pleasers" who spend their energy and "spin their wheels" trying to please all of the people all of the time. While it is important to learn cooperation and develop social interest, the "people pleaser" has an overdriven need to keep anger and conflict at a minimum. In concentrating to such an extent on other people's needs, feelings, and opinions, pleasers sooner or later end up denying and not knowing, or not experiencing, their own identity, values, self-worth, and opinions (Dreikurs, 1967, p. 113). In trying to constantly please, they end up not pleasing all the people all the time and destroy something of value within themselves.

Carolyn, age 18, a "people pleaser," was brought into therapy by her mother. She complained of depression, suicidal thoughts, and academic difficulty. As the sessions progressed, it was apparent that she was trying to please all those around her. This resulted in her following of some peer group activities which she later had difficulty accepting. She felt unable to confront her friends or break away from their influence. The following fable was told to her to illustrate how her desire to please and follow others' ideas and suggestions could easily result in the denial of her own values and ideals. It helped her reevaluate and reassess her goals and direction.

The Miller, His Son, and Their Ass

> A father, his son, and a donkey were walking along a road enroute to the fair. Some people came by and said: "Look at those fools, walking when they could be riding." The old man asked his son to ride the donkey.
>
> Some others passed by and said: "Look at that young man riding while his old father is walking. Isn't that terrible?" The father asked his son to get off, and he rode now.
>
> Later, some more people came by and said: "Isn't that awful! The man rides and has his little boy walk. How selfish!" The father then asked his son to get on the donkey, and the two of them rode.

> Then, they passed some more people, and this group said: "Two people riding a little donkey! They should be carrying him instead." The father and the son got off, tied the donkey's legs together, put a stick between them, lifted the donkey off the ground, and began to carry him. As they crossed the bridge, the donkey got scared, struggled, fell off the bridge, and drowned.
>
> *Moral*: You can't please everyone, so don't try; or; if you try to please everyone, you'll lose your ass!

DISCOURAGEMENT IN A DIFFICULT LIFE SITUATION

The presenting symptoms and problems of patients may seem so burdensome and terrifying that pessimism and discouragement become intense and overwhelming. It is important for patients to see at least a little humor or worth in their wretched situations, in order to realize that any experience is not entirely good or entirely bad. Out of their mistaken ideas and faulty decisions about life can come some positive, growth-producing changes. As the positive aspects are embraced and realized, the problem may not seem as weighty or detrimental.

Adlerians believe that we all have a choice and control over our feelings and emotions; we manufacture them for a purpose and to get a job done (Dreikurs, 1967). We have the option and freedom to choose between optimism or pessimism.

One of the most important ingredients of successful psychotherapy is the therapist's ability to encourage (Dinkmeyer & Dreikurs, 1963) and help each patient see some positive aspects of his or her problem.

To help a patient facing a crisis situation such as a loss of job, the following story can be told. It can be helpful in illustrating that what looks bad may turn out well. Initially, the unemployment may be seen as devastating, totally unfair, and humiliating, but later the experience can be used as an opportunity to develop and grow in other areas.

> Did you hear that Rosie's getting married?
> That's good.
> He's an old man.
> That's bad.
> He's very rich.
> That's good.
> But, he's very stingy.

That's bad.
But, he's very sick.
That's good.
But, he's been sick for years and years.
That's bad.
But, the doctors say he can't last long.
That's good.
He's left his money to charity.
That's bad.
But, he may change his will.
That's good.
But, his lawyer advises against it.
That's bad.
But, the old man pays no attention to anyone.
That's good.
Moral: Who knows what's good or bad?

THE TYRANNY OF THE SHOULDS

One of the tasks confronted by patients in psychotherapy is discovering their unique patterns and methods of striving from a perceived minus to a felt plus. Many times patients have modeled and patterned their lives on imitation and acceptance of other people's—especially their parents'—goals, values, and ambitions. In modeling themselves after and accepting the values of their parents or other models, patients may enter therapy confused about what they "ought to believe" and what their inner selves are directing them to believe. Patients may find themselves battling the "tyranny of the shoulds" (Horney, 1950), confused about what they feel others expect from them, and what their inner selves are trying to reveal. Patients enter psychotherapy to uncover and define their own uniqueness. Through the therapeutic use of interpreting each person's lifestyle, patients' patterns and ways of operating are illuminated and explored. They can then decide what to do with the self-imposed "shoulds," and how these "shoulds" are beneficial or destructive to their own uniqueness.

Mr. W., a 32-year-old, perpetual college student, was seen in therapy after several psychotic episodes. In exploring his lifestyle, it was discovered that he had embraced the parental values of education and achievement, pursuing a professional life and status without conscious questioning. He was rebelling, however, by continually changing majors, being placed on academic probation, and having psychotic episodes. Through the confrontation by members of his therapy group, it was pointed out how his movement or actions seemed to be suggesting negative, backward movement in pursuing a professional life. The following story was told to aid him in facing his ambivalence and imitation of others' values.

The Rabbi's Son

> When Rabbi Noah, Rabbi Mordecai's son, took his father's place as Zaddik, his followers soon saw he behaved differently from his father. They were troubled and came to ask him about this. "But, I do just as my father did," he replied. "He did not imitate, and I do not imitate." (Kopp, 1971)

This parable can also be used when a patient, who "window shops" for a therapist, makes the rounds of many therapists. He or she compares and contrasts their differing approaches and treatment plans and may, in fact, have read extensively in the field of psychology and psychiatry, quoting others in an attempt to discredit and defeat the current therapist. The therapist, in a humorous, friendly manner, can point out that he or she plans to follow his or her own style and not imitate others.

SELF-DEFEATING BEHAVIOR

One of the goals in Adlerian psychotherapy is to encourage patients to modify or change their *modus operandi*, or way of operating, if it is causing difficulty in their life or not producing the desired results.

The fable of "The Sun and the Wind" can be used in the therapeutic situation with patients who always exude hostility and anger in an attempt to get their own way. This fable can show that there are other options, producing desirable results, rather than responding with anger. The following fable illustrates that anger does not always accomplish the hoped-for results; while a lighter, warmer method may.

The Sun and the Wind

> The sun and the wind began to argue about who was the stronger. They looked below and saw a man walking along a road with a cloak wrapped around him.
>
> "Let's see who is stronger and can make the man's cloak come off!" the wind challenged.
>
> "Okay," the sun replied. "You first."
>
> The wind began to blow up a storm and blew until his cheeks cracked; but the more he blew, the more tightly the man wrapped his cloak around him. Finally, the wind gave up.
>
> It was now the sun's turn. He began to shine brightly. The weather got warm, and soon it became hot. The man loosened his cloak; and, after a while, took it off.
>
> *Moral*: Sometimes warmth succeeds when anger does not.

THE PATIENT WHO LOOKS FOR THE MAGIC ANSWER FROM THE WISE MAN

Many people approach psychotherapy with the attitude and expectations of the man seeking out the Llama. They come to the therapist wanting answers and solutions to their problems. Their own pessimism and discouragement leads them to believe some "wise seer" will magically sooth the wounds and provide the answers.

One of the cornerstones of Adlerian psychology is the belief in social equality and democracy (Dreikurs, 1971). Adler wrote about mutual respect and felt that our striving for superiority caused many problems in our relationships and interactions with other people. He approached his patients as "students," using the growth model rather than the medical model. In encouraging his students to learn and grow, he was leading them away from the inferior position that the seer (or the "Herr Doktor") had all the right answers and would magically cut out or cure the evil disease within.

If people approach therapy searching for answers, they enter treatment assuming that the therapist has all the right answers to problems and holds the magical key to life. When asked what issue or areas they want to discuss, they reply, "You decide what I should talk about."

The therapist's role is to introduce patients to new ways of problem-solving, looking at life, and confronting some of the lifestyle misapperceptions, but the therapist can't provide answers.

The following parable can be used to extricate the therapist from assuming the patient's responsibility of finding his or her own meaning to life.

The Search for the Llama

> A man was unhappy because he was searching for the meaning of life and could not find it. He went from one wise man to another but was never satisfied. He finally heard about a Llama who lived in the mountains of Tibet, and he undertook an expedition. For many months he traveled over mountains, across rivers, until finally he found the Llama and obtained an audience. He asked the wise man, "Please, tell me. What is the meaning of life?"
>
> The Llama answered, "Life is a fountain."
>
> The man was puzzled and said, "Life is a fountain?"
>
> The Llama shrugged his shoulders and said, "So, life isn't a fountain."

SELFISHNESS

Many people entering therapy are so wrapped up and enmeshed in their own problems that their world focuses almost entirely on themselves. They fail to consider others and refuse to become aware of the needs and situations of those around them. Their thoughts and actions do not focus on what they can do to help others; they see people in terms of what those people can give and do for them. Their minimal social interest and involvement with others increases their feelings of inferiority, loneliness, and isolation.

The following parable can be used in therapy to demonstrate that inferiority feelings are inversely proportional to social interest. (Dreikurs, 1953, p. 20). As patients' consideration and awareness of others' needs and situations develops, as they extend themselves to those around them, their feelings of loneliness will decrease and their connectiveness with the world will become positive.

The Two Brothers

Outside of Jerusalem on a small plot of land tilled two brothers. Their living was difficult because the soil was rocky. However, they farmed and were able to seek out a living. Whatever they grew, they shared equally. One night one of the brothers could not sleep, and he tossed and turned. It came to him that the arrangement with his brother was unjust. His brother had several children and a wife; yet, he received only one-half the crop. He thought, "My brother has all those mouths to fill, and he should have more than one-half. Tomorrow I will offer him two-thirds; this certainly would be more equitable."

That very same night, his brother tossed and turned, could not sleep, and he thought, "My brother receives one-half of what we earn. He has no children and family; in his old age he will have no one to look after him. Therefore, he deserves and needs more than one-half of what we earn. Tomorrow I will meet him and offer him two-thirds of what we grow."

The next day, they awoke and met on the Mount of Moriah and shared with the other their plans. A voice was heard saying, "This, indeed, is brotherly love!"

DISAPPOINTMENT IN LOVE

Many people come to a therapist following a broken relationship. Feeling devastated by the loss, they lack objectivity in evaluating and working through the crisis. They may feel that life has lost its meaning, having convinced themselves that this particular lover is the only one in the world. They may consider drastic responses such as an act of revenge or a suicidal gesture. The therapist can help these people explore other options and solutions.

There is a humorous fable which points out that one can live life, missing a piece of tail, but to lose one's head is fatal! What a person may consider important and vital in his or her life, may be relatively unimportant in the long run.

The Fox and the Train

A fox was out on a cold winter day foraging for food. Because he was so chilly, so hungry, and so preoccupied with his hunting, he forgot to look either way as he crossed the railroad tracks. A train bore down on him as he went across one set of tracks and amputated his tail. The fox jumped, turned around to look at what happened, and another train whizzed by and took off his head.

Moral: Don't lose your head over a piece of tail!

The Robin

There is a delightful story told about a robin living in New York who was having such a good time he failed to make preparations to fly south for the winter. As the leaves fell and the winds of bitter cold began to blow, he took to the air and began a frantic flight towards a warmer climate. As he was flying over a barnyard, frost formed on his wings, and he fell to the ground. He knew he was going to die and chided himself for not leaving with the rest of the flock. A horse passed over him and dropped some manure. The warmth revived his cold, frozen body, and some wheat seeds in the manure provided a nice lunch. He was so delighted and happy with this good fortune that he burst forth into joyful song. A cat heard the chirping, came to investigate, and began to remove the blanket of manure. When he discovered the little bird, he gobbled him up!

Several morals emerge from this story: (1) not everyone who drops manure on you is your enemy; (2) not everyone who cleans the manure off you is your friend; and (3) if you are up to your ears in manure, it may be better to keep your mouth shut.

The story can be used to point out that all events must be understood in their broader context. Hasty conclusions are often mistaken and impetuous actions make things worse.

SUMMARY

The concepts of equality, encouragement, and the use of more effective *modi operandi* can be taught in the therapeutic encounter by use of non-threatening stories. Through the techniques of humor and story-telling, patients can understand their relationships with others and their movement toward their dominant goal.

The therapist must be aware of patients' movement and not push them beyond their own pace. Humorous anecdotes are easily filed away until patients are ready to confront their situation and apply the insight to themselves. Like the parable of the Llama, no one can really provide an answer to life and one's problems. We must seek and discover our own solutions within ourselves. Parables and fables can, however, provide a source for helping a person find his or her own meaning to life.

REFERENCES

Adler, A. *The individual psychology of Alfred Adler: A systematic presentation in selections from his writings*. (H. L. Ansbacher & R. R. Ansbacher, Eds.). New York: Harper & Row, Publishers, 1967.

Adler, A. *Social interest: A challenge to mankind*. New York: Capricorn Books, 1964.

Bewick T. *The fables of Aesop and others*. New York: Paddington Press, Ltd., 1975.

Dinkmeyer, D. C. & Dreikurs, R. R. *Encouraging children to learn: The encouragement process*. Englewood Cliffs, New Jersey: Prentice-Hall, Inc., 1963.

Dreikurs, R. R. *Fundamentals of Adlerian psychology*. Chicago: Alfred Adler Institute, 1953.

Dreikurs, R. R. *Psychodynamics, psychotherapy, and counseling*. Chicago: Alfred Adler Institute, 1967.

Dreikurs, R. R. *Social equality: The challenge of today*. Regnery, 1971.

Heffner, C. F. *Parables for the present*. New York: Hawthorn Books, Inc., 1974.

Horney, K. *Neurosis and human growth*. New York: Norton, 1950.

Kopp, B. *Guru, metaphors from a psychotherapist*. Palo Alto, California: Science and Behavior Books, 1971.

Morris, W. (Ed.). *American heritage dictionary of the English Language*. New York: American Heritage Publishing Co., Inc., 1969.

Mosak, H. H., & Shulman, B. H. *Individual psychotherapy: A syllabus*. Chicago: Alfred Adler Institute, 1974.

Noel, T. *Theories of the fable in the eighteenth century*. New York: Columbia University Press, 1975.

Smith, C. *The Jesus of the parables*. Philadelphia: The Westminster Press, 1948.

TeSelle, S. M. *Speaking in parables: A study in metaphor and theology*. Philadelphia: Fortress Press, 1975.

RELIGIOUS ALLUSIONS IN PSYCHOTHERAPY

Harold H. Mosak
A clinical psychologist in private practice. He has taught at the Alfred Adler Institute of Chicago for over thirty years and is currently chairman of the board. He is also a past president of the North American Society of Adlerian Psychology.

When I was a graduate student 40 years ago, we were advised that if a client raised a "religious" question, we were not to address it but refer the client to the clergy instead. Since clients commonly brought such problems to the latter, it did not create too many problems for the therapist. However, since the clergy at that time were largely psychologically untrained, it is questionable whether the clients received the help they sought. Over the years, both clergy and those in the secular helping professions have had to meet these problems in increasing numbers (Mosak & Dreikurs, 1967). For me, the first break in the dam came with reading an article by Savitz (1955) in which a psychiatrist discussed various interventions with religious patients.

In a recent paper (Mosak, 1987a) I have treated the issues of guilt and repentance, illustrating with some approaches for dealing with these issues. In this paper I will suggest some other approaches I have developed over the years in dealing with both religious patients and religious issues. The reader is cautioned not to use these as "gimmicks"—"Use No. 5 and the client will lose his or her depression"—but as means that will help get past sticking points in the therapy. Many of these contain Biblical allusions; some come from other sources.

Individual Psychology, 43(4), December, 1987, **pp. 496–501**

LOT'S WIFE

Many patients, among them are the guilt-ridden, the "hopeless," and those who have been in past-oriented psychotherapies, dwell in therapy upon the past. Life has behaved badly or they have behaved wickedly or they still, perhaps even without being aware of it, adhere to Freud's traumatic theory of hysteria. Naturally, therapy does not move forward nor do the patients because they are not looking through the windshield; they are riveted to the rear-view mirror. Therapy becomes a forum for complaint, blaming, and castigation of self or others. This view confirms for the patient that he or she need not, and for that matter cannot, move ahead because "Thus it ever was and thus it ever shall be." The patient expresses hopelessness and, of course, is not aware of arranging his or her neurosis.

> **Therapist:** *It seems that you spend a lot of time dwelling on your sinful past.*
> **Patient:** *Well, it's all true. That's the way my life has been.*
> **Therapist:** *I won't contest the validity of what you say, but have you considered what your life will be if you continue to do so?*
> **Patient:** *No. . . .*
> **Therapist:** *Do you remember Lot's wife in the Bible? She also looked over her shoulder at the wicked past, and she turned into a pillar of salt—totally dehumanized, totally immobilized. And I wouldn't want that to happen to you. Perhaps we could look at what's ahead of you rather than what's behind you.*

"JESUS WEPT" (JOHN 11:35)

One encounters in therapy certain patients, especially men, who arrive at a point where their eyes cloud over, and it appears that they are about to cry. Seeing that the therapist has noticed, they inform the therapist, "Don't worry, I'm not going to cry (or let myself cry)."

> **Therapist:** *Why not?*
> **Patient:** *Because it's unmanly. Real men don't cry. Only weak people—no one would respect their masculinity—cry. It's an acknowledgment that they can't cope.*
> **Therapist:** *Do you know what is the shortest sentence in the New Testament?*
> **Patient:** *No . . .*
> **Therapist:** *"Jesus wept." Isn't it too bad that He was a weak person, one who couldn't cope?*

RABBI TARFON'S ADMONITION

I have previously alluded to Rabbi Tarfon in another context (Mosak, 1971). His admonition is useful with those patients who agree that they should get started on something "but it'll take forever. I may not live that long, so why get started?" Rabbi Tarfon (Ethics of the Fathers, 1984) may be quoted, "You do not have to complete the work but neither are you free to avoid it" (pp. 22–23). Many patients will take the statement to heart. Some will discuss it or argue it with the therapist. Those most susceptible to prestige suggestion will certainly grant it great consideration.

THE MOUNT OF TEMPTATION

Self-castigation when one considers responding to temptation and fighting with oneself to resist the temptation make for a fight between the "good me" and the "bad me" (Mosak, 1973; Mosak, 1987a). While there are many methods for helping resolve this conflict (Mosak & LeFevre, 1976), one I have described in another context (Mosak, 1987a) is especially effective. The described patient was a Catholic priest, behaviorally a saint, who during the session lowered his eyes to the ground and used the therapist as his confessor.

> **Patient:** *As you can see, all of my life I've been fighting my urges, fighting temptation, wrestling with the Devil.*
> **Therapist:** *Don't knock it! If wrestling with the Devil for 40 days and 40 nights was enough for Jesus, I suspect it ought to be good enough for you.*
> **Patient:** *(Laughing heartily.) I guess I never looked at it that way.*

The reframing, the converting of a minus to a plus, helped this patient develop a different perspective and halted the self-doubt.

RABBI ELIJAH, THE GAON OF VILNA

When patients ask certain questions like "What if I do it and at the end there's nothing there?" (Lenzberg, 1937; Mosak, 1987b) or "Why should I put in the effort if I don't know the outcome?," I may tell the following story:

> About 300 years ago there lived a rabbi who spent most of his waking hours studying Scripture. Apparently he was a frail man, and one night, legend has it, an angel appeared in Rabbi Elijah's dream

> to inform him that the Lord was impressed with his scholarship. "He doesn't want you to jeopardize your health, so as a reward for your good deeds, he is willing to reveal all the mysteries of the Bible to you."
>
> Rabbi Elijah responded, "Go back to your Master and tell him, 'Thanks, but no thanks.' Tell him that the fun is in the search."

The story is equally appropriate for those looking for the meaning of life.

HILLEL'S STATEMENTS

Many patients engage in the struggle between selfishness and selflessness and are fearful that if they look out for themselves at all, they will be selfish. These behaviors are treated as if they were extremes with nothing in between. Hillel corrected these notions with two statements:

> If I am not for myself, who will be? But if I am only for myself, what really am I? (Ethics of the Fathers, 1984, pp. 12–13)

The above statements are followed by a third that may be used in a confrontational manner. Some patients will express good intentions. Adlerians, not being impressed with good intentions, may respond to the patient's, "You're right. I'm going to have to get to that" with Hillel's statement, "And if not now, when?" (Ethics of the Fathers, 1984, pp. 12–13).

COMMITMENT

The issue of commitment often arises in therapy. Since Adlerians see neurosis as a "copout" from the tasks of life, it perhaps arises even more often in Adlerian therapy than in some others. Many patients attempt to intellectualize the idea of commitment. One may cut through it by pointing out the meaning by illustration. "And the Lord called unto Abraham, 'Abraham, Abraham' and Abraham answered, 'Here I am!'" (Genesis 22:1). "And the Lord called unto Jacob, 'Jacob, Jacob,' and Jacob answered, 'Here I am!'" (Genesis 46:2). "And the Lord called to Samuel, 'Samuel, Samuel,' and Samuel replied, 'Here I am!'" (Samuel, 1:7).

One may similarly employ the story of Luther nailing his theses to the cathedral door, at the same time proclaiming, "Here I stand!"

SERENITY

The well-known AA creed, which some attribute to St. Francis and others to Reinhold Neibuhr, invites the alcoholic to adopt a serenity in the face of things which cannot be changed. For patients, especially those who, like Jesus cry out, "My God, my God! Why has Thou forsaken me?," (Psalms 22:1) we may reply with the verse from the Psalms (31:5), Jesus' last words on the cross, "Into Thy hand I commend my spirit!"

HONORING PARENTS

A problem for which I had no answer until some years ago was, "How can I fulfil the commandment to love my parents when they were such bad people or parents?" Actually the question, so phrased, is a distortion of the commandment, which doesn't require that one *love* one's parents. The commandment requires honoring one's parents rather than love. Nevertheless, the therapist, having made this correction, may not have a way of approaching the problem. One rabbinic commentator (Ganzfried, 1927) offers a way of performing the commandment. It is true that it is many times more difficult to honor such parents directly, but one can live one's life in such exemplary fashion that others viewing their conduct of life would be able to say, "There is a person who would do any parent honor."

SUMMARY AND CONCLUSIONS

Since the number of spiritual, existential, and religious problems brought to the attention of the therapist has proliferated (Mosak & Dreikurs, 1967), the use of religious allusion, and the knowledge of such allusions, had best become part of the armamentarium of the therapist. Other allusions that I have used refer to Peter's betrayal of Jesus, to Moses' commission of error, to not keeping aloof from the community (Ethics of the Fathers, 1984, pp. 16–17), to the transformation of Saul of Tarsus on the road to Damascus, to King Solomon's compromise decision, to Joseph's dying and the new management in Egypt not remembering his services to the State, to the daughters of Zelaphchad, and to the parables in the Bible and in the Talmud. I have previously written (Mosak, 1984) on the role of faith, hope, and love in psychotherapy.

These allusions need not be reserved only for therapy with the "religious" patient; the messages and morals may be equally useful with patients who have fleeting interests in religion as well as with nonbelievers. The therapist will need to have a command of the sources from which these allusions are drawn. If not, he or she will at least have to possess some understanding of the client's religious knowledge. (I can remember the difficulty I encountered when I did marriage counseling with a Mormon couple and did not understand their unique form of getting married.)

BIBLICAL REFERENCES

Cohen, A. (1945). *The Psalms*. London: Soncino Press.

Hertz, J. H. (1958). *The Soncino edition of the Pentateuch & Haftorahs*. London: Soncino Press.

The New Testament and the Book of Psalms (1978). New York: American Bible Society.

REFERENCES

Ethics of the Fathers (1984). Commentary by Rabbi M. Zlotowitz. Brooklyn, NY: Mesorah Publications.

Ganzfried, S. (c. 1927). *The concise code of Jewish law: Compiled from Kitzur Shulhan Aruch*. New York: Ktav.

Lenzberg, K. (1937). Concerning wit and humor. *International Journal of Individual Psychology, 3(1)*, 81–87.

Mosak, H. H. (1971). Strategies for behavior change in schools: Consultation strategies. *Counseling Psychologist, 3(1)*, 58–62. Also in H. H. Mosak (Ed.) (1977), *On purpose* (pp. 188–197). Chicago: Alfred Adler Institute.

Mosak, H. H. (1973). The controller: A social interpretation of the anal character. In H. H. Mosak (Ed.), *Alfred Adler: His influence on psychology today* (pp. 43–52). Also in H. H. Mosak (Ed.) (1977), *On purpose* (pp. 216–227). Chicago: Alfred Adler Institute.

Mosak, H. H. (1984). Adlerian psychotherapy (pp. 56–107). In R. J. Corsini (Ed.), *Current psychotherapies*. 3rd edition. Itasca, IL: F. E. Peacock.

Mosak, H. H. (1987a). Guilt, guilt feelings, regret and repentance. *Individual Psychology, 44*.

Mosak, H. H. (1987b). *Ha ha and aha: The role of humor in psychotherapy.* Muncie, IN: Accelerated Development.

Mosak, H. H., & Dreikurs, R. (1967). The tasks of life III. The fifth life task. *Individual Psychologist, 5*, 108–117.

Mosak, H. H., & LeFevre, C. (1976). The resolution of "intrapersonal conflict." *Journal of Individual Psychology, 32(1)*, 19–26.

Savitz, H. A. (1955). The cultural background of the patient as part of the physicians' armamentarium. In D. A. McClelland (Ed.), *Studies in motivation.* New York: Appleton-Century-Crofts.

Part D
ACTING "AS IF"

VARIATIONS OF THE "AS IF" TECHNIQUE

Mark S. Carich

Currently the institutional psychologist for Centralia Correctional Center, Illinois Department of Corrections, Centralia, Illinois. He is adjunct faculty for the Department of Behavior Studies, University of Missouri in St. Louis.

Adler created the "as if" technique. It was derived from Hans Vaihinger's "as if" philosophy (Ansbacher & Ansbacher, 1956; Watzlawick, 1987). It can be defined as a cognitive, behavioral, and/or cognitive-behavioral intervention in which the client anticipates, pretends, and/or enacts a futuristic event, belief, or desired behavior. The intervention takes the form of "as if" statements or action modalities. There are variations of this intervention. For example, Zeig (1985) uses the "as if" technique combined with various Ericksonian hypnotic procedures to induce time distortion, present suggestions, age regression, and amnesia. Therapists from various theoretical orientations have also used different forms of "as if," including: cognitive, strategic, cognitive-behavioralists, systems, behavioral, and homework-oriented (Beck & Emery, 1985; Martin & Pear, 1983; O'Hanlon, 1987).

The "as if" technique is based upon the pull of a future goal. It is ideological or fictional and depends upon each person's unique life-style. Norby and Hall (1974) discuss the power/pull of fictional goals: ". . . that man is motivated more by his expectations for the future than by his experiences of the past. These future expectations may be purely fictional—that is ideals which are not capable of being realized—yet they exercise a profound influence on a person's behavior" (p. 9).

Fictional goals are beliefs or expectations concerning futuristic behaviors (Ansbacher & Ansbacher, 1956; Dinkmeyer, Dinkmeyer, & Sperry, 1987). These

Individual Psychology, 45(4), December, 1989, **pp. 538–545**

guiding fictions become self-fulfilling prophecies in that the individual tends to behave according to his/her fictions or beliefs (Beck & Emery, 1985; Watzlawick, 1987). Adler claimed that guiding fictions are typically linguistically expressed in terms of "as if" statements or modalities (Ansbacher & Ansbacher, 1956). Furthermore, guiding fictions are subjective futuristic private logic and created at both conscious and unconscious levels. Fictions are then supported by private logic and life-style. Behavior may be altered by changing the purpose(s) of the symptom or behavior.

THE BASIC "AS IF" INTERVENTION

The basic intervention consists of helping the client to think or behave in an "as if" (pretend) fashion (Dinkmeyer, et al., 1987; Mosak, 1979). The goals of this technique include: (1) to change the client's current beliefs and/or perceptions of the problem; (2) to provide insight; (3) to facilitate reorientation or actual behavior change, as the client initiates new behaviors/beliefs; (4) to encourage changes in self-esteem, confidences, concept, competence, etc.; and (5) redirect purposes/goals of problematic behaviors.

Variations of the "As If" Technique

The "as if" technique can be expressed in many different forms or ways. Some of the variations include: role play, imagery, fantasy/day dreaming, implosion, metaphor, paradoxical prescription, reframe, and non-strategic task assignment.

Role Playing. Role playing is defined as the construction and enactment of specific role(s) with the use of formal or informal scripts (Beck, 1985; Beck & Emery, 1985). An "as if" variation may include roles designed with an "as if" or "what if" contextual frame. For example, a client suffering from anxiety and inferiority because of an inability to cope with a specific individual could be instructed to play a role consisting of behaviors related to that person's feelings, such as security, calmness, relaxation, confidence, and using his/her strengths within specific communicational contexts. The client first outlines the script of the role in detail and then enacts the role. The goal of role playing is to generate new behaviors, as the individual enacts an "as if/what if" problem resolution script. For example, in sex offense group therapy, an offender is instructed to play the role of another offender's victim using specific details. The offender responds to the role player as a "what if/as if" he was the victim. This begins to instill remorse.

Role playing may be most effective when scripts include the basic sensory modalities or experiential/representative modalities associated with sensory data input (Lankton, 1980). These include: visual, auditory, kinesthetic, olfactory, and gustatory.

Imagery. Imagery consists of internally visualizing specific concrete scenes (Lankton, 1980). There may be different time dimensions associated with imagery. These include reviewing past, present, and future desires. The "as if" variation is the futuristic dimension. Mosak (1979) indicated that: "Adlerians give patients similar shorthand images that confirm the adage that 'one picture is worth a thousand words.' Remembering this image, the patient can remind himself of his goals and in later stages he can learn to use the image to laugh at himself" (p. 72).

Imagery can either be guided by the therapist or self-induced by the client. For example, a client who fears engaging in public speaking can be instructed to rehearse and visualize speaking feeling relaxed, confident, and comfortable.

Fantasy/Daydreaming Technique. Fantasy and daydreaming have been considered synonymous with each other and at times with imagery. Fantasy is defined as constructing or creating (usually futuristic, but not necessarily) make believe or pretend scenarios about possible/impossible events and situations. Fantasies may be different experiential realities including: emotions, images (visual, sensory modalities), other sensory modalities (auditory, kinesthetic, olfactory, and gustatory), cognitive-perceptual elements (thoughts, beliefs, thought processes), etc. Fantasy may be combined with imagery in order to incorporate other sensory modalities within the scenario. They can either be guided fantasies, self-induced, or ambiguously delivered. The "as if" fantasy is constructed within a "what if" context. It can be a positive, negative, or neutral experience.

For example, a sex offender (who feared rejection) was instructed to construct a negative scenario in which he approached an adult female to engage in conversation and he was rejected. The end of the scenario was for him to fantasize himself coping positively with the situation.

Implosion/Flooding. Implosion and flooding techniques have been developed by behaviorists along the lines of classical conditioning (Martin & Pear, 1983; Last, 1985; Michelson, 1985). Martin and Pear (1983) defined flooding as: "... resembles forced extinction. The therapist tried to get the patient in the presence of the feared stimulus very early during therapy and to maintain exposure for long periods of time such as an hour or more per session. Although the feared object or stimulus may be presented in vivo" (p. 247). This is distinguished from implosion as implosion is defined: "instead of requiring the client to imagine realistic scenes, the therapist requires the client to imagine high-anxiety scenes from an exaggerated unrealistic verbal description that the therapist provides" (Martin & Pear, 1983, p. 272). Implosion relies on exaggerated unrealistic brief presentations of symptomatic stimuli. Michelson (1985) claims that implosion techniques have been associated with the presentation of psychodynamic cues, horrific, frightening, and extreme stimuli. Both techniques appear to be based upon changing fictions and are variations of the "as if" technique. The variation of "as if" occurs when the symptom or problem (feared stimulus) is presented in an "as if"/"what if" fashion. In using "as if" variation, a phobic client can be instructed to imagine self as if experiencing the ultimate worst aspect of the phobia. The goal is problem resolution by ultimately shifting the meaning of the symptom.

Metaphor. A metaphor has been defined as a symbolic representation of one element to another in the form of a literary device (Barker, 1985; O'Hanlon, 1987). O'Hanlon (1987) states: "Anytime one thing is likened to another or spoken of as if it were another thing, metaphor is involved . . . The function of metaphor is to carry knowledge across contexts beyond the initial context into a new one" (pp. 71–72). At any rate, the resemblance of one item to another is symbolically transmitted without any direct connection (Barker, 1985). This includes short or long stories, stories within stories (multiple embedded metaphors), analogies, brief phrases or statements (anecdotes), puns, riddles, experiential task assignments, metaphorical objects, artistic metaphors, jokes, and humor.

The goal is to indirectly communicate various implied meanings in order for the client to gain insight, shift dysfunctional meanings, and to facilitate behavior change at conscious/unconscious levels. The "as if" technique is typically inherent in these messages. Through metaphors, the therapist can deliver the implication of thinking/acting in an "as if" manner. The delivery of metaphors requires the following steps: (1) establish goals (the type of experience and therapeutic message to be transmitted); (2) choose a symbolic representation or metaphor that has some kind of meaning to the individual; (3) create an appropriate context, choosing appropriate words or phrases to nonverbally accent; and (4) at the time of delivery, don't directly provide the meaning but allow the client to unconsciously search for the meaning. For example, a narcissistic sex offender with schizoid tendencies was instructed to look up and study a turtle. He could have been instructed to study and act "as if" he was a turtle. Thus, the inmate would experience and gain insight into his defense mechanisms and compensation strategies.

Paradoxical Prescriptions/Predictions. Paradoxical interventions are self contradictory messages delivered to the client (Mozdzierz, Macchitelli, & Lisiecki, 1976; West, Main, & Zarski, 1986). The receiver finds these messages confusing at various levels of meaning. At one level, the message consists of a logical element while at another level, it appears to be illogical. Symptom prescription is "the technique of directing the patient to do exactly what he has already been doing . . . the therapist usually provided an additional therapeutic contribution or medication to the symptomatic behavior" (Zeig, 1980, p. 16). A paradoxical prediction is making predictions that the client may or may not continue to experience the symptom. Typically, relapses are predicted to insure the client that possible relapse is okay. In both techniques, the therapist encourages and/or predicts the symptom to occur with a rationale, thus changing the contextual meaning of the problem. Adler was the first to use paradoxical techniques (Ansbacher & Ansbacher, 1956; Mozdzierz, Macchitelli, & Lisiecki, 1976). Early Adlerians have referred to these techniques as anti suggestions. Paradoxical interventions are based upon "as if" philosophy and a future orientation. The client is told to behave "as if" he has symptoms. The goal is to allow the client to experience the problem in a different context. Thus, the meaning of the problems and specific guiding fictions are changed. The "as if" variation of paradoxical predictions would take the implied form of "what if" the symptom/problem is okay.

The steps of "as if" paradoxical prescriptions include: (1) developing a cooperative rapport; (2) mutually establishing specific problems and goals; (3) creating an appropriate therapeutic context, of "as if"; (4) developing a prescription based upon a symptom, utilizing elements of the client's experiential reality; (5) providing a rationale; (6) delivering the prescription, so that it is meaningful to the client at one level and illogical at another; (7) monitoring the outcome; and (8) utilizing any consequence (West, Main, & Zarski, 1986; Zeig, 1980). The "as if" paradoxical prediction is set up similarly, except behavior is predicted, not encouraged. It is typically used after prescriptions in order to relieve the client of any worries concerning the return of the symptom. Steps include: (1) building a cooperative rapport; (2) establishing goals, problems, and consequences of previous interventions (such as prescriptions); (3) establishing an appropriate "what if" context; (4) if needed, supplementing a rationale; (5) monitoring the outcome; and (6) utilizing any consequence toward problem resolution. Predictions allow the client to experience the problem in a different way (if it occurs again). For example, in penitentiary sex offense therapy, it is common for sex offenders to become depressed and want to withdraw from group therapy. Depression occurs as the client begins to feel the remorse of his behavior. Many clients request to withdraw from therapy in order to avoid the pain. "As if" oriented prescriptions and predictions are both used to "normalize" the depression as part of the process. The client is told that depression is part of the therapeutic process. Depression is thus prescribed and predicted. As a result, clients resume therapeutic work.

Reframing. Reframing can be defined as presenting the client with a new or different way of looking at a designated event, behavior, or phenomena (Mozdzierz, Murphy, & Greenblatt, 1986; O'Hanlon, 1987). The goal of reframing is to shift one's dysfunctional view, frame of reference, and the meaning of the problem behavior to a more functional view (O'Hanlon, 1987). The individual's frame of reference and private logic changes. Adler referred to this as prosocial redefinition (Mozdzierz, Macchitelli, & Lisiecki, 1976; Mozdzierz, Murphy, & Greenblatt, 1986). "As if" reframes are hypothetical statements framed in "as if/what if" language.

The basic steps of reframing include: (1) establishing rapport and cooperation; (2) defining problems and goals; (3) choosing and selecting positive or different elements (views) from problematic behaviors depending upon the goal; (4) basing the selected view upon the client's reality and meaningfulness to the client in "as if" form; (5) emphasizing and providing the new selected view; (6) monitoring the outcome; and (7) utilizing any consequences if necessary.

For example, an inmate client indicated that it was okay to accept money from women from the outside, even if the women could not afford it. He was posed the following hypothetical situation: "What if your wife sent you money instead of taking care of the kids' needs? Would you accept it?" He retorted angrily. However, he began rethinking his position of "leeching off of women" as a form of victimization.

Non-Strategic Task Assignment. Homework or task assignments are defined as the assigning of specific (usually cognitive-behavioral) tasks for the client to engage in during or in between sessions (Shelton & Ackerman, 1976). Adler frequently used homework (task) assignments in treatment (McBrien, 1985; Mosak, 1979). The "as if" task assignment is any task delivered within an "as if" framework. For example, Shelton and Ackerman (1976) describe a marital "as if" assignment in which the couple was instructed to experience their relationship "as if" it was best.

Similarly, Adlerians use the "as if" technique as an action-oriented task in which the client is asked to act or behave as if the problem is resolved (Mosak, 1979). There are many other forms of tasks including: creating lists (of positive/negative aspects of self, problems, what would be different, the repetitive listing of "I choose" statements), writing stories, writing different types of letters (anger, guilty, goodbye, hello, acceptance, assertion, etc.). The procedure includes: (1) establishing a cooperative rapport; (2) establishing mutual goals of problem resolution; (3) selecting what type of experience and therapeutic message that you want the client to have; (4) using the "as if" format; (5) selecting the appropriate metaphor, context, and task assignment in which the message/experience is to be transmitted; (6) delivering the task; (7) monitoring the outcome; and (8) utilizing any outcome as necessary.

CONCLUSION

According to Zeig (1985): "The 'as if' technique plays on and enhances the demand characteristics of the relationship . . . (provides) powerful social cues for compliance which can lead to the subject actually having the suggested experience" (p. 330). It is a pretend intervention that alters cognitive factors (guiding fictions, subjective experience, perceptions, meanings, private logic, belief systems, etc.) and behavior as the client engages in pretend experiences.

REFERENCES

Ansbacher, H. L., & Ansbacher, R. R. (Eds.). (1956). *The Individual Psychology of Alfred Adler*. New York: Basic Books.

Barker, P. (1985). *Using metaphors in psychotherapy*. New York: Brunner/Mazel.

Beck, A. T., & Emery, G. (1985). *Anxiety disorder phobias: A cognitive perspective*. New York: Basic Books.

Beck, S. (1985). Role playing. In A. S. Bellack & M. Hersen (Eds.), *Dictionary of behavior therapy techniques*. New York: Pergamon Press.

Dinkmeyer, D., Dinkmeyer, D., & Sperry, L. (1987). *Adlerian counseling and psychotherapy*. Columbus, OH: Merrill Publishing.

Lankton, S. (1980). *Practical magic: A translation of basic neuro-linguistic programming into clinical psychotherapy*. Cupertino, CA: Meta Publication.

Last, C. G. (1985). Homework. In A. S. Bellack & M. Hersen (Eds.), *Dictionary of behavior therapy techniques*. New York: Pergamon Press.

Martin, G., & Pear, J. (1983). *Behavior modification: What it is and how to do it.* Englewood Cliffs, NJ: Prentice Hall.

McBrien, R. (1985). Managing depression: Adlerian approach. *Individual Psychology, 41*(4), 471–482.

Michelson, L. (1985). Flooding. In A. S. Bellack & M. Hersen (Eds.), *Dictionary of behavior therapy techniques.* New York: Pergamon Press.

Mosak, H. H. (1979). Adlerian psychotherapy. In R. Corsini (Ed.), *Current psychotherapies.* Itasca, IL: Peacock Publishers.

Mozdzierz, G., Macchitelli, F., & Lisiecki, J. (1976). The paradox in psychotherapy: An Adlerian perspective. *Journal of Individual Psychology, 32*, 169–184.

Mozdzierz, G., Murphy, J. J., & Greenblatt, R. C. (1986). Private logic: Relationship to the strategy of psychotherapy. *Individual Psychology, 42*(3), 339–349.

Norby, V. J., & Hall, C. S. (1974). *A guide to psychologists and their concepts.* San Francisco: W. H. Freeman.

O'Hanlon, W. H. (1987). *Taproots: Underlying principles of M. H. Erickson therapy and hypnosis.* New York: W. W. Norton.

Shelton, J. L., & Ackerman, J. M. (1976). *Homework in counseling and psychotherapy.* Springfield, IL: Charles C. Thomas.

Watzlawick, P. (1987). If you desire to see, learn how to act. In J. K. Zeig (Ed.), *The evolution of psychotherapy.* New York: Brunner/Mazel.

West, J. C., Main, F. O., & Zarski, J. J. (1986). The paradoxical prescription in Individual Psychology. *Individual Psychology, 42*(2), 214–224.

Zeig, J. K. (1980). Symptom prescription and Ericksonian principles of hypnosis and psychotherapy. *The American Journal of Clinical Hypnosis, 23*(1), 16–22.

Zeig, J. K. (1985). The clinical use of amnesia: Ericksonian methods. In J. K. Zeig (Ed.), *Ericksonian psychotherapy volume I: Structures.* New York: Brunner/Mazel.

Part E
HUMOR

LAUGHING TOGETHER: HUMOR AS ENCOURAGEMENT IN COUPLES COUNSELING

Robert J. McBrien
Director of the Center for Personal and Professional Development at Salisbury State University, Salisbury, MD, where he applies Adlerian psychology to his work counseling university students.

A couple who drove through the countryside miles from home made a wrong turn and became lost. With much laughter and a sense of adventure the couple roamed the country searching for their original route. Now they look back on that experience with pleasant memories.

Their friends had a different experience. Returning home from a drive, their car ran out of gas. This inconvenience generated an argument with massive doses of criticism and blaming. This couple does not like to recall their experience, but when they do, it rekindles the unhappiness that each felt.

Each couple had responded to an unexpected stressful situation by relying upon their typical patterns for handling adversity. In Adlerian terms, the couples cooperated with each other through their coping actions. When Adler wrote of love and marriage he focused on cooperation between the partners. He taught that the healthiest cooperative efforts occurred when each partner treated the other as coequal. Adler (1980) said, ". . . when people are equal they will always find a way to settle their difficulties" (p. 267). The first couple employed humor

Individual Psychology, 49(3/4), September/December, 1993, **pp. 419–427**

to strengthen their relationship as they transformed one of life's inconveniences into an adventure. The second couple magnified the unpleasantness of their experience, and it became a source of conflict in their relationship. The obvious difference between the two couples illustrates the benefits of a healthy sense of humor and offers an example of the Adlerian concept of converting a minus into a plus.

This article focuses on the role that humor and laughter play in marriage. Healthy humor is identified as a key to strengthening the cooperative efforts of a couple as they build their relationship. The psychology of humor, the benefits of laughter, and the uses and misuses of humor are discussed, and strategies for using humor as a source of encouragement in marriage counseling are presented.

THE PSYCHOLOGY OF HUMOR

More than 50 years before research supported him, Adler wrote of the value of laughter and the contributions humor and laughter make to psychological health. Adler (1946) said, "Laughter, with its liberating energy, its freedom-giving powers, goes hand in hand with happiness, and represents, so to speak, the keystone of this affect" (p. 276). Individual Psychology acknowledges the importance of humor and most Adlerians use it in counseling, psychotherapy, and education. Manaster and Corsini (1982) stated: "Adlerians use humor as frequently as appropriate (and as frequently as they have a good story to tell)" (p. 203).

Humor is a holistic experience which involves physical, social, and personal dimensions. Although philosophers, psychologists, and medical researchers have developed several theories regarding the ability of humans to experience humor, a comprehensive theory is lacking (Foster, 1978). However, there is agreement regarding the physical benefits of laughter. Fry (1992) summarizes evidence that laughter contributes to improved respiration through the increase of ventilation, assists the cardiovascular system by increasing circulation, and stimulates the central nervous system resulting in increased alertness and memory. A sense of humor has also been correlated with healthy adaptation over the lifespan (Vaillant, 1977).

To introduce the psychological dimensions of humor, consider this anecdote:

> While interviewing Mr. and Mrs. Johnson on their 60th wedding anniversary a journalist inquired, "Tell me Mrs. Johnson, in the 60 long years of your marriage have you ever considered divorce?"

> Mrs. Johnson replied: "Oh my, divorce? Never.
> But, murder? Quite often!"

There are several theories regarding our smiling or laughing at an anecdote. Apparently, our appreciation of humor is related to the brain experiencing a sudden shift or twist in logic when the punchline is delivered. By experiencing the incongruity, paradox, or surprise, we find delight or fun in the joke (Mosak, 1987; Fry & Salameh, 1987). Goldstein (1987) offers evidence that right brain activity is involved in appreciating a humorous event. His survey of research with brain-damaged patients offers evidence that those patients with right hemisphere damage had specific limits in their ability to appreciate certain types of humor (however, they could enjoy slapstick humor). Also, patients were limited in their ability to produce humor due to social judgment deficits.

Mosak's (1987) contribution to our understanding of humor offers explanations and practical applications from an Adlerian perspective. He describes three major categories of humor: (1) tension-release theory, (2) put-down theory, and (3) two-track theory.

Tension-release theory is probably best demonstrated by reading a well-drawn, four-panel cartoon in your daily newspaper. As you read from left to right your tension builds. When you finally read the punchline in the last panel and "get" the joke, laughter releases your tension. This release of tension confirms our understanding of the psychological benefits of laughter and supports Mosak's labeling of successful uses of humor in therapy as "wind power" (1987, p. 62).

The two components of humor can be illustrated with this anecdote:

> The coach of a nationally ranked football team was being interviewed for eyewitness news. The reporter observed that the coach's wife had traveled with him to all the away games and his team was successful every time. Smiling, the wily coach admitted, "Yes, I do bring her along. It is a question of that or having to kiss her goodbye."

The first component of tension-release theory is physiological. In the previous anecdote, the storyline creates an expectation that the coach was superstitious about bringing his wife along and winning games. The listener's brain follows the first line of logic and anticipates that the coach's response will follow that line. When the punchline occurs, we experience delight due to the sudden shift in logic. The second component, the social element, views wit and joke-telling as forms of passive aggression and is related to Freud's theory on humor and latent aggression stemming from his earlier studies on dreams, repression, forgetting, and Freudian slips (Neve, 1988).

Mosak's second category consists of put-down humor. An example of this type was taped to the back window of a pickup truck that passed me several months ago:

> Wanted: attractive woman to become my wife. Must love fishing, cutting bait, baiting hooks, and cleaning fish. Must own 16-foot bass boat with 75-horse-power motor. Send picture of boat.

This anecdote highlights one of Adler's major teachings regarding the problems that couples experience when there is a one-up, one-down relationship. Writing on love and marriage more than 60 years ago, Adler (1980) observed, "This is the reason we have so many unhappy marriages. Nobody can bear a position of inferiority without anger and disgust" (p. 267).

In put-down humor, the humorist can "revolt against the socially normal frames of reference" (Mosak, 1987, p. 21). This form of aggression or power is useful when the two frames of reference (the logic of the story-line and the twist of logic in the punchline) used to construct the joke are equal. In the anecdote of the football coach taking his wife on trips to avoid kissing her goodbye, the potential for equality is good, especially if their relationship is warm and friendly. Disparaging jokes, hurtful and demeaning, are on the "useless side of life" when the two frames of reference are unequal. The social benefits of put-down humor include subtle methods to bring down those in positions of authority. This may explain the current trend of sharing "lawyer jokes" with work mates, friends, and family. Mosak goes on to explain the usefulness of put-down humor as a humanizing element which can serve to equalize those with unequal status.

Adlerians offer a more positive interpretation of the use of humor in a social context. Rather than seeing aggressiveness, they understand the goal as striving for power (Titze, 1987). Titze employs humor to assist patients in shifting their goal from aggression to gaining control and power through the use of paradox and assertiveness.

The third category of humor consists of the two-track theory. The cognitive function in two-track theory involves following one frame of reference until being tripped up by the incongruity of a second track at the punchline. Mosak's (1987) description of Adler's teachings on joke sharing focused on the cognitive activity involved in finding the joke and having a good laugh. For Mosak, the therapeutic gains from the creative use of humor and laughter occur when a teachable moment (the "aha" experience) results.

THE HUMOR-ENCOURAGEMENT CONNECTION

Using healthy humor during counseling can increase the number of positive experiences the couples share and serve as a means of strengthening their relationship. Humor and laughter can also be introduced as a strategy to achieve a key Adlerian goal for counseling: encouragement. Sperry and Carlson (1991) list "choosing to encourage each other" as one of the 10 skills needed for a well-functioning marriage. When couples maximize their potential for humor, their relationship will continue to be strengthened long after counseling ends.

But humor can also be misused. Adler taught that any human quality has the potential to be used for either a positive or a negative purpose. Adlerians use the concepts of "useful side of life" and "useless side of life" to guide their investigation of the purpose of an act. The two important questions to ask regarding purpose is whether the act moves the client in the direction of a goal and whether the goal is on the useful side of life (Manaster & Corsini, 1982).

Individual Psychology addresses the duality of human nature when it investigates both sides of any situation. This anecdote is an example of this focus on the opposite of a situation:

> A mother was explaining the reason the bride wore white to her young son who was attending his first wedding. "She wears white because she is celebrating a joyful event. This is the happiest day of her life." "Well then," said her son, "Why is the groom wearing black?"

This duality of purpose guides our understanding of the misuses of humor by therapists. Sensitivity is essential when introducing witty comments, jokes, and laughter in the session. Offended couples might be laughing to please their therapist. They might perceive the session as a form of joke-telling social which belittles their concerns. Finally, there is also the risk that both counselor and clients could use humor as a means to evade painful feelings (Fry & Salameh, 1987).

Salameh (1987) and Mosak (1987) suggested these positive uses of humor with couples:

1. Establishing and maintaining rapport.
2. Using jokes, cartoons, or anecdotes to enhance corrective feedback.
3. Maintaining focus on the couple. This is achieved when the shared laugh is perceived by the clients as evidence that the counselor is metaphorically "reading from the same music."

4. Unblocking creativity. The release of tension resulting from laughter can free cognitive blocks. This promotes creativity, shared problem solving, and enhanced cooperation.
5. Releasing tension. The ability to laugh at a life situation detaches the person from the emotions associated with the event, may prevent somatic complications, and sends a signal of hopefulness to the couple.
6. Avoiding burnout. Using various forms of humor along with accompanying laughter prevents professional burnout. With a healthy sense of humor as a major component of one's style of doing therapy the environment is pleasant, the people are comfortable with each other, and each day stimulates creativity and is filled with variety and challenge.

Additional goals benefitting marriage counseling include role modeling, assigning the experience of healthy humor at home as well as in counseling, and using humor to encourage the couple. By guiding couples to appreciate a healthy humor style the counseling goals of both encouragement and social interest are met (Manaster & Corsini, 1982).

Viewing their clients as being discouraged by their life situation, Adlerian counselors strive to encourage them. Dinkmeyer and Losoncy (1980) include humor in their discussion of this process. They believe that when counselors guide discouraged couples toward an encouraged outlook on life, the use of healthy uplifting humor qualifies as an encouragement strategy. Through vignettes and written exercises, Dinkmeyer and Losoncy use humor to help clients overcome discouragement. Their creative uses of humor help clients to identify alternative solutions, to resolve conflicts, and to manage negative emotions. As an example of a creative application of humor, Dinkmeyer and Losoncy (1980, p. 206) have couples list five good reasons why they *should* get upset when things go wrong. The resulting laughter at the unusual request can help the couple find new ways to view their coping patterns and help them break out of their one-way approach to dealing with concerns.

Nontoxic forms of humor also meet the Adlerian standard for encouragement in these ways:

1. Healthy humor is *accepting* one's fallibility and helps the person have the courage to be human with all its imperfections.
2. Enjoying a joke with its subsequent laughter facilitates *creativity*. When a person's mind detaches from the tension of concern at the moment of "getting" the joke, the opportunity for insight into alternative solutions is possible.
3. Healthy humor produces feelings of *hopefulness* and contributes to optimism.

4. Humor and laughter produce *movement* toward improving mood, feeling accepting of others, progressing toward goals.
5. The use of nontoxic humor is evidence of *developing social interest.* When one spouse shares a joke, cartoon, or makes light of a stressful situation (thus lowering stress and brightening the other spouse's day), we can say that social interest is being developed.

STRENGTHENING MARRIAGES WITH ENCOURAGING FORMS OF HUMOR

Ziv and Gadish (1989) assessed the impact of humor on marital satisfaction with 50 married couples. They found that the marital satisfaction of husbands was related to their perception of their partner's sense of humor. The results for wives were not as conclusive.

Blumenfeld and Alpern (1986) promote humor as a necessary condition for longevity in relationships. They state, ". . . a sense of humor can help you be more accepting of your own imperfection as well as those of your spouse" (p. 153). They also give evidence that rates humor as an important factor for success in marriage.

Beecher and Beecher's (1966) chapter on marriage focused on Adler's understanding of the dominance-submissive struggle associated with discouraged, doomed marriages. Their description of Adler's use of humor to assess couples extends our appreciation of Adler's creativity:

> Dr. Alfred Adler used to say that marriage should be a partnership of two people for the world and not a side show of two people against the world. Or against each other. There is no room for mutual exploitation. Adler, told that Miss X was going to be married, commented, "Against whom." (Beecher & Beecher, 1966, p. 106)

The active-directive style of Adlerian counselors provides a wide range of opportunities for including healthy forms of humor. Assigning homework to increase the couple's understanding and use of healthy humor to strengthen their relationship is a key strategy for counselors and trainers. The following strategies are offered as basic tools for counselors to use in their work and to assign as homework for their clients and themselves.

1. Ad lib humor. A witty comment, story, or joke that is directly related to the self-disclosures offered by the couple.

2. Story telling and joke telling. Requires the counselor to have an encyclopedia of jokes, stories, and one-liners stored in memory, as well as skill in telling the joke in an encouraging manner. (Most joke books are filled with disparaging jokes.)
3. Didactic cartoons. Requires the counselor to build a library of cartoons which are relevant, meet the standards for healthy humor, and teach a lesson.
4. "Happy Hour" homework. Assignment which allows the couple to share laughter resulting from watching videotapes or listening to audiotapes of comedy.

SUMMARY

Encouragement is one of the essential skills couples need to strengthen their marriage. It is also a key technique used by Adlerian counselors. Healthy forms of humor and the resulting joy from laughter create opportunities for the couple and the counselor to feel encouraged. Sharing a joke, cartoon, or humorous comment in a creative and instructive manner meets the characteristics required by Dinkmeyer and Carlson (1984) for encouragement in marriages. They describe humor as encouraging when it generates enthusiasm, strengthens positive feelings the couple has for each other, and promotes creative solutions to challenging situations by helping the couple find positive meanings and alternatives to those challenges.

Marriage counselors are encouraged to include humor, both during therapy and as assigned homework, as a means to achieving their goal of encouraging couples to encourage each other. Not only will clients benefit, but counselors too will find they have added an element of joy to their work.

REFERENCES

Adler, A. (1946). *Understanding human nature.* New York: Greenberg.

Adler, A. (1980). *What life should mean to you.* New York: Perigee Books.

Beecher, W., & Beecher, M. (1966). *Beyond success and failure.* New York: Julian Press.

Blumenfeld, E., & Alpern, A. (1986). *The smile connection.* New York: Prentice-Hall.

Dinkmeyer, D., & Carlson, J. (1984). *Time for a better marriage.* Circle Pines, MN: American Guidance Service.

Dinkmeyer, D., & Losoncy, L. (1980). *The encouragement book.* New York: Prentice-Hall.

Foster, J. A. (1978). Humor and counseling: Close encounter of another kind. *Personnel and Guidance Journal, 56,* 46–49.

Fry, W. F. (1992). The psychologic effects of humor, mirth and laughter. *JAMA, 267,* 1856.

Fry, W. F., & Salameh, W. H. (Eds.). (1987). *Handbook of humor and psychotherapy.* Sarasota, FL: Professional Resource Exchange.

Goldstein, J. (1987). Therapeutic effects of laughter. In W. F. Fry, Jr., & W. A. Salameh (Eds.), *Handbook of humor and psychotherapy.* Sarasota, FL: Professional Resource Exchange.

Manaster, G. J., & Corsini, R. J. (1982). *Individual psychology: Theory and practice.* Itasca, IL: F. E. Peacock.

Mosak, H. H. (1987). *Ha ha and aha: The role of humor in psychotherapy.* Muncie, IN: Accelerated Development.

Neve, M. (1988). Freud's theory of humor, wit and jokes. In J. Durant & J. Miller (Eds.), *Laughing matters: A serious look at humor.* New York: Wiley.

Salameh, W. (1987). Humor in integrative short-term psychotherapy (ISP). In W. E. Fry, Jr., & W. A. Salameh, (Eds.), *Handbook of humor and psychotherapy.* Sarasota, FL: Professional Resource Exchange.

Sperry, L., & Carlson, J. (1991). *Marital therapy: Integrating theory and technique.* Denver: Love.

Titze, M. (1987). The "conspirative method": Applying humoristic inversion in psychotherapy. In W. E. Fry, Jr. & W. A. Salameh (Eds.), *Handbook of humor and psychotherapy.* Sarasota, FL: Professional Resource Exchange.

Vaillant, G. E. (1977). *Adaption to life.* Boston: Little, Brown.

Ziv, A., & Gadish, O. (1989). Humor and marital satisfaction. *Journal of Social Psychology, 129,* 759–768.

Part F
PARADOX AND "SPITTING IN THE SOUP"

THE RELAPSE TECHNIQUE IN COUNSELING AND PSYCHOTHERAPY

Raymond J. Corsini
A clinical psychologist living in Honolulu.

A number of years ago, out of a feeling of mischief, I counseled a family to do exactly the opposite of what they had been doing before counseling, *after* the presenting problem had been solved!

IN FAMILY COUNSELING

Mother had stated that she struggled daily with her two boys (ages 8 and 10) about going to bed. She would start about 7 P.M. and fight with them until 9 for them to go to bed, and finally they would drop off to sleep about 9:30. The fight exhausted her and disturbed her husband. I advised her to give the children complete freedom to go to bed whenever they wanted, but then to wake them up mornings in time to go to school—and to do nothing else. She complained that this would not work since her kids "never needed sleep." She was so insistent on this that I was annoyed (my annoyance led to my later use of the "relapse technique," as shall be explained). Nevertheless, she followed my advice and, sure enough, within two weeks the problem was solved. The children were going to bed on their own and were asleep by 9:30, as they had been before. Things were much more peaceful at home, and the mother was surprised and gratified.

Individual Psychology, 38(4), December, 1982, **pp. 380–386**

However—and here is where the relapse technique comes in—I told the mother that now there was an additional, extremely important aspect of the treatment. She was now to keep the kids up at least one hour past 9:30 P.M. and to attempt whatever methods to achieve this she and her husband could imagine—such as playing games, telling stories, pointing out that there would be something very good on television—and to insist that they stay up. Mother thought that I was out of my mind, and even the regular members of my family counseling group wondered about this strange suggestion; but I insisted—and mother finally, reluctantly, agreed to try it. When she returned, her account of what happened generated considerable amusement; she described one evening in which she and her husband were pushing on the children's bedroom door with children at the other side pushing back, yelling that they needed their sleep and should be let alone. I got my mischievous satisfaction in proving to her and to others that she was wrong in her original assessment that her children didn't need sleep. And that was the end of this technique for a while.

IN MARRIAGE COUNSELING

In marriage counseling I generally employ a contract method (Corsini, 1967; Corsini, 1970; Phillips and Corsini, 1982), which in essence asks the husband and wife what major often-occurring behaviors of the mate they would like to see stopped and what other behaviors started. The desires are clearly demarcated and defined by the counselor, and then each partner is asked to agree to do as the other wants for one week. On the second week, further extension of the contract is made. This apparently simple and logical method works quite well for some clients, but not for others, who eventually appear to revert back to their old behavior.

To illustrate with a sample problematic couple: At Session 1 the husband requested (a) no smoking in the bedroom, (b) a home cooked meal five evenings a week, and (c) sex three times weekly; the wife asked for (a) her husband to come home at an agreed time at night, (b) her husband to take her out at least twice weekly, and (c) her husband to visit her mother with her. Both partners agreed to all three of the propositions and, at the second session, both agreed that each had lived up to the contract. Also at the second session, the following further requests were made: The husband asked his wife to pay bills on time and the wife asked for a pet in the house. Both agreed to these additional requests, and on follow-up at Session 3 all was working out well, everyone living up to the agreements. As time went on, however, relapses began, and eventually the wife was again smoking in the bedroom, the husband not coming home on time at night, and so forth, with each complaining about the other.

With another couple who came to their third conference with each partner expressing satisfaction with the other's new behavior, I insisted, to their consternation, that they were now to relapse to their old behavior. Both were shocked when I suggested that for one week the husband was:

1. To tell the wife what she was thinking and feeling.
2. To gain weight by overeating.
3. To refuse to do any chores whatever.
4. To be rude to guests.
5. To hog the conversation when guests visited.

The wife also had to do five things that she had stopped doing:

1. Be late for every single appointment with her husband (who would meet her at work to drive her home).
2. To nag him daily for at least a half hour about his not helping around the house.
3. To leave at least ten items of clothing on the floor of the bedroom and the bathroom.
4. To play at least one hour of solitaire daily.
5. To talk to her mother on the phone in the evening at least a half hour daily.

We spent practically the whole session in argument, both partners adamant in their refusal to follow my directions. I, in turn, was insistent on their following my directions explicitly; I told them I would no longer see them if they refused to cooperate. Puzzled, they finally agreed to relapse to their old behavior for one week. I typed out specific directions for their misbehavior, gave each a carbon, had them sign my original, and warned them that I would not continue to see them unless they lived up to their agreement.

On the following week, they both confessed that, although they had tried every one of the misbehaviors, they had not succeeded, and that the two of them were in constant laughter at the stupidity of their own prior behavior. For example, when the husband would begin, "I know just what you are feeling—," the wife would attempt to listen with a straight face and then both would get to laughing so that he could not finish his sentence. When the wife was late in meeting him she would be late by about a half minute instead of her usual ten minutes. When she tried to play solitaire, she would be bored and just toss the cards without looking at them for an hour; after three or four days she just gave it up.

What do clients learn from this paradoxical therapy of relapse? The answer I consistently obtain from clients is that they learn the silliness of their prior behavior, and that they come to realize full well that the former behavior is an example of unintentional sabotaging revenge behavior. What is important is this: In my experience, when couples have agreed to relapse, they never really succeed, but the old behavior does not reappear as readily as when the relapse technique is not used.

My major difficulty with this technique is that I am not always successful in getting couples to relapse. Some, so delighted with the new behavior of the other and so happy with their own giving up of such punitive behavior, will not even begin to listen to me when I suggest (no matter how strongly) that they relapse.

THEORY

It is evident that this technique is only another example, although perhaps an unusual one, of paradoxical intention. Of the two instances cited, in one case a mother was conned into doing precisely what she was afraid of originally, that is, allowing her children to stay up past their official bedtime, and in the other case a couple was asked to repeat their original, precontract errors. In both cases, there was massive resistance and the usual development of a better understanding of the futility of their original behavior.

However, for a theoretician, which all therapists should be, whether or not a technique works is not as important as understanding why it works and under what conditions it should or should not be employed. Also, it seems urgent to know when and by whom it should be used. Let us attempt to discuss these points.

Why

The reason this system works is that a person who has made an error (the mother in trying to get her kids to bed before they were ready; the couple in doing a variety of things to annoy one another) and corrects it is generally so happy with the new behavior and its result that there is a reluctance to go over the reasons for employing the ineffective method in the first place; there is a strong possibility, however, that the person who tries something new and better has not really learned in any depth the basic motivations and dynamics of the old behavior and is therefore likely either to go back to it or else to attempt something new, different but similar. The relapse technique could well be called "rubbing one's nose in it" or forcing a person to see an original error quickly, thereby generating a deeper understanding and a stronger desire to avoid similar behavior in the future.

What

The proper time to employ this procedure is only after there is satisfaction on the part of clients, who are induced to repeat the previous sabotaging behavior only after they have succeeded in correcting it. Whether they actually engage in the misbehavior is not very important, I am convinced. What is important is that there be an argument with the counselor/therapist leading to the clients' agreeing to repeat their error. The discussion alone has paradoxical elements that force the clients to argue against the previous behavior; even after both parties (as in a marriage) agree to go back to their bad behavior, in my experience, they really never are able to repeat it. For example, one who uses bad language may go back to saying the same words, but without the original tone of voice.

Who

The person using the relapse techniques should, of course, be a capable counselor who has the complete confidence of the client(s). In a sense this is what occurs:

> **Client:** *You are wonderful; things are so much better because of you.*
> **Counselor:** *I am pleased. Now, I want you to do something very important. Will you do it even though you don't know what it is that I am going to ask you? [Devil's Contract]*
> **Client:** *Why no—I can't promise to do something in advance. I must know what it is.*
> **Counselor:** *Okay, but I want to assure you it is very important and I am sure you will honor my request.*
> **Client:** *I trust you. What is it?*
> **Counselor:** *I want you to do this: Keep your kids up until 10:30 P.M. every night from now on for a week. [Or, Smoke in your bedroom every night for a week; or, Refuse to do any chores for a week.]*
> **Client:** *No. That's crazy. Why do you want me to do that?*
> **Counselor:** *I have my reasons. [. . . and so on . . .]*

When

This technique should be used when the counselor feels certain that good results have been obtained but that there is a chance for the person to revert to old behavior; it is also desirable for the client to be well satisfied with the results of counseling so far.

SUMMARY

The relapse technique is an example of paradoxical intention or negative practice—doing what is wrong, useless, ineffective, or previously feared, but doing it consciously. The purpose of employing this technique of relapses, paradoxically, is to prevent relapses. It seems especially useful with strong-willed individuals who have pursued their goals with great energy but without success, and who have finally tried new ways that have worked without their really understanding why. By forcing them to argue why they should not go back to their old behavior or to do exactly the opposite of what they had been doing before, one helps them find insight into the stupidity and futility of their old behavior. By actually doing what the counselor suggests, the client almost always finds the result to be humorous and insight producing. It is an example of what Saposnek (1980) considers the Aikido model employed in brief strategic therapy. This conceptualization is found in a number of therapeutic systems including Adlerian therapy and logotherapy as well as some of the newer family therapies. Its main value is that it hastens effective counseling and tends to prevent relapses, which are ordinarily so common under most counseling conditions.

REFERENCES

Corsini, R. J. A first aid kit for marriage problems. *Consultant*, 1967, *7*, 40.

Corsini, R. J. The marriage conference. *Marriage Counseling Quarterly*, 1970, *5*, 21–29.

Philips, C., & Corsini, R. J. *Give in or give up*. Chicago: Nelson-Hall, 1982.

Saposnek, D. G. Aikido: A model for brief strategic therapy. *Family process*, 1980, *19*, 227–238.

DISCUSSION: COLUMN EDITORS

The technique presented here could be effective only under certain conditions: (a) The counselor must first of all assist in the client's changing the original behavior; (b) the new behavior must be learned and the client must value the changes; (c) the counselor must believe in the effectiveness of the relapse technique to present it with conviction; (if it is presented only as a gimmick, its effectiveness could be questioned).

Although in the case material presented for the marriage counseling example one could say that each of the spouses was in fact engaging in sabotaging behavior (revenge), that wasn't the case in the family example. The mother there was not seeking revenge, but rather was showing lack of faith in the judgment of her children. She was fearful that they would not get enough sleep and therefore assumed a "good mother" role. In so doing she attempted to be the only thoughtful one and thus deprived the children from assuming responsibility for their bedtime behavior.

The question for a counselor proposing to use the relapse technique is, can the client generalize from the presenting problem—that is, from bedtime problems to other areas. If the mother allows the children to get themselves to bed, does she then continue her "good mothering" in other areas of the children's lives. If the mother sees the absurdity of her former actions in one area, can she look at other areas with similar understanding?

A similar question can be asked with respect to the couple: If the former ways of sabotaging the relationship are made explicit, does the sabotaging take on a different form or is it actually eliminated? If one is asked (required) to reenact one's former behavior and one can see the absurdity of it, what has one learned? A by-product of this relapse technique for use with couples might be the cooperation of the couple working against the therapist's request to do what they formerly did. Now that they are required to do that former behavior they can look at it in a new light.

The therapist using this technique is really giving the clients the choice between the former behavior and a new effective behavior. Perhaps other therapists could use the relapse technique with clients whom they judge to be likely candidates for relapse. We need to collect more data on this unique technique.

THE PARADOXICAL PRESCRIPTION IN INDIVIDUAL PSYCHOLOGY

John D. West
An associate professor of counselor education at Louisiana State University and co-director of the program's family counseling center.

Frank O. Main
An associate professor of counselor education at the University of South Dakota and has recently been a visiting scholar at Louisiana State University.

John J. Zarski
A professor of counselor education at the University of Akron.

Adler has been identified as the first person in Western civilization to use and write about paradoxical interventions in psychotherapy (Mozdzierz, Macchitelli, & Lisiecki, 1976). Mozdzierz et al. (1976) have provided the following description of a paradoxical intervention: "It consists of seemingly self-contradictory and sometimes even absurd therapeutic interventions which are always constructively rationalizable, although sometimes very challenging, and which join rather than oppose symptomatic behavior while containing qualities of empathy, encouragement and humor, leading to increased social interest" (p. 169). The paradoxical prescription is thought to place the client in a therapeutic bind, and Adler frequently employed "prescribing the symptom" as a means of defusing the client's resistance to the therapist's influence (Ansbacher & Ansbacher, 1978). While the content of the therapist's words recommends that the client continue with the problematic behavior, the nonverbal message challenges the client to behave in a "normal" manner and reflects concern as well as empathy for the client (Haley, 1976; Weeks & L'Abate, 1982).

Individual Psychology, 42(2), June, 1986, **pp. 214–224**

From an Individual Psychology perspective, Mozdzierz et al. (1976) presented five essential principles of the therapeutic paradox:

1. The paradoxical technique is used to transform the client's symptomatic asocial behavior into cooperative behavior.
2. The paradoxical technique is used to prevent or remedy power struggles in therapy and thereby block the client's attempts to depreciate or oppose the therapist.
3. The client is often defending against external control and influence, and the paradoxical technique aids the therapist in joining with the client in an unconditional manner.
4. The paradoxical technique moves the client toward rather than away from the symptom, even to the point of the client's experiencing the original symptom more intensely than before.
5. The paradox may also be a context for humor; that is, the client sees the symptomatic complaint in a humorous and, therefore, more detached manner. Through this new perspective, the power of the symptom is lessened.

Authors not directly aligned with Individual Psychology have also studied paradoxical interventions. These include Bateson, Jackson, Haley, and Weakland (1956), Dunlap (1928, 1939, 1942), Frankl (1960, 1975), Erickson (1967), Haley (1963, 1976), Jacobson and Margolin (1979), Lankton and Lankton (1983), Raskin and Klein (1976), Newton (1968a, 1968b), Rossi (1980), Watzlawick, Weakland, and Fisch (1974), and West and Zarski (1983a, 1983b).

This article expands on the Adlerian perspective offered by Mozdzierz et al. (1976), integrating the ideas of those authors not directly aligned with Individual Psychology for implementing paradoxical prescriptions. The following discussion describes a method for implementing paradoxical prescriptions framed within an eight-step model developed by Haley (1976), whose model is elaborated on by reference to related studies. Ansbacher and Ansbacher (1978) point out that Haley's work ". . . blends very smoothly with Adlerian theory" (p. 320).

INITIAL STEPS IN DELIVERING A PARADOXICAL PRESCRIPTION

The first three steps of the model (Haley, 1976) insure (1) that the client is committed to "change" as the goal of therapy, (2) that the presenting problem is clearly defined, and (3) that the objectives of therapy are clearly articulated. Individual Psychology (Dreikurs, 1956) has also suggested the importance of establishing a therapeutic contract. Being placed in a therapeutic paradox requires that the client believes she or he is moving against an expressed desire, that is, the desire to change. Furthermore, before the presenting problem can be prescribed, it needs to be explicitly defined.

DEVELOPING A RATIONALE FOR THE PARADOXICAL PRESCRIPTION

Haley's (1976) fourth step in providing a paradoxical prescription includes developing a rationale or justification for the intervention. Rohrbaugh, Tennen, Press, and White (1981) describe two frameworks within which to utilize paradoxical prescriptions, each of which relies on Brehm's (1976) concepts of "psychological reactance" and "freedom of behavior." Rohrbaugh et al. (1981) define "psychological reactance" as the ". . . desire to avoid being subject to any directive that threatens to eliminate the individual's 'free behavior'. . . . Whenever a therapist offers suggestions, assigns tasks, or in other ways attempts directly to influence a client, the therapist runs the risk of threatening behavioral freedoms and arousing reactance, thus increasing the likelihood of noncompliance or rebellion" (p. 457). In turn, "freedom of behavior" refers to the client's perception that the target complaint is being voluntarily expressed.

Paradoxical prescriptions that are designed to *reduce* psychological reactance encourage cooperation (Rohrbaugh et al., 1981). With implementation of the directive, the client learns that the presenting complaint is under voluntary control and/or experiences the complaint as an ordeal. On the other hand, paradoxical prescriptions designed to *increase* psychological reactance stimulate the client to rebel against implementation, resulting in resolution of the complaint (Rohrbaugh et al., 1981).

In part, the effectiveness of the paradoxical prescription lies in its accompanying rationale. For example, Rohrbaugh et al. (1981) suggest that when a client demonstrates a low degree of psychological reactance and describes the problematic behavior as "unfree" or involuntary, an appropriate rationale may be ". . . that learning to turn the symptom off will be greatly facilitated if he [the client] can first learn to turn it on" (p. 462). A rationale used with the psychologically sophisticated client may consist of informing the individual of the necessity to practice the complaint in order to understand better his or her life-style and its fictional goal (Rohrbaugh et al., 1981). Illustrations such as these (low "reactance" combined with a reasonable rationale) suggest that the client will implement the paradoxical prescription. Implementing the prescription enables the client ultimately to view the symptom as a voluntary act and/or as an ordeal. Either of these outcomes may extinguish the behavior.

Rationales framed in a manner *congruent* with the client's own language or construct system are likely to reduce the reactance level and enhance the probability that the client will *comply*. Tennen, Rohrbaugh, Press, and White (1981) credit Fisch et al. (1975) for conveying a fundamental Ericksonian principle: Clients are more likely to accept and implement paradoxical directives that ". . . begin in and represent extensions or variations of their own views" (Tennen et al., 1981, p. 17). For example, when working with a client whose behavior characterizes a "driver" life-style (Mosak, 1971), the rationale for the prescription may be stated as follows: "Because you are conscientious, you'll want to persist in understanding the basis of the compelling workaholic behavior. You will need to become a steadfast spectator of your own behavior in order to thoroughly understand how the workaholic behavior is perpetuated. Therefore, this week it might be important to (prescribe the symptomatic behavior)." The framework for this paradoxical prescription also incorporates a rationale described by Weeks and L'Abate (1982), that is, recommending that the client learn from observing her or his own symptomatic behavior.

When the client displays a high degree of reactance, the therapist may preface a paradoxical prescription with a rationale that is *incongruous* with the way the client would like to see herself or himself (Rohrbaugh et al., 1981) in order to increase the probability of a *noncompliant* response. Here, the therapist realizes that human movement consists of striving from a "felt-minus" toward a "felt-plus" position (Ansbacher & Ansbacher, 1956). By assuming a one-down subordinate position to the client, the therapist utilizes the client's desire to "overcome" and channels the client's behavior toward the useful side of life. By refusing to implement the prescription the client defeats the therapist and also resolves the presenting complaint. For example, an adolescent may respond to his younger brother with the mistaken goal of power (Dreikurs & Soltz, 1964) and the siblings may find themselves embroiled in conflict. The rationale for the paradoxical prescription to the adolescent may be stated as follows: "It appears that your brother is quite skillful at tricking you into quarrels or fights. Evidently, your brother discovered he can make you upset by simply entering your room, changing the television station, or accusing you of something that isn't true. He is so skillful that it would be very difficult to step out of these conflicts. Perhaps you need to realize that he can force you into becoming angry. Rather than experiencing failure in trying to change, you may need to learn to live with a clever brother. Therefore, this week consider (prescribe the symptomatic behavior)." This rationale also incorporates the idea of the client's learning to live with the present situation (Rohrbaugh et al., 1981).

DISQUALIFYING SIGNIFICANT OTHER AND PRESCRIBING THE PARADOX

Haley's (1976) next two steps consist of (1) disqualifying significant others who are involved in maintaining the client's presenting problem, and (2) prescribing the problematic behavior. Frequently, these steps can be interchanged and suggested within the same session.

Zeig (1980) suggests several issues to consider when prescribing a paradox: (1) the symptom's cognitive, affective, and/or behavioral components can be prescribed, (2) contextual factors of time and place can be incorporated, and (3) elements can be prescribed in ways that highlight the role of the symptom in the client's relationship with significant others. Weeks and L'Abate (1982) have illustrated a procedure that stimulates both intrapersonal and interpersonal insight for the client: "Whenever you feel, think of, hear, see, etc., I want you to (prescribe some concrete behavior)" (p. 143) or "The next time John does—, I want you to (prescribe the symptom)" (pp. 143–144). Both prescriptions foster the client's ability to make associations between feelings, thoughts, or behaviors, and the symptom. As a result, the client learns how his or her problematic behaviors are elicited or motivated, and learns to recognize that the behavior is a voluntary action.

In discussing guidelines for prescribing and scheduling symptomatic behavior, Newton (1968a) mentions that the schedule can be developed in a manner that produces stress for the client. Haley (1984) and Madanes (1984) describe a procedure for making implementation a therapeutic ordeal. These special ordeals expand on Milton Erickson's use of paradox and focus on making a seemingly involuntary act, or symptom, voluntary (Haley, 1984). For instance, the symptomatic behavior can be scheduled for a time when the client would rather be doing something else, or the prescription can direct the client to repeat the symptom deliberately each time it "involuntarily" occurs (Haley, 1984). The prescribed ordeal leads to the client's experiencing ". . . distress equal to or greater than that caused by the symptom" (Haley, 1984, p. 6). As a consequence, the client may give the symptom up in order to avoid the ordeal. When the severity of the ordeal is not rigorous enough to extinguish the symptom, the magnitude of the ordeal can be increased. Haley (1984) also emphasizes that the ordeal must be something the client can legitimately do without producing harm or violating moral standards.

When the level of psychological reactance is high and the symptomatic behavior is described as "unfree" or involuntary, the therapist may focus on prescribing a "free collateral" client behavior (Rohrbaugh et al., 1981). For example, the client who "needs to be right" (Mosak, 1971) may describe her or his *covert* evaluations of others as problematic but unavoidable, while accepting *overt* criticalness (a collateral complaint) as "free" or voluntary behavior. In such a situation, the therapist can prescribe the *collateral* behavior, for example: "You may not be right about wanting to change the nature of your relationship with others. When I provide clients with the opportunity to listen for the hidden meanings of their symptoms, they often realize that they've been mistaken. You could be wrong about wanting to change. Consider giving up your effort to change. During the next week share your critical evaluations while working with colleagues, socializing with friends, and playing with family members." The rationale in this paradoxical prescription is, in part, based on comments by Rohrbaugh et al. (1981) and Weeks and L'Abate (1982). The rationale is framed *incongruently* with the client's self-image (needing to be right) and suggests that the client needs to listen for hidden messages contained in the problematic behavior. The prescription places the client in a position to defeat the therapist *and* to resolve the complaint by refusing to practice the "free collateral" behavior. Since the "free collateral" behavior (overt criticalness) can be influenced, it is hypothesized that the client's interactions with others will improve, in turn bringing about a change in the client's "unfree" or involuntary complaint (covert critical evaluations).

The need for therapeutically disqualifying significant others (Haley, 1976) is congruent with Adler's observation that human beings are social animals and, therefore, client complaints can be understood as problems of cooperation (Ansbacher & Ansbacher, 1956). Indeed, Adler asserted, "It is an irreparable mistake to tear symptoms from their natural context and to regard them in isolation" (Ansbacher & Ansbacher, 1978, p. 406). The therapist may find that significant others in the client's life are inadvertently maintaining or reinforcing the client's presenting complaint. For example, the therapist may ask a significant other, "If Ben's (the client's) procrastination were resolved, how would your relationship change and in what ways would you be required to change?"

At other times, the therapist may disqualify a significant other by relabeling the problem-maintaining behavior with a positive interpretation: "While completing and fulfilling Ben's obligations shows your concern and interest in his work, I wonder if this interaction between you encourages him to be more accountable?" The wife's "control" priority (Mosak, 1971) may complement and reinforce the husband's procrastination. Relabeling the wife's over-involvement with positive intent encourages her to realize that her style helps to maintain the husband's demonstrations of inadequacy. Palazzoli, Boscolo, Cecchin, and Prata (1978) note that positive relabeling decreases the danger of the therapist being disqualified by the client and poses a paradoxical question: "Why does such a good thing (e.g., display of concern and interest) produce difficulties in our relationship?"

Rohrbaugh et al. (1981) suggest utilizing *tandem* paradoxical prescriptions to disqualify significant others and state: "This paradoxical approach tends to be the most effective when the spouse, parent, or friend to be influenced is bothered about the problem and 'sweating' as much or more than the person defined as the problem bearer" (p. 464). In the previous illustration, a rationale for the tandem prescription may have benevolently described the husband-wife interactional pattern as preserving family stability (Papp, 1981): "Ben's (the husband's) failure to complete obligations and your willingness to finish his projects provides many topics for discussion and, thus, provides many opportunities for remaining close and involved with one another." A tandem prescription could direct the husband toward procrastinating during the week, while the wife could be directed to refine or complete those projects that the husband attempted: "During the week, in order to preserve your togetherness, you (the husband) need to continue failing at obligations while you (the wife) continue to complete the projects your husband initiates." If either the client or the significant other ". . . defies the prescription, some change in the usual pattern is inevitable" (Rohrbaugh et al., 1981, p. 464).

Prescribing the paradox at the end of the session prevents the client from commenting on the therapeutic directive and, as a consequence, the client is placed in a double bind (Weeks & L'Abate, 1982). A double bind is experienced as the client leaves the therapist's office and realizes she or he will be accountable for implementing a prescription or a set of behaviors that have previously been identified as problematic and counterproductive. As a result, the client is often forced to encounter her or his egocentricity and, perhaps, private logic. Hence, as Andolfi (1980) suggested, the paradoxical prescription can facilitate a personal and private confrontation without resulting in the client's "losing face."

FOLLOWING UP THE PARADOXICAL PRESCRIPTION

Steps seven and eight in Haley's (1976) model relate to following up the paradoxical prescription. Rohrbaugh et al. (1981) recommend having the client follow through on the ". . . prescription with more the same when the strategy seems to be taking hold" (p. 465). The general rule is when the client discontinues the problematic behavior, the therapist follows up by suggesting that the client is changing too soon or too fast (Weeks & L'Abate, 1982).

If during a follow-up the client reports that the symptomatic behavior has suddenly disappeared, a "paradoxical prediction" may be delivered in which the client is informed that the symptom is likely to reappear (Weeks & L'Abate, 1982). Weeks and L'Abate (1979) mention that the ". . . predictive paradox is designed to help maintain control over the symptom. It is set up so that if the symptom disappears, the client has control over the symptom; and if the symptom continues, then the therapist predicted it, and it is under his control. . . . One way to increase the power of a predictive paradox is to make the prediction and discuss ways the client can make it come true or have the client think of ways to make it come true" (p. 65). If the symptom does reappear, the therapist may follow up with one of two procedures. He or she may provide another paradoxical prescription that incorporates the qualities of an ordeal. Or, clinical judgment may suggest that reappearance of the symptom has confirmed the therapist's predictive powers, which, in the client's eyes, may elevate the therapist to an "expert" position (Minuchin & Fishman, 1981). As a result of the therapist's increased level of influence, it may be possible for him or her to utilize "compliance-based" directives.

When following up a case in which the client has demonstrated a high level of psychological reactance, the therapist may decide to enumerate the protective or stabilizing properties of the symptom (Papp, 1981) and represcribe the original presenting complaint. Or, the therapist can follow up the prescription by actively searching for any part of the prescription that was overlooked or carelessly implemented and critique the client's efforts to exhibit or practice the presenting complaint (Rohrbaugh et al., 1981). Finally, before "prescribing a relapse," the therapist may provide an Ericksonian rationale (Haley, 1973): "I want you to go back and feel as badly as you did when you first came in with the problem, because I want you to see if there is anything from that time that you wish to recover and salvage" (p. 31).

When therapeutic progress is noticed, the therapist avoids accepting credit for client change and may express puzzlement relative to the progress (Haley, 1976). Not accepting credit for client change is an Adlerian device utilized to prevent a client relapse (Ansbacher & Ansbacher, 1956): "One of the most important devices in psychotherapy is to ascribe the work and success of the therapy to the patient at whose disposal one places oneself in a friendly way, as a coworker" (p. 338). Eventually, the presenting problem is dropped and, perhaps, the therapist and the client can decide to explore other issues.

SUMMARY

Haley's (1976) eight-step model and the accompanying references provide a conceptual framework for expanding the Adlerian perspective on implementing paradoxical prescriptions. The primary purpose of the paradoxical prescription is to disrupt nonproductive behavioral patterns. Proficiency with paradoxical prescriptions is associated with skill development: Conceptual skills are developed with a theoretical understanding of Individual Psychology; conceptual skills are also developed with a theoretical understanding of the paradoxical procedure (some pertinent reviews are listed in the reference section); and therapeutic skills are enhanced by receiving supervision in the delivery of paradoxical prescriptions.

The reader should realize that paradoxical prescriptions are not panaceas in psychotherapy, but that therapeutic outcomes are dependent on interventions that precede and follow the paradoxical prescription (Zeig, 1980).

REFERENCES

Andolfi, M. (1980). Prescribing the families own dysfunctional rules as a therapeutic strategy. *Journal of Marital and Family Therapy, 6*, 29–36.

Ansbacher, H. L., & Ansbacher, R. R. (1956). *The individual psychology of Alfred Adler: A systemic presentation in selections from his writings.* New York: Basic Books.

Ansbacher, H. L., & Ansbacher, R. R. (1978). *Cooperation between the sexes.* Garden City, New York: Anchor Books, Doubleday.

Bateson, G., Jackson, D. D., Haley, J., & Weakland, J. (1956). Toward a theory of schizophrenia. *Behavioral Science, 1*, 251–264.

Brehm, S. (1976). *The application of social psychology to clinical practice.* Washington, D. C.: Hemisphere.

Dreikurs, R. (1956). Goals in therapy. *American Journal of Psychoanalysis, 16*, 18–23.

Dreikurs, R., & Soltz, V. (1964). *Children the challenge.* New York: Hawthorn Books.

Dunlap, K. (1928). A revision of the fundamental law of habit formation. *Science, 67*, 360–362.

Dunlap, K. (1939). Repetition in the breaking of habits. *Scientific Monthly, 39*, 66–70.

Dunlap, K. (1942). The technique of negative practice. *American Journal of Psychology, 55*, 270–273.

Erickson, M. H. (1967). The use of symptoms as an integral part of hypnotherapy. In J. Haley (Ed.), *Advanced techniques of hypnosis and therapy: Selected papers of Milton H. Erickson, M.D.* (pp. 500–509). New York: Grune & Stratton.

Fisch, R., Weakland, J. H., Watzlawick, P., Segal, L., Hoebel, F. C., & Deardorff, C. M. (1975). *Learning brief therapy: An introductory manual*. Palo Alto, CA: Mental Research Institute (not available on the open market).

Frankl, V. (1960). Paradoxical intention: A logotherapeutic technique. *American Journal of Psychotherapy, 14*, 520–535.

Frankl, V. (1975). Paradoxical intention and dereflection. *Psychotherapy: Theory, Research and Practice, 12*, 226–237.

Haley, J. (1963). *Strategies of Psychotherapy*. New York: Grune & Stratton.

Haley, J. (1973). *Uncommon therapy: The psychiatric techniques of Milton H. Erickson, M.D.* New York: W. W. Norton.

Haley, J. (1976). *Problem-solving therapy: New strategies for effective family therapy*. San Francisco: Jossey-Bass.

Haley, J. (1984). *Ordeal therapy: Unusual ways to change behavior*. San Francisco: Jossey-Bass.

Jacobson, N., & Margolin, G. (1979). *Marital therapy: Strategies based on social learning and behavioral exchange principles*. New York: Brunner/Mazel.

Lankton, S. R., & Lankton, C. H. (1983). *The answer within: A clinical framework of Ericksonian hypnotherapy*. New York: Brunner/Mazel.

Madanes, C. (1984). *Behind the one-way mirror: Advances in the practice of strategic therapy*. San Francisco: Jossey-Bass.

Minuchin, S., & Fishman, H. (1981). *Family therapy techniques*. Cambridge: Harvard University Press.

Mosak, H. (1971). Lifestyle. In A. G. Nikelly (Ed.), *Techniques for behavior change: Applications of Adlerian theory* (pp. 77–81). Springfield: Charles C. Thomas.

Mozdzierz, G. J., Macchitelli, F. J., & Lisiecki, J. (1976). The paradox in psychotherapy: An Adlerian perspective. *Journal of Individual Psychology, 32*, 169–184.

Newton, J. R. (1968a). Considerations for the psychotherapeutic technique of symptom scheduling. *Psychotherapy: Theory, Research and Practice, 5*, 95–103.

Newton, J. R. (1968b). Therapeutic paradoxes, paradoxical intentions, and negative practice. *American Journal of Psychotherapy, 22*, 68–81.

Palazzoli, M., Boscolo, L., Cecchin, G., & Prata, G. (1978). *Paradox and counterparadox: A new model in the therapy of the family in schizophrenic transaction.* New York: Jason Aronson.

Papp, P. (1981). Paradoxes. In S. Minuchin & H. Fishman (Eds.), *Family therapy techniques.* Cambridge: Harvard University Press.

Raskin, D., & Klein, Z. (1976). Losing a symptom through keeping it: A review of paradoxical treatment techniques and rationale. *Archives of General Psychiatry, 33,* 548–555.

Rohrbaugh, M., Tennen, H., Press, S., & White, L. (1981). Compliance, defiance, and therapeutic paradox: Guidelines for strategic use of paradoxical interventions. *American Journal of Orthopsychiatry, 51,* 454–467.

Rossi, E. L. (Ed.). (1980). *The collected papers of Milton H. Erickson on hypnosis. Volume III: Hypnotic investigation of psychodynamic processes.* New York: Irvington.

Tennen, H., Rohrbaugh, M., Press, S., & White, L. (1981). Reactance theory and therapeutic paradox: A compliance-defiance model. *Psychotherapy: Theory, Research and Practice, 18,* 14–22.

Watzlawick, P., Weakland, J., & Fisch, R. (1974). *Change: Principles of problem formation and problem resolution.* New York: W. W. Norton.

Weeks, G. R., & L'Abate, L. (1979). A compilation of paradoxical methods. *The American Journal of Family Therapy, 7,* 61–76.

Weeks, G., & L'Abate, L. (1982). *Paradoxical psychotherapy: Theory and practice with individuals, couples and families.* New York: Brunner/Mazel.

West, J., & Zarski, J. (1983a). Paradoxical interventions used during systemic family therapy: Considerations for practitioners. *Family Therapy, 19,* 125–134.

West, J., & Zarski, J. (1983b). The counselor's use of the paradoxical procedure in family therapy. *The Personnel and Guidance Journal, 62,* 34–37.

Zeig, J. K. (1980). Symptoms prescription techniques: Clinical applications using elements of communication. *The American Journal of Clinical Hypnosis, 23,* 23–33.

TRAPS AND ESCAPES: AN ADLERIAN APPROACH TO UNDERSTANDING RESISTANCE AND RESOLVING IMPASSES IN PSYCHOTHERAPY

Richard Royal Kopp
A professor at the California School of Professional Psychology, Los Angeles. He is on the faculties of ICASSI and of the Americas Institute for Adlerian Studies, is on the board of Individual Education International, and is a consulting editor for *Individual Psychology*. Kopp maintains a private practice in Sherman Oaks, California.

Carol Kivel
Lives in Tucson, Arizona.

The purpose of this article is to present an Adlerian approach to understanding resistance in therapy and to resolving the impasses which result. It will be seen that Adlerian theory is an effective framework for integrating paradoxical (humanistic and cognitive-behavioral) approaches to psychotherapy, offering a rationale for using therapeutic paradox which is grounded in a psychodynamic and interpersonal theory of resistance. (The term "psychodynamic" refers to a group of theories which emphasize unconscious [or what we in this paper refer to as "nonconscious"] motivation.)

The authors wish to thank Terese Bell, Ph.D. and Kathy Brownell for their contributions to this article, and Bernard Shulman, Harold Mosak, Stanley Pavey, and Arthur Kovacs for their helpful comments.
Individual Psychology, 46(2), June, 1990, **pp. 139–147**

SYMPTOMS AND RESISTANCE

According to Adler (1964), "All neurotic symptoms have as their object the task of safeguarding the patient's self-esteem and thereby also the lifeline [later, life-style] into which he has grown" (p. 263). The life-style consists of a system of beliefs about oneself, life, and others; a psychological (nonconscious) goal representing a person's subjective view of what would constitute a sense of significance, security, and self-esteem; and those behavioral strategies a person typically uses to move in the direction of his/her goal. As a creation of the client, the life-style functions relatively well until an "exogenous factor" appears. The exogenous factor is "a change, a shift, or an interruption in life for which the individual does not feel adequately prepared, and to which he or she makes a mistaken response" (Griffith & Powers, 1984, p. 26). In the current literature, the terms "stress" or "stressors" refer to examples of exogenous factors. Symptoms appear as part of that "mistaken" response to the exogenous factor: mistaken because, while they serve to safeguard the self-esteem and the life-style, they also prevent an effective solution to the situation the person confronts. While the client does suffer from the symptom, he or she has a nonconscious investment in maintaining the symptom for the protection it affords the self-esteem and life-style. This threat to the self-esteem generates a fear of change, rooted in what Adler termed the fear of being proven worthless (Adler, 1964). Thus, the interest in maintaining the symptoms and the life-style is a basic characteristic of resistance in therapy. The therapist may also be seen by the client as an obstruction to the client's neurotic strivings, and the client "will attempt to depreciate the physician, to deprive him of his influence" (Adler, 1964, p. 337).

PHASE 1: SETTING THE TRAP— THE CLIENT'S RESISTANCE

"Traps and Escapes," a model developed by the senior author, seems to offer a useful metaphor for understanding and resolving client resistance: (a) the trap is first set by the client, (b) then sprung by the therapist, after which, (c) the therapist feels stuck and must, (d) "escape" if therapy is to proceed. The client communicates resistance by sending a paradoxical message. For example, stating that "My marriage is bad and I want to make things better," while acting so as to continue the conflict represents a paradoxical message. Or, "I pressure myself to keep busy. I want to slow down and relax," while continuing to stay busy and complain about the pressure and fast pace of life. The trap is set only if the message is paradoxical, and the message is paradoxical only if there is an inconsistency between the client's *stated message* and the client's *actual intent*, whether conscious or nonconscious. The actual intent or "hidden message," is reflected in the client's behavior. Thus, inconsistency between *words* (stated message or intent) and *action* (real message or intent) typically characterizes the paradoxical message and represents what is referred to as resistance.

PHASE 2: SPRINGING THE TRAP—IMPASSE RESULTING FROM THE THERAPIST'S ACCEPTANCE OF THE CLIENT'S PARADOXICAL MESSAGE

The trap is sprung only when the therapist steps into it. The goal is not to prevent the patient from setting traps, but rather to help the therapist avoid stepping into them. The trap is sprung when the therapist accepts as valid the *stated* aspect of a paradoxical message. An impasse is the inevitable result. In the examples mentioned above, the trap is sprung if the therapist accepts the stated message from the client (e.g., "I want to improve my marriage" or "I want to relax"), and thus works with the client for improvement as expressed in words rather than actions. Note that if there were no resistance (i.e., if the stated message was consistent with the client's behavior) the client would be less fearful of change and would be inclined to respond cooperatively and positively to the therapist's support, advice, and direct encouragement.

RESISTANCE AS A CONFLICT BETWEEN THERAPIST AND CLIENT

From the Adlerian view, the resistance is a conflict of movement and goals between therapist and client. Every individual is seen as always in movement from a perceived "minus" position (i.e., a position of feeling inferior, insecure, or worthless), to a perceived "plus" position (i.e., a position of feeling superior, secure, or worthwhile). "'Movement' includes all thought, feeling and action; the 'law of movement' of the individual is therefore the basis of the Style of Living" (Griffith & Powers, 1984, p. 10). Movement concerns what is actually happening, not what the client says is happening. Thus, movement expresses the client's life-style based on the cognitive frame of reference and the nonconscious goal the individual has created. The self-consistent unity of the life-style requires the individual move in only one direction.

Adlerian therapists assess life-style movement by observing behavior and using techniques such as interpreting early recollections (Baruth and Eckstein, 1981; Mosak, Schneider & Mosak, 1980; Olson, 1979; Powers & Griffith, 1987), dreams (Dreikurs, 1967; Gold, 1981), and family constellation (Mosak, 1972; Powers & Griffith, 1987; Shulman, 1962).

PHASE 3: BEING STUCK—THE DOUBLE-BIND OF A TRAP WHICH IS SPRUNG

Once the trap has been sprung, the therapist is in a *double-bind* since the therapist is working in conflict with the client's actual movement which is designed to safeguard the client's self-esteem. The therapist must free him/herself from this double-bind if the impasse is to be resolved. In the first example, the double-bind is created because the therapist's efforts are in conflict with the client's movement, i.e., (a) resistive, aggressive, or critical behavior toward the spouse, (b) the ways in which such behavior is believed by the client to maintain his/her sense of security, and (c) fears associated with improvement in the marriage. In the second example, attempts by the therapist to help the client slow down and relax conflict with the client's use of keeping busy as a safeguard or protection against perceived, anticipated failure.

The therapist's disjunctive feelings, (e.g., anger, inattention, day-dreaming, allowing interruptions in the therapy session, feeling interrupted by the fact of the client's appointment, and boredom) often indicate an impasse.

Often there is "parallel transference" between the therapist and client, that is, the therapist's countertransference issues are related in content and structure to the paradoxical dilemmas of the client. Becoming aware of the complementary relationship between the movement and goals of the client and therapist can help the therapist understand how these issues contributed to acceptance of the stated message and thus to the resistance/impasse (Kopp & Robles, 1989).

PHASE 4: THE ESCAPE—THE THERAPIST RESOLVES THE IMPASSE BY ALIGNING HIS OR HER MOVEMENT WITH THE ACTUAL MOVEMENT OF THE CLIENT

When there is resistance, a "tug of war" is taking place as therapist and client struggle to move in opposing directions. To escape the impasse, the therapist "puts down his or her end of the rope," thereby acknowledging that the client's resistance involves a resistance to the therapist's attempts to produce change in the client. The "escape" occurs when the therapist aligns his/her movement and goal with the client's real life-style movement and goal. In Adler's words, "I know that if I allow it, he will no longer want to do it. I know that if I hinder him, he will start a war. I always agree" (1964, p. 347).

One method of escape is by what Adler called "spitting in the patient's soup" (Dreikurs, 1967). With this metaphor, Adler suggests that the therapist does not take away the soup (the behavior or symptom) but does render it distasteful for the client (by "reframing" its meaning). "What we must always look for is the purpose for which the symptom is adopted and the coherence of this purpose with the general goal of superiority" (Adler, 1980, p. 63). Often, the goal of the symptom must be changed or the client will retain the same goal and, through symptom substitution, simply find another means to reach it (Mosak, 1968).

Another way of describing this very effective means of dealing with the paradoxical message is the therapeutic paradox (Riebel, 1984; Weeks & L'Abate, 1982). From the Adlerian viewpoint, what makes the paradox so powerful is that the client is forced to cooperate, either with the therapist by following the paradoxical prescription or with the world at large by opposing the therapeutic suggestion (Mozdzierz, Macchitelli, & Lisiecki, 1976). Since the neurotic goal involves a perceived position of superiority over others, it is contrary to the cooperation and social interest (Gemein-schaftsgefühl) of healthy functioning. "All my efforts are devoted toward increasing the social interest of the patient. I know that the real reason for his malady is his lack of cooperation, and I want him to see it too. As soon as he can connect himself with his fellow men on an equal and cooperative footing, he is cured" (Adler, 1964, p. 347). One way to create a therapeutic paradox is through reframing (Riebel, 1984; Weeks & L'Abate, 1982). This approach changes the meaning of a symptom from a negative to a positive. It also enables the therapist to maintain a nonthreatening, noncombative posture, aligned with the real movement of the client. If, for example, a client complains of wanting to be independent by moving into his or her own apartment away from his or her parents but claims this is not possible ("I want to be independent. Can you help me?"), the therapist might respond, "It sounds as if you want to be on your own but have decided the time isn't right, so you've made the decision to stay where you are for a while." This response does not threaten the client's real movement, it supports and encourages the client, showing that, by being responsible for his or her own acts, he or she is choosing to remain at home.

Prescription of the symptom may also be helpful and can be presented in a number of ways. The first author has found it helpful to group symptom prescription strategies in order of decreasing intensity and paradoxical confrontation: (a) intensify or exaggerate the symptom, (b) continue the symptom, (c) give up the symptom if you want, but do it slowly, or (d) give up the symptom, but keep it ready in case you need it.

For example, in response to the trap "I want to slow down and relax," the therapist might say, "I'm not sure it would be a good idea for you to relax like other people. If you slowed down, you wouldn't get as much accomplished, and then you wouldn't feel as good about yourself" (spitting in the soup, reframing the behavior). Possible paradoxical confrontations might be to tell the client: (a) you might profit from increasing the pressure you put on yourself (intensification), (b) you ought to continue to keep busy (continuation), (c) you should relax only for short periods while cutting back on your schedule a little at a time (slow discontinuation), (d) you ought to be ready to resume your busy schedule if you feel unproductive or lazy (discontinuance insurance).

Each of these methods may enable the therapist to escape from the trap.

CASE EXAMPLE

Background

Barbara initially came to the clinic because she was having difficulty with her adolescent son. Her son was consistently in trouble at home and at school, had very poor interpersonal relationships, and poor academic functioning.

A theme running through the sessions had been Barbara's complaints about her mother's "constant interference" in Barbara's life. Eighteen months ago when Barbara had discovered her husband in bed with a neighbor, Barbara's mother had virtually planned, paid for, and moved Barbara and her children across the country. Barbara lived with her parents until her mother found and made all the arrangements for Barbara to move into an apartment two blocks away. Mother loaned money, bought food, clothes, etc., and since Barbara did not have a car, mother let her share the family car.

Mother and daughter call each other every day. Lately mother has done the calling because Barbara doesn't want this "interference" and yet will not tell her mother this. By doing this Barbara puts the responsibility for the interference on mother while still having mother around to tell her what to do.

The Paradoxical Message: "Yes, But"

Barbara takes a "yes, but" stance, presenting herself as a victim of her terrible life, feeling entitled to be taken care of. Lately this has been uncomfortable for her so she rearranged her environment so she would still be taken care of and be able to complain about it at the same time. Barbara talked about being "independent" (yes: "I want to live my own life without my mother always telling me what to do"). She has made no moves to become independent or less dependent in any way (but: "I can't afford my own car"; "I don't want to hurt my mother's feelings").

The Intervention

At this session Barbara was again complaining about her mother's interference and her own desires to be independent. Since the therapist was almost certain that she did not want to be independent, that she was afraid of it, a paradoxical intervention was chosen.

> **Barbara:** *I just want to be independent. I don't want to be so dependent on my mother; I'm tired of her making all the decisions.*
> **Therapist:** *Barbara, I've been thinking a lot about this lately because it is so important to you. I think it might be too soon for you to break away from your mother (her words from an earlier session).*
> **Barbara:** *What do you mean? I'm tired of being dependent; I'm so tired of her and it's frustrating. I want to be on my own.*
> **Therapist:** *I can really appreciate that. It must be difficult to have your mother so tied to you. I still believe it might be better for you to be dependent for a while longer. In fact I think that some of the things you've done lately such as not calling her may have been premature. For a while, at least, you may need to become more dependent.*
> **Barbara:** *I'm not so sure of that. She likes it but I don't.*
> **Therapist:** *Still, perhaps it's best not to break away too soon. You deserve to be taken care of by your mother.*

The Outcome

The therapist reported that within the week Barbara began to look for an apartment that was further away from her parents' house; she moved the following month and didn't seek out advice or help from her mother or father through the whole procedure. She arranged for and got a car loan and bought a car. She told her mother that she wasn't going to call her every day and told her not to call either (mother responded with, "I'm sure glad because I'm tired of having to tell you what to do all the time. It's about time you grew up"). She told her son he was going to have to accept the responsibility for his behavior, that she wasn't going to intervene every time he got into trouble at school. She's lost much of the weight she's talked about losing for years and has started doing things with her friends on the weekends. She's also lost much of the whiny, little girl quality that was so pervasive in her style of communicating. She reported that the "kids must be finally growing up because they aren't into so much trouble and Susan (her nine-year-old) doesn't whine all the time like she used to."

Barbara said that the therapist had been wrong after all, that she didn't need to be more dependent. She also stopped seeking the therapist's advice for every thing that went wrong or every problem she had with her children. The family began developing problem-solving techniques on their own, experienced success, and gained confidence in their abilities.

SUMMARY

A model, "Traps and Escapes" based on Adlerian principles was described, which offers an understanding of resistance in therapy as a paradoxical, conflictual interaction between therapist and client, and a method of resolving the impasses which can result. A case example illustrated this approach and its outcome.

REFERENCES

Adler, A. (1964). *The Individual Psychology of Alfred Adler*. H. L. Ansbacher & R. R. Ansbacher (Eds.). New York: Harper Torchbooks.

Adler, A. (1980). *What life should mean to you*. New York: Penguin Books.

Baruth, L., & Eckstein, D. (Eds.). (1981). *Life style: Theory, practice, and research* (2d ed.). Dubuque, IA: Kendall/Hunt.

Dreikurs, R. (1967). The meaning of dreams. In R. Dreikurs, *Psychodynamics, psychotherapy and counseling*. Chicago: IL: Alfred Adler Institute.

Gold, L. (1981). Lifestyles and dreams. In L. Baruth & D. Eckstein (Eds.), *Life style: Theory practice and research* (2d ed.). Dubuque, IA: Kendall/Hunt.

Griffith, J., & Powers, R. L. (1984). *An Adlerian lexicon.* Chicago: The Americas Institute of Adlerian Studies, Ltd.

Kopp, R., & Robles, L. (1989). Single-session, therapist-focused model of supervision of resistance based on Adlerian Psychology. *Individual Psychology, 45*(1, 2), 212–219.

Mosak, H. (1968). The interrelatedness of neurosis through central themes. *Journal of Individual Psychology, 24*, 67–70.

Mosak, H. (1972). Life style assessment: A demonstration focused on family constellation. *Journal of Individual Psychology*, 28, 232–247.

Mosak, H., Schneider, S., & Mosak, L. (1980). *Life style: A workbook.* Chicago: Alfred Adler Institute.

Mozdzierz, G., Macchitelli, F., & Lisiecki, J. (1976). The paradox in psychotherapy: An Adlerian perspective. *Journal of Individual Psychology, 32*, 169–184.

Olson, H. A. (1979). *Early recollections: Their use in diagnosis and psychotherapy.* Springfield, IL: Charles C. Thomas.

Powers, R., & Griffith, J. (1987). *Understanding life-style: The psychoclarity process.* Chicago: The Americas Institute of Adlerian Studies.

Riebel, L. (1984). Paradoxical intention strategies: A review of rationales. *Psychotherapy: Theory, Research & Practice, 21*(2), 260–272.

Shulman, B. (1962). The family constellation in personality diagnosis. *Journal of Individual Psychology, 18*, 35–47.

Weeks, G. R., & L'Abate, L. (1982). *Paradoxical therapy: Theory and practice with individuals, couples, and families.* New York: Brunner/Mazel.

Part G
HYPNOSIS

INCORPORATING HYPNOTHERAPEUTIC METHODS INTO ONGOING PSYCHOTHERAPY

Len Sperry
Associate professor of psychiatry and preventive medicine at the Medical College of Wisconsin and a diplomate of both the American Board of Psychiatry and Neurology and the American Board of Professional Psychology.

What practical value does hypnotherapy have for psychotherapists who have no formal training—or inclination to undertake formal training—in hypnosis? I believe certain hypnotherapeutic methods have considerable value and utility for clinicians whose primary identity and work is with insight-oriented psychotherapies. The plan of this paper is to describe five such hypnotherapy techniques and their value and application in the course of ongoing psychotherapy. None of these methods require formal trance induction or deepening. All are easily learned and compatible with the therapeutic style of a clinician who believes that treatment should be respectful, cooperative, and a collaborative relationship with a client or patient (Adler, 1956; Barber, 1985).

THE NEW HYPNOTHERAPEUTIC APPROACH

Psychotherapists who value personal enrichment, patient self-mastery and responsibility, as well as establishing a collaborative treatment agreement with the patient tend to find that the emphasis and the focus of traditional hypnosis is

Individual Psychology, 46(4), December, 1990, **pp. 443–450**

somewhat alien to their values. In the past few years, the pendulum has swung away from the Traditionalist view of hypnosis with its emphasis on pathology, hypnotizability, and therapist authority and ability. Ellenberger (1970) has carefully traced the history of two opposing orientations to psychotherapy from the beginning of western civilization until today. In describing the history of hypnotherapy, Ellenberger notes that the two opposing orientations were embodied in the Salpetriere School of Charcot, Janet, and, later, Freud. The other orientation was associated with the Nancy School of Bernheim and Liebault. Today, descendents of the Salpetriere School are called Traditionalists, while descendents of the Nancy School are called Naturalistic (Erickson & Rossi, 1979), Experiential (Barber, 1985), or the New Hypnosis (Araoz, 1982, 1985).

The Naturalistic and Experiential approaches are quite compatible with the theory of Individual Psychology. In both these hypnotherapy approaches and Individual Psychology, a premium is placed on the cooperation and collaboration between clinician and client. Respect and a focus on patient strengths, growth, and education are common. Self-hypnosis is considered the basis of the "new" approach (Barber, 1985; Araoz, 1985). So also is an emphasis on tailoring treatment to the needs and styles of the patient. Erickson is quoted by Zeig (1982): "Each patient is an individual. Hence, psychotherapy should be formulated to meet the uniqueness of the individual's needs, rather than tailoring the person to fit the Procrustean bed of a hypothetical theory of human behavior" (p. VII).

Five hypnotherapeutic techniques gleaned from the Experiential tradition are outlined below with their suggested applications. None of these techniques require the induction of a formal trance. Each has been shown to be powerful in altering the course of insight-focused psychotherapy. The techniques are: the somatic bridge, the emotional bridge, a dissociative technique, story telling, and reframing.

SOMATIC BRIDGE

The somatic bridge is a variant of the affect bridge described by Watkins (1978). It is also similar to Gendlin's focusing method (1978). The somatic bridge is a way of utilizing awareness of an individual's body to facilitate awareness of unexpressed feelings. The somatic bridge is particularly effective with individuals who are overly rational, logical, and left-brained, or who have underdeveloped intuitive, symbolic, and affective capacities, which are functions of the right brain. This technique is particularly effective for patients who have difficulty in identifying feelings. Araoz (1985) notes that the usual outcome of using this technique is that a host of meaningful memories of psychological connection rush to the patient's awareness, providing significant therapeutic material.

The purpose of utilizing the somatic bridge is for the patient to become aware of somatic sensations, focusing attention on these sensations and letting them develop, while paying attention to mental images, memories, and psychological connections. The technique is introduced in the course of psychotherapy when the patient states they have nothing to talk about or that their emotions are "flat." The therapist begins by asking the patient to sit quietly and focus their attention on their body. She tells the patient that the purpose is not to talk about the sensations but to experience them. The therapist encourages the patient to be silent and let distractions come and go. When the patient has been able to focus on one body part, the therapist says: "Now, let the awareness of your body lead you to something which was hidden in the recesses of your mind. Just wonder what will come up: memories, images, joys, pains. Whatever comes is okay. Your inner mind will speak to you in a new way through your body. Take your time. Let it happen and you'll learn important things about yourself. You will be surprised and pleased" (Araoz, 1985). Both Watkins and Araoz indicate that the careful diagnosis is assumed before using this technique. They note that psychotic-prone individuals should not be exposed to this method carelessly, since it can result in dissociations with a sense of lack of control.

EMOTIONAL BRIDGE

This hypnotherapeutic intervention has been described by Watkins (1978) and modified by Araoz (1985). This intervention is particularly useful when a patient is experiencing an emotion which the therapist believes may be related to past experiences of events, but for which the patient is not able to make the connection. The idea is that the current emotion can act as a "bridge" to other past instances of the same feeling, allowing the patient to broaden his awareness and thus to new knowledge about self. Araoz (1985) describes an example of a female patient who experienced a significant degree of confusion whose origin could not be understood in terms of current events in her life. The therapist suggested that the patient stay with her confused feeling and concentrate on physically experiencing the confusion to its utmost. The therapist added that she could allow any memories and mental images connected in any way to the confusion to emerge. This was sufficient to establish a psychological link between the patient's present confusion and significant past events where confusion was also experienced. If there is no immediate reaction, Araoz becomes more explicit and says: "You have been confused before. Perhaps not exactly like now. Allow your inner mind to connect this confusion with some other confusion of the past. Take your time, relax, and just let confusion—here and in the present—absorb all your being" (Araoz, 1985).

DISSOCIATIVE TECHNIQUE

Dissociative techniques are ways of separating the patient's self from problematic feelings, behaviors, and thoughts. Too often, patients will overidentify with a concern: "I am . . ."; "I feel . . ."; or "I keep thinking . . .," so that they become convinced that the thought, feeling, or behavior is their very self. The psychotherapist's role then becomes to aid patients in recognizing that such life-denying thoughts, feelings, or words do not emanate from the whole self, but are coming from a part—a less healthy part—of themselves. In short, the therapist helps the patient to dissociate the negative feeling, thought, mood, or action from the self.

Next time the patient says "I feel . . ." the therapist asks the patient to check what the opposite part in them is thinking, feeling, or saying. For example, if the patient is anxious, the therapist asks the patient to listen to what the anxious part is saying inside, if there is another part that is not agreeing with the anxious part, and then to verbalize what this part is saying. The goal is to encourage the patient to identify with the new part, to become the new part, and to be aware of how this new part feels. Just as with the emotional bridge and the somatic bridge, it is not sufficient for the patient to talk about this sensation or the feeling or the new part but to become the sensation, the feeling, or the new part. It is suggested that the patient be allowed to take some time to deeply experience this new part before discussing the experience and the memories and other feelings that are triggered by it.

There are several dissociative techniques that are described in the hypnotherapy literature (Erickson & Rossi, 1979). These techniques have many possibilities and permutations that are limited only by the psychotherapist's creativity.

STORY TELLING

Story telling is also called parable and metaphor by different writers. It is basically a technique of presenting a short story containing a message or moral unique to the patient, though it is not explicit. The purpose is to bypass consciousness (i.e., resistance, evaluation, analysis, and intellectualization) so that the therapist can metaphorically implant strategies for change which match the needs of the patient.

Stories told with animation, changing tones, and appropriate body posture and gestures encourage right-brain imagery and thus bypass conscious resistance of the patient. When stories are told confidently in a natural, casual manner and with some clear rationale, the patient will usually listen attentively to the story. A rule of thumb in story telling is that the therapist not analyze or process the story but rather go right into another topic after completing the story. Stories may be personal, involving the therapist's own life or friends, or they may be pulled from any number of sources including source books of therapeutic metaphors such as that of Rosen (1982). Suppose a patient is overly dependent and fearful of risk taking. Through direct discussion and interpretation the therapist may have pointed out the illusions of overprotective living and that failing to take risks is a defeat in the long run. When the patient shows indications of resistance, the therapist might turn toward the storytelling intervention. He might tell about the minister who is preaching to his congregation one Sunday morning about a much heralded basketball game in South Bend, Indiana. The minister said that even though it was a heralded game, it actually wasn't much of a game because one side was much bigger and stronger than the other side. The minister went on to describe the game in some interesting detail and noted that toward the end of the game the underdog team was losing—but only by six points. As time was running out, the underdog's coach called a time out and said to his team, "Look guys, we can win this game. Even though they are bigger than us, Marcus is quicker than any of them. Give the ball to Marcus, and we can win this game." The team went back on the floor and immediately passed the ball to Marcus who doubled-dribbled, resulting in the ball being turned over to the other team. The second time the underdogs got the ball they didn't pass it to Marcus and nothing much happened. Again the coach was bewildered and angry. The same thing happened the third time the team got the ball. Time ran out and the team lost the game. When it was over, the coach said to the two guards, "Why didn't you pass the ball to Marcus?" The guards answered, "Marcus didn't want the ball!" The minister went on to explain the moral by discussing Marcus' reluctance to take a risk and by using such metaphors as "You don't swing at anything—you don't hit anything," and "You can't steal second with one foot tied to first."

Adlerian psychotherapists from Adler to Dreikurs and, more recently, Mosak have utilized therapeutic story telling. Mosak (1987) has collected 150 such therapeutic stories and anecdotes to be incorporated into ongoing psychotherapy.

REFRAMING

Reframing is an integral part of most psychotherapeutic approaches. In some approaches, such as the Adlerian and the strategic, reframing is highlighted as a therapeutic intervention. In many other approaches its use is implied. Sherman and Dinkmeyer (1987) say that Adlerians use reframing as a major device throughout therapy to: "change negatives into positives, to assign good intentions to participants, to change the climate in the system, to help disengage power plays, and to provide encouragement in place of discouragement." They also note that reframing has been called "positive interpretation." Reframing assumes that an unhealthy pattern of behavior has payoffs—that is, it benefits the patient in some way or ways. And treatment must take these payoffs into account. Reframing recognizes the payoffs present with any unhealthy pattern. Reframing is respectful of the patient and his or her behaviors. When a therapist communicates an understanding that the destructive pattern has actually been helping the patient, resistance seems to lessen. Instead of fighting with the patient, as many other persons have done, the clinician is able through reframing to "ally" himself or herself with the patient or the patient's resistance. In reframing, the patient, not the clinician, does most of the therapeutic work. Reframing utilizes the patient's own inner power and resources to construct alternate patterns of thought and behavior. Reframing has been discussed in detail by several persons including Bandler and Grinder (1982) and Citrenbaum, King, and Cohen (1985). Both these sources suggest six basic steps of reframing. They are: identify the habit to the pattern to be changed; establish communication with that part of the patient that has been responsible for the pattern; separate the positive intentions of the pattern from the payoffs or benefits to the patient; suggest that the patient generate new behaviors that provide the needed payoffs; check to see that the alternative patterns are acceptable to all parts of the person; and check out alternative patterns of behavior within relevant future contexts. The following case study demonstrates the use of full-scale reframing done as part of ongoing psychotherapy.

The patient was a 42-year-old married male who worked as an account executive. He had been employed by the same brokerage firm for 10 years and had begun to experience intense anxiety and insomnia following a severe downturn in the market about two months before seeking therapy. He had been involved in psychotherapy for 11 sessions before mentioning his concern about weight. He weighed 40 pounds more than his ideal weight and had made numerous attempts in the past two years to lose this weight with little success. As a result of the psychotherapy he was now sleeping better and had much more tolerable levels of anxiety. He asked the therapist if the focus of treatment could now include his weight. The therapist agreed and assisted the patient to become relaxed with the use of some guided imagery. During the reframing process, the patient experienced that part of him that was responsible for his overeating and being overweight as a "hard, scary feeling in the pit of my stomach." However, the patient was unable to sway the object of his fear. Next, the therapist proceeded to identify the task for the overeating and overweight. The therapist presented several possible payoffs: "I really don't know what your payoffs are for being overweight, but I can recall what some other patients have become aware of. One man who was here yesterday became aware that his eating was a way to comfort and gratify himself when he felt lonely. Another man who was in a troubled marriage relationship became aware of the fear that losing weight would be the first step in leaving the marriage to find a more suitable spouse, and he wanted to avoid the hurt of separation and divorce. He was also afraid to be alone if he did separate from his wife. A woman who was here approximately three weeks ago discovered that she couldn't diet because she was angry and resentful of her father's demands that she lose weight."

The patient noticeably reacted to these last two payoffs. After mentioning a few additional payoffs, the therapist focused on the two payoffs that the patient had reacted to resulting in the patient's awareness of these payoffs to the situation. Prior to this point, the patient had maintained that his marriage was healthy and supportive. He was now able to articulate some of the concerns that he had previously been unwilling to admit. The therapist and patient explored healthier alternatives to overeating and being overweight that would provide the patient the safety he needed but would be more satisfying. He decided to risk beginning to lose weight with the realization that this might "lead to a lot of other changes" but that it was always his choice to go with it or not. Following this session, the patient was able to be assertive and honest with his wife instead of passively resisting her by not giving in to her demands to lose weight. These alternative patterns helped the patient to feel more powerful and to deal more constructively with the problems of his marital relationship. Six conjoint sessions focusing on marital issues occurred before treatment was successfully terminated and the patient had met his goal of losing 40 pounds.

CONCLUDING NOTE

This paper has sketched the utility of five representative techniques derived from hypnotherapy that can be easily incorporated into the course of nearly any ongoing psychotherapy. These and similar techniques which do not require a formal trance induction are quite compatible with the tenets of Individual Psychology and basically all other humanistic psychotherapy systems.

REFERENCES

Adler, A. (1956). *The Individual Psychology of Alfred Adler*. H. Ansbacher and R. Ansbacher (Eds.). New York: Basic Books.

Araoz, D. (1982). *Hypnosis and sex therapy*. New York: Brunner/Mazel.

Araoz, D. (1985). *The new hypnosis*. New York: Brunner/Mazel.

Bandler, R., and Grinder, J. (1982). *Reframing: Neuro-linguistic programming and the transformation of meaning*. Moab, UT: Real People Press.

Barber, T. (1985). Hypnosuggestive procedures as catalysts for psychotherapies. In S. Lynn and J. Garske (Eds.), *Contemporary psychotherapies: Models and methods*. Columbus, OH: Charles Merrill.

Citrenbaum, C., King, M., and Cohen, W. (1985). *Modern clinical hypnosis for habit control*. New York: W. W. Norton.

Ellenberger, H. (1970). *The discovery of the unconscious: The history and evolution of dynamic psychiatry*. New York: Basic Books.

Erickson, M., and Rossi, E. (1979). *Hypnotherapy: An exploratory casebook*. New York: Irvington.

Gendlin, C. (1978). *Focusing*. New York: Everest House.

Mosak, H. (1987). *Ha, ha, and aha: The role of humor in psychotherapy*. Muncie, IN: Accelerated Development.

Rosen, S. (Ed.). (1982). *My voice will go with you: The teaching tales of Milton H. Erickson*. New York: W. W. Norton.

Sherman, R., and Dinkmeyer, D. (1987). *Systems of family therapy: An Adlerian integration*. New York: Brunner/Mazel.

Watkins, J. G. (1978). *The therapeutic self*. New York: Human Sciences Press.

Zeig, J. K. (Ed.). (1982). *Ericksonian approaches to hypnosis and psychotherapy*. New York: Brunner/Mazel.

REORIENTATION: THE USE OF HYPNOSIS FOR LIFE-STYLE CHANGE

Barbara Fairfield
A marriage and family therapist in private practice in Lanham, Maryland. She is on the staff of the Pediatric Genetics Department at The Johns Hopkins University in Baltimore.

"I know what to do but I just can't seem to do it." How many times does a therapist hear those words from clients? The challenge for the therapist is to somehow assist the client in unifying the insight achieved through therapy, the desire for change, and the change itself. Therapy is never completed until this unity is achieved. Such a "meeting of the minds" within the individual involves a hypnotic process which facilitates movement beyond the limitations/impasse toward solving the life problem by recognizing and embracing the resources previously hidden from the client's awareness.

Reorientation of the individual's life-style is the final, but most difficult, step in the four-step counseling process proposed by Rudolf Dreikurs: (1) Establishment of the relationship; (2) Analysis of the life-style; (3) Interpretation/Confrontation; and (4) Reorientation (Dreikurs, 1967, p. 6). Once the life-style is revealed (step 2) and the client has been confronted with his or her mistaken goals (step 3), it would seem that if the client is willing to alter (reorient) these goals, he or she would do so. But since the life-style is established early in childhood and has become automatic and unconscious in its execution after years of practice, change is extremely difficult. Furthermore, in order for the change to be complete, it must involve the deeper unconscious level, lest the solutions arrived at consciously be eventually

Individual Psychology, 46(4), December, 1990, **pp. 451–458**

sabotaged by the client still influenced by his or her hidden and powerful unconscious goals.

Given the holistic nature of the individual, therapy always reaches in some way the "unconscious" or "other mind" of the person. The usefulness of the hypnotic process is that it allows the therapist to communicate more directly and more intensely with the client's unconscious.

The individual "knows" at many levels and in many ways, but the person does not always know that he or she knows. As Adler put it, "Man knows more than he understands" (Adler, 1956, p. 232). The choice of life-style beliefs made before age five or six is based on the experience of life as perceived by the client in his or her family of origin. Having drawn conclusions about self, others, and life from this relatively ignorant state of experience, the child nevertheless *believes* he must follow these private rules of life or risk absolute rejection and/or total powerlessness. Thus, a child chooses early on to "ignore" or "forget" other possibilities in order to single-mindedly pursue the goal of belonging in this family in the only way that he or she thinks possible. Consciously, then, the individual has become doubly "ignorant": first, he or she does not understand the life-style goals and how narrowly they were selected; and second, he or she "forgets" the other possibilities of living (common sense). Thus "ignorant," the person can more easily continue to choose whatever advantage is perceived in his or her narrow set of life-style beliefs. If the therapist speaks primarily to the person on the conscious level, the client is likely on the unconscious level to reject the idea that change is possible and thus the frustration when he or she "tries" to change but is unsuccessful. The hypnotic process allows the therapist to contact the person on the unconscious level where he or she *knows* all of the possibilities. In a direct but gentle way, the therapist is then able to encourage the client to believe in his or her ability and responsibility to change. In trance, the therapist can re-mind the client of all the forgotten learnings, skills, strengths, and resources. The hypnotist taps the client's past experiences by creating visual, auditory, kinesthetic, and emotional cues to those hidden memories of success and empowerment. In the unconscious memory are stored all the learnings, all the past masteries, all the wonder at life's beauty, all the curiosity about others—everything is there that the client needs to solve his or her problem. The therapist using the hypnotic process is thus able to align himself or herself with all of the most positive goals of the person.

Reorientation, then, is essentially a process of encouragement of the client. Dreikurs goes so far as to say that the "success of the therapist depends entirely on his ability to provide encouragement" (Dreikurs, 1967, p. 13). He describes the encouragement process as a "means to restore the patient's faith in himself, the realization of his strength and ability and the belief in his own dignity and worth" (Dreikurs, 1967, p. 13). The ultimate goal of therapy, therefore, is a process of reeducating the client to his or her own real value. This belief must occur at the deepest level of the self if it is to be a complete change. The person must come to trust himself or herself wholly.

The hypnotherapeutic process can be viewed then as an educational (or reeducational) process whereby the therapist creates with the client's permission and cooperation an openness to receiving new ideas, reconnections to previously forgotten or abandoned healthy ideas, and access to an increased number of creative possibilities. In this way, the therapist is allied with the client's conscious cognitive process as it becomes *informed* by the client's unconscious processes. There are many ways of structuring a hypnotherapeutic experience to achieve this goal of reeducation or reconnection, but the four-step Adlerian counseling process articulated by Dreikurs can serve as a guide for the trained hypnotherapist.

1. Relationship Building: The Induction. The first part of the hypnotic process, the induction of the trance, can be viewed as gaining the client's cooperation, i.e. step 1 of Dreikurs' counseling process (establishing the relationship). Therapists will usually develop one of several induction techniques that fit their own style as well as the style of life of the client. A more cautious client, for example, may be more comfortable with an eyes-open induction.

2. Life-Style Utilization: Deepening the Trance. In the next step, the therapist deepens the trance, creating a climate for openness. Here, the Adlerian therapist will frequently make use of the various life-style characteristics of the client previously gained during formal life-style assessment sessions. For example, the client may be directed to focus on a particular symbol, color, scene, or thought from a previously obtained early memory. Or, a client who is known to be anxious in new experiences may be invited to relive a familiar, comfortable experience.

3. Confrontation: Guiding the Re-Search of Life-Style Goals. The therapist may then guide the client in trance in an examination of his or her own life-style goals by using various metaphors, stories, images, words, etc. This is a very creative part of the hypnotic process for the therapist and usually involves the therapist being in her own trance in which the focus is very intently and expansively on the client and the client's life problem. This is not an analytical process, but having previously conducted an analysis of the client's life-style, the therapist is now free to "explore" the client's private logic in new ways—to walk around in it, as it were, and shine a light into new recesses of the client's belief system. The client

then "discovers" at a deeper, intuitive level new meanings or understandings of himself or herself and his or her life situations.

Milton Erickson was a master at utilizing the naturalistic (life-style) patterns of the patient in his hypnotic interventions to change problems into solutions. In *Therapeutic Trances*, Stephen Gilligan explains nine different hypnotic communication techniques the hypnotherapist can use to stimulate re-search by the client of his or her own internal experiences that can form the basis for positive change (Gilligan, 1987, chap. 6). Using such hypnotic techniques, the Adlerian therapist can facilitate the client's discovery of the multiple roles that life-style goals play in his or her unique symptomatic movement toward discouragement, self-devaluation, and a sense of powerlessness.

4. Reorientation: Expanding the Life-Style Possibilities. Finally, the most important part of the hypnotherapeutic process is the reorientation phase of the trance. Here, the Adlerian therapist will enable the client to "look past" the narrow constrictions of his or her own life-style themes/attitudes to see the world of expanded possibilities. In a trance, the client can see the land of "both/and" as contrasted to the private logic world of "either/or"; he or she can grasp solutions as real and attainable and view himself or herself as powerful enough to take charge of his or her own choices and embrace the whole of life. This phase requires the therapist to be truly optimistic about the client—to see the client as fully capable of health and joy. It is this optimism about the individual which the therapist "suggests" to the client and is the actual source of the encouragement in Adlerian hypnotherapy.

CASE EXAMPLE

The following is an illustration of this four-step hypnotic process used with a female client whose presenting problem was constant migraines which had not responded to aggressive medical treatment. Life-style evaluation revealed a major life theme of high achievement and over-responsibility for others. The woman is a firstborn of highly successful professional parents. She has followed their lead and now heads a department of studies at a large university. She also admits to being a "good" wife and mother. She says that she starts each day by "worrying about everything from the moment I wake up."

1. Relationship Building: The Induction. After talking with the client about her understanding of hypnosis and some common experiences of natural trance, the client was invited to go into a light trance by focusing on her breathing. The emphasis by the therapist was on the ease of this process, that it was natural and

that there was no "right" way to do it. Permission was given to listen or not to the therapist's voice, assuring the client that in either case she would receive all the benefit from the process that she needed at any moment.

2. Life-Style Utilization: Deepening the Trance. The client was invited to focus on two different scenes, one an early memory that she had previously related of herself as a toddler playing in the snow and the other a current backyard scene of her fish pond. Both of the scenes were pleasant and inviting and were used by the therapist to deepen a positive alliance between the conscious and unconscious processes of the client as well as between the therapist and the client.

3. Confrontation: Guiding the Re-Search of Life-Style Goals. Using the snow memory and the fish pond scene, the therapist began to explore the restrictions of the life-style with such rhetorical questions and observations as: "I wonder when the little girl stopped knowing how to play in the snow?"; "This is no ordinary fish pond, is it? There are 72 fish and one is an albino!"; "There is a lot to do to take care of so many fish."; "Do you think the little girl's mother will be angry if she puts the snow all over her face and head?"; "Sometimes there are so many fish to feed that there's no time to throw snowballs."; and "Do you remember—maybe you can feel in in your hand right now—that urge to pick up the snow and throw it at someone?"

In the trance state, the therapist's own unconscious processes can play with the client's life-style material to shed more light on the goals and narrow learnings of the past and begin to suggest alternative choices.

4. Reorientation: Expanding the Life-Style Possibilities. Now the client was directed to wonder at what she may be missing out on by trying too hard to achieve so much. When the therapist noticed a twitching of the client's fingers, the suggestion was made that "Things are occurring right now that are interesting and enjoyable and you can begin to focus now on what is happening that is pleasant like that slight movement in your middle finger. And you don't know just how that is happening or which finger will move next (another one does), but isn't it interesting—that pleasant feeling there in your hand—and isn't it nice to just concentrate on what is happening there that is curious (the client smiles) and even amusing and not to have to think about anything else right now?" The therapist continued to play with the ideas of letting go, permission to enjoy the present moment, curiosity about what might happen next, and delight in being rather than doing. Using the small hand movements (which actually increased in frequency as they were noted by the therapist) and referring back to the pleasant images of playing in the snow and watching the fish, the hypnotherapist planted the suggestion that the client could be both productive *and* peaceful.

Since the physical symptom of migraine involves a dilation of blood vessels in the head, the therapist also introduced some images of cold and warmth related to the early memory in order to effect some change in these vessels during headaches. Specifically, references were made to the snow being placed on the little girl's face and to her hands being warmed inside her mittens.

Finally, the therapist gave two post-hypnotic suggestions to re-mind the client of her ability to choose pleasant and easy tasks to focus on. "And perhaps tonight at dinner or at some other meal or snack tomorrow or another day, you will be surprised at how you will suddenly realize how good this bite of food tastes. And when you put your head on the cool pillow, for just an instant you will really notice how pleasant that coolness is on your face just like the little girl in the snow."

This type of trance was conducted on two subsequent visits using other metaphors, memories, and experiences, but with the same themes in mind. Each week, the client noted that she had fewer and less severe headaches. She said after the third session that she had not had such a succession of good days since her headaches began more than a year ago. She was, she admitted, still skeptical that the hypnosis sessions could account for the change. "Maybe the one medicine I am still taking (which hadn't worked before) has started to work." The therapist's response was to smile and say "Well, I won't be any more or less effective whether you believe in hypnosis or not!"

Finally, several of my clients have offered their experiences of the use of hypnosis in their own therapy. These first-hand accounts clarify the kind of reorientation/reeducation effect of hypnotherapy.

> **Client A:** *"While in the trance I was very aware of the therapist as a separate person. I was aware of her words and the progression of them as well as my ability to respond or not (to her directions) as I chose. Physically, I felt very relaxed and was aware of the loss of feeling in my hands—I had no sense of their position, no sensation of their touching, etc. After coming out of the trance, I felt like I was moving in slow motion. The world hadn't changed but I had. I had a sense that everything is OK—I didn't have to be concerned about anything specific. I felt I had all the time in the world to do whatever I wanted to do. In the first two or three weeks following the experience, I found myself at times suddenly becoming aware of viewing something from an entirely fresh perspective. It seemed as though barriers were falling or perhaps as though something that was rattling around, loose and random, suddenly found a setting, a niche, a groove in which to rest. Things fit better. Life became smoother. I was able to function well with much less effort."*

Comment: *Notice the client's experience of herself as changed, both immediately after the trance ("The world hadn't changed, but I had") and weeks later (". . . an entirely fresh perspective").*

Client B: *"My experience with hypnosis in counseling has been a powerful one. I recognized my own strength by visualizing in a trance a symbol of it. Initially, the symbol I saw was a gold brick—solid, impenetrable, and priceless. This felt incomplete, so I searched for a living representation of strength. It emerged as a man, strong and smiling, holding the golden brick. He encouraged me to accept my strength, telling me to dare to be strong, to be assertive and to smile as I enjoy my power."*

Comment: *Directing the client during the reorientation phase of the trance to "receive a symbol of their strength or success" allows the client to open themselves up to their own reservoir of positive suggestions. The client makes his or her own suggestion to the unconscious to achieve a healthy solution to life problems.*

Client C: *"Several years ago in a therapy session I was wanting to understand my feelings of fear of men better. During a trance, the therapist suggested that I recall a past scene where I had been afraid of men. The scene that appeared was quite vivid—I was a 22-year-old college student on my way to take a test to qualify for a civil service job. I arrived at the building downtown early in the morning. When I entered, I heard voices and saw some men in one room. When they saw me they started whooping and hollering in my direction. In the trance, I actually seemed to be back in that corridor and I felt the fear. Still in the trance, I began to cry, though I had not cried in the real scene. As I came out of the trance, I realized for the first time, consciously, just how frightened I was that day and how I probably carry this fear around with me every day. I was then angry that men did this to me—they had no right to intimidate me. And I was also angry at myself for allowing myself to feel so intimidated. Now, years later I am sometimes aware when this old fear of men is operating in my everyday life. For example, if a man criticizes me and I feel uncomfortable, I try to step back and look more objectively at my reaction. I ask myself if some of my discomfort may be just because I'm dealing with a man. I may ask myself, 'If a woman had made that remark, would I feel differently? Am I overreacting? Is this my old fear of men?' I tell myself, 'This is not the way I want to relate to men in my life. My fear is unreasonable.' Then, I re-evaluate my reaction and decide how I am going to proceed in the situation."*

Comment: *Even years later, a powerful trance experience can motivate the client's continued challenge of old life-style beliefs. The trance can intensify the experience of an early memory and reveal the intensity of feelings that accompanied the life-style choice/conclusion.*

SUMMARY

Hypnosis is a powerful tool available to the Adlerian therapist for reaching and reorienting the client's hidden goals of behavior. Communicating with the client in trance allows the therapist to cooperate with the client's inner resources for growth and change and "suggest" to the client more healthy life-style beliefs with which he or she may live life more fully and easily.

REFERENCES

Adler, A. (1956). *The Individual Psychology of Alfred Adler*. H. L. Ansbacher and R. R. Ansbacher (Eds.). New York: Basic Books.

Dreikurs, R. (1967). *Psychodynamics, psychotherapy, and counseling*. Chicago: Alfred Adler Institute.

Gilligan, S. (1987). *Therapeutic trances: The cooperation principle in Ericksonian hypnotherapy*. New York: Brunner/Mazel.

HYPNOSIS, TAILORING, AND MULTIMODAL TREATMENT

Len Sperry
Associate professor of psychiatry and preventive medicine at the Medical College of Wisconsin and a diplomate of both the American Board of Psychiatry and Neurology and the American Board of Professional Psychology.

Jon Carlson
A professor of counseling and psychology. at Governors State University, a faculty member at the Alfred Adler Institute of Chicago, and a psychologist in private practice.

Within the past two decades there has been a dramatic shift in the practice of psychotherapy. Whereas, treatment had been primarily unimodal, today it is becoming more multimodal (Lazarus, 1981). Whereas psychotherapeutic interventions had been basically uniform in scope, today it is more likely that interventions are consciously tailored to client or patient needs and styles (Sperry, 1989). This is particularly evident with habit change programs which involve hypnosis. Early smoking cessation programs, for example, involved only hypnotherapeutic suggestions which tended to be generic suggestions. Then, due to the relative ineffectiveness of such unimodal interventions, programs became more multimodal. Here, generic hypnotherapeutic suggestions were coupled with behavior modification strategies, as well as adjunctive treatments such as exercise, relaxation, and diet modification. Additionally, a self-hypnosis cassette tape was usually provided for intersession use. The American Lung Association single-session smoking cessation program is such a multimodal intervention.

In reviewing studies on hypnosis as a treatment for smoking, Holroyd (1980) concluded that under favorable treatment circumstances, at least half and frequently more than two-thirds of the smokers who begin treatment stop smoking and remain

Individual Psychology, 46(4), December, 1990, **pp. 459–465**

abstinent for at least six months. In comparison, only 30% of people treated by non-hypnosis interventions remain abstinent after three months. Holroyd's conclusion is based on a metanalysis of some 89 studies. She concludes that tailoring hypnotherapeutic suggestions to a given patient's underlying motivation proves much more effective than giving the same suggestion to all patients regardless of their particular motivation.

It has been our experience that effective psychotherapeutic interventions and particularly habit change programs such as smoking cessation require that treatment be tailored to particular individual differences. We have found utilizing life-style information to be particularly valuable. The following case illustrates a multimodal tailored treatment program.

CASE STUDY

Jilian is a 42-year-old divorced female with a 25-year history of smoking 1-1/2 packs of cigarettes per day. A detailed assessment, which included background information, a smoking history, a health assessment, and life-style data including early recollections (ER) yielded the following. The patient was a relatively healthy woman with no concurrent medical problems except for chronic neck pain sustained as a result of a car accident approximately 12 years before her consultation. Her smoking history was quite unique in that the majority of her smoking occurred at only three times throughout the day: upon rising, on retiring at night, and while engaged in her livelihood as a portrait artist. Furthermore, her smoking was strictly a solitary activity which gave her a feeling of safety and a sense of satisfaction. Unlike the typical smoker, Jilian would absent herself from social situations to smoke, never smoking in the presence of others. None of her social friends smoked, and her decision to quit smoking was primarily for health reasons. She reported that smoking seemed to exacerbate her neck pain. In fact she noted that she had nearly no neck pain during two previous attempts to quit. She had a positive family history of heart attacks and stroke among smokers both male and female. Her father was a three-pack per day smoker who died suddenly at age 43 of a heart attack. Her mother was a nonsmoker and did not permit smoking within the house itself. Jilian recalls that during her parents' marital quarrels, her father stopped fighting abruptly and left to go outside to smoke. Further inquiry showed that Jilian learned to "solve" conflicts by "walking out" of a difficult situation and lighting up a cigarette.

Smoking appeared to serve at least two functions for Jilian: first as a stress reducer; and secondly, as a "trigger" for creative productivity, that is, for painting and artistic efforts. Psychologically, she was an only child and "daddy's girl." Father was a hard-working and successful businessman with strong perfectionist strivings. Father was described as intense, nice, and fun to be around. Mother was described as serious, artistic, and a loner. On the *Kern Life-Style Scale* (1986), Jilian scored highest on perfectionism and lowest on the need to please. Her ERs suggested that she was guarded and aloof and cordoned herself off from others following conflicts. It also seemed that she utilized withdrawal as a means of controlling other's feelings as well as her own. She viewed the world as hostile, unpredictable and unsatisfying.

It is interesting to note that her smoking behavior occurred in places and situations where she was withdrawn from others—such as in her art studio—just as it is a general theme throughout her early recollections. She appeared to use smoking as a socially acceptable way of absenting herself from a social group when she became anxious and uncomfortable. When it was suggested that perhaps she feared she might not be able to control herself or others if she was successful in quitting smoking, a recognition reflex was elicited.

Based on this information, a treatment program was tailored for Jilian. The program consisted of four interventions: education, diet and exercise, behavioral change strategies, and hypnosis. The reader is referred to Carlson (1989) for a detailed description of this treatment program. A handout provided Jilian with information on smoking cessation. It was recommended that Jilian make diet changes that would influence the acid-alkaline balance in her body. Nicotine is a very strong alkaline substance. When her acidity levels rise, her alkaline levels would need to be changed to keep this in balance. When her acidity levels would go up, her alkaline level would drop and she would crave cigarettes. By making dietary changes, it is possible to minimize changes in the pH balance. This was done by getting her to eat more fruits and vegetables; stay away from meat, eggs, and alcohol; eliminate refined sugar products; and decrease stimulant usage. It was further suggested that she drink lots of juices and water.

On the behavioral level, it was suggested that Jilian practice deep diaphragmatic breathing and muscle relaxation each hour. A daily exercise program was developed. This would improve her health, burn off calories, and give her something to occupy her time. She decided that walking and biking would be good for her and that she would rotate these on a daily basis. It was further suggested that she make an appointment to get her teeth cleaned in order to get rid of any residual tobacco stain or taste in order to have a fresh, clean mouth. This was to be followed by regular brushing.

Suggestions were made to break up the routines in the places where she smoked and to plan other ways to use her time upon rising and retiring at night, and also while she was engaged in thinking. It was suggested that Jilian further plan to keep very busy during the next few weeks and to increase her daily activity patterns. It was suggested that she take walks, shower, go to church, bicycle, pray, swim, make love, play tennis, engage in activities that would keep her hands busy. She was asked to think of times where it was going to be difficult for her to not smoke and to schedule things which she could do instead. Since Jilian used smoking primarily to reduce stress, particularly interpersonal stress, and to induce creativity and productivity, an important behavioral change strategy was to collaborate with Jilian to find more effective substitutes for stress reduction and creativity. She recalled that taking a walk through a small horticultural park or looking through a particular art portfolio seemed to have a similar effect of inducing a creative mood. She also decided to join two of her friends for an aerobics class and lunch, thinking that this would be an interpersonal stress reducer. An assertiveness class was also suggested, as was chewing sugarless gum as further means of reducing her own discomfort among other persons.

A mainstay of this two-session treatment program was the hypnotic suggestions. These were of two types: positive affirmations and self-hypnosis. The sheet with six affirmations tailored to Jilian's underlying motivations was provided to her. She was asked to write out each of these affirmations five times in the morning and then to repeat them aloud to herself. The affirmations were:

1. "Taking care of myself physically is important to me. I know I will live a longer and a more satisfying life."
2. "I have more energy and less pain than ever before. I enjoy life and I'm glad to be here."
3. "I have no habits which control or influence me in any harmful way. I am in control of myself and everything I do. I always do what is best for me, myself, and my future."
4. "All of my senses are clear and alive. I am more productive and creative than when I was a smoker."
5. "I give myself permission to relax, feel good, breathe deeply and fully, and enjoy being a healthy nonsmoker at all times and in all circumstances."
6. "People enjoy being around me. And, I like being around others. I have self-confidence and self-respect. I like myself, and it shows!"

The self-hypnosis component began near the end of the first session. Standard breathing, relaxation, and guided imagery were utilized along with directives for smoking cessation. The induction was audiorecorded, and Jilian was given a copy of this tape for personal use outside this session. She was told to listen to the tape at least once a day when she could be without interruption for at least the next two weeks. This was to reinforce what she had learned during our sessions together. The following is a script of the self-hypnosis tailored to Jilian's situation.

> "Begin to become aware of your breathing . . . breathe slowly and deeply . . . breathe freely and easily . . . sit back comfortably in your chair, close your eyes and let yourself begin to relax . . . feel your muscles relaxing and your mind relaxing . . . sitting quietly and peacefully, more at ease . . . your body is slowing down . . . time is slowing down . . . there is lots and lots of time . . . lots and lots of time . . . we're in no hurry . . . you feel more at ease, at peace with your surroundings, at peace with yourself . . . so peaceful, relaxed, calm, and tranquil . . . as you breathe easily and gently, you feel yourself relaxing more and more . . . calmness is present throughout your body and your mind . . . calmness, peace, and relaxation are spreading throughout every part of your body and your mind as you feel more and more relaxed . . . you feel as if you're floating along on a soft, soft cloud . . . floating gently and easily . . . so relaxed and calm and comfortable . . . soft, gentle, quiet, peaceful, and restful relaxation . . . as your mind and your body are relaxing more and more . . . your thoughts are fading away . . . a feeling of well-being now exists as though all of your cares have been rolled away . . . breathe peacefully and comfortably and imagine your worries, uncomfortable thoughts and problems being carried away with each breath . . . stop worrying, being anxious, being afraid, being tense, being upset, and being frustrated . . . instead you feel calm, free, at ease, confident, and peaceful . . . allow any distractions, whether thoughts or outside noises to drift away . . . imagine clouds drifting smoothly across the sky, carrying with them all distractions, all worries, all uncomfortable thoughts and problems . . . allow stress, tension, worry, and anxiety to float away as clouds with each breath you take . . . allow them to drift easily and effortlessly away . . . feel your pressures disappearing, drifting easily and effortlessly away . . . now imagine yourself at the top of a large hill . . . I'm going to count backward from 10, and I want you to imagine yourself going down the hill . . . as you ease down, you will move further and further into a deeper, more comfortable state . . . when you reach the bottom you will find yourself in a special place . . . that's the place, whether it's real or imaginary, where you are peaceful and comfortable . . . whether it's by the sea, on a mountain top, near a brook, in a meadow . . . wherever it is that you are peaceful and comfortable . . . breathe in slowly and deeply as I begin to count: 10, deeper and deeper; 9, 8, feel yourself easing into deeper and deeper relaxation; 7, 6, a deeper relaxed state; 5, 4, breathe in the clean, fresh air as you feel a healthier, happier person; 3, 2, you are

deeper and deeper . . . feel yourself fully relaxed as if a cloud of relaxation has covered you; 1 . . . now imagine yourself deeply relaxed and deeply alive and aware in your special place . . . breathe in the clean and fresh air . . . notice the colors, scenery, noises, smells, your good feelings . . . imagine them on a canvas now in front of you . . . feel how warm you feel. Warmth has spread throughout your body . . . such a pleasant experience . . . notice how good you feel and how good your body can feel . . . you can be calm, relaxed, and feel good like this whenever you want . . . whenever you feel tense, you will hear the words, 'calm and relaxed and peaceful . . . calm and relaxed and peaceful' and they will trigger this good feeling for you . . . the quality of your life depends on what you do and think . . . smoking is a poison to your physical health and to your creativity . . . therefore, make a private commitment to be healthier and more creative . . . smoking is a poison to your body and to your mind . . . therefore make a private commitment to be healthy and more creative . . . raise your finger once you've made this commitment . . . each day this commitment becomes stronger . . . every day, in every way, your commitment is stronger and stronger . . . you don't ever want to say to yourself when you die that you didn't live your life well, that you wished that you would have quit smoking . . . when you learn to smoke you had to train your body to really take it and then want it and then need it . . . feel how it was . . . really experience it . . . you learned that smoking gave you a way from other people when conflict and bad feelings came up . . . experience that now . . . feel how it was . . . starting today you are going to live your life fully . . . you are going to be comfortable and charming being around other people . . . the beautiful person you are fully emerge . . . the message now is going through all your mind and all throughout your body . . . programming all throughout your mind, all throughout you body, on down into your smoking arm and your smoking hand, programming all of you: no smoking . . . your whole system is now programmed . . . you are now a nonsmoker . . . you are now a nonsmoker . . . you are now a nonsmoker . . . you want to live and will choose to live well . . . when you have the urge to smoke, breathe deeply and say to yourself, 'I have a commitment with myself to be a nonsmoker and live well. I have a commitment with myself to be a nonsmoker and live well . . . I have a commitment with myself to be a nonsmoker and live well' . . . let these words go deep . . . deep . . . deep . . . into your unconscious mind . . . so they will be there when you need them . . . breathe in now and breathe out . . . nothing will get in your way . . . you are free from tension, worry, disruption, and smoking . . . you are free in your life works . . . and you are in control."

SUMMARY

Research on the efficacy of tailored multimodal interventions suggests that these interventions are more effective than standard treatments (Holroyd, 1980). Our clinical experience matches these findings. Approximately 80% of persons who have undergone this single-session tailored treatment have been abstinent from nicotine for at least 12 months. We have found that tailoring hypnotic suggestions to life-style themes is a key factor in treatment effectiveness.

REFERENCES

Carlson, J. (1989). Brief therapy for health promotion. *Individual Psychology, 45*(1 & 2), 220–229.

Holroyd, J. (1980). Hypnosis treatment for smoking. *International Journal of Clinical and Experimental Hypnosis, 28*, 341–357.

Kern, R. (1986). *Lifestyle scale.* Coral Springs, FL: CMTI Press.

Lazarus, A. (1981). *The practice of multimodal therapy.* New York: McGraw-Hill.

Sperry, L. (1989). Contemporary approaches to brief therapy: A comparative analysis. *Individual Psychology, 45*(1 & 2), 3–25.

Part H
SUBSTANCE ABUSE

ALCOHOLICS AND THEIR TREATMENT: CURRENT ADLERIAN THINKING

Joseph (Yosi) Prinz
Director of special compensatory education programs for the Jerusalem District, Ministry of Education, Israel.

Since the published Adlerian literature on substance abuse was found to be sparse, the author surveyed contemporary Adlerians involved in substance abuse treatment and/or particularly knowledgeable about Adlerian theory.

The article consists of two major parts: (1) a summary of the views of contemporary Adlerians who were surveyed by the author and (2) the author's conclusions and recommendations.

An open-ended questionnaire was sent to 42 currently active Adlerians with a letter asking them to respond to five questions about alcoholics and their treatment.

Sixteen recipients of the questionnaire returned completed responses. Responses to the five questions were grouped into five topical areas: alcoholics' life-style and implication of life-style for treatment; self-determination versus the AA concept of powerlessness; the disease concept of alcoholism; Adlerian principles applicable to treatment of alcoholics; and treatment methods appropriate for alcoholics.

This article is derived from the author's doctoral dissertation, *An Adlerian Treatment Model for Problem Drinkers*, which was accepted by the Adler School of Professional Psychology in October 1991. The complete dissertation is available at the Adler School's library in Chicago.

Individual Psychology, 49(1), March, 1993, **pp. 94–105**

Several respondents, in addition to answering the questions, acknowledged the didactic value of the questionnaire. To Henry Stein, director of the Alfred Adler Institute of San Francisco, the questionnaire became "a stimulating springboard topic for one of our monthly master seminars on theory and practice." According to Stein, an audiocassette of that seminar is available. Another respondent used the questionnaire as an opportunity to clarify her thinking on this subject. "Your questions," wrote Jackie Brown, "caused me to examine my place on this topic for the first time in about three years."

The author hopes that Adlerian readers of this article will be prompted to consider and, perhaps, reconsider their own positions on treating this population after reading the views of their contemporaries.

ALCOHOLICS' LIFE-STYLE

The first question, the most comprehensive one, elicited the most detailed responses:

> Adler classified alcoholics along with perverts, suicides, neurotics, problem children, etc. What do you see that is uniquely or particularly characteristic of alcoholics—in terms of goals, etiology, symptom choice, and behavior patterns? What implications does that have for treatment?

The responses which described the characteristics, goals, and behaviors of alcoholics, which Adlerians would refer to as the life style, revealed a few common themes:

1. A gap between high-flown goals and low tolerance for accepting and dealing with the burdens of life. "Whenever a difficulty arose—they looked for some way to deny the difficulty and have it easy" (Kurt Adler). A "combination of excess ambition . . . coupled with anger at defeat" (Eva Dreikurs Ferguson).
2. Desire to escape from reality or to self-medicate. "Alcoholics want to feel good" (Guy Manaster). ". . . alcohol allows the alcoholic to medicate away his or her concerns and problems" (Richard Betts).
3. Emptiness. Jackie Brown used a metaphor to describe the hollowness, the suffering, and everlasting struggle for fulfillment: "The receipt is never enough; a hole of emptiness and pain ensues."
4. Guilt. The feeling of guilt was mentioned by Buzz O'Connell, Albert Ellis, Kurt Adler, and Bernard Shulman. Ellis stressed the self-condemnation

that alcoholics indulge in for being alcoholic, while Kurt Adler acknowledged the usefulness of AA in alleviating guilt feelings.

5. Biological component. Len Sperry and Albert Ellis found themselves in the same boat: Sperry emphasized the biological component and Ellis saw alcoholics as "largely born with a strong innate tendency to be seriously disturbed."
6. Denial. A display of entrenched denial patterns was described by Ron Pancner and Helen Cooley.
7. Nonexistence of an "alcoholic personality." Ronald Pancner expressed this idea most unequivocally: "Any personality structure can be susceptible to alcoholism." Ray Corsini thought similarly: "Every alcoholic is a unique individual."
8. Self-destructiveness. Ray Corsini echoed Alexandra Adler's (1941), characterization of alcoholism as "slow suicide."
9. Lack of social interest. This was the most frequently mentioned trait. Buzz O'Connell called it "lack of community feeling."

IMPLICATIONS FOR TREATMENT

Respondents gave the following as implications of the listed life-style characteristics for treatment: To increase their social interest (Kurt Adler, Jackie Brown): to help the "person (a) to have more confidence in own action, (b) to have more willingness to accept defeat, and (c) to reconsider concepts of 'life is unfair'" (Eva Dreikurs Ferguson).

Buzz O'Connell stressed the importance of a "solid relationship of cooperation-as-equals." Ron Pancner was concerned about the denial of the alcoholic, and he suggested dealing with it "in a rather forceful fashion." "To address the life-style convictions" was suggested by Len Sperry, Arthur Nikelly, and Jackie Brown. Brown emphasized focusing on "the art of giving . . . as opposed to receiving."

SELF-DETERMINATION OR POWERLESSNESS?

The answers to the second question: "How do you reconcile the Adlerian concept of self-determination with the AA concept of powerlessness?" can be divided into two categories:

1. Those that see no place for reconciliation. "The Adlerian concept of self-determination conflicts strongly with the AA concept of powerlessness" (Albert Ellis). "AA is entirely wrong to call these people powerless" (Kurt Adler). Ray Corsini rejected "completely" the AA concept of powerlessness; Norman Silverman stated he "cannot reconcile" the two concepts and so did Jackie Brown.
2. Those who try to reconcile the two by:
   a. Stressing the paradoxical act of admitting powerlessness at the same time one makes a decision to make such an admission and seek help. "[T]he individual who . . . accepts that 'he is powerless' over the outcome consequences of his drinking does *not* experience any feeling of helplessness or powerlessness. On the contrary, and this is the paradox, the recovering person begins to feel empowerment. . . ." (Helen Cooley). James Croake used an aphorism to express this idea: "A symptom lasts as long as one fights it." Bernard Shulman saw the AA concept of powerlessness as a useful "trick of words." Guy Manaster described it as "a ploy to allow change."
   b. Seeing the two concepts as complementary. Len Sperry saw the declaration of powerlessness as "a decision for health." Ron Pancner saw "no conflict at all" between the two concepts.

IS ALCOHOLISM A DISEASE?

The responses to the next question: "Do you agree or disagree with the notion of alcoholism as a disease? Why or why not?" are clear cut. Although there is no intention to draw statistical conclusions in this paper, it is clear that the majority of the respondents do not agree with the notion of alcoholism as a disease. The explanations differed. Kurt Adler wrote that "anything that can be cured by talking with people and explaining their wrong attitude cannot be called a disease." For Ray Corsini, a decision a person makes "to take 'something' . . . does not qualify as a disease." Arthur Nikelly described alcoholism as "a socially constructed 'disease.'"

The "minority" who regarded alcoholism as a disease included three out of the four physicians who responded to the questionnaire. Len Sperry reminded Adlerians that Adler's approach was "biopsychosocial and holistic [so] there is no basis for disagreement." Ron Pancner cited "genetic studies, adoption studies, monozygotic twin studies" to support his position. Bernard Shulman saw alcoholism as "an altered physiological state and therefore a disease." Helen Cooley described the disease concept as a useful fiction that is helpful for some patients: "It reassures them that they are not 'moral degenerates.'" For other patients she pointed out, it would be a "destructive fiction."

APPLICABLE ADLERIAN PRINCIPLES

The fourth question was: "What basic Adlerian principles are particularly applicable to the treatment of alcoholics? How do they apply?"

Many of the respondents stressed the importance of fostering social interest (Jackie Brown, Bernard Shulman, Buzz O'Connell, Ron Pancner, Norman Silverman, Helen Cooley, and Henry Stein.) Albert Ellis stated that "almost all the Adlerian principles are applicable," without mentioning specific ones. Buzz O'Connell, who believes that the feeling of guilt is an important component in the phenomenon of alcohol abuse, suggested "living with inferiority feelings without guilt."

Jackie Brown focused on the teleological point of view—"identifying the purpose of the drinking strategy (what's gained; what's avoided)." Richard Betts suggested changing environment and friends. Ron Pancner suggested teaching patients the purpose of symptoms, to think differently, and to be responsible for their behavior. He stated that "the 12 steps of AA are very compatible with the stages of psychotherapy as taught by Adlerians." Len Sperry would use "the same principles as are used with other habitual dysfunctions." He proposed to add "relapse prevention strategies."

Norman Silverman mentioned Dreikurs' (1967) four stages of psychotherapy, "establishing a relationship, understanding the patient, explaining the patient to himself/herself and reorienting the patient." He and Henry Stein stressed the first and basic principle of psychotherapy (as Shulman wrote): "The patient must be won over."

Eva Dreikurs Ferguson offered five suggestions: "(1) look at the consequences of one's actions; (2) look at myths; (3) help self-encouragement; (4) build up realistic options and action plans; (5) examine 'basic mistakes' (à la Dreikurs)."

TREATMENT APPROACH, METHODS, AND TECHNIQUES

Question five asked: "From your experience, what treatment approach, methods, and techniques have you found or would you expect to be most effective in working with problem drinkers?"

When it came to practical methods, the tendency of the answers changed; some of those who do not currently treat problem drinkers did not answer. Others advocated their particular therapeutic specialties or techniques in their answers. For example, Albert Ellis (but also Arthur Nikelly) suggested working according to Rational-Emotive Therapy. He found it "most effective in working with problem drinkers, because it includes a wide variety of cognitive, emotive, and behavioral methods." Corsini was very skeptical about success in working with alcoholics. He reported having treated "some 100 alcoholics" over a three-year period: "They did not show up for sessions." In a candid and a somewhat sarcastic way Corsini expressed his disappointment: "They would apparently get insight, etc., and then get drunk." The only successes he reported with alcoholics "was with psychodrama in one case and the behind-the-back technique in another case."

Ron Pancner stated a strong belief in the efficacy of "education about the illness." He suggested working in group therapy, involving the family, and emphasized the importance of self-help groups: "AA provides invaluable support." Helen Cooley recommended integrating "the 12 steps of AA into the Adlerian principles." In a case that she described, the aim was to help the patient "stay the center of attention" without using alcohol, in other words, moving the patient from the useless to the useful side of life.

AUTHOR'S INTERPRETATIONS AND RECOMMENDATIONS

After four and a half years of visiting and working in American alcohol treatment and prevention programs and researching Adlerian and non-Adlerian treatment methods, I have been able to clarify my own views of alcohol abusers and their treatment. Space does not permit the detailed presentation of the treatment model that was the subject of my dissertation. However, the Adlerian ideas on which the model is based (Dreikurs, 1953, 1960, 1967) and their application to substance abuse treatment are presented next, followed by specific recommendations. I gratefully acknowledge the influence of my teacher, Norman Silverman, and of Herbert Fingarette (1989); William Miller (1986, 1989); Stanton Peele, (1989); and Linda Sobell and Mark Sobell (1987) for introducing me to alternative ways of viewing substance abuse and to multimodal treatment approaches.

Since the common denominator of actual and potential clients of alcohol treatment programs is problems related to alcohol use, the term problem drinkers is used in the balance of this article and includes the minority subgroup of drinkers, commonly referred to as alcoholics, who are physically dependent on alcohol.

Adlerian Principles Applied to Treatment of Problem Drinkers

Social Interest. A major task in the treatment of problem drinkers is to create pro-social goals to replace the alcohol-focused purpose around which all of their life activity is organized.

Teleology. Problem drinking is for a purpose, and it is the therapist's task to help the client discover what that is. Goals of treatment for an individual should be a matter of informed choice by the client and not imposed by treatment staff.

Holism. Alcohol-abusing clients are to be viewed as holistic individuals with life task problems that are caused or exacerbated by excessive use of alcohol, rather than as members of an undifferentiated class labeled "alcoholics."

Self-Determination. Problem drinkers have choices to make about whether and how much they wish to drink and what type of assistance they wish, if any, to deal with their drinking.

Phenomenology. Problem drinkers are individuals with a unique pattern of perceptions and predisposing circumstances which influence their drinking behavior.

Understanding the Patient. An Adlerian therapist imbued with the described principles must come to understand the problem-drinking patient and bring the patient to share in that understanding. The usual Adlerian techniques, such as analysis of the life style, may be used with these clients, as long as they are not under the influence during the treatment. It is especially important (1) to identify and modify any unrealistic beliefs and goals that may be supporting the patient's drinking habit, such as "Everyone must like me" or "I am worthwhile only if . . ." and (2) to understand the purpose of the drinking. In looking to identify a patient's purpose for drinking, one must always ask "what is gained" and "what is avoided" by the drinking behavior (Jacqueline Brown, personal communication, February, 1991). The answer to "The Question": "If you could stop drinking, what would change in your life?" (Adler, 1932: p. 16) can lead to an understanding as to what situation or life task the patient is avoiding through drinking.

Treating Problem Drinkers versus Alcoholics. Treatment programs should differentiate between physically dependent alcoholics and the large majority of problem drinkers who are not physically dependent. Programs that offer treatment before a person "hits bottom" have a better chance of succeeding, since job and family, important sources of support, are more likely to be still intact.

Treatment programs should direct efforts toward people whose drinking is causing problems in their lives, but who are not willing to label themselves alcoholics and not ready to commit to what most treatment programs impose as an initial goal—total and permanent abstinence. These people need a less restrictive alternative, a treatment program that will respect their self-apperception and permit them to set and attempt to achieve a personally determined goal—to decrease their drinking to a level that is compatible with the meeting of their personal, family, occupational, and community responsibilities. If such a goal is found to be not achievable, the patient is likely to be more receptive to a goal of abstinence later on.

Goal Alignment versus Denial. Fighting "denial" and "resistance" are counterproductive, imcompatible with Adlerian principles and, possibly, a partial explanation for the dismal results that most treatment programs achieve. (More than 90% of alcoholics treated in American public facilities drink again within four years [Polich, Armor, & Braiker, 1981]). What is important is to establish and maintain a cooperative therapeutic alliance, with goals and treatment methods that are negotiated between client and therapist. A warm and trusting relationship is a key ingredient in motivating a problem drinker to make the difficult life changes involved in recovery.

Life Task Emphasis. Most alcohol and drug treatment programs in the United States are heavily focused on the substance, its abuse, and the resulting negative consequences. These are issues about which the patient is usually as expert as the treatment personnel. What the patients lack and need help with in treatment is developing the motivation and skills to meet the tasks of life.

The goal of treatment, then, becomes the preparation of the individual to address all the areas of life that were previously evaded or neglected for fear of failure or loss of face, evasions that were facilitated by, blamed on, or excused by the drinking. It follows, then, that treatment effectiveness should be evaluated by examining posttreatment client functioning at school, work, leisure-time activities, and in important relationships, in addition to the usual measures of substance use and involvement with the law. Adlerians also include relationship to self and the cosmos as important life tasks (Dreikurs & Mosak, 1967; Mosak & Dreikurs, 1967).

Work. Counselors should assess the degree to which the patient's job is a positive force in his or her life or a contributing factor to the problem drinking. Treatment staff should work with the patient to remedy workplace problems caused by the drinking or to encourage the patient to find alternative employment if the job environment is a major stressor.

Friendship/Community. For problem drinkers, friendships are frequently formed and held together by the common activity of drinking. Treating the problem drinker in a therapeutic group can provide important opportunities for the patient to learn socialization skills not accomplished in the family of origin (Dreikurs, 1990/1932). It is important that such groups allow the major input to be provided by the patients. Many so-called therapy groups consist largely of educational lectures and "scare tactics" by staff. Yet there is compelling evidence that the most effective teaching or counseling is that done by peers (Perry & Grant, 1988; Botvin, Baker, Renick, Filazzola, & Botvin, 1984; Tobler, 1986; Wodarski, 1987).

Training in social skills, alternative recreational outlets, and assertiveness can equip the patient to manage without the "crutch" of alcohol. Involving the patient in volunteer or community activities can overcome the deficiency in social interest that is characteristic of many substance abusers.

Love, Marriage, and Parenting. The family is an important source of encouragement and should be included as an integral part of treatment, if possible. The common practice of referring spouses and children to separate support or codependency groups may drive a deeper wedge in an already divided family and is recommended only when the problem drinker is uncooperative with treatment efforts. Central to rebuilding good will in the marital and family relationship that has been disturbed by alcohol abuse is developing the mutual conviction that each member of the family has positive intentions toward the others. If this is done, displeasing behaviors will not automatically be viewed and responded to as personal attacks. For detailed treatment of marital and family therapy with alcohol-affected couples, see the article by Arkin, Lewis, and Carlson in the June 1990 issue of *Individual Psychology*.

Self. Problem drinkers often become a nuisance to others but, most of all, they hurt themselves through neglect of proper nutrition, exercise, and healthful recreation. A comprehensive treatment program should encourage the valuing and development of a healthy life-style, not simply teach health rules (Bergin, 1991). As Buzz O'Connell has said, treatment must restore the ability to get "high" without the use of alcohol or other substances (1988).

Cosmos. In addressing the fifth life task, the counselor's challenge is to help the client deal with the existential issues of the meaning of life in ways that are consistent with his or her level of spirituality. It is important for problem drinkers who have lost faith in God, self, and others to deal with issues of spirituality. However, religious terminology or beliefs should not be imposed on clients who are strongly secular in orientation.

Creative Eclecticism. Adlerians have described many tools for understanding patients and bringing about changes in their attitudes and behaviors, such as role playing, psychodrama, and paradoxical interventions (Mosak, 1989;

Mozdzierz, Macchitelli, & Lisiecki, 1976). O'Connell (1975; 1988) and Starr (1977) described the application of several of these techniques specifically to substance abusers. The 4 R's of Corsini (Ignas & Corsini, 1979), respect, responsiveness, responsibility, and relationships. Kelly's (1955, 1964) technique of having patients try new roles and behaviors by acting "as if" can also be useful.

There are many other treatment techniques compatible with Adlerian principles and which have been used effectively with substance abusers. The reader is encouraged to explore the Behavioral Self-Control Training of Hester and Miller (1989); the cognitive therapy of Albert Ellis and his colleagues (1988); the community reinforcement approach of Sisson and Azrin (1989); the relapse prevention methods of Marlatt and Gordon (1985); and the self-efficacy theory of Bandura (1989).

Adlerian Social Clubs. A final recommendation to Adlerians who wish to provide services to substance abusers is to establish Adlerian clubs in various cities. In the tradition of the Vienna coffee houses, these clubs would provide a healthy and intellectually stimulating social outlet for people who share Adlerian ideas—a place to meet, exchange ideas, share happiness and sorrow, discuss problems, and get support. In the beginning, these "coffee houses" could be held periodically in a room or area of an existing coffeehouse or restaurant. Lectures on chosen topics could be offered. Small group discussions could be organized around "table topics." People who wish to discuss particular issues put a sign on a table at the beginning of an evening naming their topic and inviting people to join them. The advantage of this type of club is that it is open to all and not simply a segregated place just for people who share a common problem.

EPILOGUE

There are many factors which discourage Adlerian practitioners from dealing with problem drinkers. Some shy away because they anticipate poor results (Ray Corsini, personal communication, February 1991), or because "failure" (resumption of drinking on the part of the client) is so much more obvious than backsliding by other neurotics we like to believe we've helped (Alexandra Adler, 1941). Some don't take them on because they think that their treatment can only be done in groups, though research shows that there is no difference in results of individual versus group treatment (Miller, 1986). Other practitioners don't enter the field because they are not recovering alcoholics, an unproven credential that more then 60% of counselors of alcoholics are estimated to have (Bradley, 1988).

A major purpose of this article is to encourage Adlerian counselors to treat problem drinkers and to assure them that they have the right frame of thought and the appropriate tools with which to stop drinking. Alfred Adler referred to therapists who treat addicts as a "fellowship of lifesavers" (1932, p. 16). If one life is spared or one family's life is enhanced because an Adlerian counselor influenced by this paper had the courage to treat a problem drinker, the task shall have been worth the effort.

REFERENCES

Adler, A. (1932). Rauschgift (Intoxicant). *Internationale Zeitschrift für Individualpsychologie, 10*, 1–19.

Adler, Alexandra, (1941). The individual psychology of the alcoholic patient. *Journal of Criminal Psychopathology, 3*, 74–77.

Arkin, S., Lewis, J. A., & Carlson, J. (1990). Marital therapy with alcohol-affected couples: Treatment strategies. *Individual Psychology, 46*, 125–132.

Bandura, A. (1989). Human agency in social cognitive theory. *American Psychologist, 44*, 1175–1184.

Bergin, A. E. (1991). Values and religious issues in psychotherapy and mental health. *American Psychologist, 46*, 394–403.

Botvin, G. J., Baker, E., Renik, N. L., Filazzola, A. D., & Botvin, E. M. (1984). Cognitive behavioral approach to substance abuse prevention. *Addictive Behaviors, 9*, 137–147.

Bradley, A. M. (1988). Keep coming back. The case for a valuation of alcoholics anonymous. *Alcohol Health & Research World, 12*.

Dreikurs, R. (1953). *Fundamentals of Adlerian psychology*. Chicago: Alfred Adler Institute.

Dreikurs, R. (1960). Are psychological schools of thought outdated? *Journal of Individual Psychology, 16*, 3–10.

Dreikurs, R. (1967). *Psychodynamics, psychotherapy and counseling*. Chicago: Alfred Adler Institute.

Dreikurs, R. (1990). Drug addiction and its individual psychological treatment. *Individual Psychology, 46*, 209–216. (Original work published 1932)

Dreikurs, R., & Mosak, H. (1967). The tasks of life II. The fourth life task. *Individual Psychologist, 4*, 51–55.

Ellis, A., McInerney, J. F., DiGiuseppe, R., & Yeager, R. J. (1988). *Rational-emotive therapy with alcoholics and substance abusers*. New York: Pergamon Press.

Fingarette, H. (1989). *Heavy drinking: The myth of alcoholism as a disease.* Berkeley: University of California Press.

Hester, R. K., Miller, W. R. (1989). Self-control training. In R. Hester & W. Miller (Eds.), *Handbook of alcoholism treatment approaches* (pp. 141–149). New York: Pergamon Press.

Ignas, E., & Corsini, R. (1979). *Alternative educational systems.* Itasca, IL: Peacock.

Kelly, G. (1955). *The psychology of personal constructs: A theory of personality.* New York: Norton.

Kelly, G. (1964). The language of hypotheses: Man's psychological instrument. *Journal of Individual Psychology, 20*, 137–152.

Marlatt, G. A., & Gordon, J. R. (Eds.). (1985). *Relapse prevention: Maintenance strategies in addictive behavior change.* New York: Guilford.

Miller, W. R. (1986). Haunted by the Zeitgeist: Reflections on contrasting treatment goals and concepts of alcoholism in Europe and the United States. *Annals of the New York Academy of Sciences, 472*, 110–129.

Miller, W. R. (1989). Increasing motivation for change. In R. K. Hester & W. R. Miller (Eds.), *Handbook of alcoholism treatment approaches*, (pp. 67–80). New York: Pergamon Press.

Mosak, H. (1989). Adlerian psychotherapy. In R. Corsini (Ed.), *Current psychotherapies*. Itasca, IL: Peacock.

Mosak, H., & Dreikurs, R. (1967). The life tasks III. The fifth life task. *Individual Psychologist, 5*, 16–22.

Mozdzierz, G. J., Macchitelli, F. J., & Lisiecki, J. (1976). The paradox in psychotherapy: An Adlerian perspective. *Individual Psychology, 32*, 169–184.

O'Connell, W. (1975). *Action therapy and Adlerian therapy.* Chicago: Alfred Adler Institute.

O'Connell, W. (1988). Natural high theory and practice: A psychospiritual integration. *Journal of Integrative and Eclectic Psychotherapy, 7*, 441–454.

Peele, S. (1989). *Diseasing of America: Addiction treatment out of control.* Toronto: Lexington Books.

Perry, C. L., & Grant, M. (1988). Comparing peer-led to teacher-led youth alcohol education in four countries. *Alcohol Health and Research World, 12*, 322–326.

Polich, J. M., Armor, D. J., & Braiker, H. B. (1981). *The course of alcoholism: Four years after treatment.* New York: Wiley.

Shulman, B. (1973). *Contributions to individual psychology.* Chicago: Alfred Adler Institute.

Shulman, B. (n. d.) *Individual psychological psychotherapy: The Adlerian model.* Unpublished manuscript.

Sisson, R., & Azrin, N. (1989). The community reinforcement approach. In R. K. Hester & W. R. Miller (Eds.), *Handbook of alcoholism treatment approaches* (pp. 242–253). New York: Pergamon.

Sobell, M. B., & Sobell, L. C. (1987). Conceptual issues regarding goals in the treatment of alcohol problems. *Drugs and Society, 1*, 1–37.

Starr, A. (1977). *Rehearsal for living: Psychodrama.* Chicago: Nelson Hall.

Tobler, N. S. (1986). Meta-analysis of 143 adolescent drug prevention programs: Quantitative outcome results of program participants compared to a control or comparison group. *Journal of Drug Issues, 16*, 537–567.

Wodarski, J. S. (1987). *Field Assessment of social learning approach to teaching adolescents about alcohol and driving.* Athens, GA: University of Georgia Research Foundation.

ALCOHOLISM AND DRUG DEPENDENCY: SOME MISTAKES WE CAN AVOID

Helen K. Cooley
Directs a private practice, interactions Institute, in Evergreen Park, Illinois. One of the primary programs offered there is the diagnosis and holistic treatment of chemical dependencies in the individual and family.

Alcoholism and drug dependency have become the second largest health problem in the United States today. In some sections of the country it has reached epidemic proportions. In the United States there are approximately 12 million alcoholics and drug dependents. Each of these persons affects the lives of at least 4 other persons who also will be in need of professional help. Thus, we are considering 48 million people who suffer directly or indirectly from alcohol or chemical dependency (HEW, 1978). For the Adlerian clinician, teacher, counselor, or parent it becomes an immediate and constant challenge to first detect the problem, and then do something concrete to help these individuals and their families recover from this illness.

Long before chemical dependency (CD)[1] became such a national and international problem Alfred Adler gave some helpful insights into the problems of treating persons who develop this emotional disorder. He spoke of the CD person as often displaying "an acute feeling of inferiority marked by shyness, a liking for isolation, oversensitivity, impatience, irritability . . ." (Adler, 1956, p. 423). Dreikurs added to our understanding of addiction by presenting us with an important guideline for treatment. He stated "the only therapy that seems to affect them

[1][The term "chemical dependent" or CD is used in this paper to cover both alcohol and/or drug dependency. It implies a chronic use over time, although in some cases the usage may be of a "binge" type interspaced with periods of abstention.]

Individual Psychology, 39(2), June, 1983, **pp. 144–155**

(alcoholics and drug addicts) is *group* therapy. They resist personal treatment in most cases . . ." (1967, p. 139, my italics).

This paper presents some of the reasons for client resistance and suggests practical methods for overcoming that resistance and avoiding the most common treatment pitfalls. A holistic model of treatment will be offered that has proven successful with many CD persons (Cooley, 1977).

CLIENT RESISTANCE AND METHODS TO OVERCOME DENIAL

The Significance of the Denial System

Those who have attempted to help the alcoholic or drug dependent person on a one-to-one basis may know what a discouraging process it can be. Unlike other clients who complain clearly of their primary symptom, the alcoholic or drug user rarely presents his or her addiction symptom as the basis for his or her suffering. This is but the first indication of the pervasive use of denial by the chemically dependent client, hereafter referred to as CDC.

The basic component of chemical addiction is the complex and rigid denial system that the individual sufferer creates. This denial system functions to protect the person from the facts and destructive evidence of his or her chemical usage (Hazelden Educational Services, 1975b). For example, it is not unusual for a CDC to be totally unaware of the connection between his or her high rate of job absenteeism and repeated intoxication with its ensuing withdrawal syndrome (hangover). This denial system has misled many well-trained and experienced professionals (Banta, 1980).

A very important way the denial system interferes with counseling is in the area of the presenting symptom. Unlike persons with other symptoms who detail each episode or "attack," the CDC has a desperate need to avoid disclosing the primary symptom. This client will go to great lengths to convince himself or herself and those closest to him or her, *particularly* the counselor, of a host of other problems, ranging from insomnia, a brutal employer, or psychosis to secret confessions of sexual deviation. In short, the counselor should anticipate this pervasive denial system when dealing with the CDC.

Unless the helpers have been trained in diagnosing and treating CD they may unwittingly become enablers of the illness (Banta, 1980). In other words, the CDC is extremely adroit at incorporating the therapist into his or her denial system. This is an essential element of this particular illness. Not only is drug usage the primary symptom, it is also the CDC's most important relationship! Johnson's four-step process describes how this relationship develops (Kinney & Leaton, 1978). The foremost goal, although mostly hidden from the awareness protection of this relationship with his or her drug *at all costs* (Hazelden Educational Services, 1975b).

The Critical Time Factor

Experience has been that the Adlerian procedure of doing a Life Style diagnosis, disclosing faulty conclusions, or giving assignments will rarely be effective in the treatment of the CDC. Too often the helping person spends months of time and professional energy (often along with the client's money!) doing Life Style work that has little chance of being useful until the sufferer has, first, recovered from his or her chemical addiction.

This time-lapse factor has serious consequences. Many other symptoms tend to diminish, with or without appropriate treatment. With alcohol and drug dependency this is seldom true. Sadly, the illness follows a steady, although often unseen, progression (Kinney & Leaton, 1978). During this period a well-intentioned and often well-trained helper may be using treatment procedures that are appropriate for treating other types of illnesses, but inappropriate for treating chemical dependency. Meanwhile the client's addiction is becoming more entrenched, complex, and creative. Psychological and physical deterioration that may not be easily recognizable is progressing The most disturbing changes are those that concern the client's private logic. His or her denial system is becoming more pervasive and rigid in order to shield the sufferer from the evidence of the advancing illness, as well as barricade himself or herself from all consensual validation (Hazelden Educational Services, 1975b).

Erroneous Use of Prescribed Medication

Meanwhile the helping person is becoming more perplexed and frustrated. Just when it appears that progress is starting to be made, the client's life becomes even more tumultuous. The client may exhibit intense emotional agitation or a "manic" kind of enthusiasm, to be followed at the next meeting by a mood of despair and depression. Many well-trained professionals have diagnosed the client as cyclothymic, manic-depressive, borderline, or having an anxiety neurosis, when in actuality the client may be presenting the complex and subtle three-part behavior cycle of the hidden addict.[2] The helper observing the erratic moodswings may decide that the client would benefit from prescribed medication. This is often a serious error that compounds the problem by inviting cross-addiction or establishing the belief that a pill will solve the addiction (Banta, 1980).

When the helper is untrained in the recognition of the CD cycle he or she may easily misinterpret the client's behavior. Without realizing it the therapist may be observing either stage two, the chemical withdrawal period, which involves both fearful anxieties and reactive depression, or stage three with the manic anticipatory build-up toward the next chemical episode. Less frequently the counselor may witness the first stage of the cycle where the client is in an artificial calm or euphoric drug state. When the person's drug of choice is a sedative in pill form, rather than liquid alcohol, he or she runs less risk of detection. This person may more frequently meet with the helper in the euphoric first stage of the cycle. The alcoholic client may attempt to be more prudent by delaying his or her drug intake until after the scheduled meeting with the helper. This often requires the person to endure painful withdrawal symptoms. Even with the best intentions many clients will succumb to the physical demands and drink before their appointment. Then to protect themselves from possible discovery they may not show up for their meeting. Last minute cancellations are a common avoidance technique with the active alcoholic person.

While the CDC is pursuing his or her addiction, which includes the three-part cycle of euphoria (drug state), withdrawal from toxic effects, and anticipatory build-up, his or her erratic mood swings are not reliable indicators of any particular underlying mental disorder. In most cases to prescribe medication that may relieve the symptoms is to ensure misuse.

There are three exceptions where medication may be necessary. The first is when the person is hospitalized for the purpose of drug withdrawal. Under medical monitoring, on an in-patient basis only, Valium and other drugs are given to avoid convulsions or delirium tremens (West, 1974). Once the patient is discharged from the hospital it is preferable to avoid giving medication. Tendency to seek instant relief from discomfort, along with a high sensitivity to all medications, makes these clients poor candidates for chemotherapy. Cross addiction or a new addiction is all too often the unfortunate result (Kinney & Leaton, 1978). The second exception involves persistent mood swings. When they continue, even after prolonged abstinence and systematic counseling, lithium carbonate has proven effective in the control and leveling of these mood swings. Since there is

[2]In some cases chemical dependency can best be understood in terms of multiple diagnosis. Effective treatment, however, depends upon focusing on the addiction and abstinence first.

a high potentiality for toxicity, medical monitoring is essential (Baldessarini, 1978). The third exception that should be mentioned concerns the CDC who also has an underlying psychosis. Very few CDCs will be found in this category, but when psychosis is the accompanying diagnosis additional treatment is needed. Along with CD counseling the patient will need psychiatric supervision that may include prescribing one of the major tranquilizers (Kinney & Leaton, 1978).

The Problem of Confrontation

To successfully assist the CDC in recovery, the helper must be able to unmask the denied and hidden symptom. Often this must be done without overt help or cooperation from the client. It is essential, therefore, that the helper be knowledgeable in the subtle physical signs and behavioral clues. Some of these signs and clues may include such things as a bulbous, enlarged nose, jaundiced skin and eyes, spider angiomas, scabbing, hoarse voice, fiery red palms, protruding abdomen indicating a swollen liver, shrunken arms and legs, multiple bruises, perspiration, abnormal blinking and movement of the eyes (either too slow or jerky and rapid). Other alerting signals are the continual use of mints or gum, reports of home violence, job or appointment absenteeism, sexual escapades, complaints of hypertension, palpitation, insomnia, anxiety alternating with depression, and evasiveness about specifics of daily routine. When several of these signs and symptoms are presented the possibility of CD is strongly suggested (Kinney & Leaton, 1978).

Confronting the person with this conclusion is no simple task. A combination of firmness, tact, and factual evidence along with a personal refusal to be drawn into the role of *enabler* are basic ingredients of successful confrontation.

Process of Bereavement and Prolonged Panic

When CDCs stop using their chemical they may experience grief. This bereavement period usually abates within six months, but may last as long as a year. This sadness at having ended the intense relationship with a chemical often is diagnosed as reactive depression. Professional counselors should resist the temptation to suggest or prescribe any medication to ease a recovering CDC's discomfort. Medication is inappropriate for not only the reasons stated previously, but also because it interferes with the resolution process that is necessary for recovery from the grief (Kellermann, 1979).

Emerging panic is another stage of the recovery from chemicals. Clients may cover this sense of panic with a deceptively nonchalant attitude, or they may display excessive activity, irritability, or manic behavior. As they become more aware of their personal powerlessness over chemicals, they fear emotional bankruptcy. Their past neglect of the business of living coupled with an urgency to put their lives in order all at once often cause them to take on more than they can handle (Alcoholics Anonymous World Services, 1979, p. 21). Unlike other clients who present plans that are obviously lacking in common sense, CDCs can convince a counselor that their judgment is sound and their plans appropriate. It takes wisdom and firm directiveness to restrain impatient clients from moving too fast, overloading themselves with responsibility and risking a relapse.

AVOIDING SOME COMMON THERAPEUTIC PITFALLS

Life Style Interpretation

It is risky to attempt formal Life Style collection and presentation within the first few months of treatment. To focus the client into the past during his or her primitive stage of recovery is antitherapeutic. In most cases it is appropriate to consider the client to be in an on-going state of crisis for at least six months, and in many cases longer, no matter how calm or confident he or she may appear. Naturally, there are exceptions to this, but as a standard procedure it is suggested that counselors avoid Life Style work when an individual is in the early stages of recovery. The CDC often recalls the past with an exaggerated horror and sense of degradation. It is wise therefore to follow the traditions of the AA program, which instructs its members to stay in the present, forget the past, and live twenty-four hours at a time (Alcoholics Anonymous World Services, 1976). In the first months of treatment the appropriate question is, "What are you doing to stay sober, or straight, today?" not "Describe to me the kind of person your father was when you were six." Caution in this area cannot be overemphasized! What may appear to the helper as an ordinary, inoffensive question may be experienced by the client, in his or her highly sensitized state, as a callous intrusion.

At the same time it should be remembered that without Life Style collection and presentation, we are limited in our ability to help clients change their faulty conclusions about themselves and their world. And without this change their abstinence is precarious! Even with the most skilled counseling and comprehensive treatment program, relapse back to chemical use happens with many clients, so it is essential that clients eventually move into the Life Style work. Each client is individual, but as a rule of thumb it is prudent to delay formalized Life Style work until the person has six months to a year of basic recovery treatment and abstinence. That does not mean that the counselor will not tactfully raise some Life Style issues as they present themselves during that first year. In fact, it is the creative and subtle introduction by the helper of new ways of perceiving life during those initial treatment months that makes it easier for the client to "hear" the formal Life Style presentation when it is finally given. In other words, clients will have already started to reconsider some of their faulty notions, *before* they are presented with the specific interfering ideas. It is understood that Life Style work need not always be done in a formalized manner to be effective, but whatever approach is chosen, it is vital to the recovery of clients that they correct their distorted attitudes.

When the counselor decides to present Life Style information, it is recommended that care be taken to use the most tactful language and spread the presentation out over several weeks. The reason for this elongated process is that bombarding clients with too many insights can trigger the reactivation of their denial pattern and possibly bring on relapse into chemicals. Or it may cause them to terminate treatment. Worst of all, the ill-timed disclosures may cause them to do both. Life Style presentation at any time with CDCs can be risky, but, nonetheless, until they have reconsidered their faulty ideas, their abstinence remains in a primitive state (Cooley, 1977).

Identifying the Subtle Signs of Impending Relapse

The counselor must keep in mind during that first year of abstinence that the client is sicker than he or she appears. The recovering person may present convincing arguments and evidence in order to withdraw from a structured therapy program. This "flight-into-health" is a common phenomenon of the illness and signals, in most cases, a hidden yearning to return to the chemical relationship. It is in the private sessions that the counselor can establish a strong enough bond with the client that he or she will be able to later "hold" the client in treatment, until he or she is firmly committed and regularly attends meetings of one of the community self-help programs such as Alcoholics Anonymous or Narcotics Anonymous. This does not mean that helpers are to engage in power struggles. It does mean, however, that positive pressure should be applied to influence the client to continue participation in the support program. How is this done? Reminding the client firmly that most CDCs who leave treatment before the first year return to their chemical often "buys" the helper some time. Bringing the issue up to the support group is a potent therapeutic tool. The group tends to react with unanimous concern. Many members will recount their own past experiences of withdrawing prematurely from treatment, thinking they could do it on their own, and then experiencing painful relapse. Group pressure can be the helper's greatest ally!

A HOLISTIC TREATMENT PROGRAM

In the first year of abstinence from chemicals a therapy and educational program should be available. This program should guide the recovering person and his or her family through the difficult period of adjusting to the dramatic changes that result not only in the recovering person, but also in the family dynamic. Treatment that only involves individual counseling is rarely successful. The application of a holistic program is needed that is able to do the following:

1. Continue to confront the denial pattern that tends to reactivate during the primitive stage of recovery (Cooley, 1977).

2. Be sensitive to the grief process and provide a climate of acceptance for this stage where little is expected from the individual in terms of Life Tasks. (It takes courage enough to abstain from one's painkiller one day at a time!) Many clients are too depressed in the beginning of recovery to work on life problems. Others, however, rush in all directions trying to do everything at once. This overenthusiasm to make up for lost time is one way a person may attempt to relieve the sense of panic. This behavior is ill-advised, and these clients need to be reminded that they may jeopardize their sobriety by overextending themselves. Their energies need to be focused on the number one priority, their recovery program.

3. Educate the client to understand the physiological process of repair. Up to a year or longer is often needed for the body to neurologically heal and become rebalanced chemically.

4. Monitor the client's weekly events and have regular contact with family members and other persons involved in the client's recovery.

5. Involve the client in group support. This often includes three to five group experiences each week. Ideally, some of these groups would be Alcoholics Anonymous meetings.

(a) *Topic Group.* Through discussion and lecture, client and family are taught the physical, emotional, and cultural aspects of addiction, withdrawal, and long-term recovery.

(b) *Support Group.* Facilitated by the primary helping person, this group is designed to expand social *interest* through identification and problem sharing. Another important goal of this group is to train the members to have a "permanent awareness of the possibility of relapse" (Chicago Area AA Service Office, 1973).

The tone of the meeting is practical. Discussion of options is encouraged, while introspection and analysis are discouraged. The leader's role is directive and encouraging, providing a structured and protective environment. In this primitive recovery stage the group must allow for the particular type of sensitivity, the pampered nature, plus the neurological impairments of the members. Faulty conceptualization, disorientation, occasional inability to abstract, problems with concentration and thought organization, as well as unreliable memory must be expected. Extreme tolerance with members' mistaken notions is an important factor. The exception to this is the issue of chemicals. Private logic in this area is never allowed to go unchallenged. Most other exaggerated ideas and denial "pockets" can be accepted during the primitive stage of abstinence (Cooley, 1977).

(c) *Spiritual Needs Group.* Most CDCs seem to have a heightened need to deal with the Spiritual Task almost at once in order to move themselves out of the center of their universe as well as to replace what has been a very powerful god in their lives. Addicted persons tend to have made a total commitment to their drug and have given it absolute power over them. When they finally abandon this destructive commitment there is a vacuum. Recovering persons respond more rapidly to treatment when they can find "a power greater than themselves" (Alcoholics Anonymous World Services, 1976, p. 59). Carl Jung (1976), in a letter to one of the founders of Alcoholics Anonymous, describes the alcoholic's spiritual situation. He says, "His craving . . . was the equivalent, on a low level, for the spiritual thirst; [for] a union with God" (1976, p. 2). Even though this spiritual need may be present, many clients express antipathy toward churches and view them as guilt producing and punishing or hypocritical and bigoted. Others feel it is childish and unscientific to believe in God. As is stated in the section, "We Agnostics" of the Alcoholica Anonymous Big Book, many "thought that faith and dependence upon a Power beyond ourselves was somewhat weak, even cowardly" (Alcoholics Anonymous World Services, 1976, pp. 45–46).

Since traditional religious groups may seem unappealing to many recovering persons, it is useful to guide clients to alternative groups. Alcoholics Anonymous, Narcotics Anonymous, Alanon for the families, and Natural High groups (O'Connell & Bright, 1977) are either available or can be organized by the helping person to aid clients in dealing with the "spiritual thirst."

(d) *Family Group.* This group focuses on the needs of persons closest to the CDC. It encourages family members to examine their own participation, which often includes the role of the enabler, within the context of the illness (Hazelden Educational Services, 1975a). New roles are discussed, along with individual responses to the recovery process. Family dynamics are explored. Members provide mutual sharing and encouragement. The CDCs are usually not included in these family meetings.

6. Provide individual counseling. Private sessions can add a useful component to the recovery program, one that may not be found within the group setting. These meetings with the primary helping person provide the intimacy that allows the client to develop a trust bond with another human being, something he or she may not have had in years (or perhaps never). In this setting clients, with their fragile pride, may be able to risk exposing their needs for the most elementary guidance in life skills. Clients often carefully conceal their need for basic instruction in matters of day-to-day business. The primary helping person may be the only one during the initial recovery stage that the client will allow to see his or her inadequacies or accept advice from.

Private sessions are also important because they provide undivided attention, which meets the needs of the pampered or indulged Life Style. The group experience requires the recovering person to share the counselor with other members. While it is essential to eventually expand clients' social interest, at first the helper must accept them just as they are, recognizing, and to some degree meeting, their exaggerated need for individual attention. As clients become more emotionally invested in their groups and learn that they have a place of respect among their peers, their need for exclusive attention will diminish. They become willing to share the leader's attention, as well as give their own attention to other members' concerns. Eventually, they learn to place their dependency upon the group rather than making demands upon one or two persons.

SUMMARY

Being a well-trained member of the medical or professional helping community does not necessarily qualify a person to successfully diagnose and treat alcoholism or drug dependency.

The first priority in helping CDCs is to correctly identify their symptoms and then confront their denial pattern. To do this we must understand the hidden goal of their denial, which includes a desperate need to protect and preserve their relationship with their chemical.

Helpers must understand the paradox of the illness. Even when clients become aware of the destructiveness of their symptoms, they will continue to yearn for a return to the chemical relationship. We can expect clients to experience a prolonged grieving process, not unlike the kind that we would associate with the loss of a beloved family member.

For the first year of recovery clients are not as well as they appear. Despite a calm and confident appearance their balance is precarious and their sobriety fragile. During this initial recovery period a comprehensive treatment program that includes individual counseling and peer self-help groups (such as AA, family, and educational groups) along with medical monitoring should be provided. Formalized Life Style collection and presentation must be pursued cautiously. Ill-timed disclosures may initiate relapse or flight from treatment. Nonetheless, clients have to have a personality change to maintain stable sobriety. As the basic text of Alcoholics Anonymous states, those who try to "hold on to old ideas [find] the result was nil until [they] let go absolutely" (Alcoholics Anonymous World Services, 1976, p. 56). In order for the recovering person to grow out of this primitive abstinence stage and comfortably solve the Life Tasks, disclosure of faulty conclusions must eventually be completed.

The principles of Individual Psychology that focus on holism and social embeddedness offer unique opportunities for successful treatment. The emphasis on group fellowship and expanding social interest, with a thrust toward the Spiritual Task, is essential for recovery from alcoholism or drug dependency.

REFERENCES

Alcoholics Anonymous World Services, Inc. *Alcoholics Anonymous big book: The basic text for Alcoholics Anonymous*. New York, N.Y.: Alcoholics Anonymous World Services, Inc., 1976.

——. *Twelve steps and twelve traditions*. New York, N.Y.: Alcoholics Anonymous World Services, Inc., 1979.

Ansbacher, H., & Ansbacher, R. (eds.). *The Individual Psychology of Alfred Adler*. New York, N.Y.: Harper and Row, 1956.

Baldessarini, R. Chemotherapy. In A. Nicholi (ed.), *The Harvard guide to modern psychiatry*. Cambridge, Mass.: Belknap Press, 1978, pp. 387–482.

Banta, R. Why certification? *Illinois Alcoholism Counselor Certification Board, Inc. Newsletter*, 1980, 3, 6–7.

Chicago Area Alcoholics Anonymous Service Office. *Alcoholism and the A.A. program by a doctor in A.A.* Chicago, Ill.: Alcoholics Anonymous Service Office, 1973.

Cooley, H. Alcoholism-outpatient and follow-up treatment in a general hospital. *Illinois Medical State Journal*, February 1977, 135–139.

Dreikurs, R. *Psychodynamics, psychotherapy and counseling*. Chicago, Ill.: Alfred Adler Institute, 1967.

Hazelden Educational Services. *Dealing with denial* (Caring Community Series, no. 4). Center City, Minn.: Hazelden Foundation, Inc., 1975a.

——. *Reviewing the enabling role: The crisis* (Caring Community Series, no. 6). Center City, Minn.: Hazelden Foundation, Inc., 1975b, pp. 20–21.

HEW. *Third special report to the United States Congress on alcohol and health*. Rockville, Md.: United States Government Printing Office, June 1978.

Jung, C. The Bill W./Carl Jung letters. *Here's How Newsletter*. Chicago, Ill.: Alcoholics Anonymous Service Office, February/March 1976, 1–3.

Kellermann, J. *Grief: A basic reaction to alcoholism*. Center City, Minn.: Hazelden Foundation, Inc., 1979.

Kinney, J., & Leaton, G. *Loosening the grip: A handbook of alcohol information*. St. Louis, Mo.: C. V. Mosby Co., 1978.

O'Connell, W., & Bright, M. *Natural high primer*. Houston, Tex.: Natural High Associates, 1977.

West, J. Alcoholism: A general hospital meets the challenge. *Illinois Medical Journal*, August 1974, 96–99.

MARITAL THERAPY WITH ALCOHOL-AFFECTED COUPLES: TREATMENT STRATEGIES

Sharon Arkin
A clinical psychology intern at Charter Beacon Hospital in Fort Wayne, Indiana, and a Psy.D. candidate at the Alfred Adler Institute in Chicago. Arkin worked as a vocational counselor, substance-abuse counselor, and employee assistance program coordinator for the District of Columbia and federal government from 1964 to 1983.

Judith A. Lewis
A professor of Alcoholism and Drug Abuse Sciences at Governors State University.

Jon Carlson
A university professor in the Psychology and Counseling Department at Governors State University in University Park, Illinois.

When problematic drinking interferes with an individual's physical health or life functioning, the alcohol use itself must be interrupted. Before a therapist can address other life-style issues, he or she must help the client to change the specific behaviors related to alcohol consumption. Thus, the treatment plan for an individual with alcohol-related problems must focus, at least in part, on measures that promise to alleviate the immediate problem of alcohol use. Depending on the severity of the alcohol problem, these measures may include detoxification and inpatient treatment. Treatment focused narrowly on alcohol consumption, however, provides

Individual Psychology, 46(2), June, 1990, **pp. 125–132**

a short-term solution at best. Long-term sobriety requires a holistic approach and attention to all elements of the client's life-style.

Adlerians know that individuals can be understood and treated only in a social context, that each human is "embedded in the community of his fellow man, which furnishes both the resources and the problems of his life" (Rattner, 1983, p. 4). This is as true of alcoholics as of any other group of clients. Alcoholism, like all problems, develops in a social milieu and can best be resolved in the social context. In the case of adult alcoholism, the most important social system affecting treatment outcome has been found to be the family; in fact, "the more cohesive and supportive the family . . . the better the prognosis for an individual who has been treated for alcoholism" (Finney, Moos, & Mewborn, 1980, p. 27). Within the context of the troubled alcoholic family, the spousal subsystem plays a major role in the development and maintenance of alcohol problems and must play an equally important role in their resolution. Steinglass (1979), after studying the interactions of a number of marital couples affected by alcoholism, determined that these couples tended to use the alcoholic's intoxication as a way of dealing with conflict and as a way of stabilizing their interactions. Clearly, effective therapy for alcohol problems must be directed toward helping couples to change these highly dysfunctional patterns. Although a large number of treatment alternatives are available, treatment strategies can best be categorized in terms of three general types: (1) alcohol-focused interventions aimed at supporting the alcohol abuser in modifying or quitting his or her drinking, (2) interventions aimed at improving the quality of the marital and family relationship, and (3) relapse prevention strategies.

ALCOHOL-FOCUSED INTERVENTIONS

Interventions with alcohol-affected couples need to begin by helping them to interrupt the ongoing patterns that have characterized their past interactions (Lewis, in press). Part of the therapist's role at this point involves helping the nondrinking individual to decide whether it is possible or appropriate to press the alcoholic into treatment. In some cases, the best alternative may involve disengagement; the nonalcoholic spouse may seek a more positive life-style with or without the participation of the alcohol abuser. If the nonalcoholic spouse has previously behaved in ways that enabled the alcoholic to drink without negative consequences, a change in this pattern might precipitate a change in the alcoholic's drinking even without direct confrontation. "The alcoholic who is sheltered from the reality of his behavior has little reason to stop drinking. He continues to derive satisfaction (no matter how unhealthy) from his drinking and if he does not have to face the consequences, why should he stop?" (Krimmerl, 1975, p. 16). Forcing the alcoholic to face the consequences of his or her drinking behavior might bring about a crisis that leads to change.

The ideal situation, however, is one in which the couple decides as a unit to move in the direction of recovery. In this case, the alcoholic and his or her spouse must come to a clear and specific agreement between them about the goal for the alcoholic's drinking and the role of each in achieving this goal. If moderation in drinking is the mutually-accepted goal, then agreement must be reached concerning acceptable limits, drinking situations, and consequences of excessive drinking. If abstinence is the goal, an initial target time period for such abstinence needs to be established, at the end of which the goal should be reviewed. The benefits to be gained by adherence to the agreement, as well as the effects of violations, must also be clearly identified.

Some alcoholics use disulfiram (Antabuse), a drug that produces violent nausea when combined with alcohol. If Antabuse has been prescribed, it is taken daily in the hope of discouraging impulsive alcohol use. Couple involvement in Antabuse procedures has been used with some success (Azrin, 1976) to ensure daily Antabuse ingestion and to prevent nagging and arguments between the alcoholic and the spouse. When this approach is used, the alcoholic agrees to take Antabuse each day in the presence of the spouse. The spouse agrees to take Antabuse each day in the presence of the spouse. The spouse agrees to record the event on a calendar provided by the therapist and not to mention past drinking or any concerns about future drinking. As O'Farrell (1987) stresses, this process must be viewed by the couple as a cooperative, trust-building procedure, not as a surveillance operation.

Another issue of importance involves the behavior of the nonalcoholic spouse and other family members with regard to alcohol use. Decisions must be made about whether to keep alcoholic beverages in the home, whether to accept invitations to social events where alcohol will be served, and whether to socialize with friends who drink heavily (O'Farrell, 1987). In their consideration of these issues, the alcoholic and his or her spouse are, in effect, agreeing together on the life-style changes that they hope to make.

Destructive communication or interaction patterns that generate tension also need to be identified and addressed if drinking behaviors are to change. Frequently, married couples engage in behaviors that exacerbate alcohol abuse or allow drinking to substitute for problem solving and conflict resolution (Steinglass, 1978). The couple working toward abstinence or moderation in alcohol use needs to analyze the true goals of their behaviors and, at the same time, learn new skills that can take the place of dysfunctional interactions.

GENERAL MARITAL IMPROVEMENT STRATEGIES

Improving a marital relationship involves work on attitudes, behaviors, and feelings, with improvements in feelings seen as a by-product of improvements in the other two areas. Partners in an alcohol-affected marriage often have a history of resentments, breaches of trust, and disappointments. They are typically enmeshed in a circular pattern of blaming behavior, with *both* members feeling that they are unappreciated for their contributions and *neither* willing to take responsibility for difficulties.

The overriding task of a marital therapist is to build in such couples the mutual conviction that each partner has positive intentions toward the other. This process, like the encouragement process used with individuals (Dreikurs, 1953), increases the individual's confidence in himself or herself and in the efficacy of the relationship. If a conviction of positive intentions exists, displeasing behaviors by one's partner, when they occur, will not automatically be escalated into a personal attack or viewed as a deliberate effort to hurt or annoy. Such misinterpretations and faulty conclusions are the crux of interpersonal conflict. Creating positive conviction requires regular demonstrations of good will and good faith by each partner toward the other, as well as recognition of past contributions and demonstrations of good intentions.

The process can be summarized in terms of the "4 R's" (Manaster & Corsini, 1982). It begins cognitively, with *respect*. "I decide to respect my partner and believe in his or her good intentions." The next step is positive action: *responsibility*. Instead of worrying about the other's doing his or her share, each behaves "as if" he or she were responsible for 100%. Only after a pattern of positive, responsible action is demonstrated and acknowledged can feelings begin to change and *responsiveness* become a reality. *Resourcefulness*, the fourth R, is demonstrated when a couple begins to solve problems flexibly and creatively, exploring and drawing upon many alternatives instead of using the old, automatic ways that are typical of alcoholic families.

The importance of good intentions is stressed in the following adaptation of O'Farrell's (1987) Increasing Pleasing Behaviors exercise. A series of activities can be initiated to increase a couple's appreciation of their mutual good intentions, as well as their knowledge about what actually pleases the other. Each spouse is asked to complete a list of five things the partner has done that demonstrated his or her good intentions *and* which were pleasing. Another list identifies things the partner has done that were *not* pleasing but that probably were done with good intentions; in this list, the good intentions are also described. The two lists are then read aloud and discussed. The first list provides encouragement and mutual awareness of the other's appreciation. The second list provides an opportunity for reframing or refocusing on positives; even though displeasing behavior is mentioned ("husband is working too much overtime; wife is nagging me about my drinking"), there is acknowledgment that, in performing the behavior, the partner's well-being is being considered ("he wants to provide financially for the family"; "she is worried about my health and safety"). The discussion might conclude with the couple negotiating alternative behaviors that might be performed in place of the well-intentioned ones that were not pleasing.

If a couple is finding they are having difficulty pleasing each other, it may be that they are unaware of what the other wants or needs. "Give the customer what he or she wants" is an unquestioned maxim in the retail world, and market researchers constantly work to discover what desires customers have so that these desires can be met. Yet, at home, many people are in the dark as to what pleases their partner. The woman who prepares elaborate meals for her husband may be sabotaging the partner's attempt to maintain a normal body weight. The man who massages his wife's back before lovemaking in the hope that she will do the same to him may very well *not* be pleasing her; he may not get what he wants unless he tells her specifically what he likes. Many couples need to be taught how to get more of what they want by articulating their wants in positive, clear, and specific terms.

One issue that may be important for couples involves leisure time. Quitting or curtailing drinking creates a vacuum for many couples in terms of how to spend nonworking time. A common solution is for the alcoholic spouse to commit large blocks of time to Alcoholics Anonymous meetings. The spouse's response may be one of resentment, along with feelings of being neglected or left out. Some will choose to join Al-Anon, thereby getting their own needs for support met but, on occasion, increasing the distance between the spouses. Although involvement in mutual help groups should be encouraged, the alcohol-affected couple should also be encouraged to cooperate in planning and carrying out leisure time activities without an alcohol focus.

Sometimes, new competencies are needed by couples in order to carry out previously untried behaviors. The need for skills in communication, assertiveness, problem solving, and conflict resolution might have been covered up by the couple's previous focus on alcohol. Now, the leisure time vacuum may be joined by a communication vacuum and intensive skill-building efforts become imperative.

Good communication involves a cooperative interaction. The therapist can teach the couple how to structure communication sessions (Hahn, 1984) that begin with positive or neutral topics. In such a planned, face-to-face discussion, each partner takes a turn expressing his or her point of view without interruption. When one partner is finished, the listening partner responds by repeating back both the words and the feelings of the speaker's message, thereby checking to make sure that the intended meaning was received. Only when the feedback loop is complete does the second partner begin his or her turn. As skill increases, communication sessions can be increased in duration and frequency and attempted with more controversial topics. Couples can use *Time for a Better Marriage* (Dinkmeyer & Carlson, 1984), a self-contained marriage enrichment manual that includes communication exercises and daily discussion topics.

RELAPSE PREVENTION

No matter how motivated the client may be or how effective the therapy, the danger of relapse is always present when dealing with addictions. The recovering couple has to remain vigilant, working together to recognize the signs of incipient relapse and to prevent minor slips from developing into major binges.

Effective relapse prevention work depends on the counselor's ability to view the client from a holistic orientation that sees the person as a unity (Mosak, 1989). The most frequently used relapse prevention model, which is based on the work of Marlatt and Gordon (1985), depends on a recognition of the complex interactions among psychological and social factors. Drinking behaviors are seen as important but are addressed in the context of the person's general life-style, environment, and emotional well-being.

In the Marlatt and Gordon approach, relapse prevention begins with an analysis of the alcoholic's typical drinking patterns. High-risk situations are identified and coping strategies developed and practiced. Typical strategies employed are assertive drink refusal, avoidance of high-risk situations or people who drink, relaxation routines, and use of substitute activities. Homework assignments are aimed at providing a feeling of mastery or confidence that can help in dealing with future high-risk situations. Role-playing or rehearsal in the therapist's office also helps to prepare the client for forthcoming activities, such as office parties. The more success experiences the person has, the more encouraged he or she becomes concerning the ability to master difficult situations in the future.

Alcoholics also need to learn to distinguish between "cravings" for alcohol and states of emotional arousal brought on by conflict, stress, or crisis. The Marlatt and Gordon model uses a number of self-monitoring activities, suggesting that clients keep logs of cravings, alcohol refusals, drinking incidents, and the circumstances and feelings associated with each incident. The self-knowledge that is enhanced through these methods can lead in the direction of life-style changes, with clients learning how to avoid situations that threaten their sobriety and how to create positive growth opportunities for themselves.

In addition to addressing situations and skills that are directly related to alcohol use, the Marlatt and Gordon model stresses the use of global intervention strategies that are designed to increase the client's overall ability to deal with stress, to train the client in identifying early warning situations, and to address the need for a balanced daily life-style. The recovering client needs to lead a life that balances work and leisure, growth and stability, self-control and reasonable indulgence. Threats to this life-style balance, whether personal or situational, need to be recognized early if relapses are to be prevented.

Clearly, the nonalcoholic member of the couple has a major role to play in relapse prevention. Early training regarding the nature of the relapse process and its prevention needs to be provided to both members so that they can work together in the relapse prevention effort. The kinds of life-style changes that can prevent relapse require the joint effort of the alcohol-affected couple. This effort can become a reality only if both members agree on the steps that they will take together and only if both members carefully maintain an awareness of their own goals and behaviors. In the final analysis, alcohol problems are resolved when couples recognize the purpose that alcohol has played in their relationship and find better ways to meet their life goals.

REFERENCES

Azrin, N. H. (1976). Improvements in the community-reinforcement approach to alcoholism. *Behaviour Research and Therapy, 14*, 339–348.

Dinkmeyer, D., & Carlson, J. (1984). *Time for a better marriage*. Circle Pines, MN: American Guidance Service.

Dreikurs, R. R. (1953). *Fundamentals of Adlerian psychology*. Chicago: Alfred Adler Institute.

Finney, J. W., Moos, R. H., & Mewborn, C. R. (1980). Post-treatment experiences and treatment outcome of alcoholic patients six months and two years after hospitalization. *Journal of Consulting and Clinical Psychology, 48(1)*, 17–29.

Hahn, J. M. (1984). Growing ourselves up: An exercise for learning to love unconditionally. *Individual Psychology, 40(2)*, 154–161.

Krimmerl, H. E. (1975). The value of a crisis. *Al-Anon faces alcoholism.* New York: Al-Anon Family Group Headquarters.

Lewis, J. A. (In Press). Treating the alcoholic with the family. In L. L. L'Abate, J. Farr, & D. Seritella (Eds.), *Handbook of differential treatments for addictions.* Boston: Allyn and Bacon.

Manaster, G. J., & Corsini, R. J. (1982). *Individual psychology.* Itasca, IL: F. E. Peacock.

Marlatt, G. A., & Gordon, J. R. (1985). *Relapse prevention: Maintenance strategies in the treatment of addictive behaviors.* New York: Guilford Press.

Mosak, H. H. (1989). Adlerian psychotherapy. In R. J. Corsini & D. Wedding (Eds.), *Current psychotherapies, 4th ed.* Itasca, IL: F. E. Peacock.

O'Farrell, T. J. (1987). Marital and family therapy for alcohol problems. In W. M. Cox (Ed.), *Treatment and prevention of alcohol problems: A resource manual.* New York: Academic Press.

Rattner, J. (1983). *Alfred Adler.* New York: Frederick Ungar.

Steinglass, P. (1978). The conceptualization of marriage from a systems theory perspective. In T. J. Paolino & B. S. McCrady (Eds.), *Marriage and marital therapy: Psychoanalytic, behavioral, and systems theory perspectives.* New York: Brunner/Mazel.

Steinglass, P. (1979). Family therapy with alcoholics: A review. In E. Kaufman & P. Kaufman (Eds.), *Family therapy of drug and alcohol abuse.* New York: Gardner Press.

Part I
MISCELLANEOUS

INTERRUPTING A DEPRESSION: THE PUSHBUTTON TECHNIQUE

Harold H. Mosak
A clinical psychologist in private practice. He has taught at the Alfred Adler Institute of Chicago for over thirty years and is currently chairman of the board.

In listening to the depressed client one hears certain themes recited recurrently. This litany centers around pronouncements which interfere with the forward motion of therapy and sometimes prompt the therapist to feel that "if I hear this once more . . ." These statements may be lifestyle-related or situation-related. The therapist hears:

1. "I am a victim of my depression." Following this statement are numerous complaints concerning the severity and tenacity of the depression, complaints about sleep, appetite, concentration, sex.

2. "I am a victim of life." In this attribution of blame the client may refer to a single "trauma" (the precipitating incident) or to a lifelong series of unfairness committed by others or by life itself. This other-blaming often alludes to the parental role in bringing up the child. One hears people say, "My mother loved me but she died." In addition, there are the laments of "Why did this happen to me?" as if the person should have some special exemption from the vicissitudes of life, and often "Why is God punishing me?"

3. "I am a victim of myself." Clients describe themselves as inadequate, a recent failure, a chronic failure, persons who have once or always done the wrong thing. Like Job the client questions, "What have I done so wrong that God

---

Individual Psychology, 41(2), June, 1985, **pp. 210–214**

is punishing me?" Sometimes this is given as an affirmative statement. The person knows what he has done wrong to incur the wrath of God or Fate.

4. "I am helpless." There is little or nothing that clients feel that they can do either about past events, the current situation, or themselves. "I've felt this way so long." "I know I should do something but I can't get myself to do it." "I tell myself I have to stop crying but the tears still keep coming." Such clients feel that they have little or no control over life. Seligman (1975) describes depression as "learned helplessness."

5. "I am hopeless." Again attribution of blame may fall on life, others, or the self. "Life has really shafted me." "If only I had done something before, but now it's too late." "I loused myself up so badly, I'll never get out of this. I might just as well kill myself." "The past was terrible, the present even worse if that is possible, and the future is hopeless."

It is such cognitions and their concomitant feelings which therapists must interrupt before they can discuss the dynamics of the depression which may lead to the elimination of the depression.

Since no discouraged therapist has ever helped a discouraged client, it is sufficient that only the client is discouraged at the initiation of treatment. Therapists might more profitably devote time and energy to determining what can be done to help their clients overcome their initial discouragement sufficiently so that therapy may progress. To accomplish this end it is advisable to interrupt the client's depression.

Adlerians generally use four interruption techniques. Those Adlerians who are legally licensed to do so may prescribe medication (Mosak & Phillips, 1980). Adler (1964) suggests an excellent technique for what I call "turning the client's eyeballs outward." It interferes with the client's self-absorption and attempts to mobilize the client's social interest. Wolfe (1931), recognizing that depression and humor are incompatible, engages in task-setting (Mosak, 1984), the "homework" consisting of telling people jokes until the client has succeeded in making them laugh. Another group of Adlerians base their theory of depression upon what the Freudians call "repressed hostility" or "aggression turned inward" (although their formulations are in Adlerian rather than Freudian terms). They encourage their clients to express anger openly and outwardly. All of these techniques are selectively effective. When I found them to be so, I experimented with various methods and discovered the Pushbutton Technique.

In administering this technique I give the following instructions after some prefactory remarks about the specific client's depression, especially the client's view of it.

> This is a three-part experiment. Please close your eyes and keep them closed until all three parts are over. First, I'd like you to dig into your memory and retrieve a very pleasant memory—a success, a beautiful sunset, a time when you were loved—and project that in front of your eyes as if you were watching it on a TV screen. Watch it from beginning to end and attach to it the feelings you had when the incident occurred. Go! Remember how wonderful it was! When you are through, hold up a finger to signal that you are through, and we'll go on to the last part.

When the client signals that the "TV movie" is over, we proceed to the second part:

> Now I'd like you to fish back in memory and retrieve a horrible incident. You failed. You were hurt or ill. Life screwed you. Someone died. You were humiliated. Watch that one from beginning to end as if it were on TV and attach to it the feelings you had at the time the incident occurred. Go! Remember how terrible it was! When you are through, hold up a finger to signal that you are through, and we'll go on to the next part.

When the finger signal has been given, the therapist gives the concluding instructions:

> Now I'd like to go into your memory and retrieve another pleasant memory. If you can't come up with another pleasant memory, go back to the first pleasant memory you had. Watch it on the TV screen from beginning to end and attach to it the feelings you had when the incident occurred. Go! Remember how wonderful it was! When you are through, please open your eyes.

When the experiment is ended, we invite clients to discuss their impressions of the experience with us. They usually conclude that their feelings generally followed their images—"When I had a good memory, I felt good. When I had a bad memory, I felt bad."[1] Using this as a point of departure for task-setting I tell the client:

> What a person feels goes along with what a person is thinking about. If you think good thoughts, you feel good. If you think bad thoughts, you feel bad. The problem with the people who feel depressed is that they only think bad thoughts. [I may here refer to the bad thoughts in the client's litany.] No wonder you feel bad! But one thing we've discovered is that you are not a victim of your

[1]For theoretical statements paralleling this view, see Dreikurs (1967), Ellis and Harper (1976), Mosak (1984), and Raimy (1975).

> depression. You can make it come and you can make it go. We just saw you turning it on and off and on again[2] merely by deciding what you were going to think about. You are not helpless. You are not hopeless, and getting rid of your depression doesn't have to take forever. You can change it anytime you want. So I'm going to send home with you two make-believe pushbuttons—a happy button and a depressed button. If you press the happy button, you'll think happy thoughts and have pleasant feelings. If you press the depressed button, you'll have lousy thoughts and lousy feelings. However, if you come back next week and are *still* depressed, I'm going to ask you to explain why you *choose* to continue to feel depressed when you have the happy button at your disposal. We'll find out what your investment in being depressed is.

With this tactic we undermine the client's "misunderstandings of the self" (Raimy, 1975). The client is not a victim or helpless or hopeless or lacking control. The task encourages in these ways at the same time that it teaches. It gives the client hope and removes the pessimistic thought that eliminating the depression has to take "a long time" or "forever." If the client says that after feeling good the negative thoughts return, we may encourage with "Most learning requires practice, so you'll have to practice it more until it becomes automatic." If the client resists with "You expect me to change just like that?" sometimes accompanied with a snap of the fingers, I relate the following story, a favorite of Dr. Dreikurs':

> A millionaire from Long Island decided to take a motor trip to Los Angeles. He and his chauffeur drove until they arrived at the outskirts of Chicago. At this point the millionaire told his chauffeur, "I've changed my mind. Turn left here. I'd like to go to New Orleans instead." The chauffeur turned around peevishly and exclaimed (accompanied with a snap of the fingers), "You expect me to change directions just like *that*?"

If the client maintains that he has no pleasant memories, we may jog the client's memory or encourage with "Everyone must have at least one pleasant memory" or we may instruct the client to think of a funny movie or we may ask the client to construct a pleasant memory, perhaps of what it's going to be like when the depression lifts. However, resistance to the task is minimal since built into the final discussion is what my students call a "Godfather technique," "an offer you can't refuse." The client will have to explain why he or she *chooses* to be depressed if the depression continues.

[2]We ask the client to think of a second pleasant memory to reinforce the notion that the feelings can be switched on and off and also to "leave a good taste in the client's mouth."

Once the depression is interrupted, we can begin to discuss the depression and its purposes.

The Pushbutton Technique, like other techniques, is selectively effective. It merely adds to the repertoire of the clinician. Brewer (1976), however, has compared the effectiveness of this technique with that of other techniques used in treating state depression and concludes:

> Results supported conclusively that Autobiographical Recollections[3] was the superior method for inducing not only depression, but also elation in a population of both sexes. Moreover, the data indicated in every case that subjects receiving Autobiographical Recollections-Happy were left, at the conclusion of the experiment, better off than they were at the beginning of the experiment, and better off than subjects receiving Mood-Elation and the controls.
>
> Results demonstrated that Autobiographical Recollections was also the superior method for inducing and altering anxiety. (pp. 72–73)

REFERENCES

Adler, A. (1964). *Problems of neurosis: A book of case histories.* New York: Harper Torchbooks. (Originally published 1929.)

Brewer, D. H. (1976). The induction and alteration of state depression. Ph.D. dissertation, University of Houston.

Dreikurs, R. (1967). The function of emotions. In R. Dreikurs, *Psychodynamics, psychotherapy, and counseling*. Chicago: Alfred Adler Institute. (Reprinted from *Christian Register, 130*(3), 11–14, 24.)

Ellis, A., & Harper, R. A. (1976). *A new guide to rational living.* Hollywood, Calif.: Wilshire Book Co.

Mosak, H. H. (1984). Adlerian psychotherapy. In R. J. Corsini (ed.), *Current psychotherapies*. Itasca, Ill.: F. E. Peacock.

[3]Brewer uses this name for the Pushbutton Technique.

Mosak, H. H., & Phillips, K. (1980). *Demons, germs, and values*. Chicago: Alfred Adler Institute.

Raimy, V. (1975). *Misunderstandings of the self*. San Francisco: Jossey-Bass.

Seligman, M. (1975). *Helplessness: On depression, development and death*. San Francisco: W. H. Freeman.

Wolfe, W. B. (1931). *How to be happy though human*. New York: Farrar & Rinehart.

SECTION IV
CHILD COUNSELING

EDITORS' COMMENTS

Perhaps the pragmatic approach of Adler's work is best seen with children. Dreikurs's four goals of misbehavior have provided the treatment profile for much of the work. Use of role-playing with children in schools is commonplace. Using this procedure effectively is a different story. Grunwald showed the definite steps that must be followed for the effective use of role-playing.

Dr. Rudolf Dreikurs differed from the Adlerian approach as he demonstrated how to counsel a child alone without his family. Adlerians traditionally see problems within context. This interview shows how Dreikurs is able to help Bruce understand the purpose of his actions and realize that he has options.

Adler viewed children's play as an opportunity to view their characteristic way of behaving. Information about the child's present status and future direction is available. Yura and Galassi highlighted several techniques to understand child's play.

Understanding the purpose of children's behavior is imperative for effective treatment. Hartwell-Walker and Belove used the "loyalty" dilemma as a way to conceptualize misbehavior in children. These writers also offered alternative ways for children to disengage from their dilemmas.

Borden has found early recollections (ERs) to be important sources of information in helping children understand the goal of their misbehavior and how to take a more constructive course. West and Dann used stories to help children gain self-understanding. Brief stories can be used to change socially destructive behaviors into positive ones.

Use of Adlerian play therapy has been growing. Kottman and Warlick presented some practical considerations when using this play media technique. Kottman and Stiles described the mutual storytelling technique in the context of Adlerian child therapy. This procedure is used to gain insight into mistaken goals, redirecting goals, changing faulty beliefs, and developing social interest.

COUNSELING A BOY: A DEMONSTRATION[1,2]

Rudolf Dreikurs[3]

Former emeritus professor of psychiatry, Chicago Medical School, and founder of the Alfred Adler Institutes in Chicago and Tel-Aviv, the Community Child Guidance Centers of Chicago, as well as the *Individual Psychology Bulletin* which he also edited and which was the forerunner of the present Journal. He devoted his life to the propagation of Adlerian thought through teaching and demonstrations throughout the world. He was the author of numerous books and articles translated into many languages.

Before we start I should like to make some comments. What I am about to do is unusual for me. When there are problems with a child, we normally work with the whole family—the father and mother, and also brothers and sisters who often have a much greater influence on the development of the personality than the parents. Thus, if a child has problems, I would work with the family. On the other hand, the school counselor works with the children individually, sometimes even without calling the parents in at all.

We have, however, thought—and a start has already been made in Israel—instead of having a center for the guidance of parents, to have a center for children to find out what to do with their parents and teachers. Thus interviews with the child alone will become more frequent. But, to repeat, this is not characteristic of the Adlerian approach.

---

[1]Demonstration at the Fourth Brief Psychotherapy Conference, Chicago Medical School, Chicago, March 24–25, 1972.

[2]Comments addressed to the audience are in roman type; the interview proper is in italic type.

[3]Since Dr. Dreikurs was ill at the time Mr. Robert L. Powers sat beside him during this demonstration. Mr. Powers made some comments toward the end.

Journal of Individual Psychology, 28(2), November, 1972, **pp. 223–231**

I am fully aware that at this meeting here there are many with a different orientation, and it may be very difficult for some to understand and to approve of this demonstration. There will probably be one rather frequent complaint, namely, the danger of an interview without follow-up. As it happens, in our two cases this morning, there will be follow-ups, in that both are presently in treatment with another counselor. But I want to state very emphatically: It does not do any harm if there is no follow-up. If what we have done has no effect, we do not need a follow-up. If it has an effect, this is worthwhile in itself. The patient knows more, and one never can tell how much he has gotten out of an interview.

Many with a different orientation call our approach a stunt, not believing that one can accomplish anything of significance with a child by what I did this morning. But we know from experience that sometimes children remember for the rest of their lives the first time they encountered somebody who could explain to them why they are doing what they do. For example, a boy may have been convinced, "I am a bad boy," so long as he did not realize how he gets involved in a power conflict.

Our job is to help a child to understand his problems. We may understand more, or understand less, but no harm can come from our attempt. One of the most devastating aspects of present psychiatric, psychological, and social attitude is this horrible fear of what we might do to the client. We must stop being afraid. We are convinced that whatever we have to offer, the child may do something positive about.

Dr. D.: *Now, what is your name?*
Bruce: *Bruce.*
Dr. D.: *And how old are you?*
Bruce: *Twelve years.*
Dr. D.: *I heard you wanted to talk with me. Right?*
Bruce: *I wanted to meet you.*
Dr. D.: *Just to see me?*
Bruce: *Yeah, I never met you before.*
Dr. D.: *You just want to sit there and see me talk? Do you want me to talk about you and your problems?*
Bruce: *Fine, do what you planned to do.*
Dr. D.: *No, I think you must have something in your mind. Did you think I would ask you about your problems when you came here?*
Bruce: *Uh, I don't know what you planned to do. I've never actually been counseled, except with Mrs. Rosenberg.*[4]

[4]Dr. Bina Rosenberg is an associate of Dr. Dreikurs.

Dr. D.: *Are you helped already? Now it is the same with me too. I want to understand what problems you have and to see whether I can help you to understand them and change them. Do you have any problems?*
Bruce: *I think everybody does.*
Dr. D.: *Will you tell us about yours?*
Bruce: *Fine. I think that one of my main problems is that instead of turning kids on, since I have only one friend, I think I turn kids off.*
Dr. D.: *How do you do that?*
Bruce: *Probably by aggravating them, making them mad somehow.*
Dr. D.: *Do you do similar things otherwise too, besides with your friends?*
Bruce: *Pardon?*
Dr. D.: *Do you do it with your teachers too, with your parents, that you get them mad?*
Bruce: *I don't think I do it with my teachers or parents . . .*
Dr. D.: *No?*
Bruce: *Maybe with my mother and dad.*
Dr. D.: *What do you do with your mother and dad?*
Bruce: *Let's see, uh, sometimes I do things like, uh, you know, I can't really describe it . . .*
Dr. D.: *Oh yes, you can; if you want to you can.*
Bruce: *Let's see how can I say it, uh . . .*
Dr. D.: *Are you ashamed to say what you are doing?*
Bruce: *No.*
Dr. D.: *You can openly talk, we can . . .*
Bruce: *I can talk.*
Dr. D.: *You're not afraid to me?*
Bruce: *No.*
Dr. D.: *Nor of them?*
Bruce: *No.*
Dr. D.: *You're not afraid of anybody?*
Bruce: *No. They are just people.* (Laughter from audience.)
Dr. D.: *Very well. Now tell me what you're doing with your parents?*
Bruce: *Well, there is really nothing. Sometimes they get into fights and then I try to stop it.*
Dr. D.: *You're a peacemaker?*
Bruce: *Or else I get involved in it somehow or other, and then I get kicked out of it.*
Dr. D.: *Don't you think your mother and father have any problem with you? If I would ask them, what would they say about you?*
Bruce: *That I have no friends. That I can't keep myself, you know, I don't keep myself busy. Usually I'd ask my mother before my dad started to work. He's now a projectionist. But before, he had the complete week-*

ends off. So I would, you know, ask him: Dad where are you going this week, you know. Every weekend.
Dr. D.: *Well that doesn't seem like much of a problem.*
Bruce: *I don't know how to keep myself busy. That's about the way I am trying to say it.*
Dr. D.: *Ah hah! Now may I make a guess why you can't keep yourself busy?*
Bruce: *Well?*

You see, here we have what I call a gold mine, a statement which requires immediate exploration, because there may be the opportunity of revealing something very important.

Bruce: *I think that the reason why I don't have many friends . . .*
Dr. D.: *No, the question I asked was: Why can't you keep yourself busy?*
Bruce: *I guess because I don't want to do anything without others with me, you know. I'm lonely.*
Dr. D.: *Why?*
Bruce: *Why? Because I have no brothers and no sisters.*
Dr. D.: *And if you have no brothers and no sisters you should be lonely for life?*
Bruce: *I mean like, I'm lonely, you know. I . . .*

If I may, I should like to read here a statement by the teacher. It could be written by any one of the hundred thousands of teachers in this country. Without the slightest understanding of what goes on, if you don't mind my saying this, the teacher had suggested: "Complete assigned work on time. Be present in reading class more. Study for tests. Stop daydreaming. Be more organized. Take more time in preparing assignments. Be in class on time." It is a wonderful plan, but who will carry it out I don't know. It is a tragedy when we encounter children, up to high school, up to college, who always had some troubles, and nowhere did anybody ever explain to them why they have these problems. And without knowing why, you can't do anything about it. Here is a wonderful opening for a strong statement. Why can Bruce not keep busy?

Bruce: *I wish I could answer that.*
Dr. D.: *Would you mind if I tell you?*
Bruce: *Fine, tell me, please do, I need help. That's what I came to you for.*
Dr. D.: *No, you came only here to see me. Please.* (Long laughter.)
Bruce: *Right!*
Dr. D.: *In that case it wasn't true. Could it be that you can't keep yourself busy because you try to keep the other people busy with you?*
Bruce: *That might be true.*

Dr. D.: *You see, it looks to me that you are an only child . .*
Bruce: *That's true.*
Dr. D.: *That you got all the attention, and for some reason you probably do a lot of things to keep people busy. That is what we call the goal of attention. As long as you can get the attention in a nice way, you are a wonderful kid—nice, pleasant, everything. But if you don't get enough attention in a nice way, you don't mind disturbing others, keeping them busy with you.*
Bruce: *That's true. I do disturb people, I got it, because it does turn out that I get a bad reaction from that.*
Dr. D.: *Now you don't mind that there is a bad reaction as long as there is any reaction.*
Bruce: *I'd rather get a good one.*
Dr. D.: *But you don't mind disturbing, and it is much easier to get attention by disturbing.*
Bruce: *True. It is.*
Dr. D.: *And that's what you're doing.*
Bruce: *I guess, most likely true.*

Now you see, it is actually a fact that he disturbs in order to get attention. Of course I can't prove it, but the discussion which I have with this boy this morning, can have a lasting effect on him when he now realizes that whatever he is doing is to show his power.

Dr. D.: *If you want to help yourself, I will give you some advice.*
Bruce: *Please do.*
Dr. D.: *Whenever you do something wrong, like provoking people, then say to yourself, "Aha, I want to keep them busy." Pinch yourself.*
Bruce: *But sometimes I do it without myself knowing it.*
Dr. D.: *Now I invite you to know it. I disturb your innocence.* (Laughter.)
Bruce: *What?*
Dr. D.: *You see, until now you could do all these things because you didn't know why, you were a helpless victim . . .*
Bruce: *I'm not saying I was helpless.*
Dr. D.: *There are two things you can do: You can get attention in a pleasant way, or you can do your job even if you don't get attention. But that you don't know; you always are trying to get attention.*
Bruce: *I must admit that's why I came here.* (Long laughter.)
Dr. D.: *Now you see . . .*
Bruce: *I don't see myself. You see I have a friend who always makes personal comments. I think I'm taking up his practice, and if something comes along that turns out to be a little bit slow I try to liven it up.*

Dr. D.: *And to liven it up you don't care whether what you are doing is pleasant or not.*
Bruce: *Oh, I do.*
Dr. D.: *Yes, you would like to.*
Bruce: *I don't do any of that unless I think the people like me.*
Dr. D.: *No, you don't mind that people don't like you as long as you keep them busy.*
Bruce: *No, that is not true. I don't have anything to do with people that stay away from me. I stay away from them. If they don't like me . . .*
Dr. D.: *You told me before, and I think you were right, that you can't make friends because you stir them up.*
Bruce: *At times I do get them angry, or else at other times they might get me angry.*
Dr. D.: *I don't want to argue with you. And do you know why I don't want to argue with you?*
Bruce: *I'm not sure.*
Dr. D.: *Because I am sure that nobody can win an argument with you anyhow.*
Bruce: *Here I must agree. It's never turned out that anybody has won.* (Laughter.)
Dr. D.: *That's right.*
Bruce: *My mother and my dad and me are all stubborn, in the same sense.*

You see, children can really catch on and can see that there are alternatives to them. We can now look at the statement from the teacher. Why does Bruce need special assignments? He should do all the things that he is supposed to do. Why should he?

Dr. D.: *You'd rather do what you feel like.*
Bruce: *I feel that I should do it because it is assigned.*
Dr. D.: *Yes, but you are not really doing it. We can't expect from you, that just because the teacher wants you to do something, you should do it.*
Bruce: *Oh, may I ask, did you get that from one of my teachers?*
Dr. D.: *Yes, yes. Now, the main thing is, do you think I could be right? That your trouble is that you always want people to be busy with you? Wherever you are?*
Bruce: *I think that's true.*
Dr. D.: *It is up to you whether you want to continue or not. You can change.*

The important therapeutic feature in our cognitive approach is the so-called "Aha" situation. It means the patient suddenly begins to realize, "Aha, the doctor is right." We will improve only to the extent to which we are willing to say, "Aha here I go again."

Bruce: *But see, I'm going about it a different way, in the sense that I don't think that way is the right way, and that's why I'm coming to you.*
Dr. D.: *Now do you think you will do what I say?*
Bruce: *Yes.*
Dr. D.: *I don't think so.*
Bruce: *Well, I sure won't waste $50 to see . . .* (Drowned by long laughter.) *If I wasn't here for free, it would cost a lot of money, and I wouldn't waste your suggestions and let them go up into the air.*
Dr. D.: *Now I will you why I don't think you should accept my suggestions. If you would stop keeping people busy, you would feel normal.*
Bruce: *That's true.*
Dr. D.: *You wouldn't be the center. And you want to be the center, you want people to be impressed with you.*
Bruce: *I don't want to be the center of attraction all the time; I want a little rest in between there too.*
Dr. D.: *There's time enough when you sleep.*
Bruce: *Yeah, that's good enough. And then when I'm playing with my friends I like to be quiet a little bit.*
Dr. D.: *Yes, but you see, that is very difficult. You are a clever boy.*
Bruce: *Thank you.*
Dr. D.: *And all your life long you learned how to keep people busy—the teachers, parents, anybody.*
Bruce: *I guess so.*
Dr. D.: *Now to give all that up and to be like anybody else, that is not for Bruce.*
Bruce: *Yeah, it is. If I could learn how to do it, I'd be . . .*
Dr. D.: *Well you can do it, if you want to, but I don't think you will.*
Bruce: *Uh . . . let's see, how can I put this? If you stayed here in Chicago and if I could see you again for free, I'd bet you that I'd be changed. Just because of this.*
Dr. D.: *And if you can't see me for free, you can't change?*
Bruce: *There you're wrong. Well, we can give you a report. Mr. Doe can give you a report.*
Dr. D.: *Yes, I can hear what the outcome of our discussion is. But my job here is to open your eyes. You don't have to do these things. It is your decision to be the center, it is your decision to upset other people, to keep them busy, and you are something special.*
Bruce: *But what I'm wondering is, if I get a reaction out of a person, how do I get a good reaction instead of a bad one? I mean like . . .*

Dr. D.: *Come on, you can't always get good reactions. For you the main thing is to get any reaction—good or bad, it doesn't make any difference.*
Bruce: *See, I want to try to make friends instead of enemies and I think I've turned them into enemies instead of friends.*
Dr. D.: *Do you want to have your own way?*
Bruce: *At times, yes. I must admit I do.*
Dr. D.: *Usually. Then how can you have friends?*
Bruce: *But I'm starting to give in to them instead of me. I mean, in my sense it's giving in . . .*
Dr. D.: *In your sense it's giving in. If you do the things the teachers and the friends want, you feel you are giving in. "I am something special."*
Bruce: *Well I must admit everybody is special.*
Dr. D.: *No, not everybody is. Many aren't, but you certainly are. You are different. You want to be different.*
Bruce: *I don't really want to be different. I'd like to be like some other people, like my kids, like my fellow students in some senses and in other senses I wouldn't.*
Dr. D.: *Yes, but I'm not so sure that you really find it easy, without saying: "Here I am giving in on something. I won't come in time. I won't do my assignment." And the more the teacher presses you, the more you get discouraged. "I can't do the things which the teacher wants. So I won't do it." Are you satisfied with yourself? Do you think you are good enough?*
Bruce: *I'm very satisfied with myself, since I've proved to myself . . ., since I've done a couple exams and I've gotten a good grade on a lot of them, and so I'm pretty happy with myself.*
Dr. D.: *That is worth the $50 that you paid.*
Bruce: *The $50 I had in the bank, sitting in my account.*
Dr. D.: *Anyhow, is there another problem? How about in the morning getting up?*
Bruce: *No problem. I get up and I get dressed.*
Dr. D.: *Is there anybody who has to wake you up?*
Bruce: *At times, yes, because my dad always drives me to school, because I go early in the morning.*
Dr. D.: *And who wakes you up?*
Bruce: *My mother.*
Dr. D.: *Does she have to wake you up several times?*
Bruce: *No, once.*
Dr. D.: *Uh, how about eating?*
Bruce: *As you see, there is no problem in that.*
Dr. D.: *There* is *a problem in it.*
Bruce: *Yes. I'm fat.*

Dr. D.: *Why are you fat?*

Bruce: *Because I'm nervous. But I haven't eaten this afternoon, which proves I'm not nervous with you.*

Dr. D.: *Aha. Now, may I tell you, may I guess, why you eat too much?*

Bruce: B*ecause I get hungry, I guess. I don't know.*

Dr. D.: *Well, that is your opinion. Do you mind if I tell you?*

Bruce: *Fine, tell me, please.*

Dr. D.: *Who makes a fuss when you eat too much?*

Bruce: *My mom.*

Dr. D.: *That's the reason why you eat.* (Laughter.)

Bruce: *Right.*

Dr. D.: *Now you admit it yourself. It is you who had the other opinion.*

Bruce: *Uh, I have other techniques than that one to get her angry.*

Dr. D.: *Let me hear some of your tricks.*

Bruce: *Umm . . . "Mother do this, Mother do that for me."*

Dr. D.: *Keeping her busy. "I want service."*

Bruce: *I won't say I'm not like that. When I was younger they used to call me king of the Jews, but . . .*

Dr. D.: *Ha, ha, ha. King of the . . . ?*

Bruce: *King of the Jews. That's what they call Christ now, in Jesus Christ, Super Star.*

Dr. D.: *You are King of the Jews. Nothing else but that will do.*

Bruce: *I must admit that I don't think I am now* (laughter) *though people are treating me like that.*

Dr. D.: *And that's the reason when they don't treat you like that, you may disturb them.*

Bruce: *True, But . . .*

Mr. P.: *They crucified the other one too.* (Laughter.)

Dr. D.: *Now tell me, we have to come to an end, do you think you learned something today?*

Bruce: *I do.*

Dr. D.: *Honestly?*

Bruce: *Honestly and truly. I think that my problem was that I tried to attract attention. You are telling me how not to attract; instead of go go go, do the opposite of the go, go, go.*

Dr. D.: *Now the main thing is . . .*

Bruce: *I mean, I pushed my way. Instead I've got to reverse that and let them push me.*

Mr. P.: *Uh . . . What Dr. Dreikurs is trying to say, Bruce, is that there are times when you can't stand it if you don't get attention. Everyone likes some attention, Dr. Dreikurs likes some, I like some. That's why I sit so close to him, and that's why we are all concerned that we all notice each*

other when we go places. But there are some times when we don't get it. The question is, can we stand it at those times? And he thinks, when you don't get it, you would rather have bad attention than no attention.
Bruce: *Yeah, bad attention rather than none.*
Mr. P.: *Right. You feel that you're in danger, if you're overlooked, of being ignored, of being disregarded, that you won't count. You feel discouraged and frightened.*
Dr. D.: *Yes. And before you change that, you have to learn to catch yourself. And the moment when you do it, say. "Aha, here I go again."*
Bruce: *I don't think I should say that right out loud. The kids will call me a fool.*
Dr. D.: *No, no I didn't mean telling the others; tell yourself.*
Bruce: *Oh, you mean: "Aha, here I go again."*

Now I want to ask a question. How many of you think that Bruce learned something fundamental today? (*Counting hands.*) How many of you doubt that he learned something? (*Counting hands.*) These are the different "religious" groups. (*Laughter.*)

Bruce: *What do you mean by that?*
Dr. D.: *There are religions that have different beliefs—the Moslems, the Jews, the Christians. And so in psychology, there are also different religions—the psychoanalysts, the Gestalt people, the Adlerians, and so on. And each one of these religions has its own ideas, and they don't agree with each other. And all those who have not an Adlerian training, will find it difficult to believe that you really learned. They always say that this is superficial, and they can't understand it. And so we have to realize that at this stage there are different churches, different popes, different bibles, and there is the same confusion in psychology as in life.*
Bruce: *Uhmm, may I ask you one question? I was sort of afraid of psychiatrists and psychologists. What makes a person this way? Is it a normal reaction for a person to get scared, like I was nervous when I came here.*
Dr. D.: *Oh yes.*
Bruce: *Then I calmed down.*
Dr. D.: *When one doesn't know what will happen, we all get nervous. I appreciate your help and hope you got something out of this meeting.*
Bruce: *Thank you very much. I've enjoyed it very much.*

ADLERIAN USAGE OF CHILDREN'S PLAY

Michael T. Yura
Assistant Professor of Counseling and Rehabilitation Services, College of Human Resource and Education, West Virginia University, Morgantown, West Virginia.

Merna D. Galassi
Presently completing a dissertation for the doctorate from West Virginia University at the University of North Carolina at Chapel Hill, North Carolina. She received the Master's degree from Harvard University and the B.S. from Brandeis University.

The present paper attempts to explore and expand on Adler's view of children's play. Initially, there will be a description of his predecessors' and contemporaries' views of play, followed by statements of Adler and other proponents of Individual Psychology. The article includes a discussion of a child's misdirected goals, life style and the concept of social interest as reflected in his play. Finally, examples of play techniques are drawn from both the authors' personal experiences in which they employed play for psychological investigation and reorientation of the child's misdirected goals. These examples should be useful for counselors, teachers, and parents.

HISTORICAL

A child's play has been the object of much theorizing and hypothesizing. As early as the fourth century B.C., Plato stated in the *Laws* that "a child's character will need to be formed while he plays" (Plato, 1970, p. 273). In addition, he also

---

Journal of Individual Psychology, 30(2), November, 1974. **pp. 194–201**

recognized the practical value of play. By having children play with various objects, Plato helped them to learn their arithmetic lessons (Plato, 1852, p. 302). Through the years, others such as Aristotle, Comenius, Rousseau, Froebel, Schaller and Lazarus have noted the educational importance of play (Millar, 1968). At the turn of the century, Spencer in his Surplus Energy Theory (1887, pp. 627–648), G. Stanley Hall, in his Recapitulation Theory (1906, p. 74), and Groos in his Instinct-Practice Theory (1908) attempted to explain the nature of play. Freud regarded play among other things, as a means for the child to learn to master disturbing events. In play, the child can be a grown-up, a parent, a professor, a fireman—whatever he wishes (Millar, 1968).

Child analysis originated with Freud's (1955) analysis of "Little Hans" in 1909. Hermine Hug-Hellmuth (1913), a follower of Freud, introduced play directly into the therapy situation. By providing the child with toys and other material, she allowed him to express himself through his play. Melanie Klein (1955, 1961) in her work with children, interpreted the child's play in psychosexual terms. For instance, if a child put a male and female doll on top of each other, Klein might say that the child was disturbed by his parents' sexual relationship. However, Anna Freud (1965, p. 31) thought play to be of secondary importance to the child's relationship with his therapist and used play to a great extent to establish a relationship with the child.

ADLER'S VIEW

In Adler's view, play provides information not only on the child's present status but also on his future. "There is in the life of a child an important phenomenon which shows very clearly the process of preparation for the future. It is play . . . the manner in which a child approaches a game, his choice, and the importance which he places upon it, that indicates his attitude and relationship to his environment and how he is related to his fellow men" (Adler, 1954, p. 81). Based on Adler's assumption that the child's characteristic way of behaving is apparent in his play, many "guesses" (hypotheses) can be confirmed by watching him at play. For instance, if the child's misdirected goal is assumed to be getting attention, one would expect him to engage in boisterous play activities to get others involved with him, or perhaps, to pretend to be a movie star or famous singer performing before a large audience. The child who seeks power might in his play, take the role of the leader or boss, of the commander of a large army, or of a school principal. A revengeful child may beat his dolls or break his toys, whereas the withdrawn or defeated child may engage in very little play or in solitary play. The extremely defeated child may not risk joining in play activities for fear of another unsuccessful experience.

Expressive Behavior

Adler believed that by the way the child thinks and behaves and by its characteristic perceptions, its interest is being specialized for its future occupation. Thus, a great interest in playing with toy soldiers may be a preparation for military life, may also be the prelude to success as the director of a department store (Adler 1929b, p. 148). The information to be gained from observation of a child at play can be used in directing or redirecting him at an early age.

One of Adler's major hypotheses was that of the unity of the individual—each individual is guided by a central theme (Adler, 1929a). This central theme, or life style, is present in every expression of the personality. Thus we can observe and decipher a child's life style by both his verbal and non-verbal behavior (Adler, 1956).

Social Interest

Somewhere between the ages of two and three, children usually begin to play with other children. However, if the innate aptitude of "social interest" has not been developed, the child will lack that important interest in cooperation with others. "Social interest is the expression of capacity for give and take" (Dreikurs, 1953, p. 9). Thus, the play of a child whose social interest has not been developed may be either solitary or aggressive toward other children.

A child's ability to participate in group games perhaps reflects his social feelings better than other play activities. Group games generally incorporate rules which the group has decided on and each member is willing to adhere to, at least for the length of the game. Adler stated, "Above all else, games are communal exercises. They enable the child to satisfy and fulfill his social feelings. Children who evade games and play are always open to the suspicion that they have made a bad adjustment to life. These children gladly withdraw themselves from all games, or when they are put on the playground with other children, usually spoil the pleasure of others. Pride, deficient self-esteem and the consequent fear of playing one's role badly are the chief reasons for this behavior. In general, by watching a child at play we shall be able to determine with great certainty the quantum of his social feeling" (Adler, 1954, p. 82).

In his play a child not only reveals his social feelings but also gets a chance to develop them further. Therefore, if a child has not yet developed acceptable ways of finding his place in the group, opportunities should be made available by which the child is encouraged to join group play activities in which he is likely to meet success.

Since play not only gives clues to the child's life style, misdirected goals, and private logic, but also to his relationship to his environment and his fellow man, greater use of a child's play should be made in understanding and redirecting him.

In one of the few articles (Bader, 1936; Friedman, 1951; Lewis, 1947), which seem to appear in the Adlerian literature concerning the importance of a child's play. Bader reports on a pampered three and one half years old who is the youngest of three boys. He is over-protected by his parents and grandparents. He always plays alone usually building with blocks. He builds a "secluded enclosure" in which he places an animal or human figure. Bader believes that his buildings reflected "his interpretations of his experiences as the smallest and weakest in the midst of adults" (Bader, 1936, p. 90).

PLAY TECHNIQUES

Play is a powerful medium which counselors, teachers, and parents can use in educating children. Play activities can be used either with a single child or with groups of children.

1. Puppets have been used quite effectively by counselors in working with children. The counselor could have a variety of puppets—a puppet family, puppets that represent the child's age, and animal puppets. The counselor can either suggest a situation for the child to dramatize with the puppets, or leave the structuring of the situation to the child. The child's puppet can represent himself or someone else while the counselor usually plays a number of roles.

In the first stage of Adlerian counseling (building a relationship), puppets often facilitate the conversation between the child and counselor. In addition, by observing a child structure his own puppet shows, the counselor can gain much information on the child's life style and private logic.

A five-year-old boy, Alan, was aggressive and bossy. He reacted to most situations at home and nursery school by throwing temper tantrums, hitting, and arguing with others. Puppets were used to demonstrate ways other than fighting to cope with situations he didn't like. Situations were arranged where the counselor had the aggressive puppets and Alan had the victimized puppet. Alan began to see himself in a new way. He also was given the opportunity to play the aggressive puppet while the counselor verbalized the feelings of the victimized person through her puppet.

After the first session with the puppets, Alan's teacher reported that to her surprise he returned pensively to the class room and remained quiet the rest of the morning. In the case of Alan, puppets were useful both in helping him see his own behavior as well as providing him with an opportunity to try some new patterns of behavior. After three sessions, Alan began to play with the other children instead of fighting with them.

2. A miniature house and doll family were used in the following case to gain information about a six-year-old boy's interactions with his parents and siblings and to understand a typical day in his life. The child was referred because he constantly cried during school when confronted with tasks he felt he couldn't complete successfully. He was presently failing and was to be retained in the first grade for the following school year. Michael is the "baby boy" in a family with two older sisters. During the course of the second play session, using the miniature house and family, Michael revealed how his mother and sisters did everything for him. He displayed himself in the play family situation as a helpless and dependent child. The counselor then discussed with Michael what he had revealed in his play and asked him to tell what the different family members did each day and what his role in the family was. In the following sessions Michael was asked to play with the doll family again but now to let the "littlest child" do some things for himself—for instance, pretend mamma is busy and the other children are out. On this occasion, Michael pretended to play by himself in his room. In addition, suggestions were made for how Michael could become independent at school.

3. Game activities can probably be arranged even more easily by a teacher than a counselor. A teacher is used to scheduling the children's play time and thus she should use her position and knowledge to redirect as many children as possible.

(a) *Attention-getting children* can be redirected from their useless goals by special types of group activities. The case of Susan, a six-year-old attention-getter, will illustrate the point.

Susan was a first grader who always wanted to be the center of attention. She would call out constantly, make funny faces, sing when everyone else was working, tell wild stories and ask irrelevant questions just to be sure everyone knew she was there. In order to help redirect Susan's behavior from this goal of attention, activities were planned in which she had to not call attention to herself. *For instance, Susan was chosen to steal the bone in the "dog and bone game."*[1] In this game, one child is the guesser who has a bone and all the other children are puppies. The teacher chooses one child (puppy) to steal the bone while the guesser

[1]This is a game that M. Galassi learned as a young child. It was both played at school and neighborhood parties.

closes his eyes. The guesser has three tries to find the child who stole his bone. If the child who stole the bone is not picked, then he gets a turn at being guesser. In the case of Susan, she had to sit quietly so as not to be selected by the guesser, if she wanted a chance of being guesser. At first such activities were difficult for her but eventually she learned to enjoy them. This not only gave Susan experience at not calling attention to herself but also a chance to be a participating member of the classroom group. At the same time, her attention-getting devices were being ignored by both the teacher and classmates and she was being encouraged for her participation in group activities.

(b) *Bossy children* can be helped if play activities are arranged where the three or four of them are put together. In one first grade class there were three bossy girls. They were always arguing over something or bossing someone. Two were the youngest at home who got their own way often, and the other was the oldest girl at home who helped mother take care of and boss the younger children. The three girls were told that they could put on a puppet show together, if they wanted, and could practice during recess. The rest was up to them. At first they quarreled a lot as to who would make the stage and who would have the lead puppet, etc. They even tried to have the teacher appoint one of them as leader. When this failed they each wanted to put on their own show. Their requests were refused, but they were told that they didn't have to be in the show if they chose not to. Finally, after three weeks they worked out the difficulties and put on a show. Somehow they had learned to share both the work and play aspects.

Another play activity in which bossy children often have struggles is jumproping. The bossy child doen't want to turn the rope; he just wants his turn to jump and then wants to leave the game. A teacher can give the rope to a *group* of such children. Then their characteristic strategy, to jump first and hold the end last, doesn't work very well. Left on their own, the children usually find a solution. The choice for each in such a group is either not to play at all or to cooperate with the others, thus the natural consequence of the situation is quite effective.

(c) *The withdrawn child* is proabably best aided through arranging play situations in which he is central to the game or activity. Of course, it must be determined ahead of time that the child has the necessary skills or understanding for the activity. For instance, in the case of Robert, a very quiet first grade boy who rarely played with the other boys or spoke in class, the teacher gave him the football, basketball, or kickball on various days to be in charge of and take out on the playground. In this way the other children had to interact with him in order to play with the desirable object.

In the classroom, Robert was chosen to be the caller in a game of bingo. Robert was not given a turn until after a few other children had already had a turn so that the teacher was sure he knew what to do. In this way Robert met with success while learning to become a more active class member.

These cases are a few concrete examples of how play can be used in working with children, especially within their natural environments. Not only can counselors make use of these techniques in a playroom, but so too can teachers and parents.

When the child comes to the play room for the first time he is usually told that he can play with any toys or objects he likes, and can do anything he wishes as long as it is not destructive to himself or another person. During the course of the play session with the child, the counselor will often ask the child to tell what he is doing. When the time is appropriate, disclosures can be made to the child and appropriate alternative plans for redirecting the child's behavior can be suggested.

CONCLUSION

The authors believe that a child's play is of use in revealing and redirecting his useless goals, and in indicating the degree of development of his social interest. Further study of these functions of play, and development of techniques adapted to them are needed. Adler stated, "Play is, so to speak, a kind of profession and must be considered as such. Therefore, it is not an insignificant matter to disturb a child in his play. Play should never be considered as a method of killing time" (Adler, 1954, p. 82).

REFERENCES

1. Adler, A. *Problem of Neurosis: A Book of Case Histories.* London: Kegan Paul, Trench, Trubner & Co., 1929a.

2. Adler, A. *Science of Living.* New York: Greenberg Publisher, 1929b.

3. Adler, A. *Understanding Human Nature* (1927). Greenwich, Conn.: Fawcett Publications, 1954.

4. Adler, A. *The Individual Psychology of Alfred Adler.* Ed. by H. L. & R. R. Ansbacher. New York: Harper and Row, 1956.

5. Axline, V. M. *Play Therapy.* Boston: Houghton Mifflin Company, 1947.

6. Bader, H. Glimpses of the Life-style in Dreams, Fantasies and Play of Children. *Int. J. Indiv. Psychol.*, 1936, *2*(1), 84–90.

7. Dreikurs, R. *Fundamentals of Adlerian Psychology.* Chicago: Alfred Adler Institute, 1953.

8. Freud, A. *The Psycho-Analytical Treatment of Children.* New York: International Universities Press, Inc., 1965.

9. Freud, S. *The Case of "Little Hans" and the "Rat Man." Standard Edition.* Vol. 10, London: Hogarth Press, 1955.

10. Friedman, A. Observations in a Play Group of Young Children. *Indiv. Psychol. Bull.*, 1951, *9*(1), 25–30.

11. Groos, K. *The Play of Man.* New York: D. Appleton & Company, 1908.

12. Hall, G. S. *Youth.* New York: Appleton-Century, 1906.

13. Hug-Hellmuth, H. *Aus dem Seelenleben des Kindes.* Leipzig: Deuticke, 1913.

14. Klein, M. *Narrative of a Child Analysis.* New York: Basic Books, 1961.

15. Klein, M. The Psychoanalytic Play-Technique. *American Journal of Orthopsychiatry*, 1955, *25*, 223–237.

16. Lewis, A. Developing Social Feeling in the Young Child Through his Play Life. *Indiv. Psychol. Bull.*, 1947, *6*(1–2), 58–60.

17. Millar, S. *The Psychology of Play.* Harmondsworth, Middlesex, Great Britain: Penguin Books, 1968.

18. Nikelly, A. (Ed.) *Techniques for Behavior Change.* Springfield, Ill.: Charles C. Thomas, 1971.

19. Plato. *The Works of Plato.* Translated by G. Burges. Vol. 5. London: John Childs & Son, 1852.

20. Plato. *The Laws.* Translated by T. J. Saunders. Harmondsworth, Middlesex, England: Penguin Books, 1970.

21. Spencer, H. *The Principles of Psychology.* Vol. 2, New York: Appleton, 1897.

THE LOYALTY DILEMMA

Marie Hartwell-Walker
Director of the Adlerian Counseling Center of Amherst, Massachusetts.

P. Lawrence Belove
Clinical coordinator at the Adlerian Counseling Center of Amherst, Massachusetts.

> The first cooperation among other people which (a child) experiences is the cooperation of his parents; and if their cooperation is poor, they cannot hope to teach him to be cooperative himself. (Adler, 1931, p. 133)

Much of the so-called "inappropriate" behavior of teenagers and younger children is commonly attributed to "mistaken ideas" in the mind of the child or young adult. However, it is just as reasonable to assume that the behavior is, in fact, quite appropriate and that the ideas are not mistakes but perhaps reasonable and insightful interpretations of a real situation. It is the purpose of this paper to suggest a way within the framework of Adlerian psychology to see the misbehaving child's motivations as benign, and the thinking of this child sound, even though the child's behavior is disturbing to others.

According to Adlerian theory, the overriding motive in human behavior is fundamentally benign. It is to join and become one with the human community. "The leading idea of the Individual Psychology of Alfred Adler is found in his recognition of the importance of human society, not only for the development of the individual character, but also for the orientation of every single action and emotion in the life of a human being" (Dreikurs, 1953, p. 1). Adler's term for the way a person finds a unique place in the human world is "life style," which is a thoroughly interactional concept. The child is working to achieve a place; others in the world are acknowledging, allowing, and supporting the place the child achieves.

Individual Psychology, 38(2), June, 1982, **pp. 161–172**

In Adlerian terms, living the human life and contributing to the human community is understood as the process of meeting a continuing series of tasks and challenges. The "healthy" person is one who steps directly forward into life with arms outstretched to meet the challenges of life with courage. Disturbing behavior, "neurotic" behavior, is understood as an avoidance of a life challenge. "All neurotic symptoms have as their object the task of safeguarding the patient's self-esteem and thereby also the life-line (later, style of life) into which he has grown" (Adler, 1956, p. 263). Self-esteem is threatened when a person feels he must either address a life challenge and fail or avoid a life challenge and preserve the life-line. Adler described this either/or, win/lose thinking as the central characteristic of neurotic mental life (Adler, 1956). A healthy person does not feel that a choice has to be made or that the challenges of life endanger their place in a social context.

We are suggesting that although the antithetical, either/or thinking which produces "neurotic" behavior may stem from a mistaken notion or perception in the mind of the child, it may also stem from a perfectly clear and accurate perception of immediate circumstances. The pathology, the "either/or," the sense of forced choice—all this may be inherent in a class of commonly occurring situations in family life.

THE LOYALTY DILEMMA

Disturbing behavior is a response to a new situation which challenges a child's sense of place. One of the most commonly troublesome situations for people is when they find themselves as part of a triangle. Triangles have been systematically studied in many of the new schools of family therapy (Haley, 1978; Bowen, 1978; Minuchin, 1974). We wish to examine a triangular situation, not so much as a whole, but rather as it appears to a person—the child—caught at one corner of the triangle; we have found that one useful way of characterizing that perspective is as a "loyalty dilemma."

In a two-parent family, a growing child must deal with both parents. The child intuitively knows that any dealings with Mother have implications for dealings with Father and vice versa. As long as the parents are in acknowledged agreement or even comfortable disagreement, it is possible for the child to be close to both Mom and Dad. To have a special relationship with one is not perceived as a threat by the other.

However, when the parents are in an uncomfortable disagreement, such that they cannot agree to disagree or to acknowledge their disagreement, the child is in the position of being asked to resolve a conflict the parents have not been able to resolve themselves. Furthermore, the child has to resolve that conflict in order to maintain a relationship with both parents. To join with only one parent is not an acceptable alternative as it implies the "loss" of the other. It is the child's relationship with each as separate individuals, and with other members of the family, that forms the prototype for life style (Shulman, 1973).

The dilemma is rarely a chronic phenomenon but more likely specific to developmental situations. It generally occurs when the developmental challenges of a child's life require that a stand be taken on an issue which is an unresolved dispute between the parents. For example, a young teen may find herself in a dilemma about how to handle her sexuality if the parents are in disagreement about it. She would not face such a dilemma as a 7-year-old girl.

We see loyalty dilemmas in single-parent families too. The significant other who is on the other side of the argument from the parent with whom the child lives may be more difficult to identify. That individual may be the other parent (wherever that parent may be), the "myth" of the other parent and what he or she stood for (in the case of the deceased or abandoning parent), a grandparent, or, in a number of the cases we have seen, an agency worker who has an important relationship with the child. A child could be forced to choose between allying with a teacher and allying with one or both parents. The forced choice could be between a group of peers and one or both parents. A well-intentioned therapist could inadvertently force a child to choose between allying with the therapist and allying with one or both parents.

THE DILEMMA AS PRIVATE LOGIC

When we speak of motivation in an Adlerian framework, we often speak of it in terms of "private logic" (Dreikurs, 1953). To understand a person we need to understand their private logic. In this section we will discuss the dilemma as a kind of logical form.

Formally, a dilemma is a hypothetical argument. It is future-oriented thinking. The major premise of a dilemma is a compound hypothetical phrase. The phrase states that if certain things, "antecedents," are true, then other things, "consequents," must inevitably follow. The form is this:

If A then B and if C then B.

The minor premise is a disjunction; a forced choice. The form is this:

Either A or C.

The disjunctions may be either "strong" or "weak"; that is, the alternatives may be mutually exclusive or there may be some compromise position. The stronger the disjunction, the more difficult the dilemma.

The dilemma in its entirety can be formulated as follows:

If A then B and if C then B.
Either A or C.
Therefore, B.

The conclusion simply and logically follows. There is no flaw in the logic of a dilemma. Dilemmas always make some sort of sense.

Translating this to a clinical example, we have this kind of situation from the child's point of view. In the Smith family, Mother strongly supports the importance of education. Father believes the kids should be "allowed to be kids" and that schools expect too much of them. The child could construe things as follows:

Major Premise: If I do well in school, I discredit Mom in her argument with Dad and if I don't do well in school, I discredit Dad in his argument with Mom.

Minor Premise: I have to do either well in school or not well in school.

Conclusion: I'm going to discredit one of them and lose my relationship with one of them.

We could identify this conclusion as a "mistaken idea," but is it? The child's logic is flawless. We could say to the child, "Could it be that you feel you are in danger of losing the love of a parent?" and the child might respond with a recognition reflex, but how does that help?

Since dilemmas are in themselves valid, the way to deal with them is to look for, or to create, material faults. In other words, ways must be found to make the premises no longer accurately reflect the material reality of the situation. Either the premises must be shown to be mistakes in interpretation of the situation (which is a more orthodox method of Adlerian counseling) or the situation must be reorganized such that the premises come to be mistakes (which is more in keeping with the work of Dreikurs, 1964, and his parent training work and the work of certain strategic therapists like Haley, 1978). In the example of the Smith family it is reasonable to conclude that the child is in danger of alienating one or the other parent. The way out is either (a) for the child's reading of the situation to change or (b) for the situation itself to change.

GETTING OUT OF THE DILEMMA: METHODS

In formal logic there are three ways of meeting a dilemma. All three ways can work; no method is inherently preferable. Misbehaving children can be understood as using methods that do not work well. It is as if that which was designed to solve the problem has become something which makes the problem worse. A successful therapist is able to introduce methods of meeting the dilemma that work. The three ways of meeting a dilemma are as follows: (a) taking it by the horns, (b) escaping between the horns, or (c) rebuttal.

The way to "take a dilemma by the horns" is to challenge the major premise and to suggest that the consequents do not necessarily and inevitably follow from the antecedents. If the major premise is "If A then B and if C then B," then a successful taking of the horns results in a major premise that goes if "A then X if C then Y."

To escape between the horns is to challenge the minor premise. If a person believes that he must choose either A or C, then the way out is to allow A and C or a little of A and a little of C. "Escaping between the horns" means softening the disjunction, blurring the line between "either" and "or."

Technically speaking, rebuttal involves negating and transposing the consequents of the major premise. With simpler dilemmas, a rebuttal changes "If A then B and C then B" into "If A then not B and if C then not B."

The consequents in the example above stated that doing well or poorly would discredit one parent in their argument with the other. To refute the dilemma the child would have to arrange things (in Adler's, 1965, sense of the neurotic arrangement) so that performance in school did not effect the parents' arguments about school. The child could develop a symptom as a way of rebuttal. A symptom is often a way of having a problem that cannot be resolved by parents. Since it cannot be resolved, the child is able to remain loyal to both parents. Both parents could "forgive" a child's apparent alliance with the other if they also believed the child was "sick," or "depressed," or had a "learning disability." In the case above, father thought kids should be allowed to be kids and mother thought that school was important. The child using rebuttal as a kind of method could arrange to do very well academically, but also to be a behavior problem.

Before proceeding to case examples, we will summarize. The features of the loyalty dilemma are these: (a) Two significant people in a child's life are in a disagreement they cannot resolve. (b) Not only can they not resolve it, but also they cannot acknowledge, comment on it, or in other ways agree to allow it to remain unresolved. In other words, they are locked into the fight. (c) For the child to move forward with his/her life, the fight between the two others has to be dealt with.

The therapeutic implications are as follows: (a) the therapist assists the parents (or whomever) to resolve their differences, *or* (b) the therapist finds a way for the child to proceed without the differences being resolved.

CASE EXAMPLE: CHALLENGING THE MAJOR PREMISE

Susan is a 34-year-old mentally retarded adult living in a state-supported home, an ordinary house in an ordinary neighborhood with three "direct-care" workers who rotate shifts. She has been in this kind of setting or a state school for the retarded since she was 4 years old. Currently, she visits her parents two to three times per month for weekends. Susan has a history of "acting up" in the group home when she returns from weekend visits with her parents. We were involved in the case as consultants by the people who ran the group home.

When we talked to the staff, we learned that Susan's parents had a reputation for being "difficult." We decided to talk to Susan's parents and we learned that they had a number of deeply felt dissatisfactions with the way these various facilities were run but they were afraid to voice their concerns because they did not want to anger those who cared for their daughter. It was as if they felt that their daughter was being held hostage to keep them, the parents, on good behavior. When Susan came home for the weekend, the parents would talk about how poorly the home was run and Susan would overhear their conversations.

Susan's dilemma was how to be loyal to her parents without alienating the staff and how to be friends with the staff without betraying her parents. Her answer was to challenge the either/or part, the minor premise. Therefore, when she was good, she was very, very good and when she was bad, she was horrid. The staff was confused. Sometimes it seemed that Susan was doing so well, and then "out of nowhere" she would have setbacks. The staff took to blaming the parents and medicating Susan.

Our solution was to challenge the major premise and attempt to put the staff and parents in better relationship. We held a series of meetings with Susan's parents and the staff of the group home and the management of the home. The purpose was to get the people who knew Susan best all together in the same room to discuss what were the best ways to work with her. Our private and unstated agenda for the meetings was to put Susan's parents and the staff in cooperation around the joint task of caring for Susan. As unobtrusively as we could, we directed the meetings so that Susan's parents and the staff members would come to have more respect and friendly feelings for one another.

In the cooperative atmosphere of the meetings, the participants were also able to develop a number of rules for dealing with Susan that provided her with firmness and structure. Those who dealt with Susan were able to act much more decisively with her, knowing that they had the support and cooperation of the other adults involved.

Assessing the results of this intervention, we are pleased to report that Susan's acting up diminished considerably. Dreikurs used to say that children always know when the jig is up. Perhaps in this situation, Susan knew that the situation had changed and the pressure was off. There are certainly other potential difficulties in this situation but the series of meetings successfully resolved the presenting problem.

CASE EXAMPLE: CHALLENGING THE MINOR PREMISE

Sally, age 17, was referred to the center by her school guidance counselor because of "chronic depression." She was complaining about always having to do her sister's chores, failing in school, having to rely on her sister for social contacts and being always sad. Because she was living at home, we asked for the whole family to come in. Resistance by the family to coming was overcome by our stating that they were to come merely to help us understand Sally. Family members were Mom, Dad, and a sister Alice, age 15.

When we met the family we were struck by how much Sally was like her Dad, a low-key, carefully spoken, don't-make-waves kind of person. Alice, on the other hand, was very much like Mom: social, engaging, bright, full of mischief. In an infectious and charming way she saw responsibilities as a bother, something to be handled as quickly as possible in order to leave time for fun. It was evident that the parents' differing styles of problem solving caused many disagreements. However, the most relevant disagreement was their on-going argument about how to help Sally grow up and become a young adult.

In Sally's dilemma, the major premise was: If I take Dad's advice, then he wins his long standing argument with Mom, and if I take Mom's advice, then she wins. Minor premise: I'm 17, finishing high school and a growing young woman, and I have to meet the tasks of life according to the traditions of my family, which means, either Dad's way or Mom's way. The conclusion: Either Mom wins or Dad wins and I can't upset either.

Sally's unproductive solution to the dilemma was a rebuttal, a negation of the major premise. Her answer was to accept advice from both parents and to guarantee, by means of a "depression," that the advice wouldn't work. Our task was to find another solution to the dilemma for Sally. Our first attempt was to take it by the horns and challenge the major premise. The way to do that would have been to resolve the differences between Mom and Dad. We quickly learned that that tactic would require too much work and that the parents were not interested in the project.

We then decided to try to find an escape for Sally through the horns by challenging the minor premise. The minor premise for Sally was that she was dealing with a strict win/lose situation. Sally had told us in an initial interview that she was concerned about her parents' relationship. We had to find a way to soften the disjunction, to allow one of the parents to be successful without the success reflecting negatively on the other parent.

Here is how we did it: First, we decided to characterize Dad as the expert on Sally's problem because they were so much alike. Then we found ways to define Alice as also having a problem—not a difficult task—and we characterized Mom as an expert on Alice's problems. We then asked each parent to solve their particular child's "problem" in the limited time frame of two weeks. In this way, Sally could accept her father's help without discrediting her mother. Mom was busy with Alice. We also stated that we would be interested in seeing who could do better. This final statement capitalized on the unspoken competition between the parents and blocked the well-intentioned interference by each parent in the other parent's project.

The intervention effectively eliminated Sally's depression and, incidentally, took her out of the role of being the "sick" one in the family. This constituted the end of the first phase of therapy.

CASE EXAMPLE: REBUTTAL

Ellen, age 14, was referred to us by her natural father. She was the middle child and only girl of three children. Both brothers were characterized by both natural parents and Mother's new husband as perfect in every way. Ellen was brought in because of rapidly escalating misbehavior, which included drunkenness, thefts, and evidence of promiscuity. After the initial interview, none of the involved adults would participate in therapy.

It became clear to us that although Ellen's parents had been divorced for 10 years, the fight was far from over. Ellen's mother had left Dad to marry one of Dad's business partners. The whole affair had been a particularly scandalous event in the small town in which they lived. Dad maintained a close relationship with his children. They spent every weekend, holiday, and two evenings a week at his apartment.

Each parent blamed the other for Ellen's misbehavior. Each had brought her to a succession of therapists, treatment centers for psychological testing, and alternative schools, each parent accusing the other of sabotage.

Ellen's dilemma was similar to that faced by Sally in the previous case. To do better in any particular context would be only to add fuel to Mom and Dad's continuing battle. The adults were, of course entrenched, and unwilling to come to therapy. To do so was a threat to the carefully maintained balance between them. Even to come to us would have been perceived by Mom as a point for Dad's side.

Since we were unsuccessful in drawing in the adults, we decided that we could only offer Ellen some explanation of her behavior that made it make sense to her. We could also suggest and set the stage for alternative behavior.

We described Ellen's behavior in positive terms. We praised her for being willing to sacrifice her own life for the sake of her parents. We told her that she was to be commended for helping the two of them to stay "married" and in balance with one another. We also suggested to her that since she knew her parents far better than either of us, she should keep it up for the time being so that her parents wouldn't have to face the painful reality of their divorce and the community scandal and could instead focus on her.

She greeted this explanation with some relief, stating that it was nice to know that at least she wasn't crazy. However, she didn't know what she could do about it. We said we didn't know either and restated that maybe she should just keep it up for awhile until she could think of something else. (We decided to do this rather than to offer suggestions because Ellen, like the rest of her family, was highly oppositional and was likely to greet any suggestions with a myriad of reasons why she couldn't act on them.)

Ellen did keep it up for almost a year and a half, accumulating a police record of minor offenses. On her 16th birthday (the earliest opportunity in our state for a child legally to leave home), she declared to both of her natural parents that she had had enough and that they were all welcome to one another. She moved out of the house to a boarding house, got a job, and took the high school equivalency course at night—managing to catch up with her high school class. This year she graduated with her class in spite of a four-year history of truancies, suspensions, and failing grades.

This last case illustrates the best we have been able to do using a rebuttal as a way of meeting a dilemma; it is worth some formal analysis. A rebuttal is an attack on the major premise. If the major premise is "If A then B and if C then B," then the rebuttal is "If A then not B, and if C then not B." In Ellen's case, the major premise went like this: If Mom's tactics cure me, then she wins a fight with Dad; and if Dad's tactics cure me, then he wins a fight with Mom. Hence, the rebuttal we offered went like this: If Mom's tactics cure me, then she makes peace with Dad and if Dad's tactics cure me then he makes peace with Mom. The conclusion is that it is best to keep needing a cure in order to stop the fight.

Ellen accepted our new way of perceiving her situation but was not willing to give up on her parents. Since we could not convince her to give up on her parents' marriage, all we could do was offer her a way of not feeling crazy. At any rate, we had offered her a way out of the dilemma, and when she was old enough to take it she did.

CONCLUSIONS AND COMMENTS

We have found the loyalty dilemma one useful way to conceptualize the purpose of misbehavior in children. It seems to suggest interventions that can change a situation and result in changed behavior in disturbing children and teens. It represents a moderately successful attempt on our part to incorporate into Adlerian thinking the recent work of Haley, Minuchin, and Bowen. Finally, it seems to have strong implications that we have yet to explore for life style assessment and therapy with individuals.

REFERENCES

Adler, A. *The Individual Psychology of Alfred Adler*, Ed. by H. L. & R. Ansbacher. New York: Basic Books, 1956.

Adler, A. *What life should mean to you*. New York: Putnam, 1958.

Bowen, M. *Family therapy in clinical practice*. New York: Jason Aronson Press, 1978.

Dreikurs, R. *Fundamentals of Adlerian psychology*. Chicago: Alfred Adler Institute of Chicago, 1953.

Dreikurs, R. *Children: The challenge*. New York: Hawthorne, 1964.

Haley, J. *Problem solving therapy*. San Francisco: Jossey-Bass, 1978.

Minuchin, S. *Families and family therapy*. Cambridge, Mass.: Harvard University Press. 1974.

Shulman, B. The family constellation in personality diagnosis. In *Contributions to Individual Psychology*. Chicago: Alfred Adler Institute of Chicago, 1973.

COMMENTS COLUMN EDITORS

This presentation of the loyalty dilemma is a very creative endeavor to help us as counselors to reexamine some of our conceptions of presenting problems. We need to be aware of the total situation of the people with whom we work. We have been presented a model for looking at disturbing behavior as an individual's creative response to a no-win situation. If we can enter the perceptual world of the client then we, too, can come to better understand the response of the client. People do what makes sense to them. The dynamic tension that involves the client in the three-way situation keeps all parties stuck. Here we have been given three alternative ways to help clients remove themselves from the triangle.

Although the presenters indicated no preference as to which method is to be used to get the client out of the dilemma, it seems that a first choice for a counselor would be to try to see if the significant disagreers could resolve their dispute. Thus, it would seem that if the counselor could assist the two parties to cooperate and thereby challenge the major premise as was done in the case of Susan, the situation would be or could be resolved. If cooperation is not possible and if neither party is willing to change or broaden their stance, then challenging the major premise is not possible and the counselor will have to help the client through other means.

Using the two other methods outlined here, "escaping between the horns" and "rebuttal," the counselor assists the client to maintain the relationships with the two others but to change the terms of the relationships so that the client does not have to make a choice between the two disputing parties and their valuing systems. In essence, the counselor assists the client in broadening his view of the situation and his part in it.

It seems like many children who are identified as needing assistance are ones who are using rebuttal and are choosing to be excused from the battle by being depressed, having special needs, or having learning disabilities. These children are really using a rebuttal in a reactive stance and are willing to be "sick" or "unable to learn" in order not to lose their place in the family unit. By scrambling the major premise as in the case of Ellen, the client is able to make an effective rebuttal that is pro active in their own behalf and thereby to remove themselves from the tensions between the two other parties.

The methods presented here have tremendous potential as strategies for counselors. Try them and see how they work for you.

EARLY RECOLLECTIONS AS A DIAGNOSTIC TECHNIQUE WITH PRIMARY AGE CHILDREN

Barbara L. Borden

A counselor in private practice. She has led children's, women's and public family counseling sessions for the Chicago area Family Education Association.

Interpreting early recollections, a vital projective diagnostic technique used extensively by trained Adlerian therapists, is an essential means of revealing a person's life style, his own unique way of thinking, feeling, acting, or responding to himself and to his environment.

Early recollections, those moments from the first four, five, or six years of life that a person chooses to remember from all his myriad experiences, are "the prototype of the individual's life style or useful hints as to why his life plan was elaborated into its own particular form" (Adler, 1979, pp. 17–18). In early recollections, persons reveal through the remembered incidents and their feelings about them, their nascent attitudes toward themselves, their relationships to others, and their views of life. Through skilled interpretation of early recollections as well as of other such diagnostic measures as the family constellation and dreams, the therapist can form a picture of the individual's life style.

While early recollections have been significantly utilized in Adlerian therapy with adults and adolescents, a scan of the literature concerning early recollections with children reveals that their diagnostic and therapeutic potential has remained virtually untapped. In speculating on a reason for the limited use of

Individual Psychology, 38(3), September 1982, **pp. 207–212**

early recollections with children, it is suggested that since the life style of the child is fairly well formulated by the age of 6 (Dreikurs, 1957) recall might either be too premature or unreliable based upon the chronological age of the child. Should a child, for example, report an incident that had happened yesterday, one might consider it neither reliable nor valid in terms of its relevance in the formation of attitudes consistent with the emerging life style.

For these very reasons, however, the child's recall is valuable. "Since the life style of the child is fairly well formulated by the age of six, and since the child is extending himself beyond his immediate family and environment more than ever before where he is forming new relationships, and meeting new conflict situations, it is the most opportune time in which to redirect goals of misbehavior and social interactions in the home, school and community; and it is the most opportune time in which to assess how the individual child finds his place within his family constellation in terms of the child's own life style" (Borden, 1973, p. 22), before it becomes too solidified. The child's recollections are thus seen to be a reliable, valuable adjunct resource in working with the child therapeutically (Dreikurs, Grunwald, & Pepper, 1971).

Experienced clinicians, working with adults, can make accurate diagnostic judgments only to a limited extent on the basis of early recollections alone (Hedwig, 1965, p. 188). Just as early recollections would not be used as the sole determinant of an adult's life style, neither would or should they be so used in determining a child's life style.

USE OF EARLY RECOLLECTIONS WITH CHILDREN

The use of early recollections with the primary age child, 5 through 8 years old, was initiated four years ago on a yearly basis in a well-established Adlerian Children's Discussion Group (Borden, 1973, 1978) and has proven to be a successful adjunct diagnostic tool in confirming the emerging life style. Before examples of early recollections with the primary-age child are presented, a short explanation of the Children's Discussion Group is needed to understand the relevancy in utilizing early recollections.

The purpose of the almost decade-old group is to explore the goals of behavior of the children and to employ their own insights and abilities to counsel one another with the interpretations and guidance of an Adlerian counselor. Through a school year's involvement in the group, meeting weekly for one hour, many and varied diagnostic and interpretive modalities are utilized in helping the children understand, and gain an appreciation for, their developing life style. The children then have an opportunity through the presentation of alternative behavior repertoires to modify or change their life style.

In using early recollections with children, timing is of utmost importance. In the children's group the same phases operate as in adult counseling: relationship, psychological investigation, disclosure or interpretation resulting in new insights, and reorientation resulting in attitude and/or behavior change (Eckstein, Baruth, & Mahrer, 1975, pp. 2–3).

Before eliciting early recollections from children, one should establish a relationship of mutual trust and respect. Psychological investigation (into what the child says are his problem areas and how he acts within the group setting), interpretation or goal disclosure (gaining awareness of a child's unique private logic), and reorientation (practice of new attitudes and behavioral responses) are all interrelated and should be on-going.

To optimally utilize early recollections, it is vital, therefore, for the counselor to have (a) established rapport with the child, (b) developed an understanding of the child's modus operandi and goals of misbehavior (Dreikurs, 1964), (c) exposed the child to the goal disclosure process. Once this condition is attained, and early recollections are interpreted, the child can realize how his recollections are fitting in with his conceptions about life, with his private logic.

Regarding the question of the value of a child's early recollection when it is of a relatively recent incident, the important point is that the child has chosen that particular incident. Its selectivity correlates with the impression the incident has made and, therefore, its relevance to the child's schematic attitude towards life. Generally, with adults and adolescents, more than one early recollection is needed in order that recurring themes within the person's life become apparent. However, with young children, a single early recollection can provide significant information. If one can get more than one recollection, so much the better.

EXAMPLES OF CHILDREN'S EARLY RECOLLECTIONS

While early recollections from children are not reported with the same verbal proficiency that an adolescent's or an adult's would be, the following examples from those reported by the children in the discussion group illustrate their integral worth as a validation of a child's emerging life style. "What the counselor is looking for in the memories the child relates is not *Truth* with a capital *T*, but clues to the very personal logic of that child" (Janoe, 1979, p. 231).

> Greg, age 7, exhibited behavior that indicated all four goals of misbehavior. Since he was so discouraged, he sought constant attention, positively and negatively, and used power and revenge in interactions with his peers. When asked how he kept himself from growing up, he stated "I want new things all the time"—an indication for him that being given to is being accepted. Wearing a "Darth Vader" costume at Halloween time could be symbolic of his negative self-image, as well as could the "mask" he uses for his power plays. Greg's desire to receive a robot as a present could be interpreted as his desire for more self-control. As these responses occurred during the course of the group and appropriate goal disclosures were provided by the counselor and group members, progress was observed. Greg became a more cooperative group member. Towards the end of the group, however, he reported this recollection from the age of 3: "I kept on biting my friend. Once I bit her so hard, she had a bump for a month. I bite anyone who gets in my way." (Feeling: "Me—mean man.") While progress had been made, the recollection still emphasized Greg's attitude of revenge and of being able to do whatever he wanted, which at that time was his modus operandi. His discouragement comes through in "Me—mean man."
>
> The next example concerns Dan who was in the group through the latter half of his kindergarten year and most of first grade. During this time, his life style shifted from one of having to have life on his terms in every respect, to that of cooperation and respect for others. By the end of kindergarten, he stated, "I changed to being happy and cooperative. I can think for myself." He no longer had to prove his power. His early recollection showed him playing with his younger sister cooperatively, and wishing for her to grow up, but with the control element of being a first-born: "I am playing ball with my sister, and I sat on the ball". Feeling: "I want her to give up her bottle and blanket."
>
> During his second year in the group, he was positively involved in all aspects of group behavior. This year's recollection indicates a positive change, consistent with a positive self-image: "I am playing with my sister on a hill. Mother took a picture of us together." (Feeling: "I am happy.") One can note Dan's progress in his self-development, verified by the difference between the two recollections. In therapy, patient or client progress can often be depicted through a change in early recollections.
>
> Having siblings within the group affords a counselor the unique experience of seeing a family constellation process in the

making and sibling interaction in an objective setting. Brett, age 5, was smothered by a brother two years older, who played the "big brother" role to the hilt. On the day that early recollections were taken, the older brother was absent and Brett remembered the following incident from the age of 4: "My brother was playing ball and didn't want me to play, so I broke up the game." (Feeling: "Proud.")

Besides the obvious recognizable competition between the brothers, one can see that Brett felt competent to handle situations despite his brother's attempt to maintain his number-one position. As the group proceeded through the year, Brett became an independently functioning group member, and his brother retreated from his protective role, allowing the younger sibling to think, speak and do for himself.

Susie, the only girl among three brothers and the third born, bore her position with keen persistence through her manipulations to achieve whatever it was she wanted. During the beginning sessions of the group, it was not uncommon for her to cry, cling to the counselor for attention or speak in an almost inaudible tone. When she discovered that her manipulations were for naught, through goal disclosure and the group process, her behavior changed. She became a leader, thinking for herself and holding her own. During the group's final evaluation of one another's progress, although progress was mentioned on an on-going basis throughout the year, she stated that "I've learned to grow up." Susie's early recollection, from age 3, depicts her independence, as well as her persistence in getting her own way. "Everyday I went to my friend's house. One time she said she couldn't play with me. I kept ringing her doorbell until she came to the door. Afterwards she came outside." (Feeling: "I did it.")

SUMMARY

Some guidelines to be used when eliciting and interpreting a child's early recollections are:

1. To have established prior rapport.
2. To understand the family constellation.
3. To understand the goals of behavior and modus operandi of the child.
4. To ask for early recollections with such questions as "What is one of the first things you can remember?"
5. To write down the early recollection exactly as it is reported.
6. To ask for the feeling associated with the recollection.

7. To look for recurring themes if more than one early recollection is given.
8. To interpret the meaning of the early recollection. Once the family constellation is understood and the movement of the child is known, the early recollection should be a validation of the emerging life style. A recognition reflex (Dreikurs, et al., 1971) will indicate if the interpretation is correct.
9. To use the early recollection as an adjunct in explaining the child's emerging life style.

The primary-age child's life style is conducive to change; it is still in a malleable state. Early recollections are a source of information to use in helping a child to understand the direction and movement of his behavior as his attitudes about himself, other people, and life in general are taking shape.

REFERENCES

Adler, A., Significance of early recollections. In H. A. Olson (Ed.), *Early recollections: Their use in diagnosis and psychotherapy*. Springfield, Ill.: Charles C. Thomas, 1979.

Ansbacher, H. L., & Ansbacher, R. R. (Eds.), *The Individual Psychology of Alfred Adler*. New York: Harper & Row, 1956.

Borden, B. Children's groups, a first year report of F.E.A. *The Individual Psychologist,* 1973, *10* (1), 22–26.

Borden, B. Children's discussion groups: A positive force in behavioral change. *The Individual Psychologist,* 1978, *15* (1), 53–61.

Corsini, R. J. (Ed.) *Current personality theories*. Itasca, Ill.: F. E. Peacock, 1977.

Dreikurs, R., & Soltz, V. *Children the challenge*. New York: Meredith Press, 1964.

Dreikurs, R. *Psychology in the classroom*. New York: Harper & Row, 1957.

Dreikurs, R., Grunwald, B. B., & Pepper, F. C. *Maintaining sanity in the classroom: Illustrated teaching techniques*. New York: Harper & Row, 1971.

Eckstein, D., Baruth L., & Mahrer, D. *Life style: what it is and how to do it.* Alfred Adler Institute (Distributor), 1975.

Hedwig, E. Children's early recollections as a basis for diagnosis. *Journal of Individual Psychology, 1965, 21* (2), 187–188.

Janoe, E. & B. Using early recollections with children. In H. A. Olson (Ed.), *Early recollections: Their use in diagnosis and psychotherapy.* Springfield, Illinois: Charles C. Thomas, 1979.

CHILDREN'S STORIES FOR PSYCHOLOGICAL SELF-UNDERSTANDING*

John D. West
An associate professor of counselor education at Louisiana State University.

Linda K. Dann
A counselor at an elementary school in the East Baton Rouge Parish school systems. She has an undergraduate degree in Art from Tulane University and a Masters in Counseling from Louisiana State University.

In order to assist children in understanding and managing their classroom behavior, Dreikurs, Grunwald, and Pepper (1971) recommend that elementary and middle school counselors consider using children's stories for psychological self-understanding. Since being referenced by Dreikurs et al. (1971), children's stories for psychological self-understanding have not received widespread attention in Individual Psychology literature.

This article demonstrates, by way of illustration, how stories for psychological self-understanding are constructed and used. The stories are conceptually grounded in children's goals of disruptive behavior (Dreikurs, Grunwald, & Pepper, 1971; Dreikurs & Soltz, 1964). Since these goals have been thoroughly explained elsewhere, the article does not describe motivations for disruptive behavior. The article does, however, demonstrate how the goals of misbehavior can be assimilated into story telling. The illustrative story is followed by a conclusion outlining procedures in developing and using stories for psychological self-understanding.

---

*The authors would like to express appreciation to the fourth and fifth grades at Glen Oaks Park Elementary School and Episcopal Elementary School in Baton Rouge, Louisiana, for helpful comments in the preparation of this article.

Individual Psychology, 41(4), December, 1985, **pp. 461–470**

The story is about a fifth grade student, Carrie, who attends Shadyside Elementary School. The principal, Ms. Wickerschmidt, has asked Carrie to write a diary describing herself and her classmates. Carrie's teacher is Ms. Gentry and the other students in the story are Mary, Denise, Ellie, Carl, Jeff, Andre, Laura, and Tanya. The adult reading this story may want to place the characters' names on the blackboard and ask the children if they know what a diary is or if they have ever kept a diary. The story depicts each student demonstrating a goal or motivation of disruptive behavior and includes discussion questions that can be used to assist children in developing psychological self-understanding.

A STORY FOR PSYCHOLOGICAL SELF-UNDERSTANDING: "CARRIE'S DIARY"

Monday

Ms. Wickerschmidt, she's the principal of our school, asked me to write a book called a diary. Ms. Wickerschmidt told me to do this because I sometimes talk with my friends during class and I sometimes don't pay attention. Ms. Gentry's our teacher, and yesterday while she was writing on the blackboard I was feeling sort of bored so I told Tommy a real funny story. We both laughed so hard that Ms. Gentry had to remind me about not disturbing others and the importance of finishing my work. One other time this week Ms. Gentry was busy with some of the students in our class and since I was again feeling kind of bored I made a few funny faces. The kids on my side of the room almost fell out of their desks laughing. Anyway, Ms. Gentry reminded me again about getting back to my work.

Questions

1. Why do you think Carrie tries to make the other students laugh? (Active Destructive Attention Getting)
2. What other ways do students behave when they want to be "noticed"?
3. What are some of the ways students can be "noticed" that do not interfere with others completing their work?

So, today, Ms. Wickerschmidt said, "Carrie, I want you to notice all the things Mary does to get along with people and write some of those things down in your diary."

Mary never gets into trouble; she's sooo good. She always says, "Yes, Ms. Gentry" and "No, Ms. Gentry."

Yesterday, when Ellie asked to play jump rope with us, some of the girls told Ellie "No." They said Ellie's not like the rest of us. She won't even try to do her school work without someone helping her, and besides, she's in the slow reading group. But Mary told her to come on and play with the rest of us. Mary even let Ellie go first just because she saw Ms. Gentry watching us.

While Ms. Gentry was still watching, Mary asked Tanya to play and Tanya never says anything in class. Even if Ms. Gentry calls on her, Tanya looks like she's going to cry. Anyway, Mary said real loud, "We should be kind to others, especially people who aren't as fortunate as we are. Ms. Wickerschmidt and Ms. Gentry said so." I bet Mary said it that loud so Ms. Gentry could hear her.

Mary really tries hard to make other people think she's sooo good. She always tries to be Ms. Gentry's favorite student.

Questions

4. Why would Mary want others to think she is "sooo good"? (Active Constructive Attention Getting)
5. What are some of the other ways students behave when they want to be noticed as being "sooo good"?
6. How might wanting to be "noticed" as being "sooo good" lead to problems for Mary?

Tuesday

Yesterday, when we were playing Red Rover, Mary picked Denise instead of Laura. When we got on the bus to go home Laura told Mary that her feelings had been hurt. Mary said she didn't think she needed to apologize since Laura was eventually chosen and was allowed to play anyway. That's when Laura *accidentally* stepped on Mary's foot. Then Mary started yelling at Laura to get off her foot and the bus driver eventually got mad at Mary.

Later, after we got home, Laura asked me to go over to Mary's house. Laura said she was sorry about *accidentally* stepping on Mary's foot, and, then, Mary said, "The reason I chose Denise for Red Rover was because earlier in the morning she had given me some stickers. That's why I chose Denise. Besides, I saw

Ms. Gentry on the playground today and she told us that we should be friends with everyone and, anyway, you shouldn't tell me who to choose in Red Rover."

Then, Laura told Mary that her mother had invited me to spend the night at their house and that we had to go since Laura's parents were also taking us to the movie. Sometimes I think Laura imagines things, because her mother hadn't asked me to spend the night at their house.

Questions

7. Why do you think Laura stepped on Mary's foot? Why do you think Laura told Mary that her mother had invited only Carrie to spend the night at their house? (Passive Destructive Revenge)
8. When students' feelings are hurt, what other ways do they behave in order to "get even"?
9. Instead of "trying to get even," what other ways could students use to let others know when their feelings have been hurt?

Wednesday

Boy! Jeff sure got in trouble today. He's always late for school in the morning. Well, not only in the morning. Lots of times he comes in late from recess and doesn't finish his seatwork on time and almost always forgets his homework. When Ms. Gentry tells Jeff to do something he'll often stick out his lip and say, "I won't and you can't make me." Jeff never says this very loud, and because I sit next to Jeff, only I can hear him.

On Monday Jeff was late getting to school and Ms. Wickerschmidt told him to never ever be late again. This morning Jeff's mother found him skipping school and brought him to the principal's office around lunch time. Ms. Wickerschmidt said, "Who do you think you are, young man? The other children have been here all morning. You need to get to school on time." Ms. Wickerschmidt sure sounded angry.

And then Jeff's mother said, "Jeff, I never want to hear of you skipping school again and from now on you *will* be at school on time."

Jeff didn't say anything. He just stuck out his lip, scratched his ear, and stared at the floor.

Jeff doesn't care what anybody thinks about him. Nobody can make him do anything. Ms. Wickerschmidt said he's incorr . . . incorrig . . . incorrigible.

Questions

10. Why do you think Jeff is often late for school? Why do you think Jeff forgets to finish his homework? (Passive Destructive Power)
11. What other ways can students behave in order to show that "Nobody can make me do anything"?
12. How can the belief that "No one can make me do anything" create problems for everyone in the classroom?

Thursday

I know that Ms. Wickerschmidt said for me to write this diary about myself and what I'm doing in school, but I really am doing very good, I mean well, now. Ms. Gentry only had to remind me three times this week about not talking with Tommy during class and about the importance of paying attention. Actually, I think Ms. Wickerschmidt ought to make Ellie keep a diary. Instead of doing her work, Ellie always wants Ms. Gentry to help her. Ellie will raise her hand and whine, "Ms. Gentry, I can't do this. Won't you please help me?"

When Ellie completes her work she says, "This isn't very good, is it? Do you think this is good enough?" It sems like Ms. Gentry is always helping Ellie.

This whole week our class has been making science projects. We've been drawing different bugs and stuff and writing reports about our drawings. Ellie didn't know what animal to pick so Ms. Gentry told her to draw caterpillars. I think that's good for her because Ellie's as slow as a caterpillar. Then, Ellie didn't know how to find a book in the library so Ms. Pintle, she's the librarian, ran all around the library trying to help Ellie pick out a book. Finally, after Ellie chose a book, she sat staring at the picture of the caterpillar until Ms. Gentry stopped at her desk. Ellie said, "Ms. Gentry, I can't decide which color to draw the caterpillar. What colors do you think I should use?"

Questions

13. Why do you think Ellie often wants Ms. Gentry and the other students to help her? (Passive Destructive Attention Getting)
14. What other ways do students behave when they want to be "noticed"?
15. What problems can arise in the classroom when someone believes "I must be noticed by the teacher and the other students"?

Friday

I sure am glad today's Friday! I don't understand that Denise at all. Denise is sort of pretty and always wears really cute dresses, but at recess Denise just sits on the grass and watches everyone. That is, she watches until we invite her to join the rest of us in kickball or jump rope. It never takes long before someone yells, "Hey, Denise, come play with us." Ms. Wickerschmidt hardly ever fusses at Denise because her mother is our "Room Mother." Ms. Gentry sometimes tells the class that we should use Denise as our model. Like yesterday, after Denise finished her arithmetic she closed her book, folded her hands on top of her desk, and waited quietly until Ms. Gentry told us what to do next. Sometimes when our class walks to the lunchroom Ms. Gentry reminds us to be quiet in the hall, and then, Ms. Gentry tells us to be more like Denise. Denise is rather quiet and shy but she always has her hands washed for lunch, she's quiet in the hall, and she never leaves her table messy after lunch.

Questions

16. How does Denise try to get Ms. Gentry and the other students to "notice" her? (Passive Constructive Attention Getting)
17. How does Denise's behavior differ from Ellie's behavior?
18. In what way is the purpose for Denise's behavior and the purpose of Ellie's behavior similar?

Monday

I hate Andre. I had a new yellow dress on today and Andre said I looked just like a banana. Nobody really likes Andre, he's nothing but a mean bully. Actually, everybody hates him because he's so rotten. He picks on all the little kids and tells them if they don't give him their lunch money that he's going to sit on them and pound them into the ground.

Today at recess Andre asked Carl and Jeff if he could play kickball with them and they said, "No, because you always get mad when you lose." Only this time Andre didn't wait to get mad. Right then Andre got mad and punched Carl in the face, and Carl's nose started to bleed. I've never seen so much blood in my whole life. Carl hit him back and then all the kids on the playground came running to watch the fight. We all watched until Ms. Gentry pulled Andre and Carl apart and made them stop fighting. She really fussed at Andre and sent him into the principal's office where he got in a lot of trouble. Carl was sent to the nurse's office.

When we got back to our classroom I saw Andre take Ms. Gentry's grade book, and I have a good idea she's going to find it on the playground next to the swing set all torn up. I think maybe I won't tell her I saw Andre take it because I don't want a bloody nose too.

Questions

19. Why do you think Andre is often angry and mean toward the other students? (Active Destructive Revenge)
20. When students feel that other classmates or teachers are mean or unfair toward them, what are some other behaviors that students use to "get even" or "hurt back"?
21. What more appropriate ways can students respond or behave when their feelings have been hurt?

Tuesday

This morning Ms. Gentry told us about making friends and how to be a good friend. She said, "I think it would be helpful if all of you learned how to get along better with each other. Lately there have been so many problems."

Ms. Gentry told the class, "I want everyone to pick a person in class that they don't know very well and every day I want you to say or do something nice for that person. You must keep your choice a secret and next week we will see if you can guess who was trying to be nice to you."

Carl said he didn't think that was such a good idea. "That's not a good way to make friends. I think a better idea would be to give them some candy or gum and then they would *have* to be your friend." No one was surprised that Carl didn't agree with Ms. Gentry's idea. He always likes to argue.

Ms. Gentry said, "I don't think others would *have* to be your friend just because you gave them candy, Carl."

Of course Carl had an answer for Ms. Gentry. "If that didn't work, you could tell them that you have a new football and, then, they would *have* to be a friend if they wanted to play with your football."

Ms. Gentry told Carl that she'd like for him to try her suggestion this week and see what happened.

But Carl wouldn't stop arguing and said, "If I can't make friends my way than I'm not going to do it at all. My way would work the best. What if I did something nice every day and no one wanted to be my friend?"

Ms. Gentry mentioned that Carl was right and others wouldn't *have* to be our friends just because we had done something nice for them.

Then Carl said, "So we should use my plan and not your idea for making friends."

After that Ms. Gentry changed the subject. She's good at changing the subject.

Questions

22. Why do you think Carl argues with Ms. Gentry? (Active Destructive Power)
23. What other behaviors might a student use to show teachers and classmates that "no one can tell me what to do"?
24. When someone is trying to show you that "no one can tell me what to do" or that "I'm going to be the boss," what is a good way for you to respond?

Wednesday

Tanya hasn't been to school all week. Last week, when I was outside the principal's office writing my diary, I heard Ms. Wickerschmidt and Tanya talking. Ms. Wickerschmidt left her door part way open so I couldn't help but hear what they were saying. I just happened to hear Ms. Wickerschmidt tell Tanya that she had to improve or she wouldn't be promoted to the sixth grade. Ms. Wickerschmidt said, "I don't understand how a child can sit in school all day long and not learn anything. Ms. Gentry will be helpless unless you make an effort in class."

Tanya didn't respond to Ms. Wickerschmidt. She's usually quiet and hardly ever says anything. Tanya even sits by herself in our classroom and never raises her hand to answer Ms. Gentry's questions. I think Ms. Gentry would like to help Tanya because sometimes she asks Tanya really easy questions in class. At recess Tanya sits over by the fence, watches us, and hardly ever plays with anybody.

Anyway, Ms. Wickerschmidt scolded Tanya. She asked why Tanya misses the bus so often and why she doesn't even try to complete her homework. Tanya sat with her head down and tears rolling down her face but, again, Tanya didn't say anything.

I bet Tanya won't ever come back to school in her whole life. Ms. Gentry will probably be upset if Tanya doesn't come back. She helps Tanya a lot. She doesn't even get mad at Tanya and lets her do lots of stuff like take care of the hamsters and give out papers. Ms. Gentry really likes Tanya and says that we all have "potential," whatever that is.

I don't know, it seems to me that Tanya has "given up" and that she isn't even interested in trying to do better in school.

Questions

25. Why does Carrie think that Tanya has "given up"? Why do you think Tanya isn't interested in doing better in school? (Display of Inadequacy)
26. What other behaviors do students use to show the teacher and classmates that they have "given up" trying to do well in school?
27. When a student has "given up" trying to do well in school, how could the teacher and classmates help him/her?

Thursday

This is the last day I have to write in my diary. I sure have observed a lot in the past ten days. Ms. Wickerschmidt would probably appreciate me summarizing my ideas about the reasons why students sometimes misbehave in school. Let's see, what should I write in my diary? [The school counselor can then assist the students in summarizing the Dreikursian goals of children's misbehavior.]

CONCLUSION

When asked why students demonstrate disruptive behavior one group responded, "We want friends and we want to fit in." In part, stories for psychological self-understanding are used to help students gain a better understanding of disruptive motivations, and a story depicting a particular motivation need not be much more than a paragraph in length. While issues that arise at school and in the classroom provide themes for the stories (e.g., loneliness, conflict, forgetfulness, cheating), experience suggests that the stories are most appropriate for students in the upper grade levels of the elementary school. That is, students in the first and second grades seem to have difficulty generalizing Individual Psychology principles from the stories to their own everyday lives.

Initially, students may not openly identify with or own disruptive motivations demonstrated in the story. We believe they can vicariously learn about cooperative behavior by attending to the story and participating in the group discussion. After a few sessions, however, it is not unusual for defenses to be lowered and for some students to start self-disclosing. The students can be allowed to disclose and discuss their own disruptive behaviors and motivations; however, as Dreikurs et al. (1971) suggest, they are discouraged from accusing others of demonstrating disruptive motivations. If the student identifies with a particular motivation, role play can be used to help differentiate cooperative from disruptive behavior. On one occasion two boys mentioned that a story depicting a revenge motivation sounded somewhat similar to their own situation. In class the boys discussed their anger and with the assistance of class members they reviewed more constructive means for expressing their feelings. Finally, the boys role played a scene that typically would have elicited resentment and conflict. The role play offered an opportunity for the students to practice behavior that countered the more destructive expression of resentment.

When delivering a story for psychological self-understanding, it is helpful to work with a group of approximately ten students as opposed to an entire class of perhaps thirty students. The students seem to appreciate a "simple" or "straightforward" story. While they like having a central character present throughout the story (e.g., Carrie), a lengthy description of the characters can become boring. On the other hand, students enjoy hearing about how the characters find themselves in "trouble" with friends, teachers, and parents and, as one group commented, "We get tired of hearing about kids who never do anything wrong."

The adult should remember to thoroughly discuss each story. A thorough discussion can stimulate an awareness of how disruptive motivations create problems for the entire classroom, e.g., "What problems can arise in the classroom when someone believes 'I must be noticed in order to feel good about myself'?" As previously suggested, the adult can also develop discussion questions that are designed to increase coping strategies. For instance, students can be asked for alternatives to the character's means of letting others know "I'm angry" or that "I've had my feelings hurt" (see questions 3, 9, and 21). Younger students may draw pictures in response to discussion questions and pictorially demonstrate constructive alternatives to disruptive motivations. Homework for older students may include written responses to discussion questions; for example, responses may clarify similarities and differences between particular motivations (see questions

17 and 18). In general, the stories, questions, and ensuing discussion are oriented toward helping students learn problem solving in a democratic atmosphere where self-discipline is valued, rather than in an autocratic atmosphere where decisions are governed by adult dictates.

In order to utilize stories for psychological self-understanding, counselors must become familiar with children's goals of misbehavior. Furthermore, the counselor needs to be able to disclose motivations for the story character's behavior and, therefore, may want to consult Grunewald and Platt's (1975) comments on goal disclosure.

REFERENCES

Dreikurs, R., Grunwald, B. B., & Pepper, F. C. (1971). *Maintaining sanity in the classroom: Illustrated teaching techniques*. New York: Harper and Row Publishers.

Dreikurs, R., & Soltz, V. (1964). *Children: The challenge*. New York: Hawthorn Books, Inc.

Grunewald, S., & Platt, J. (1975). Goal disclosure techniques. In C. Asselin, T. Nelson, & J. M. Platt (eds.), *Teacher study group leader's manual*. Chicago: Alfred Adler Institute of Chicago.

ADLERIAN PLAY THERAPY: PRACTICAL CONSIDERATIONS

Terry Kottman
Currently the director of the Pupil Appraisal Center at the University of North Texas. She is also an assistant professor in the Counselor Education Department.

Jayne Warlick
In private practice in Arlington, Texas. She specializes in working with children and their families.

Young children have not yet completely mastered the abstract symbols and concepts necessary to verbal communication and may have insufficient experience in the use of language to adequately express their thoughts and feelings (Hansen & Stevic, 1969; Walsh, 1975). Since children use play to express feelings, explore relationships, and explore themselves (Barlow, Strother, & Landreth, 1985; Nelson, 1968), play is the logical medium through which to communicate with children who are experiencing some type of difficulty in their lives. Play therapy, a therapeutic interaction between a child and a therapist through the utilization of toys or other play materials, is one of the most widely accepted methods of working with children who are exhibiting some type of emotional or behavioral problem (Phillips, 1985).

The concepts of Individual Psychology and many of the techniques of Adlerian counseling can be combined with the basic premise of play therapy to create a unique procedure for helping children. While conceptualizing children in terms of Adlerian personality theory, the Adlerian play therapist can creatively choose techniques such as encouragement, family constellation, early recollections, goal

Individual Psychology, 45(4), December, 1989, **pp. 433–446**

disclosure, and tentative hypotheses to help children. The Adlerian can use play therapy to teach children to catch themselves at self-defeating behaviors, gain insight into their purposes, and develop alternative methods of coping successfully with life. Although several authors (Nystul, 1980; Yura & Galassi, 1974) have suggested that therapists could combine Adlerian concepts and methods with some type of therapy utilizing play media, little has been written about practical methods of incorporating attitudes and techniques based on the theory of Individual Psychology into the practice of play therapy. This article was designed to provide an explanation of different ways Adlerian attitudes and methods can be utilized in the practice of play therapy.

RELATIONSHIP

In Adlerian counseling, the first phase of therapy is the establishment of a democratic relationship (Manaster & Corsini, 1982). In the process of building a relationship with the child, the play therapist can choose from a variety of different techniques: tracking behavior, restating content, reflecting feelings, encouragement, giving explanations and answering questions, asking questions, and playing with the child. The democratic relationship between the child and the play therapist can also be enhanced by the attitude of the therapist toward setting limits in the play room and the phraseology of the limit-setting.

The foundation of the relationship in most forms of play therapy consists of three primary elements: (a) tracking of behavior, (b) restatement of content, and (c) reflection of feeling (Axline, 1969). As the child plays, the therapist provides a running account of the child's behaviors and rephrases any utterances that the child may make. A tracking statement is simply a description of the child's actions, such as, "Now you're picking that up," or "You're going over to the sandbox." Restatement of content could include statements like, "Oh, you're painting a yellow sun," or "Your mother said you had some trouble this morning." Tracking behavior and restatement of content are intended to let the child know that the play therapist's attention is focused on the child; that whatever the child does or says is important and worthy of attention.

The play therapist also tries to reflect the feelings expressed through the child's play activities and/or words. It is important to reflect both the child's stated feelings (e.g., "You say you're really happy today") and to reflect underlying emotions and the feeling tone expressed in the child's play (e.g., "You look really angry when you hit the punching bag," or "You seem kind of sad this morning"). The reflecting of feelings is intended to communicate the therapist's emphatic understanding of the child's perception of the world and the child's place in that world.

Encouragement

Encouragement can be used in play therapy to help build a relationship in which the child's efforts at self-understanding and self-reliance are acknowledged and enhanced. An Adlerian play therapist would utilize encouragement to help enhance the interaction with the child in the playroom, both in the initial, relationship-building sessions and in the subsequent stages of therapy. Encouragement in a play therapy situation could be manifested in several ways. The play therapist could make encouraging comments about behaviors which actually occur in the playroom, such as "You really are working hard on the painting," or "You look proud of yourself for hammering that nail all the way into the log." The play therapist could encourage the child's efforts in activities which occur outside the playroom, such as "You sound like you liked working on that science project," or "So you figured out a way to get your brother to play with you without throwing a tantrum." The Adlerian play therapist could also use encouragement to help a child to be more resourceful and confident in solving problems by making comments such as, "I bet you can figure that out for yourself," or "You can decide which one you want to use."

Open Communication

In order to establish open communication and develop trust in the relationship, the Adlerian play therapist strives to honestly and openly answer children's questions: those regarding play therapy process and procedures, reasons they were brought to play therapy, their own lives, and any other query. The therapist makes every effort to allow children freedom to decide for themselves about materials and activities in the playroom, but is careful to provide explanations when requested. For instance, in answer to a question about how a certain toy is used, the therapist might initially say, "You can decide that." If the question was repeated, the therapist might reply, "I bet you can think of something for yourself," or "You could use it to play catch, or bowl, or lots of things you could think of." Although it is important to accurately answer questions, the play therapist should also listen for covert messages in questions, and attempt to reflect the feelings and address the concern expressed in the implicit question. One common example of this type of communication would be children asking where their mother is. This question usually really means, "Will my mother leave me or will she still be in the waiting room when I get out of here?" The Adlerian play therapist must be alert to this type of two-tiered question and provide answers to both levels.

Asking Questions

Another element in building the relationship is the Adlerian play therapist's attitude toward and method of asking questions. The therapist can ask for clarification about events or conversations that occurred in the playroom or in the child's life outside the playroom, can ask for information connected to family constellation, family atmosphere, or early recollections, or any other relevant topic. While it is permissible for the therapist to ask these types of questions in the playroom, the attitude of the questioning must convey respect for the child's right to answer, to refuse to answer, or to simply ignore the question. In order to establish that the play therapist is different from most of the other adults in the child's life, the number of questions should be kept at a minimum. There are two appropriate methods of asking questions in Adlerian play therapy: (a) direct questioning, and (b) tentative questioning. In the direct questioning method, the therapist simply asks for information or clarification (e.g., "Did you have any fights in school this week?"). In the tentative questioning method, the therapist couches the question in terms similar to the delivery of a tentative hypothesis (e.g., "I wonder if anyone ever talks to you that way?" or "I wonder it that's something you do at home sometimes?"). The tentative questioning method can be used to gather information from the child, to make interpretations, and to give the child more freedom to gracefully refuse to answer a question.

Actively Interacting

The Adlerian play therapist can further enhance the therapeutic relationship by actively interacting with the child, either at the child's invitation or the therapist's instigation. When a child asks the therapist to play, the therapist may choose to do so. At times, in order to further convey respect for the child's position in the relationship, the therapist may leave the direction of this type of interaction to the child. One possible method of allowing the child to "lead" during active interaction is the "whisper technique." As the play progresses, when it is the therapist's turn to do or say something, the therapist whispers, "What should I do next?" to the child. This gives the child the opportunity to decide upon the direction and the content of the play. When the Adlerian play therapist thinks that a child must quickly deal with a specific issue, however, it is permissible for the therapist to initiate and direct the interaction. In this situation, the therapist would suggest the play and dictate, at least initially, the direction and content of the play. For example, when a child is about to go into the hospital, the therapist might say,

"Let's play out what will happen tomorrow when you go to the hospital. First you and your mom will hop into the car. Then what?' "

Limit-Setting

Limit-setting is another important aspect of relationship-building in Adlerian play therapy. There are certain nonnegotiable rules in the playroom, such as the prohibition of harm to the material and to self and others. There are other rules, however, such as the disposition of the sand and paint, which are more flexible. In setting limits on this type of behavior, it is important for the therapist to negotiate the terms of the rule with the child. For example, if a certain amount of water is permissible in the sandbox, the therapist might say, "How much water do you think would be a fair amount for you to put into the sand?" Negotiations can go on from this point. If a child is actively involved in setting the limits for the variable rules and actively involved in generating the logical consequences for both types of infringements, rule infractions and power struggles can be reduced and the relationship with the therapist will be enhanced. Setting the limit in Adlerian play therapy is a four-step process: (a) state the limit; (b) reflect the feeling expressed by the child and acknowledge the child's desire to perform the prohibited behavior; (c) encourage the child to generate alternative behaviors which would not violate the limit and agree upon an appropriate substitution; and (d) if the child does not abide by the new arrangement, encourage the child to generate logical consequences for transgressions. With many children, simply including them in this process makes the fourth step unnecessary.

In another example, if a child was angry and aimed a dart at the mirror, the Adlerian play therapist would state that the behavior was unacceptable by saying, "The mirror is not for shooting." Then the therapist would acknowledge the feeling with the phrase, "I can tell that you are really angry right now." In the next step in the process, the therapist would engage the child in the generation of alternative behaviors by saying, "I bet you can think of something else you can shoot with the dart that wouldn't break if you shot it." The therapist and the child would then reach an agreement about an appropriate alternative behavior, and, if necessary, discuss possible consequences if the child chooses not to abide by the agreement.

EXPLORATION OF THE LIFE-STYLE

In order to facilitate the exploration of the child's life-style in play therapy, the Adlerian play therapist utilizes three methods of exploration common to Adlerian therapy with adults: (a) family atmosphere, (b) family constellation, and

(c) early recollections. These techniques must be adapted slightly for working with children in play therapy.

Family Atmosphere

The therapist gathers the family atmosphere information both from the child's parents during parent consultations and from the child in the playroom. When conducting the initial interviews with the child's parents, the therapist asks questions about the discipline methods used by each parent, the level of ambition for the children manifested by each parent, the relationship between the parents, family values, and any other questions which will help the therapist to understand the atmosphere present in that particular family (Dewey, 1971). During the course of play, the therapist pays close attention to any comments the child may make about discipline, ambitions, and the relationship between the child's parents. The Adlerian play therapist also attends to any play involving the doll house or the kitchen area for subtle clues about family atmosphere. If a child always has the father doll yelling at the children in the doll house, or spends much time in the kitchen banging pots and pans and talking about how the children must come and eat right now, this can probably be considered an indication that this is a family with an authoritarian atmosphere. With an older child or a younger child with good verbal skills, the therapist could also ask questions about family discipline practices and the relationship between the parents during a play therapy session.

Family Constellation

Gathering family constellation information can also take place both in the interactions during parent consultation and during play therapy. The best method of gathering birth order information from the parents is to ask them the standard questions about the order in which the children were born and then to ask them to describe each child and the interactions between the children. These questions should be designed to determine who takes care of whom, who plays with whom, who is jealous of whom, etc. The parents should also be asked to rate the siblings on dimensions such as intelligence, cooperativeness, strength, and desire to please (Eckstein, Baruth, & Mahrer, 1975).

Although it may be helpful to gather some of this data from the child's parents in order to understand their perspective on the children, it is essential to give the greatest weight to the information provided by the child. This information can be gathered in several different ways. The Adlerian play therapist can simply ask the child questions about the family constellation (Dinkmeyer, 1977) during the course of the initial play therapy sessions, either relating the questions to things that are acted out or mentioned in the play or simply asking them directly. The play therapist can also find out much about the family constellation through the child's drawings. A therapist can ask the child to draw a picture of the family and to describe the various siblings, or wait until the child chooses to draw a picture of the family, and then ask them to talk about the family constellation.

Early Recollections

The collection of early recollections can also be valuable in helping the Adlerian therapist understand the child's life-style (Borden, 1982). Early recollections could be gathered during a play session in several ways. The therapist could simply ask the child to recount several incidents which happened when the child was younger. With a less verbal child, the therapist could ask the child to play out an early recollection with the dolls in the doll house or with the puppets. Another possible means of soliciting early recollections in play therapy would adapt a technique discussed by Nelson (1986). This procedure facilitates the gathering of early recollections through a child's drawings or other art work. The therapist could wait until the child was getting ready to paint a picture or draw and request an illustration of an early recollection, and, after the completion of the picture, elicit the story and feelings related to the incident. In order to gain a complete understanding of the patterns implicit in early recollections, these procedures would probably have to be repeated several times over different sessions.

INSIGHT

During the insight phase of therapy, the Adlerian play therapist uses goal disclosure, shares inferences about life-style through interpretation of verbalizations and play, self-disclosure, and points out parallels between the child's behavior in the playroom and behavior outside the playroom to help facilitate the child in gaining insight into relationships, purposes, and behavior. The Adlerian therapist can use these techniques in the play therapy in order to confront (Sweeney, 1981) the child about mistaken beliefs and goals, which will encourage the child to change and work toward more attainable, useful goals.

The phrasing used in the insight phase is extremely important. Goal disclosure, inferences about life-style, and connections between the playroom and the rest of the child's life should be made gently, in the form of guesses or tentative hypotheses (Dinkmeyer, Pew, & Dinkmeyer, 1979). This allows the play therapist the freedom to make mistakes, lessens the possibility that the child will feel cornered and defensive, and encourages both the therapist and the child to consider alternative explanations. In a play therapy situation, the therapist might say, "Could it be that the way that mother doll talks to the baby doll is the way your mother talks to you?" or "I have an idea that when you go right ahead and shoot the dart at the mirror even though you know it's against the rules, you are wanting to feel kind of powerful and important. You might be wanting to show me that I can't stop you from doing that if you want to do it."

Goal Disclosure

In order to help clients stop themselves at self-defeating perceptions and behavior, Adlerian counselors frequently reveal the purpose of the clients' behaviors to them. Dreikurs (1957) labeled the four goals of children's misbehavior as (a) desire for attention, (b) desire for power or superiority, (c) desire for revenge, and (d) display of inadequacy. By observing their own reaction to children's behaviors and observing the children's response to correction, therapists can begin to understand the purposes of children's behavior (Dinkmeyer, Pew, & Dinkmeyer, 1979). The Adlerian play therapist can use incidents which occur in the playroom to disclose children's goals to them, and thus help them gain insight into themselves and their motivation. It is essential that the counselor pay close attention to children's nonverbal reactions to goal disclosure in order to recognize any recognition reflexes, which confirm that children have gained some insight from the disclosure (Smithells, 1983).

One method of goal disclosure appropriate for use in the playroom would involve a therapist-generated dialogue between two dolls or puppets about the purpose of a specific behavior. For example, one puppet could say to the other puppet, "Do you have any idea why Michael talks so loudly in the playroom?" The other puppet could reply, "Could it be that he wants to get everybody to pay attention to him?" The toy telephone could also be used so that the therapist can carry on a conversation about the purposes of behaviors, either with an imaginary third party or with the child.

Sharing of Inferences

The Adlerian play therapist shares inferences about children's life-styles with them based on the information collected about family atmosphere, family constellation, and early recollections. The therapist looks for patterns in children's behaviors and perceptions about themselves, others, and the world. Themes are evident in children's activities and verbalizations in the playroom, their interactions with their parents and other family members, their parents' attitudes toward discipline, and their psychological position in the family. The disclosure of these inferences is designed to help clients gain insight about how mistaken, self-defeating ideas and behaviors keep them from leading a successful, fulfilling life (Dinkmeyer, Pew, & Dinkmeyer, 1979). In play therapy, inferences about life-style should be shared through interpretations of children's behaviors and verbalizations in the playroom. These interpretations help facilitate children's insight into the patterns in their behavior by linking the abstraction of the pattern to the concrete experiences in the playroom. By communicating to children through the language of play, the therapist can help them to understand concepts that young children are not capable of discussing because of their limited abstract reasoning skills and limited verbal abilities.

Some of the sharing of the play therapist's inferences concerning a child's life-style can be made directly to the child in play therapy, without the utilization of some type of metaphoric play. The therapist could simply say, "Sometimes it seems like you have to be responsible for making sure that everything happens just the way your mom and dad want," or "You'd like everybody to take care of you and make sure you get what you want." Patterns in the child's life-style can also be revealed in a less direct manner, through the use of the play media in the setting. For example, while the child is playing with the dolls and the dollhouse, the therapist could point out that, "The big sister is always in charge of taking care of the littler kids. I bet sometimes you feel like that's what happens in your family." Inferences about life-style could be addressed even more subtly, with the therapist not specifically mentioning the parallel between the child's situation and the situation presented in the play. In response to an abused child repeatedly burying the mother and father doll in the sand, the Adlerian play therapist could merely say, "Sometimes it might feel nice for children to be able to make things that hurt them disappear for a while."

Feedback about the Relationship

In their relationship with the therapist, children will usually duplicate some of the attitudes and behaviors manifested in their relationships with the other important adults in their lives. This duplication gives the therapist the opportunity to experience children in ways which are similar to the ways in which significant other adults experience them. The reactions felt by the therapist probably, at least to some extent, reflect the reactions felt by these other adults. Sometimes it is important for the Adlerian play therapist to self-disclose to children and share these personal reactions to what is happening in the play therapy situation. The timing and phrasing of these statements is critical. The therapist should use this technique sparingly and should be certain that children with whom it is used are capable of gaining insight from such feedback. Since the therapeutic relationship in the playroom may be more democratic and trusting than the children's other relationships with adults, it is extremely important to couch any revelations about the therapist's responses in an encouraging, noncritical way. Again, the play therapist must choose whether to address the issue directly or subtly. The Adlerian play therapist should be sure to couch direct self-disclosing messages in the form of "I-statements," in which the feeling is stated in a matter-of-fact, nonjudgmental tone of voice in such a way that the child can understand that there is no blame attached to the statement. This would help avoid defensiveness on the part of the child and encourage the child to gain insight about his or her interactions with other people. This straightforward method of giving feedback should only be used after the therapist is certain that the relationship with the child is firmly established.

If the direct manner is chosen, the therapist could say, "Sometimes I feel kind of angry when you yell at me in a loud voice like that," or "I feel really sorry for you when you look so lonely and sad. I wonder if that's the way other grown-ups feel when you look like that." A more indirect method of giving the child feedback about the play therapist's personal reactions to the interaction in a session would utilize the play media to communicate with the child. If the child repeatedly hits and kicks the punching bag, session after session, the therapist could say, "I bet that punching bag is getting tired of being hit and kicked all the time, and is wondering if you could think of something else to do today." If the child is playing with the dolls in the doll house and the little boy doll constantly yells at the mother doll, the therapist could say, "Sounds like the little boy is angry at the mother. I bet the mother feels kind of angry at him for always yelling at her though."

Pointing out Parallels

It is frequently important for the Adlerian play therapist to point out parallels between the behaviors, relationships, and feelings manifested in the playroom and the behaviors, relationships, and feelings in the rest of the child's life. Although this technique, too, can be done either directly or indirectly, it is usually executed in a straightforward, expository manner. Pointing out parallels is usually done in connection with one of the other techniques utilized in Adlerian play therapy. When utilized in conjunction with other techniques such as reflecting emotions or sharing inferences, the parallel statement follows the statement representing the other technique (e.g., "Seems like you're really angry today. I wonder if that is how you express anger at home?" or "You act like you're used to getting your own way. I bet that's how you act with the other children at school."). A less direct method of pointing out parallels would make use of the communication possibilities inherent in the play media. Two therapist-controlled puppets or dolls could carry on a conversation about how excited a little boy is getting about his "correct" answers to problems he is writing on the chalkboard. The puppets could then make some guesses about how he wishes that would happen at school.

REORIENTATION

The closing stage in Adlerian counseling is reorientation. During this phase the counselor attempts to help the client use the new understanding gained during the insight phase to change behaviors and ways of interacting with others (Sweeney, 1981). In Adlerian play therapy, the reorientation phase consists primarily of helping the child generate alternative behaviors to replace inappropriate behaviors, encouraging the child to try new behaviors and patterns of interaction, and working with parents on different types of discipline and ways of relating to the child.

Generating Alternative Behaviors

Although children may have learned to better understand the purposes of their behaviors during the insight phase of therapy, they probably will not be able to change their behavior patterns without some guidance in how to generate alternative behaviors. One method of helping children learn how to do this during a play therapy session is to teach simple problem-solving skills. Another method is to ask children how they could have done something differently. A third technique, used in Adlerian limit-setting, is to model the generation of alternative behaviors.

In teaching problem-solving, the therapist needs to help the child learn to define the problem, brainstorm possible solutions, choose one of the possibilities, test to see whether that solution works, and evaluate the process of decision making. The therapist will need to lead the child through this process for the first several times a problem occurs in the playroom to firmly establish the skills needed. If a child is having trouble deciding how to get a finished painting down from the easel, the therapist could say, "What is the problem?" When the child has defined the problem, the therapist could then say, "What are some possible ways to solve this problem?" After several choices have been listed, the therapist could encourage the child to choose one to execute by saying, "Which of these would you rather do?" After the child chooses one of the alternatives and carries it out, the therapist could help evaluate the process by asking, "Did it work? What could you have done differently?" This last question can be used during the process of play therapy sessions whenever a child seems to be struggling with a decision. By asking, "How can you do it differently?" or "What else could you do?" the therapist encourages the child to think of possible alternative behaviors. In situations in which it is important that the child generate at least one alternative, such as setting limits, it may be helpful for the Adlerian play therapist to model the behavior. For instance, if a child is having difficulty thinking of an alternative target for the darts, it is appropriate for the therapist to "prime the pump" by supplying the child with several alternatives (e.g., "You could shoot the darts at the punching bag or the wall. Can you think of some other places you could shoot it?").

Encouragement

Encouragement is an essential part of the reorientation process. As children formulate new goals and new ways of gaining significance and try out new behaviors, it is essential that they get positive feedback based on effort, rather than results. During a play therapy session, the Adlerian play therapist must constantly be aware of possibilities for encouraging comments about behavior and about attitudes.

It is important to monitor both the words expressed by the child and the themes and patterns evident in the play. When a child says, "Look at my tower!" the therapist could say, "You really worked hard on that and you seem really proud of all your hard work." If the therapist notices that a child's play in the dollhouse is much calmer than it had been, the therapist might say, "Seems like things are much quieter in that house lately. I bet the children feel good about that."

Consultation with Parents

Based on the Individual Psychology concept that the individual is socially embedded (Ansbacher & Ansbacher, 1956), one of the unique aspects of Adlerian play therapy is the inclusion of the parents as active participants in therapy. The interaction in the playroom between the child and the therapist can be enhanced by additional consultation with the family outside of the playroom. One important adjunct to every play therapy session, especially during the reorientation phase, is a discussion with the parents about weekly progress at home and school. Information supplied by the parents at that time is later integrated into the playroom setting if appropriate.

At times the parents may be invited into the playroom. The purpose of including parents is to help them understand the child's world and enhance family cohesion and cooperation. This inclusion of the parents in the process of play therapy should occur only after the initial phase of relationship-building is well established. Therapists may, indeed, decide not to include parents in the playroom until the reorientation phase. When including parents in the playroom for the first time, the initial part of the session should be designed to allow the child to "show Mom and Dad around your playroom." This procedure can be practiced before the session which will include parents. The child should be allowed to be an equal partner in the planning of sessions which will include the parents.

Introducing the parents to the playroom affords the Adlerian play therapist an opportunity to model more appropriate behaviors to the parents. Demonstrating limit-setting, active listening, and tracking can provide the parents with the confidence to try these techniques at home. Parents may benefit from being taught a home-play technique recommended by Moustakas (1959), Baruch (1949), and Guerney (1982). Parents can be taught to do a form of play therapy to use with their children at home. The goal of this filial therapy is to foster good parent-child relationships. Adlerian play therapy may be complimented by the same therapist working with the parents toward changing family relationships to encourage the child's behavioral adjustment.

SUMMARY

Concepts and techniques used by Adlerian therapists with children can be enhanced by introducing play media to form a unique procedure for helping children. Adlerian play therapy utilizes such basic tenets as the democratic relationship, assessment of life-style, goal disclosure, confrontation, and encouragement to help children develop more confidence and approach life tasks in a more useful manner.

REFERENCES

Ansbacher, H., & Ansbacher, R. (1956). *The Individual Psychology of Alfred Adler*. New York: Harper Torchbooks.

Axline, V. (1969). *Play therapy* (rev. ed.). New York: Ballantine Books.

Barlow, K., Strother, J., & Landreth, G. (1985). Child-centered play therapy: Nancy from baldness to curls. *The School Counselor, 28*, 347–356.

Baruch, D. (1949). *New ways in discipline*. New York: McGraw-Hill.

Borden, R. (1982). Early recollections as a diagnostic technique with primary age children. *Individual Psychology, 38*, 207–212.

Dewey, E. (1971). Family atmosphere. In A. G. Nikelly (Ed.), *Techniques for behavior change* (pp. 41–47). Springfield, IL: Charles C. Thomas.

Dinkmeyer, D. (1977). Concise counseling assessment: The children's life style guide. *Elementary School Guidance and Counseling, 12*, 117–124.

Dinkmeyer, D., Pew, W., & Dinkmeyer, D. (1979). *Adlerian counseling and psychotherapy*. Monterey, CA: Brooks/Cole.

Dreikurs, R. (1957). *Psychology in the classroom*. New York: Harper & Row.

Eckstein, D., Baruth, L., & Mahrer, D. (1975). *Life style: What it is and how to do it*. Chicago: Alfred Adler Institute.

Guerney, B. (1982). Filial therapy: Description and rationale. In G. L. Landreth (Ed.), *Play therapy: Dynamics of the process of counseling with children* (pp. 342–353). Springfield, IL: Charles C. Thomas.

Hansen, J., & Stevic, R. (1969). *Elementary school guidance*. New York: Macmillan.

Manaster, G., & Corsini, R. (1982). *Individual Psychology*. Itasca, IL: Peacock.

Moustakas, C. (1959). *Psychotherapy with children*. New York: Harper.

Nelson, R. (1968). Play media and the elementary school counselor. In D. Dinkmeyer, (Ed.), *Guidance and counseling in the elementary school: Readings in theory and practice* (pp. 267–270). New York: Holt, Rinehart, & Winston.

Nelson, A. (1986). The use of early recollection drawings in children's group therapy. *Individual Psychology, 42*, 288–291.

Nystul, M. S. (1980). Nystulian play therapy: Applications of Adlerian psychology. *Elementary School Guidance & Counseling, 15*, 22–30.

Phillips, R. (1985). Whistling in the dark?: A review of play therapy research. *Psychotherapy, 22*, 752–760.

Smithells, T. (1983). Working with children: Observation, interpretation, and psychological disclosure. In O. Christensen & T. Schramski, (Eds.), *Adlerian family counseling* (pp. 117–136). Minneapolis, MN: Educational Media.

Sweeney, T. (1981). *Adlerian counseling: Proven concepts and strategies.* Muncie, IN: Accelerated Development.

Walsh, W. (1975). *Counseling children and adolescents: An anthology of contemporary techniques.* Berkeley, CA: McCutchan.

Yura, M., & Galassi, M. (1974). Adlerian usage of children's play. *Journal of Individual Psychology, 30*, 194–201.

THE MUTUAL STORYTELLING TECHNIQUE: AN ADLERIAN APPLICATION IN CHILD THERAPY

Terry Kottman
Currently the director of the Pupil Appraisal Center at the University of North Texas. She is also an assistant professor in the Counselor Education Department.

Kathy Stiles
A doctoral candidate and teaching assistant in counselor education at the University of North Texas.

Several authors (Dinkmeyer & Dinkmeyer, 1983; Dinkmeyer, Dinkmeyer, & Sperry, 1987; Kern, Matheny, & Patterson, 1978; Kottman & Warlick, 1989) have posited that Adlerian counseling techniques work well with children. One of the primary strategies developed to help children gain insight into their own behaviors and learn new ways of solving problems involves exploration and disclosure of goals of misbehavior (Dreikurs & Soltz, 1964; Smithells, 1983; Thompson & Rudolph, 1988). As the counselor works with children using this strategy, the children's perspective toward their own behavior progresses through several stages (Thompson & Rudolph, 1988). Initially they understand the connection between their purposes, their behavior, and the consequences of their behavior, but only after the behavior has occurred. Gradually, they grow more aware of the goals of their behavior and learn to "catch themselves" as the behavior is occurring. Finally, their heightened understanding of their own purposes and the consequences of their behavior allows them

Individual Psychology, 46(2), June, 1990, **pp. 148–156**

to anticipate interactions and generate more appropriate alternatives in advance (Thompson & Rudolph, 1988).

Dreikurs and Soltz (1964) identified four mistaken goals of misbehavior: attention, power, revenge, and inadequacy. By cultivating an understanding of these four goals and helping children gain insight into their own specific goals, counselors who work with discouraged children can assist them to learn new, constructive ways of belonging (Smithells, 1983; Thompson & Rudolph, 1988).

Because they have not yet developed the expressive language skills necessary for traditional "talk" therapy, children sometimes indirectly communicate their fears, hopes, and struggles in the form of metaphors (Brooks, 1985). Santostefano (1984) defines a metaphor as "a pattern of images, symbols, words, emotions and actions which synthesizes, conserves, and represents experiences. . . . when imposed on information a metaphor not only determines how the information is construed, but also prescribes particular actions and emotions" (p. 79). This phenomenological representation of metaphor is consistent with the view presented in Individual Psychology of the role of subjective perception in the development of the life plan and life-style. One method of communicating metaphorically with children is through the mutual storytelling technique.

THE MUTUAL STORYTELLING TECHNIQUE

The mutual storytelling technique (Gardner, 1971, 1986) provides counselors with a way of utilizing their clients' metaphorical communications about their life-styles and goals. The child is asked to tell a self-created story with a beginning, a middle, and an end. While listening to the story, the counselor analyzes its metaphors and their psychological meaning for the child. The counselor then responds with a story in which the characters are the same and the plot is similar, but in which the ending represents a healthier resolution than the ending in the child's story, if the child resolved the story maladaptively. In the counselor's retelling, then, the characters solve their problems and conflicts in more adaptive ways, thereby metaphorically providing alternative ways for the child to cope with the world.

Mutual storytelling is a powerful technique when used with children who are old enough (at least five years) and verbally comfortable enough to engage in storytelling (Gardner, 1986). Of crucial importance to its effectiveness is the relationship between child and counselor. Before the counselor can understand the child's metaphors and use them effectively in the retelling, the counselor must take adequate time and care in becoming acquainted with the child and developing a democratic, trusting relationship (Gardner, 1971)—the foundation of Adlerian psychotherapy and counseling (Dreikurs, 1967).

AN ADLERIAN APPLICATION

Traditionally, the mutual storytelling technique has been used with psychoanalytically oriented child psychotherapy (Gardner, 1971, 1974). The technique, however, lends itself readily to application by Adlerian child therapists. When using mutual storytelling as a strategy in Adlerian counseling with children, the counselor can use the child's story to gain insight into the child's mistaken goals. The counselor's retelling of the child's. story presents an opportunity to help the child understand his or her mistaken goals. In the retelling, the counselor can also redirect the child's mistaken goals, correct faulty beliefs, and develop the child's social interest.

The following stories metaphorically illustrate children's goals and the behavior they use to reach their goals. In listening to children's stories, the counselor can gain further insight into children's perceptions of how they gain their significance. The counselor's retelling provides alternative ways for children to achieve a sense of belonging.

The Goal of Attention

When their goal is attention, children believe that they only belong when they are noticed. In a counseling session, children whose goal is attention often manifest behaviors that seem to be designed to keep the counselor involved with them. For example, children may remain in close physical proximity to the counselor, speak loudly and quickly, and respond negatively when the counselor's attention turns away from them. The counselor's affective response, which can be used to help in goal identification, is typically annoyance when children behave this way. In sharing the hypothesis about the goal, the counselor might say, "Could it be that you only feel important when I am paying very close attention to you?"

The following is an example of the application of mutual storytelling with a child whose goal is attention. When asked to tell a story using any of the toys in the play room, the child walks over to the doll house and gets the mother, father, little boy, and little girl dolls and acts out the following story:

It was Sally's birthday and the whole family was having a party. When Sally started opening her presents, her little brother, Ted, asked their mom if he could go to the bathroom. She said "Yes," but he wanted her to go with him. Their father told him that he didn't need anyone to take him to the bathroom anymore. He could go by himself now. Ted didn't go to the bathroom. He stayed in the room where Sally was opening her presents. After a few minutes, he asked his dad to get him a glass of water. His dad told him to wait until Sally had finished opening her presents or go to the bathroom and use the glass he could reach. He still didn't go.

After a few minutes, he told his mom that he wanted to go outside to play. She told him it would be nice if he would stay and watch Sally open her presents. He started crying and said he wanted a present, too. His parents both told him that it wasn't his birthday and that he would get some presents on his birthday. He told them he would like a drum, a paint set, and a bicycle with a horn. They said they would see. Then their mom brought in the birthday cake. Ted sang "Happy Birthday" very, very loudly. Ted told their mom that he wanted the biggest piece of cake. She told him it was up to Sally to decide, so he asked Sally if he could have the biggest piece and she said, "Yes."

Using the same dolls and roughly the same plot the client used, the counselor retold the story:

The whole family got together to celebrate Sally's birthday. There were presents and a cake at the party. When Sally started opening her presents, her little brother Ted asked Mom if he could go to the bathroom. She said "Yes," but Ted would only go if she went with him. Father said "Ted, it seems like you're feeling left out because Sally is in the spotlight today. Well, even though this is her birthday and she's getting extra attention doesn't mean that we've forgotten you. You are an important part of this party and of this family."

Ted smiled because he was glad his father had said that, but he still didn't go to the bathroom. After a few minutes, he asked his mom to get him a glass of water. She said, "Ted, that's something you can do for yourself. We'll be right here when you come back." Ted hesitated a little, then went off to get himself a glass of water. When he came back, Sally was still opening presents, and Ted was getting a little tired of the birthday party. He complained that he wasn't getting any presents, and Mom said, "Even though it's Sally's birthday and her day to get presents, we still think you are a valuable part of the family." Then Sally cut the cake and they all sang "Happy Birthday" to her. She hugged Mom, Dad, and Ted and thanked them for her party, and Ted felt happy that he was there to help make Sally's day special.

The Goal of Power

When their goal is power, children behave as if they only belong when they are refusing to do what others want them to do. In a counseling session, children whose goal is power often test the limits set by the counselor on the use and misuse of the room's toys and materials, behave aggressively toward the counselor or a symbol of the counselor (such as the punching bag), behave stubbornly, and throw temper tantrums. The counselor of "power-hungry" children typically feels angry in response to these and other behaviors designed by children to prove their superiority over the counselor. In checking out a hypothesis about this goal, the counselor might say, "Could it be that you only feel important when you are in charge?"

The following is an example of the application of mutual storytelling with a child whose goal is power. When asked to tell a story using any of the toys in the playroom, the child selects from the animal shelf a lion, bear, and elephant. She brings them to the sand box and acts out the following story:

These three animals live together in the jungle. The lion was the king of the jungle and he liked to tell everybody what to do. This made the bear and the elephant mad because they didn't like it when someone else told them what to do. The bear said to the lion, "You can't tell me what to do. You are not the boss of me. I am my own boss." The lion said, "You have to do what I say because I am king." The bear said, "No, I don't. If you tell me what to do, I will bite you and I will be king. Then I can tell you what to do." The elephant said, "You can't boss me around. I am bigger than you. I can tell you what to do. If you don't do what I say, I will step on you and squish you." The bear said to the elephant, "We don't have to do what he says. Let's show him who is boss. Let's fight with him so he can't tell us what to do." The bear and the elephant said to the lion, "You can't make us follow your rules. We don't want to do what you say. If you try and make us, we will bite you and step on you and then we will tell you what to do." So the bear bit the lion and the elephant stepped on him. After that, though, they both wanted to be king, so they had another fight, and the elephant won, so he got to be king and told all the other animals what to do.

Using the same animals and following a similar plot, the counselor retells the following story:

These three animals live together in the jungle with a bunch of other animals. Everybody knew that the lion was the king of the jungle—he had always behaved like a king, telling others what to do, and it seemed like he always would. One day the bear and elephant were chatting by the river about life in the jungle. Because all the animals were afraid of the lion, they never talked about him behind his back. But that day the bear and elephant admitted to each other that they were not happy with being bossed around by the lion. The bear suggested that he bite the lion and become the king himself. The elephant said that he could just as easily step on the lion and squish him, and then he, the elephant, would be king. The bear and elephant looked at each other in shock—they each had just realized that to bite or step on the lion would be treating the lion the same way he treated them and the other animals. "Surely there's another way to bring peace to our jungle and relief from the lion's bossiness," they said.

They decided to get all the animals together to hear their ideas about how to solve this problem. The others agreed with the bear and elephant that life in the jungle with the lion as king was getting out of hand. The zebra suggested that they invite the lion to their meeting so that he could hear how unhappy they were. When he arrived, they said, "We need to let you know that we are angry with you because you always boss us around. We want to take turns being king, so everybody gets a chance to be the boss." "I'm not too sure about this," the lion said. "I like being the boss. But since you aren't happy, I'm willing to try taking turns at being king."

The Goal of Revenge

Children whose goal is revenge believe they have been hurt in some way by another person or by life circumstances. They feel that the only way for them to gain significance is to avenge themselves on others. In a counseling session, vengeful children may try to hurt the counselor or other children in the session—either emotionally, physically, or both. For example, they could attempt to shoot the counselor or others with a dart gun, try to break a mirror with a hammer, or comment negatively about the counselor. When this happens, the counselor may feel deeply hurt and may even feel a desire for retribution. When the goal of behavior is revenge, the counselor might hypothesize, "Could it be that you only feel important when you are hurting me or others?"

Children whose goal is revenge frequently also act out or talk about getting revenge on others, such as teachers, friends, parents, or siblings. For example, they may play out a scene in which they have been punished by a teacher. As part of the play, they may have the teacher repeatedly fall down a flight of stairs or get run over by a car. During this process, they might make comments about "getting even" or "paying her back for being mean to me." When children act out in this manner, the counselor's personal reaction will be less likely to serve as an accurate barometer in determining the goal of behavior. In response to this type of behavior, the counselor might say, "Could it be that you feel hurt by someone and want to get back at them for hurting you?"

The following is an example of applying mutual storytelling in counseling a child whose goal is revenge. When asked to tell a story using any of the toys in the playroom, the child goes to the doll house and gets the mother, father, little boy, little girl, and baby dolls. He puts them all into a large plastic dune buggy and acts out this story:

This family is going to the store. The father is driving, but the little boy wants to drive. The little boy asks the father if he can drive. The father says "No." The little boy asks his mom if she thinks he should be able to drive. She says, "No." The little boy asks his sister if she thinks he should be able to drive. She says, "I don't think so. You're too little." The road gets very twisty and the father drives fast. The little boy says, "I think you're driving too fast, Daddy." The father says, "Shut up, kid," and starts hitting the little boy. The mother hits him, too. His little sister says, "Hit him harder." Suddenly the car goes out of control. It runs off the road and falls off a cliff and crashes. The whole family gets killed, except the little boy and the baby.

Using the same characters and a similar plot to this story, the counselor retells it in this way:

This family is going to the store. The father is driving, but the little boy wants to drive, and he asks his father if he can. The father says, "No, little boys need moms and dads to do the driving so they can stay safe and healthy." The little boy asks his mom if she thinks he should be able to drive. She says, "You can drive when you're 16, but until then, Daddy and I will do the driving." The road twists and turns and the father drives too fast for the boy to feel safe. The boy says, "I get scared when you drive fast, Daddy. You said you would drive so we could be safe, and I don't feel safe right now. Please slow down." The father slows down and drives more carefully.

The Goal of Inadequacy

When the goal of children's behavior is inadequacy, they believe that they are incapable of doing anything. Children who feel inadequate also tend to feel inconsequential and behave as if they belong only when others expect nothing of them. Their behavior, often characterized as withdrawn, is designed to hide how truly discouraged they feel about life.

In a counseling session, children who feel inadequate will display an inability to take responsibility for themselves by constantly asking the counselor to do things for them that they should be able to do themselves. With extremely discouraged children, they may be unwilling to do anything or interact with the counselor at all. These children may simply stand or sit in one place, expressionless, with little or no effort to play or interact. In working with these children, the counselor will probably feel helpless, lost, and discouraged. Goal disclosure must be delivered very gently, such as, "Could it be that you're afraid to try doing that yourself because you think you might not be able to do it?" or "Could it be that you would really like me to stop talking to you and just leave you alone?"

In the following example, mutual storytelling is used in counseling with a child whose goal is inadequacy. When asked to tell a story using any of the toys in the playroom, the child just stands in the middle of the room, looking at the floor. The counselor goes to the shelf and gets two puppets. She hands them to the child, who drops them and looks down at the floor. The counselor suggests that maybe they could tell a story together. She puts one of the puppets on her hand and gives the other to the child. The child continues to hold the puppet rather than put it on her hand. The counselor tells the following story:

A mother bear was giving her little bear cub growling lessons one day. "It's time for you to learn to growl for yourself now, rather than relying on me to growl for you." The little bear cub really believed she couldn't do her own growling, so didn't even want to try. She wanted her mother to continue growling for her so she could feel safe. She just stood there and looked at the ground, and felt sad and scared. Her mother tried and tried to get the little cub to growl, but the little cub wouldn't even try. Just then, a bee landed on the cub's nose, and she growled! Her mother said, "You growled all by yourself! What a good feeling, to be able to growl for yourself!" The little bear cub smiled and felt so proud. She growled a little growl at her mom and smiled again.

CONCLUSION

The authors have used the mutual storytelling technique in counseling children. In their experience, the technique is fun to use as well as effective. Furthermore, the children with whom they have used mutual storytelling seem to have enjoyed telling their stories as well as listening to the retellings. Children tend to become very involved in the development and evolution of the plots and characters, indicating how closely their stories and the retellings parallel their own lives.

Mutual storytelling, used in the context of Adlerian counseling with children, is an effective strategy for gaining insight into children's mistaken goals. It can also be used to redirect those goals, change faulty beliefs children have about themselves, and develop their social interest. The retelling process can help children generate more adaptive ways of interacting and gaining significance.

REFERENCES

Brooks, R. (1985). The beginning sessions of child therapy: Of messages and metaphors. *Psychotherapy, 22*, 761–769.

Dinkmeyer, D., & Dinkmeyer, D. (1983). Adlerian approaches. In H. T. Prout & D. Brown (Eds.), *Counseling and psychotherapy with children and adolescents: Theory and practice for school and clinic settings* (pp. 289–327). Tampa, FL: Mariner.

Dinkmeyer, D., Dinkmeyer, D., & Sperry, L. (1987). *Adlerian counseling and psychotherapy* (2d ed.). Muncie, IN: Accelerated Development.

Dreikurs, R., & Soltz, V. (1964). *Children: The challenge.* New York: E. P. Dutton.

Dreikurs, R. (1967). *Psychodynamics, psychotherapy, and counseling.* Chicago: Alfred Adler Institute.

Gardner, R. (1971). *Therapeutic communication with children: The mutual storytelling technique.* New York: Jason Aranson.

Gardner, R. (1974). The mutual storytelling technique in the treatment of psychogenic problems secondary to minimal brain dysfunction. *Journal of Learning Disabilities, 7*, 14–22.

Gardner, R. (1986). *The psychotherapeutic techniques of Richard A. Gardner.* Creskill, NJ: Creative Therapeutics.

Kern, R., Matheny, K., & Patterson, D. (1978). *A case for Adlerian counseling: Theory, techniques, and research evidence.* Chicago: Alfred Adler Institute.

Kottman, T., & Warlick, J. (1989). Adlerian play therapy: Practical considerations. *Individual Psychology, 45*, 433–446.

Santostefano, S. (1984). Cognitive control therapy with children: Rationale and technique. *Psychotherapy, 21*, 76–91.

Smithells, T. (1983). Working with children: Observation, interpretation and psychological disclosure. In O. Christensen & T. Schramski (Eds.), *Adlerian family counseling* (pp. 117–136). Minneapolis: Educational Media.

Thompson, C., & Rudolph, L. (1988). *Counseling children* (2d ed.). Pacific Grove, CA: Brooks/Cole.

SECTION V
COUPLE AND FAMILY COUNSELING AND THERAPY TECHNIQUES

EDITORS' COMMENTS

The purpose of Adlerian counseling and therapy with couples is to help couples live in egalitarian, cooperative relationships of mutual respect. The greatest enemy of an equal relationship is the expectation that one's partner automatically will do what one wishes, that one's partner will try to please one and to avoid doing what one dislikes. The desire for superiority, expressed through these expectations, easily leads to complementary efforts of domination and resistance. Through one's lifestyle convictions, one easily can justify a goal of superiority, being best, being in control, and being dominant. The only solution to such arrangements is training and practice in techniques that shift issues from "Who will win?" to "What can we do to improve the situation?" Only when one is attuned to addressing the needs of the situation, rather than one's need to win, is equality established. Further, only when each partner is more interested in the other than in himself/herself will partnership be successful. Each paper in this section offers cognitive and behavioral techniques to aid this transition.

The Pews (1972) offered an excellent description of Adlerian marriage counseling in a traditional perspective, organized around Dreikurs's four-stage formulation of therapy. They outlined a large number of techniques. Starting with clinical "guessing" to establish rapport, they suggested that a good contract aids in maintaining the proper relationship. In assessment, they may allocate five to six interviews for family constellation and early memory assessments for both partners. At times, for faster work, they employed a history of the marriage and accounts of what initially attracted partners to one another to define areas of conflict. They also mentioned rating scales for discussion. During re-orientation, they recommended conflict resolution methods, assignment of tasks, training in listening, and modeling. Dinkmeyer and Dinkmeyer (1982) described a similar perspective on marriage therapy, emphasizing systemic ideas of communication and choice. They too expanded their ideas within Dreikurs's four stages and repeated many of the techniques that the Pews described. They incorporate other techniques, however, such as catching oneself, switching roles, and paradoxical intention, some taken from systems theory literature.

Sherman (1993) defined intimacy and discussed some common obstacles to intimacy: presumed gender differences, wanting change in one's partner, and differences in ideas of comfortable closeness. Differences in emotional intensity; differences in living styles; differences in rules, customs, and traditions; ambiguity regarding intimacy; and desires for symbiotic attachment comprise other obstacles. In his account of each, Sherman suggested a pertinent therapeutic strategy. He also described other, more specific techniques for use in developing intimacy, including clarifying one's own and one's partner's ideas of love, an intimacy genogram, enhancing attending skills, sculpting, and the couple conference.

Tuites and Tuites (1986) described straightforward and simple methods directly addressing equality in relationships. After defining equality and demonstrating inequality through examples that an Adlerian counselor will understand immediately, they suggested that four skills implement equality. Level communication emphasizes openness, honesty, consideration, and mutual respect. In using assertive criticism, one seeks to tell another that one doesn't like something being done. Conflict resolution skills aid in the resolution of difficulties. Finally, encouragement promotes acceptance of the other's competence in a confident fashion and leads to the idea that only through putting the other first can one have a noncompetitive relationship.

Complementarity in Adlerian couples counseling refers to the idea that partners choose one another to mutually meet expectations and train one another to do so. Belove (1980) developed Dreikurs's idea that what we originally are attracted to in one another may become grounds for contention later. He described a protocol for using stories of first meetings, *first encounters of the close kind* (FECK). These stories frequently aid a counselor in determining what is important for one in another's behavior, that is, the expectations one has regarding one's partner. These stories can be used to start discussions, to introduce the idea of complementarity to a couple, and to show how each partner encourages complementary behavior in the other. The technique enables a counselor to demonstrate very quickly, without extended lifestyle analysis, how individuals maintain patterned interactions in their relationships. It also aids a counselor in pointing out partners' strengths quickly and without ambiguity.

The Adlerian approach views problems within the social context. Therefore, family counseling is a natural for Adlerians. McKay and Christensen discussed the purpose of adults' emotional responses to children's goal of misbehavior and specific procedures for helping adults change their emotional responses. The authors highlighted the following techniques: avoiding the first impulse, careful attention to tones, using diversionary tactics, disrupting disjunctive beliefs, and using reminders and signals. These procedures are helpful in breaking up behavioral patterns within the family system.

Pepper and Roberson clarified issues concerning the use of consequences and discipline. The authors provided a framework for how to use this important boundary marking procedure. Nicoll and Hawes combined family counseling assessment with the family genogram. This tool allows family members and the therapist to obtain insight into the influence of family myths and family rituals. Dinkmeyer described a process of Adlerian family therapy and 10 of the predominant techniques. Dreikurs demonstrated the idea that children continue behavior that gets results. In this demonstration, he pointed out a few ways for parents not to be "conned" into the results that reinforce misbehavior. Dreikurs also pointed out to counselors how to elicit and analyze information to pursue this focus.

ADLERIAN MARRIAGE COUNSELING

Miriam L. Pew
Director of the Wilder Community Offenders Group Counseling Program, St. Paul.

W. L. Pew
Staff psychiatrist, Hamm Memorial Psychiatric Clinic, St. Paul, has had training in pediatrics, psychiatry, and child psychiatry, and Adlerian training from Dr. Rudolf Dreikurs.

The authors, a husband-wife team, have worked as co-therapists and co-counselors for over a decade in a number of settings: private pediatric practice, private marriage counseling practice, in-patient and out-patient psychiatric settings, correctional institutions, community-based correctional facility, family education centers, and marriage education centers. Our basic theoretical framework is Adlerian, but we have borrowed from communication theory, family therapy approaches (especially the Palo Alto group), psychodrama, social group work, and probably many other sources of which we are not consciously aware. We aim for flexibility and creativity, not following any rigid pattern but employing a variety of techniques.

Therapy, counseling, and education are seen as qualitatively similar processes. We depend heavily on style-of-living assessment and strive toward cognitive, attitudinal change, as in traditional therapy. Specific recommendations may be given, as in counseling. Finally, principles of improved human relationships are being taught which can be generalized to all human relationships, and are educational in nature.

Prepared for the Fourth Brief Psychotherapy Conference, Chicago Medical School, Chicago, March 24–25, 1972.

Journal of Individual Psychology, 28(2), November, 1972, **pp. 192–202**

Adlerian therapy has, as formulated by Dreikurs (e.g., 7, pp. 65–71), the following four aspects: (*a*) establishing a proper working relationship, (*b*) assessment, (*c*) interpretation, (*d*) re-orientation and re-education. They are applicable in counseling as well as therapy.

These aspects are not sharply separated steps, but may appear together. For example, the establishment of a good working relationship is greatly facilitated if we can demonstrate that something about the counselee makes sense to us. This can be done often within the first few minutes of the initial interview if we have the courage to "guess." Adlerian "guessing" is far from "coin flipping," as our colleague Maurice Bullard has lately pointed out. It is the formulation of a quick working hypothesis, or stochastic hypothesis, on the basis of cues so far obtained, and inferences drawn from them on the basis of our general understanding (2, p. 141). By our guessing correctly, the counselee becomes convinced that we understand him. Thus assessment and interpretation (*b* and *c* above) are used to facilitate the good working relationship (*a*), while some re-orientation (*d*) may be involved at the same time. If we make a wrong guess, that is, our hypothesis about the counselee is not confirmed by him, we have a chance to model "the courage to be imperfect" (see below).

ESTABLISHING AND MAINTAINING THE PROPER RELATIONSHIP

We work hard to establish the relationship quickly, gathering only a minimal history and working directly toward a contract. Generally this contract will involve an agreement to meet together as a foursome for five or six interviews (the time necessary to complete style-of-living assessments on each partner) with an agreement to re-evaluate and renegotiate the contract at the end of that time. Weekly interviews are preferred but in some instances the first interviews have been completed in a few days. The partners may be asked to defer certain areas of discussion until the life styles are completed. The married pair usually receives more help with their problems when the therapists understand both life styles.

Our bias is in favor of marriage, and we feel it is important to be explicit about our beliefs in order to reach an agreement on goals with the couple. If they can agree on a goal of maintaining their marriage and enriching it we are probably in the best situation. However, we do work with un-married couples, with couples whose goal is an amicable divorce, and sometimes with only one partner for a time before the other partner chooses to join us. The important principle is that of shared, explicit goals. When resistance is encountered, we realize it is time to renegotiate the goals of the therapy.

ASSESSMENT AND INTERPRETATION

Family Constellation and Early Recollections

A style-of-living assessment is desirable. To this end we diagram the childhood family constellation and make a few guesses about how the person may have found a place in that group. Then we ask for early recollections (ERs) and check out our guessing by finding out what attitudes, convictions, opinions of self and others, and life in general he has recorded in the ERs. Sometimes a single ER will encapsulate the broad strokes of the life style, while in other instances the life script is epitomized in a favorite childhood song, fairy tale, or nursery rhyme.

We prefer to conduct the collection of these data in the presence of the partner. Then all four of us participate in interpretation. The procedure seldom requires more than four to five hours, total, taking first one and then the other partner.

But such a comprehensive assessment is not necessary in all cases. Many times, especially in the public setting, a "mini life-style assessment" is quite adequate.

Two Shortcuts

Dreikurs has described a useful approach to understand quickly a life style, which he calls "two points of a line" (6). The unified movement toward a self-determined but unadmitted goal can be discovered by identifying two points on a line of movement on which line then an infinite number of points can be located. This technique demonstrates our understanding to the couple especially well when two apparently contradictory points can be shown to be constituents of the same line.

Dreikurs also described the "hidden reason" (6) for behavior, or the "private logic" of the individual which can be uncovered by "guessing" what he may have told himself to justify a certain behavior. If the guess is correct, an adult version of the "recognition reflex" seen in children can often be observed.

History of the Marriage

Sometimes we choose to approach the problem through a brief history of the marriage, beginning with the couple's initial meeting. This is similar to asking a family in family counseling to describe a typical day and gives a quick insight into problem areas. Dreikurs (8, p. 89) has pointed out that the very attributes that attract a couple to each other in the first place are the areas they often choose for conflict when they have decided to discontinue cooperation. The husband who admired his girl friend's verbal facilities now complains that she talks too much. The wife who liked strength of decision making, now complains of domination.

We should emphasize, however, that a long arduous history is seldom desirable and should only be considered at a later stage if therapy is not proceeding well or the therapists cannot put the picture together satisfactorily.

Rating Oneself and One's Partner

One quick technique for evaluating the current relationship and pin-pointing trouble spots is through asking each partner, in the other's presence, to rate himself in seven areas (life tasks) on a scale of 1 to 5, 1 being high. After rating himself, e.g., on occupation, he is asked how he thinks his wife would rate him, and then we turn to her for her rating. Hypothetical results of such ratings are shown in Table 1.

We see from the table that John rated himself lowest on love and marriage, highest in friendship, with Mary concurring. He also rated himself highest on leisure and recreation, but here Mary rates him lowest. Mary, like John, rates herself lowest on love and marriage, while John gives her a somewhat higher rating.

TABLE 1
Hypothetical Ratings in Seven Areas of Each Spouse (*a*) by Himself, (*b*) as He Thinks the Other Would Rate Him, (*c*) as the Other Does Rate Him

	Ratings					
	John			Mary		
Area	*a*	*b*	*c*	*a*	*b*	*c*
Occupation	2	4	2	3	1	1
Love and marriage	5	4	5	5	5	3
Friendship	1	1	1	3	3	3
Getting along with self	3	5	5	4	5	5
Finding meaning in life	2	2	2	4	5	5
Leisure and recreation	1	3	5	4	5	4
Parenting	2	4	1	2	2	2

She feels that John would rate her lowest not only on this, but also in three other areas. Sometimes a partner hears for the first time something encouraging. Other times a partner realizes for the first time his spouse's discouragement. Or both partners may be surprised to find strengths or weaknesses in their relationship that they had not recognized. Or marked discrepancies become clear. Or a pattern of one partner always accepting a one-down position may emerge.

Self and Ideal Self

We also ask each partner to place himself on a 10-rung ladder with the top rung representing his ideal self, a modification of the Kilpatrick and Cantril technique (11). Here we can often see graphically demonstrated the high-flown ambitions and the low self-esteem and discouragement.

Both the ratings and the ladder position provide a baseline which can be referred to later in therapy as evidence of improvement or to point out trouble spots still inadequately dealt with.

RE-ORIENTATION AND RE-EDUCATION

Conflict Resolution

The four principles of conflict solving delineated by Dreikurs (9) are relevant to re-orientation in cases of marital conflict. They are (*a*) mutual respect—neither fighting nor giving in; (*b*) pinpointing the problem—the underlying issue; (*c*) reaching a new agreement, and (*d*) participation in decision making and responsibility.

These four principles are *not* steps in a sequence. (*a*) Mutual respect is an ideal to be worked toward and may emerge from some of the other facets. (*b*) The "problems" presented by the couple are seldom the basic issue, i.e. common complaints concerning sex, money, child rearing, in-laws, etc., are actually only battlegrounds agreed upon by the couple. The underlying issue will always be some threat to personal status, prestige, superiority: Who's going to decide? Who will control? Who is right? etc.

(*c*) When a couple is fighting they have reached an agreement to fight. Therefore if conflict is to be resolved, a new agreement must be reached. Ultimately this means each partner speaks in the first person stating what *he* is willing to do without demanding from the other. Whenever a partner is concentrating on what his spouse should be doing, he is overlooking the part he plays and the possibility that he can change the balance by changing his own behavior. This is best exemplified when a spouse learns to deal with a tyrant.

> A severely depressed, paranoid wife had just been released from a psychiatric hospital and complained that her physically abusive husband dominated her through temper tantrums. She was advised to retire to the bathroom without comment at the beginning of each provocation. Although she protested bitterly that her husband would break down the door, she did carry out our recommendation and came back in one week describing a miraculous change in the relationship. Her husband quickly caught on that she was taking her sails out of his wind, and they could soon laugh together.

(*d*) Full involvement in the decision making process is essential for an equalitarian cooperative relationship of mutual respect. We teach this very specifically in our interviews and emphasize that decisions need not be for life, rather, often only until the next interview.

Assignment of Tasks

We give specific tasks to be carried out between interviews. One of the most effective, in the beginning, is to suggest to the couple that each continue doing exactly what the other is complaining most about, and do it on schedule, deliberately—"the benevolent ordeal," one of Haley's "therapeutic paradoxes" (10, p. 187). In this way many couples quickly recognize the absurdity of their particular conflict, and are unable to carry out the recommendation without laughing after the first few days. This is a change of behavior, and new methods of problem solving become believable.

Other tasks we may assign are of a more educational rather than paradoxical nature. We may ask each partner to list, independently, his expectations of his spouse as wife and mother (husband and father). These lists are considered at the next interview, clarified, and discussed in terms of whether they are reasonable (usually they are). Sometimes we will ask a couple to live according to these expectations for a time-limited period.

Couples in conflict often don't listen to one another. We teach them listening techniques, e.g., having to paraphrase to the partner's satisfaction what he has said before answering. A more complex technique is the marriage conference described by Corsini (3). We ask the couple to schedule three or four one-hour appointments in a place and at a time when they won't be interrupted. One partner has the floor for the first half-hour and the other partner listens and avoids disrupting. Then the process is reversed. The couple is admonished not to discuss in between appointments the subjects dealt with in the marriage conference. Some couples have found this process so helpful they have continued it on a weekly basis.

This last technique illustrates our goal, i.e., to teach the couple principles, attitudes, techniques which they can generalize to child-parent, employer-employee or and other human relationships. Some couples return occasionally for a "check-up." Others find that by the time they have terminated they can, with the support of appropriate reading (e.g., 4), work out their own conflicts.

General Adlerian Attitudes

The following attitudes which we bring to the therapeutic situation are the logical accompaniment of Adler's concept of man, developed by a therapist for its usefulness in psychotherapy. They are, of course, not exclusively Adlerian.

Courage and Optimism. Adler considered courage and an optimistic outlook as one aspect of mental health and as a requirement of any kind of leadership (1, pp. 155, 450). We share Adler's view that a human "is not obligated to his symptoms" (1, p. 292) and really believe that he can change and grow. Given a relationship of trust, mutual respect, courage and cooperation any problem can be solved. The counselees, like the patients, are likely to be fearful and pessimistic. Thus re-orientation involves the following:

Encouragement. This is effected in various ways. We list, in addition to a person's mistakes, his assets. Sometimes this involves re-definition, e.g., stubbornness, as persistence. Adlerian psychology being one of use, even apparent deficiencies may not be inhibiting, depending on how they are used. We encourage by discussing how others have similar problems; giving honest recognition for useful behavior; always minimizing useless behavior. In the Marriage Education Center we often ask the larger group to list the strengths they have noted in the particular marriage. Participation, only as an observer, may be very encouraging, not only in becoming aware that one's problems are not so hideous and unique, but also in hearing other couples report their successes. "If they can do it, so can we!"

Positive Expectations on our Part. These are revealed in the contract. "We don't see your marriage as hopeless and we care enough about what happens to schedule a series of interviews with you." Many couples have come to us after years of conflict and many disappointing marriage counseling experiences, wondering if there is any hope for their marriage. The fact that we are unimpressed with the history but willing to start from today is apparently very reassuring.

Courage to be Imperfect (12). This attribute which we deliberately try to instill in our counselees is essential for the therapist. Mistakes are seen, not as disasters, but opportunities for learning. All human failures are seen as mistaken efforts to find belonging in the human community.

Emphasis on the Present. We want to know only enough past history to identify present convictions and guidelines. Themes that are discovered in the marriage history are related to here and now problems or events. Recounting of past injustices is discouraged because both past and future are fictions; they are not concrete reality. Attempts by the marital partners to discourage themselves or each other by reliving the past or anticipating the unknown future are pointed out until they catch themselves, an "aha" experience.

FOUR-WAY THERAPY

We had been working as a therapeutic team for several years before we heard the process described as therapy of couples by couples, or conjoint marital therapy. Today this process is not uncommon. Our decision to work this way was based on the multiple therapy principles adumbrated by Dreikurs (5) and the comfort that Adlerians in general have in various group approaches.

There are certain distinct advantages in having the therapeutic couple be married. We provide a model and can share some of our own problems and give encouragement that such problems can be solved. We sometimes, almost deliberately, disagree, thereby providing an opportunity to demonstrate that conflict can be resolved peacefully. Since we are parents too we can empathize with problems involving children. Often one of us can empathize with one partner, providing a great source of encouragement. We have learned to work together in such a way that we can substitute roles comfortably, one being more observer, or more diagnostic, or more supporting, etc. Marriage therapy is often completed so much more quickly that we can justify, in our clinic, the use of two therapists purely from an administrative point of view. Co-therapy is probably the most effective teaching process. Although one therapist may be senior in some respect, this does not make him superior since his partner is sure to be senior in some other respect, e.g., a male therapist can never know what it is like to be pregnant or to menstruate or to be discriminated against as a female.

One of the advantages of four way therapy is that it is fun. We have learned to keep a rather light, whimsical, often humorous air in the face of even the grimmest tragedy with the result that both couples find themselves looking forward to the next session, with keen anticipation and we, as a therapeutic team, often don't feel that we have really been working.

MARRIAGE EDUCATION CENTERS

After many years of working in the private office, we decided to apply our experience in public, before an audience, similar to Adler's counseling centers of 50 years ago, and along the lines of the various family education centers set up under Dreikurs' guidance. We established two marriage education centers as pilot projects in which the sessions were open to the public.

The first center was in an outpatient psychiatric clinic, to which couples were referred not only by the clinic, but also by other agencies, lawyers, pastors and other clients. Other professionals interested in marriage were welcome to attend the sessions. The usual procedure was to interview a volunteer couple who had attended for a few weeks. They were identified as co-educators with us since we, through talking with them, could elucidate general principles that could be of use to anyone attending. The rest of the group was encouraged to participate through offering suggestions, testifying as to their own experience with a given approach, but, probably most important, offering encouragement. We would see a couple for a single interview or for a series of weekly interviews or for brief follow-ups. Many couples who were never interviewed described improvement in their marriage relationship through merely attending the weekly meetings. We varied the format considerably, at times relying more on lecture-discussion, at other times using psychodramatic techniques or conducting a complete psychodrama. We often gave specific recommendations to the couple and asked them to return in one week and report their experience to the group.

The second center was organized in a small theater at a theological seminary, which could accommodate up to two hundred people. The process was similar though often somewhat more formal with the separation inherent in the elevated stage which made it easier for a large group to see and hear but took away some of the intimacy. In terms of providing services economically to large numbers of people, we demonstrated that couples will discuss the most intimate details of marriage in such a setting just as families will discuss their problems in the family education centers. No one is asked to discuss anything he, or she, does not want to, and the therapist must remain sensitive to the couple they are working with while at the same time keeping in touch with a large audience. Again the team effort facilitates this: one of us might be working more intensively with the couple while the other might be more tuned in to what was going on in the larger group. The marriage education center provides a remarkably effective training ground for professionals who are working with or wish to work with marriage problems.

Each center has advantages and disadvantages. The type of center established would probably be most dependent on the skills of the leaders. Not all couples could be helped in this setting. Thus the centers became referring agencies also, if we felt that more frequent interviews, individual or group therapy, drug therapy, or hospitalization was desirable. Our choice was to work with intact couples. But we were not averse to working with one partner—always with the willingness to incorporate the other partner when he or she chose to join us. Among our couples there were failures, one partner continuing to attend after separation or divorce. And there were unexpected successes, such as the following.

> John was referred to the marriage education center immediately following a second psychiatric hospitalization. He had been both seriously suicidal and homicidal. His wife refused to accompany him, later came with him and then alone. Both were seen individually for drug therapy. The situation was very serious when John was arrested and Mary became acutely psychotic and was hospitalized. Five months later Mary called to say they had reconciled, were living peacefully with their children and John was attending the university, a life-long dream, while working part time. Independent contact with John and with their attorney confirmed Mary's optimistic report.

We think this example is crucial to our thesis that anyone can be helped, and would allay the likely criticism that only the simple problems can be dealt with in public and that these "more serious illnesses" can only be helped through a medical-model approach behind closed doors. More recently we saw this couple with their children in a restaurant and the remarkable improvement persists.

We decided we would not deny anyone attendance, though we might decide at any point in an interview to stop working, directly, in that setting at least, with the couple that had volunteered.

A preliminary report on marriage education centers was presented in 1970 at the Centennial Conference of the International Association of Individual Psychology (13). As far as we know, the marriage education center model has not been replicated. We would like to see the process tried in other settings.

CONCLUSION

We see the final goal of the marriage therapist to work himself out of business and to do this as quickly as possible. One of our greatest satisfactions as a therapeutic team has been to help a couple out of the "professional patient" role, help them to stop the rounds of interminable therapy and to learn to accept responsibility for their own behavior and to solve their own conflicts.

Because marriage is such a close relationship it tests in each partner a willingness to cooperate, and measures social interest. Cooperation and sense of community can be taught in marriage counseling or therapy and in marriage education centers.

REFERENCES

1. Adler, A. *The Individual Psychology of Alfred Adler*. Ed. by H. L. & Rowena R. Ansbacher, New York: Basic Books, 1956.

2. Adler, A. *Superiority and social interest*. Ed. by H. L. & Rowena R. Ansbacher. Evanston, Ill.: Northwestern Univer. Press, 1964.

3. Corsini, R. J. Let's invent a first-aid kit for marriage problems. *Consultant*, Sept. 1967, p. 40.

4. Dreikurs, R. *The challenge of marriage*. New York: Duell, Sloan & Pearce, 1946.

5. Dreikurs, R. Techniques and dynamics of multiple psychotherapy. *Psychiat. Quart.*, 1950, 24, 788–799.

6. Dreikurs, R. The holistic approach: two points of a line. In R. Dreikurs (Ed.), *Education, guidance, psychodynamics*. Chicago, Ill.: Alfred Adler Institute, 1966 mimeographed. Pp. 19–24.

7. Dreikurs, R. *Psychodynamics, psychotherapy, and counseling: collected papers*. Chicago, Ill.: Alfred Adler Institute, 1967.

8. Dreikurs, R. Determinants of changing attitudes of marital partners toward each other. In S. Rosenbaum & I. Alger (Eds.), *The marriage relationship*. New York: Basic Books, 1968. Pp. 83–103.

9. Dreikurs, R. Solving conflicts: four steps of conflict resolution. Unpublished paper, 1970.

10. Haley, J. *Strategies of psychotherapy*. New York: Grune & Stratton, 1963.

11. Kilpatrick, F. P. & Cantril, H. Self-anchoring scaling: a measure of individuals' unique reality worlds. *J. Indiv. Psychol.*, 1960, 16, 158–173.

12. Lazarsfeld, Sofie. Mut zur Unvollkommenheit. *Int. Z. Indiv. Psychol.*, 1926, 4, 375–381. Engl. trans. Dare to be less than perfect. *Int. J. Indiv. Psychol.*, 1936, 2(2), 76–82.

13. Pew, Miriam L. A marriage education center. *J. Indiv. Psychol.*, 1970, 26, 226.

FIRST ENCOUNTERS OF THE CLOSE KIND (FECK): THE USE OF THE STORY OF THE FIRST INTERACTION AS AN EARLY RECOLLECTION OF A MARRIAGE

P. Lawrence Belove

With Marie Hartwell-Walker, Ed.D., co-director of the Adlerian Counseling Center of Amherst, Massachusetts. He is a doctoral candidate, studying family therapy, at the University of Massachusetts.

With few exceptions, which may have diagnostic significance because they are exceptions, most married couples, when asked to recall their first encounter with each other, recall not only the impressions they had of each other but also a single, selected moment which in its visual qualities and specificity has many of the characteristics of an early childhood recollection. Even when questioned separately the partners often produce the same moment as the subject of the recollection, as if there were some unspoken agreement between them about the significance of that moment, perhaps as if the shared recollection defined for them in metaphor the nature of their current relationship. We can call this shared recollection the First-Encounter-of-a-Close-Kind (FECK) story.[1] If the FECK story is a spontaneously- and jointly-selected parable of a marriage, then we have available

---

[1]Coincidentally, "feck" is defined in the 1971 edition of *The Compact Edition of the Oxford English Dictionary* as "the purport, drift, tenor, or substance of a statement, intention, etc."

Journal of Individual Psychology, 36(2), November, 1980, **pp. 191–208**

to us a convenient assessment tool which may show how the partners themselves characterize the main themes of their marriage.

To demonstrate how FECK stories may be interpreted and to establish this thesis it is first necessary to sketch briefly the theory of Individual Psychology as it applies to the assessment of a marriage.

ASSESSING A MARRIAGE

An axiom of Adlerian Psychology is that every individual orients himself in the world according to his or her basic convictions. These convictions include expectations about life, expectations about people, the self and others as well as guiding intentions or conclusions about what it takes to live in a world so understood. This framework of basic convictions, expectations, and intentions is referred to as a person's unique, self-created style of life.

In Adlerian psychology, everything everone does is seen as an expression of and a reinforcement of the style of life. Life style is a holistic concept; people are assumed to be self-consistent. In a troubled marriage the Adlerian assumption is that each partner is acting in a manner necessarily consistent with his/her basic convictions. Each partner is seen as contributing equally to the trouble because each is seen as realizing some purpose for himself through the trouble. All behavior can be seen as making sense, albeit according to private logic.

Because all behavior, including marital behavior, is an expression of this coherent life style the selection of a mate is never seen as capricious or as something in the hands of fate.

> As personality has developed in the efforts of the child to integrate himself with others, so our resulting life style attracts us to persons who fit with our personal method of social interrelation. Sexuality and the social institution of marriage make marital choice more intimate than any other relationship. Hence the fundamental structure of the individual personality is evidenced more decisively in the choice of a mate than in any other human affiliation. (Dreikurs, 1946, p. 87)

The basic convictions, expectations and intentions which guide the life style are not only self-consistent but also constant. When people who once loved each other come to dislike each other, the assumption of Adlerian psychology is that the life styles of the partners have not changed, but, only, that those qualities which were once seen as pluses have since come to be seen as minuses.

> The factors which lead to the choice of a partner are correlated with the conflicts which later result during a marriage . . . Even when former virtues turn into faults, these faults serve to maintain the once established equilibrium. Thrift in finance is seen as miserliness; generosity as extravagance; assurance as lust for domination; orderliness as exaggerated meticulousness; fondness for home life as dull domesticity. (Dreikurs, 1946, p. 83)

If the partners are married and therefore committed to one another, and if the choice of a mate is, at some level, purposeful and part of a constant and consistent life style, then any significant interaction between the partners, painful or not, reflects an implicit agreement and a complementarity of life styles. The complementarity does not refer to traits but rather to convictions, expectations, and intentions.[2] "Each somehow senses what he can expect from the other and their agreement implies a certain acknowledgement of cooperation in pursuit of each one's goal" (Dreikurs, 1959, p. 78).

For example, if a man is convinced that in order to be a "Real Man" he must overpower women, then he needs to find a woman who resists him so that he may work to overpower her. He needs a worthy opponent, not a pushover. The ideal woman for such a man would be one who believes that in order to be a "Real Woman" she must continually prove that no man is going to overpower her. She too needs a worthy opponent. Two such people with complementary ideas about life could marry each other and live interesting lives, each using the other to con-

[2] It is in the discussion of the unique agreement formed between the partners that Adlerian theory most resembles other schools of thought. Clifford Sager, in his book, *Marriage Contracts and Couple Therapy* (1976), arrives at the most similar conceptualization. He says, "Each partner in a marriage brings to it an unwritten contract, a set of expectations and promises, conscious and unconscious" (p. ix). Sager's concept of the individual contract is almost identical to the Adlerian concept of life style in the sense that it attempts to characterize the stance an individual takes toward life, specifically toward the life task of marriage. A contract is an implicit interactional frame involving both expectations and intentions. In addition to the two individual contracts, Sager also identifies a third, explicitly interactional contract, which provides "an operational field in which each struggles with the other to achieve fulfillment of his own individual contract" (p. 28). Watzlawick, Beavin, and Jackson (1967) reach a similar conclusion. They state that when two people create a relationship they agree that certain behaviors will be allowed and certain behaviors will not. Salvador Minuchin (1974), a family systems therapist describes the contractual arrangement in the following manner: "When partners join, each expects the transaction of the spouse to take the forms with which he is familiar. Some behaviors are reinforced and others are shed as spouses accommodate to and assimilate each other's preferences" (p. 27). Satir (1967) speaks in terms of a "basic marital homeostasis or definition of the relationship" (p. 115).

firm his or her own thesis. The general rule which Adlerian psychology applies to all married partners is that each will stimulate behavior from the other which brings the reactions anticipated. It is not as important that the behavior is pleasant or not as that it confirms the self, the life style.

The problems in a relationship which bring a couple to counseling are usually precipitated by an exogenous factor. The partners who come to counseling are basically, at the level of their convictions, expectations and intentions, the same two who once loved each other and got married. However, their life situation has changed; something new has come to their life which makes it difficult for them to continue their agreement. For example, a couple whose agreement is that he be the only man in her life and that she love and nurture him will find that the birth of a child, especially of a son, can throw their basic agreement off balance. A couple with the agreement that they both be strong, independent people can find the sudden fact of being publicly, legally married and consequently obligated to each other so disturbing an idea that they will get involved in a variety of negative behaviors simply to maintain the fiction of themselves as free and independent agents. Whatever the case, when life presents situations which challenge the partners' ability to live together according to the agreement implicit in the complementarity of their life styles, one or both of the partners will strive, possibly through illegitimate methods, to defeat the life situation and restore the basic pact. It is an assumption of Adlerian psychology that even the most neurotic goal is somehow always realized, even through specious means and measures.

In the Adlerian frame of reference, marriage is not seen as a state of being, but rather as a task—a task set for two. Adler held that all people are confronted by, must respond to, certain inevitable facts of life on earth. Among these is the awareness that humans come in two sexes, must mate to procreate, and that "a good marriage is the best means we have for bringing up the future generation of mankind" (Adler, 1956, p. 433). Making a successful marriage is a task requiring the utmost cooperation. Each must feel equal in worth to the other. Thus, a married couple is seen in the light of Adlerian psychology as two separate individuals, each operating according to the guidelines of his/her basic convictions, intentions, and expectations, each striving to achieve his/her own place in life, but at the same time, each also working to build a life with the other, and in the process using more or less courage, more or less selflessness, more or less positive cooperation.

There are a variety of methods Adlerians doing marriage counseling have developed for getting at the shared agreement and the style of cooperation as well as the basic convictions, expectations, and intentions of each partner. Most Adlerian clinicians have trained themselves to guess stochastically toward these issues from the moment of first contact with the client. Pew and Pew (1972) have recommended working out formal life style assessments for each spouse in the presence of the other. Grunwald (Note 2) works with a formal questionnaire which surveys the life tasks and other basic issues and allows her to work quickly back via "gold mines," or contextual clues, to basic life style issues—a method similar in format to Dreikursian family counseling. Powers and Hahn (Note 3) have demonstrated a formal interview format in which they synthesize the life styles of each partner in tandem and simultaneously describe the couple's unique style of interaction. For Powers and Hahn, some of the strongest clues as to the dynamic of the marriage are derived from each partner's stated definition of masculinity and femininity. The FECK story interpretation may offer an additional technique arising out of Adlerian psychology for pinpointing the unique style of relationship in a marriage.

A NEW ASSESSMENT TOOL—THE FECK STORY

Dreikurs described the moment of love at first sight as a time when each communicated to the other ". . . untold impressions, opinions and promises . . . (and came) . . . to an understanding without either becoming aware of his participating in the game" (1946, p. 66). He was speaking of the moment when each partner rather intuitively recognized in the other the basic attitudes toward life and the two sexes that would complement his/her own attitudes. Rather than recognize this moment of rich but not fully, or immediately, understandable communication as happening only to those who have experienced love at first sight, the common FECK story suggests that it happens to all couples. Rather than "love at first sight," call it "the first sight of love."

FECK stories are like early recollections. They are of specific events; what was seen, heard, and spoken, by whom, in what setting, to what effect. They are brief, anecdotal stories with a beginning, an end, and a strongly implied, but rarely specified or explicitly understood, moral. The incidents described are often innocuous and would ordinarily be forgotten were it not for their unique personal significance. They are selective; one brief, but telling moment is seized and cherished from the uncountable moments which pass in the first days or hours of an acquaintanceship. It is possible that these FECK stories, so provocatively similar to early recollections, may be similarly interpreted.

Contemporary Adlerians do not agree that non-early recollections are suitable for projective interpretation. Mosak (1977) says, "It would appear that later recollections change with the present mood while early recollections reflect the basic attitudes to life. In line with this we have arbitrarily set age eight as the cut-off point for early recollections" (p. 70). Ackerknecht (1976) states, "If a person of at least average or normal intelligence cannot produce any early recollections before the age of six or seven, this may represent a resistance toward the interviewer, but more often it indicates that the reality of the early years of this person's life does not agree with the subjective fictional character of a person's life history on which his life style is based" (page 48). Pursuing this idea, Ackerknecht offers a sequence of recollections including memories from age 14 and 15. The apparent rule of thumb is that significantly early recollections begin when a person believes his or her own story begins. Some Adlerians (Note 3) occasionally use the projective interpretation of the story of the first menses as a clue to a client's attitudes and expectations concerning her role as a woman in the world, once again following a beginning-of-the-story rule of thumb.

Finally, Adler cautioned against too arbitrary a cut-off date;

> We should not distinguish too sharply between old and new remembrances, for in new remembrances also the action line is involved. . . . No memories are chance memories. Out of the incalculable number of impressions which meet an individual he chooses to remember only those which he feels, however darkly, to have a bearing on his situation. (1956, p. 352)

Nonetheless, FECK stories, like recollections of the first menses, should not be handled as if they had the same universal scope as the earliest recollections. For example, the recollection of the first menses is specifically about the recollector's view of herself as a sexual female. FECK recollections are specifically about the recollector's relationship to one other significant person.

In addition to their intentionality, or focus on a specific aspect of life, FECK stories have another suggestive quality. They are shared. FECK stories are often cooperatively selected and held in common by both spouses, and often as if by unspoken agreement. (At this point instances where FECK stories are not shared have not been analyzed.)

Powers (1973) notes that cultures and groups use myths, just as individuals use early recollections, to explain, define, and guide themselves. FECK stories seem to be like self-selected myths "spontaneously" created for self-definition and guidance. Like early recollections and myths FECK stories seem to condense the main themes of a relationship into a kind of metaphor *a deux*. The expectations and remembrances of a marriage are captured in a living story, actively remembered, as if the partners were saying to themselves and each other, "For as far back as we can remember this is how things were between us and this is probably how they will be."

Even though FECK stories are recollections from later life, they do appear to retain a stable and shared form, relatively independent of current mood, through the years in which an intimate relationship is maintained. Further, they also follow a beginning-of-the-story rule of thumb. And finally, following the assumption that there are no chance memories, the Adlerian theorist is bound to consider their dynamic importance, and to ask how they may be serving some purpose.

ASKING FOR FECK STORIES

With FECK stories, as with early recollections, it is important to follow Dreikurs' caution and carefully distinguish between specific recollections and general reports (Dreikurs, 1952). Reports have a general quality, i.e., "We used to do this or that." Recollections have a focused quality and a specific sensory component. The FECK story, to be interpreted projectively, must be a recollection, a story of one living moment which symbolized for each partner the first time each recognized in the other something which would help them realize their own plan for life.

Usually it is sufficient to ask, "Most couples have a story they share about their first encounter. What was your story?" If what comes forward is a remembrance of impressions or a saga of several weeks' events it helps to point the question further by asking, "What is the story of the first interaction you can remember with your husband (wife)?" The virtue of this terminology is that "interaction" demands a recollection of specific events and tends to prohibit the retelling of remembrances of impressions only.

As with early recollections, it is important to ask for a moment of focus, to get a clear description of the moment and accompanying feelings. Since many of the difficulties in a marriage come from "mind-reading," the imputing by one of what's going on in the head of the other, it is sometimes useful to ask the teller of the FECK story what the other one was thinking in the moment of focus.

It is important to get distinctly separate versions of the FECK stories. This may be possible by simply instructing one to keep quiet while the other tells their version. Getting separate versions may be difficult when dealing with couples involved in power struggles or battles of righteousness because often these battles focus on who has the right to define the relationship. It may be necessary to take each one's story out of the presence of the other. Also, such couples, in a manner consistent with their styles, may produce quite different versions or even different stories.

In some instances there is no readily available story. With limited clinical experience it is difficult to say what this means. There are couples now married who have known each other since childhood. Two such couples contacted claimed not to have a story. Possibly another incident serves as a defining metaphor for them. Possibly the story was not properly asked for. Possibly there is no story. One man contacted who was divorcing a woman who had been his childhood sweetheart produced an early recollection, age nine, of him and his soon-to-be-ex-wife. She was not available to be asked for a matching story.

EXAMPLES OF FECK STORIES AND DISCUSSION

Couple One

His Story. We met in a student hang-out. I saw C. sitting at a table and I said, "Who is that girl with those big tits?" to my companion. And he said, "That's C. I can fix you up with her." And he did. We had a blind date and we went to someone's apartment. There were three couples and this was a make-out party, as it could only happen in the fifties. Someone turned off the lights and there was some heavy petting going on somewhere in the room. C. demanded that the lights be turned on and all this sillyness be stopped and made inappropriate comments for that kind of party. It was somewhat embarrassing and the other people were annoyed. And that was the end of the date.

Focus: Total darkness with C. demanding that the light be turned on and saying, "What's going on here?"

Feeling: I didn't have my expectations fulfilled, but I was somewhat amused also.

Her Story. We met through a sorority sister. N. had seen me at a restaurant—a bohemian, beatnik place. He talked to the sorority sister of mine. We were having a dance; she was going to go with his roommate. She was sexy and slept around so I'm sure they thought they were going to get lots of sex. So N. picked me up and we went and we came back to their apartment and they wanted to turn out all the lights. And I turned them back on. And the night proceeded like that. It was a tug of war and I won. And N. said, "How could you have done such a terrible thing to my friend and my friend wanted that evening with the other girl."

Focus: Their apartment. The other couple on the bed and me walking around turning lights on. N. was sitting on the couch looking annoyed.

Feeling: I'm not going to allow this. And being amused at the situation. I'm not one to give in.

Discussion of Couple One's Stories. After 15 years of marriage both continue to carry the same memory and both spontaneously focus on the same moment. In his memory his expectations of her are that she's a strong, bossy woman; of himself, that there's nothing he can do about it; of others, that in collusion with this strong woman he can dominate a scene without having to do it directly, that she is a front woman for the marriage; and of his ways of responding to her strength, that he gets annoyed and embarrassed, turns his attention elsewhere, distances himself from her and sees her as a joke played on others.

In her memory her expectations of him are that he will let her have her way; of herself, that she will win; of others, that what they want doesn't count and she will dominate; and of her methods, that she will succeed through stubbornness, taking action, justifying herself through humor.

Their mutual expectations, then, are that C. is boss and N. goes along, unwilling to confront; that both enjoy C.'s power but N. covers by expressions of good intentions and C. covers with humor. Despite the fight, they will both find humor in it, although a rather cynical kind of humor.

In subsequent questioning the following themes are brought out. First, that she is, in fact, the boss. She said she liked him because, among other things, he was "physically the opposite of my Dad who was authoritative, strong, taking care of things, and taking care of me." He, on the other hand, complains that he would like her to "turn her attention away from manipulating other people and her environment, her children, and her friends and her husband."

A second theme that emerges is that she is the center of attention and needs to dominate a scene. She complains that "he doesn't know how to share his interests and I should have all the extra attention." He responds that "she is insensitive to others' feelings, but also excessively interested in others' activities but only to be critical of them."

A third theme is that he responds to her bossiness by distancing himself. She complains that "he doesn't know how to share his interests," and also that he is "tremendously self-absorbed in his own projects." And a final theme which emerges in subsequent questioning, but is also evident in the FECK story, is that being amused is important to both of them. She says she was attracted to him because he was interesting and there would "never be a boring moment." He liked her because "she was charming. I saw us having lots of fun, charming and good times."

In addition to the broad themes suggested in the FECK stories there were also some specific issues seen in the FECK stories and later coming forth in response to questions about their current situation. They are both unhappy with each other's ability to show and give affection. She says, "We disagree on style. He pinches. I like to talk." He says, "She shows affection to female friends but not to men." Further, while he rates both himself and her as "adequate" sexually, she expects that he rates her as being very poor and himself as being very good.

Couple Two

His Story. I just met my spouse through a friend in Germany. My friend and I were going to a car race and she was asked to go with us. I remember asking her to sit in the front seat of the car with me, which she did. My friend was fond of her and this bothered him when she decided to sit with me instead of with him. My first impressions were of a pretty, frail girl who was definitely a different individual.

Focus: Getting into the car. I'm in front. She's getting in. She had decided. There are three people in the back, one being her boy friend.
Feeling: Generally happy and excited to have her next to me.

Her Story. I met D. over at a friend of his in Germany. His friend was in love with me. We went together to a car race in Germany with D. I liked his quietness, easiness. He was the opposite of me. Where I wanted to be at that particular time. I had seen him the night before at a party with the American friends and he sat quietly in a corner smoking a pipe. Very introverted and absorbing. It intrigued me.

Focus: The party. Him in the corner smoking the pipe.
Feeling: He attracted me physically.

Discussion of Couple Two's Stories. Here are two separate stories without a shared focus. Her story is of a party which occurred the evening before the event in his story. The difference in the two stories suggests that they do not agree on a definition of the relationship or on who has the right to define the relationship.

He finds her, in the story, "interesting" and "different." He gives her the right of initiative: "I asked . . . she decided." She also sees herself as the one having the initiative. She had him spotted the night before he knew about her. Nonetheless, he chooses to remember their meeting at a time when he was the one in the driver's seat. Here are two people who both like to think they're running the show, each with conflicting styles of management. He works quietly by keeping control and allowing her alternatives which he selects. She works by being flexible and impulsive and doing what she wants.

In subsequent discussion she complains that he is being repressive and not offering her the alternatives she wants. "I want him to get off his conventional ideas about marriage and let me have my freedom. He is mistrusting—that's the biggest problem." She further complains he is not willing to fight and argue with her.

He complains that she should be more considerate of others and more patient with others and should think more about others. On the other hand, in the FECK story he was struck by the fact that she sat in the front with him, despite the fact that it "bothered" his friend, he cherishes the memory of her as someone who does what she wants heedless of the feelings of others. He loved her because she was a "definitely different individual," but he's unhappy with her because she is inconsiderate and impatient.

Couple Three

His Story. I remember walking down the street. It was in fall. She had high heels on. She was taller than me.

Focus: The two of us walking down the street.
Feeling: Okay.

Her Story. We were just at a club meeting. It was usual for boys to accompany some of the girls home by car or by walking them home. Somehow R. and I started walking home. I remember that it was dark out, but not too dark—you could still see quite a ways down the street. Some leaves had fallen. I didn't have warm enough clothes on, and I was shivering a little wishing I had warmer clothes. I did most of the talking. I remember him walking me to the door.

Focus: The two of us walking down the street. I wish I had warmer clothes. I see some leaves on the street and see some trees up ahead.
Feeling: I feel chilled.

Discussion of Couple Three's Stories. In the recollections, she needs warmth and doesn't think to ask, feels uncomfortable and distracted. She discounts responsibility for their being together; somehow it happened. She talks; he doesn't. He's impressed by her stature, he looks up to her, but also sees her as propped up. It could be guessed that she expects men not to understand her and not to be responsive to her and that he expects women to be admirable, or in some way above him. They do not remember communicating, only talking; both are distracted, she by her chill, he by her height. She dominates the relationship.

These guesses seem to be supported by the issues brought forward in counseling sessions. Her presenting complaint was that "We don't talk; he doesn't say what's on his mind; he watches TV." She also complains that she "wants sex more than he does." His response is that he always has to initiate sex so he winds up watching TV and going to bed late. Furthermore, he resents doing things for her in that she hints for things without asking directly. She will say, "Oh, I wish I had a glass of water" and he doesn't know whether it's a request or a put-down. She later admits in counseling that she doesn't believe men can understand women but also that she expects men to understand her by reading her mind. She wants an emotional response but instead only gets a response to her ideas. Her husband says he tries to respond to her ideas but mainly feels inadequate and sort of bewildered as to why he's disappointed her. Finally, he says he was initially attracted to her because she was a good talker and she says she was attracted to him because he was a good listener.

Couple Four

His Story. I just remember coming up the stairs to meet her and it was our first date and she had come out of her apartment to meet me and I thought she was very attractive and sexy. Felt good.

Her story. Our first date was a blind date and he had called me up. What I remember is having opened the door and gone out on the landing to meet him as he came up the stairs. I just remember how good he looked coming up the stairs—a beautiful, handsome, sexy man. I felt good.

Discussion of Couple Four's Shared Story. In these brief recollections both agree she is on a higher level than he. For both of them the memory fades before they are on the same level. When confronted with this interpretation she replied, "Yes," then, after a pause, "but," she continued, "I've always thought he had a finer mind than I and was more cultured; and also that I had the better sense of social things." When asked which was more important, a sense of culture or a sense of social things, she said social logic was more important. Both came forward with second recollections which, though not shared, do reveal more about their styles of operating with each other.

His Second Story. I took her to see a Bob Dylan concert. Dylan was a hero of mine and I wanted her to appreciate him. When Dylan came on stage to sing, many of the audience, who had not heard his voice before, started to laugh. She started to laugh, too, and it bothered me because he was someone I valued and wanted her to like. I was almost going to laugh, too, but I didn't.

Focus: She and everyone else laughing.
Feeling: Upset and tempted to go along with her in the laughing but deciding not to.

Her Second Story. We were at a restaurant that evening and I had gone to the ladies room and before I returned to the table had stopped to put on more lipstick to make myself sexier. As I was at the mirror someone opened the door to the ladies room and I realized you could see into the room and I saw him across the room smiling at me. I stopped putting on lipstick because I didn't want to appear vain to him and then left.

Focus: The door opening and me seeing that he could see me.
Feeling: Annoyed that the restaurant was so designed that you could see in.
Focus: Stopping putting on lipstick before I was finished.
Feeling: Acting casual as though I only wanted a little lipstick because I didn't want him to think I was vain.
Focus: Him across the room and smiling.
Feeling: I knew the whole thing didn't matter to him but it mattered to me.

Discussion of the Second Stories. In her story she sees herself at some distance from him and feels she needs some enhancing and masking to make herself attractive. Further, her pretense with her husband is that she doesn't care about being sexually attractive, but in fact, she does. Before counseling she was unwilling and embarrassed to initiate or share her interest in sex.

The idea of her superior social sense and his superior cultural sense comes forward in his second story. Also in his story we see him setting forward the things he admires as a substitute for himself. Also, it appears that he is less ready to accommodate to what he believes to be her expectations and values than she is to his.

Taking the stories together we see two ambitious people each admiring the other, wanting to impress the other, but also slightly discouraged and hiding from the other. She struggles to maintain her one-up position; he struggles to get up to even; neither feels quite good enough in and of themselves.

Couple Five

His Story. The first day of theater class and it was my first day transferring from the engineering department to theater. The class was structured around a series of theater exercises, and I noticed that as we were sitting around before class this blond, jeans, very hard-ass-looking girl. Very attractive. And the first thing the professor did was to pair us off. Everyone in the class. And lo and behold, I got paired off with her. We went up on stage. The whole class went up on stage and first we did some warm-up exercises, and then, to work on the concept of trust on the stage and to develop the necessary feeling that there is someone else on the stage with you and that you have to trust and relate to that person we did a specific exercise and that exercise was that one partner turned his back to the other partner and stood about three paces in front and he had to fall back and the other had to catch him. So it turned out we were the last in the exercise. Everyone had done it. You each took turns—one followed the other, and so I went first in our pair. I fell back and she caught me. Then it was her turn to fall back and she hesitated and turned to the professor and said, "But he's too slight." She couldn't be convinced to do it with me. So she completed the exercise with the professor. A few years later, after we had been dating I asked her at a party if she would like to try it again. She said, "Yes," and at that time I let her fall on her ass.

Focus: Her saying she couldn't do it and me trying to convince her.
Feeling: Degraded because she couldn't talk to me and she had turned to the professor. Shattered and embarrassed when she said I was too slight. Frustrated because it took me a lot to do the exercise and I had surrendered to it, but then she wouldn't return the trust and I couldn't reason with her. I was angry and finally relieved when it was all over.

Her Story. We met the first day, the first hour, the first class of junior year. It was a theater class and we did an exercise where you were supposed to fall into someone's arms. An exercise of trust. The professor paired us off and I was supposed to fall into G.'s arms. I turned to the instructor and said, "But he's so slight." And I wouldn't do it because I really was afraid I was going to do him in. At the time he was shorter than me, you know, smaller, and I refused. And he got very upset. And then he turned out to be in the second class also. We had the same class right after that. And that's how we met.

Focus: Saying, "But he's so slight," to the instructor. And turning and looking at G. and seeing the instructor looking and laughing and G. coming up and saying, "What did you say?" and the instructor said, "She said that she felt you were too slight and she felt she would ruin you." G. was very upset. Really. His whole little body was just shaking. He said, "Well, that's ridiculous. Of course I can." I said, "Well, I'm not going to give you the pleasure of even trying."

Feeling: How much I didn't like him and how much he liked me. I was in a good place and my whole thing was very appealing. And to me he was like nobody. In the conversation with the instructor I felt like I always feel, very much just like me. It was just a matter-of-fact thing. The feeling was soft and quiet. There was no anger. A slight cockiness. I had ruled him out as an interesting person already. Felt fine doing it. It was a matter-of-fact thing. He had only the beginning qualifications. When I said he was slight I felt kind of comical. I sincerely believed what I was saying. I felt both amused and yet, in a way, disjointed from it all because it was, as I say, kind of matter-of-fact for me. I remember him getting very upset with that. He was very distressed. He didn't like that because I think he was very attracted to me. I felt fine, the kind of satisfaction you get when you play a kind of mirthful, not malicious joke. I felt there's many a truth in jest and I did sincerely feel he was too slight, but yet it was still kind of a joke. You know, fun. I was having fun with it. Like an Irish Leprechaun would.

Discussion of Couple Five's Stories. It is occasionally useful to summarize this material in terms of a rubric similar to the Life Style rubric: "Life is . . ., Others are . . ., I am . . ., therefore. . . ." With FECK stories the rubrics are much more narrowly defined, however.

For him: (With her) I am defeated while heroically doing my best.
(With me) She is simply unreachable and unmanageable.
Therefore, I must let someone else deal with her.

For her: (With him) I am too much for him to handle. I know better than he. I am justified in not trusting him.
(With me) He is not trustworthy. He may get angry but he is unconvincing.
Therefore, I have to ally myself with someone else.

The issue for her is trust; for him, heroics, or meeting challenges. As he sees it, he does his part. They agree; he will not convince her to trust him. She maintains her position as someone who is willing to participate as an equal, but, "is my husband equal to it?" which is a position of covert superiority justified by pessimism. She does not recognize her self-fulfilling prophecy: "I don't think he is trustworthy, therefore nothing he can say or do will convince me otherwise." In this marriage we can speculate that each uses the other as an excuse to remain distant; each feels justified.

As to his reasons for being married to her, the following clues are available; he enters the new scene and assumes a macho posture as seen in his description, "Jeans. Very hard-ass." Later, during the exercise, he sees himself heroically doing his part, and he sees her as unmanageable. Possibly then, if he sees her as "unmanageable," he doesn't have to try to manage her and can retain his position as the hero struggling against the impossible. There is something of the "irresistible force meeting the immovable object" in the dynamics of this marriage. Even the professor couldn't convince her to try the exercise of trust with this man whom she subsequently married.

In their current situation she continues to use the assumption of excessive responsibility as a cover for her own discouragement. Her stated complaint about her marriage is as follows, "I want to change the day-to-day routine, the fights. We just don't have it together. He hasn't even built a coffee table so the ash trays keep falling off the couch. I'd like to see a functioning ship and we cannot be fighting every day. That's a new rule I just made up." His response to her is to get angry, play the role of the exasperated husband and become a workaholic, leaving her alone, hurt and confirmed in her pessimism.

SUMMARY

FECK stories do seem to offer a quck way to get at the basic issues in a marriage. There seem to be several ways to use them in clinical work:

A. As a discussion starter. The innocuous quality of the question allows for quick and painless movement into the basic issues of a marriage.
B. As a discussion starter in couples groups, as a way of introducing the idea of complementarity of life styles, and as a way of introducing the idea that the same qualities once seen as virtues come to be seen as faults.
C. As an opportunity to develop descriptions of the clients' behavior in the clients' own language, as a way of developing an idiosyncratic glossary for the case at hand, and as an alternative to the more rigid typology templates as a way of describing the patterned interaction in a marriage.

D. As an encouragement technique which allows the counselor to minimize past injustices. It is necessary to know very little history in order to identify present convictions and guidelines.
E. As an assessment technique in situations where only one of the couple is present. The FECK story allows the client to reveal his or her own role in the marriage.
F. Finally, there remains the possibility that the usefulness of the FECK question may be extended to friendships, partnerships, and other committed relationships.

REFERENCE NOTES

1. Powers, R. L. Demonstration of family counseling at the Alfred Adler Institute of Chicago, Fall, 1977.

2. Grunewald, B. Personal communication. May 1978.

3. Powers, R., & Hahn, J. A. *Couple Counseling Workshop.* Workshop presented at the meeting of the North American Society of Adlerian Psychology, Chicago, 1977.

4. Perman, S. Life Style Diagnosis course lecture at the Alfred Adler Institute of Chicago, Spring, 1977.

REFERENCES

Ackerknecht, L. K. New aspects of early recollections (ER) as a diagnostic and therapeutic device. *The Individual Psychologist*, 1976, *13*(2).

Adler, A. *What life should mean to you.* Alan Porter (Ed.). New York. G. P. Putnam's Sons, 1958.

Adler, A. *The individual psychology of Alfred Adler.* H. L. Ansbacher & R. R. Ansbacher (Eds. and trans.). New York: Basic Books, 1956.

Dreikurs, R. *The challenge of marriage.* New York: Hawthorn Books, Inc., 1946.

Dreikurs, R. The psychological interview in medicine. *American Journal of Individual Psychology*, 1952, *10*, 99–122.

Dreikurs, R. Adlerian analysis of interaction. In K. Adler & D. Deutsch (Eds.), *Essays on individual psychology*. New York: Grove Press, Inc., 1959.

Minuchin, S. *Families and family therapy*. Cambridge: Harvard University Press, 1974.

Mosak, H. H. Early recollections as a projective technique. In H. H. Mosak (Ed.), *On purpose—Collected papers by Harold H. Mosak*. Chicago: Alfred Adler Institute of Chicago, 1977.

Pew, M. L., & Pew, W. L. Adlerian marriage counseling. *Journal of Individual Psychology*, 1972, *28*(2), 191–202.

Powers, R. L. Myth and memory. In H. H. Mosak (Ed.,), *Alfred Adler: His influence on psychology today*. Park Ridge, N.J.: Noyes Press, 1973.

Sager, C. J. *Marriage contracts and couple therapy. Hidden forces in intimate relationships*. New York: Brunner/Mazel, 1976.

Satir, V. *Conjoint family therapy*. Palo Alto: Science and Behavior Books, 1967.

Watzlawick, P., Beaving, J. H., & Jackson, D. D. *The pragmatics of human communication. A study of interactional patterns, pathologies, and paradoxes*. New York: Norton, 1967.

ADLERIAN MARRIAGE THERAPY

Don Dinkmeyer
President of Communication and Motivation Training Institute in Coral Springs, Florida. He is an author and a consultant, and is engaged in private practice.

James Dinkmeyer
An associate of Communication and Motivation Training Institute in Coral Springs, Florida.

Adlerian marriage therapy views the marriage relationship as a system. The input from each partner either improves the relationship or stimulates dissonance and conflict. The transactions between the husband and wife are understood as purposive psychological movement. All the behavior in the system makes sense in the light of each partner's perceptions, beliefs, and goals.

The communication between partners is seen as expressing the intentions and goals of each partner. The emotional response of each spouse leads to diagnosis of the purpose. Goals may include attention, power, vengeance, or displaying inadequacy in order to be excused. These are diagnosed by observing the feeling experienced by the spouse. Feelings indicate the purpose of the transaction. If the spouse feels annoyed, the goal is attention. If the feeling is anger, the goal is power. When the spouse feels hurt, the goal is revenge; while a feeling of giving up or despair indicates the goal of displaying inadequacy.

The couple is helped to see that their goals and the ensuing conflict are chosen. Because choice is an essential component of all behavior but one frequently denied in human relationships, the couple is helped to see how, by their behavior, belief, and attitude, they choose conflict. They are helped to see how they can make new choices.

Individual Psychology, 38(2), June, 1982, **pp. 115–122**

Behavior is a function of one's perception or of what experiences mean to a person. The therapist confronts the couple with the meaning they are giving to their experience.

Our marital therapy has a comparatively simple equation which explains marital happiness. This equation is based upon the work of Walter O'Connell and the "natural high" (O'Connell, 1975). Marital happiness is a result of increasing the self-esteem of each partner and increasing the social interest or feeling of cooperation and belonging: MH = SE + SI.

Adlerian marriage therapy helps the couple improve the marital relationship. The process of therapy involves four major steps: (a) establishing the relationship, (b) understanding the couple, (c) providing insight, and (d) reorientation and reeducation (Dreikurs, 1967). These steps are not distinct but overlap. For example, it is effective to establish the relationship by showing the couple they are being understood, by empathizing or commenting on psychological movement.

Reeducation is also continuous and not restricted to the last phase. For example, the pamphlet "The Basics of Self-Acceptance" (Dinkmeyer, 1977) might be shared at the first meeting. We believe a feeling of mutuality improves as each person accepts himself. As each person learns to build self-esteem and self-acceptance the possibilities for improving the relationship are greatly enhanced.

STEP 1: ESTABLISHING THE RELATIONSHIP

The first task is to align goals and to develop a working relationship that has mutual respect. The couple is asked what they expect or hope for, and the therapist indicates how that can be achieved. The concept of mutual respect is discussed. The couple is expected neither to fight nor to give in.

The initial agreement is worked on by having each partner describe the situation as they see it. It is important to focus on the "here and now" feelings rather than "ancient history" which consists of gunny-sacking old grievances. As the couple shares what they would like to work on in therapy, it is important for the therapist to indicate that there is hope and potential for growth. Usually, the purpose of therapy becomes either (a) to maintain their marriage and try to improve it the best way they can, or (b) to work toward an agreeable divorce.

Cooperation is an important part of a relationship. Unfortunately, many couples have learned to cooperate through fighting. The therapist explains that by treating each other as equals, rather than using one-up-manship tactics or put-downs, cooperation and mutual respect can be attained. The therapist models and encourages this in interaction with the couple.

In the early stages of marriage therapy the therapist identifies how something each mate does or believes makes sense. As the therapist communicates this, the possibility of success is increased. This can be done by making guesses based on the psychological movement of each partner.

> **Bill:** *I try to listen to my wife but she doesn't always make sense so I try to do what I feel will work out best.*
> **Therapist:** *Could it be that you feel as though you need to be right so you attempt to do this by discounting your wife's ideas?*

If the guess is wrong, the therapist has demonstrated the "courage to be imperfect," or to take a risk even though the guess may be wrong. Modeling behavior on the therapist's part helps each partner develop the courage to try something new and to take a chance (Pew & Pew, 1972).

STEP 2: UNDERSTANDING THE COUPLE

This step involves exploring both partners' life styles to determine perceptions, ideas on which they operate, the basic mistaken perceptions about themselves and life, their assets and strengths, and the goals which they set for themselves. The life style is assessed by (a) determining the family atmosphere and the family constellation, (b) asking for early recollections and assessing the goals and basic perceptions of life that are the basis for current ideas and feelings about self and others, (c) determining the number-one priority and identifying what is being achieved or avoided with the priority and, (d) rating satisfaction in seven life tasks to pinpoint trouble areas. The therapist can have each partner guess what their partner will think they feel is their level of satisfaction and then obtain that estimate from their partner to verify how close their guess has been. This "taking the temperature" of a marriage provides quick insight into the amount of empathy that exists in the relationship.

In taking the temperature of a marriage, the therapist should ask each spouse to rate from 1 to 10 their satisfaction in the following challenges of living, then to identify how they believe their spouse perceives their satisfaction. By comparing the ratings, one can identify the amount of empathy possessed by each partner.

The ratings in Table 1 indicate lack of empathy between Jack and Laurie with respect to work, sexual relationships, and their use of leisure. The temperature shows a high empathy in friendship, self-satisfaction, and parenting.

It is also helpful to have both partners describe what first attracted them to their mates. Dreikurs (1967) found that the very attributes that initially attracted a couple to each other frequently became conflict areas.

> **Example.** Tom is very outgoing and enjoys dancing, eating out, and concerts. When Tom first met Julie they enjoyed doing all of these things together. Julie is more of an introvert and enjoys reading, talking, and staying at home. When they first met they were attracted to each other because they were so different and they enjoyed learning to do different things. However, now they have found that what each really hoped for in their marriage was for their partner to adopt their own interests.

STEP 3: PROVIDING INSIGHT

The therapist gives feedback to each partner on themes and patterns, on the person's beliefs, expectations, and his or her operational rules. The therapist also has the couple list each other's strengths. This changes the "mental set," as quite often the couple has been emphasizing only the negative aspects of the relationship.

The therapist's focus is on increasing each partner's awareness of the purpose of behavior, an important step in motivating subsequent changes.

> **Mike:** *You say that I put down Gloria because I need to prove that I am superior. I suppose you expect me to never give my opinion to her!*
> **Therapist:** *You can continue.*
> **Mike:** *I don't understand why you would say that?*
> **Therapist:** *What I am saying is that there is possibly a different way to express yourself that would make your opinion more meaningful to Gloria and you could feel good helping her. But you can certainly continue to get her to look up to you by putting her down if you wish.*

This is known as "spitting in the client's soup." The person can choose to continue the old behavior, but once revealed it is not as appealing.

The couple's marital system is revealed by understanding the life styles and purposes of behavior. Differences can either begin to enhance the marriage, or they

TABLE 1
Challenges of Living and Spouse Ratings of Satisfaction

	Jack	Laurie Perceives Jack's Satisfaction	Laurie	Jack Perceives Laurie's Satisfaction
Work	5	8	6	3
Friendships and Social Life	8	8	8	7
Relationships with Opposite Sex & Sexual Relationships	5	8	7	5
Purpose & Meaning of Life	4	7	8	8
Self-Satisfaction	5	6	7	6
Parenting	6	5	5	4
Leisure	5	8	3	6

can continue to be a source of conflict. Areas of commonality or agreement can be identified, as couples often have not made the most of these shared interests.

Dreikurs found that persons most likely choose a partner who will treat them in the way they expect to be treated. We let someone get close to us based on our private logic. For example, an individual may wish to be looked upon as being very attractive. Instead of choosing a partner that is attractive, an average appearing mate is chosen, to make the person look better by comparison. We look for someone who can give us

> an opportunity to realize our personal goals, who permits us to continue plans which we have carried since childhood. We even play an important part in evoking and stimulating in the other precisely the behavior which we expect and need. (Dreikurs, 1946, p. 69)

STEP 4: REORIENTATION AND REEDUCATION

Reorientation is a process that occurs during all stages of therapy, but has special importance after insight has been attained. The therapist educates the couple in conflict resolution techniques. The therapist helps them confront faulty beliefs about their relationship. Each learns to formulate internally consistent values and attitudes toward themselves, their partners, and the world. The goal of reorientation is a new set of behaviors and skills consistent with the new agreements, focusing on cooperation and give-and-take.

The therapist stresses the difference between wanting to change and trying something new, actually changing by doing something. It is necessary for the couple to make a commitment to their new agreement.

The Process of Change in Marriage Therapy may take considerable time and effort. It is important that the therapist model patience for the couple. Elements of the marriage often get worse before they get better. This is especially true in relationships where both couples withhold their emotions. When one begins to express feelings, the other partner may feel threatened.

Marriage therapy is concerned with understanding the system and helping each partner learn to encourage their spouse so that both self-esteem and a desire to cooperate for the common good are developed.

There are two important ideas for the couple to remember in their marriage:

1. Neither partner is either all good or all bad; one should avoid striving to be superior and making the partner appear inferior.
2. Each partner must have the courage to be imperfect. One should accept that one's partner can and will make mistakes, that one can still continue to function without feeling devastated.

ADLERIAN TECHNIQUES IN MARRIAGE THERAPY

Catching Oneself

The therapist asks the partners to practice "catching themselves" in any behavior they want to change. At the start they will have difficulty in catching themselves before falling into their old traps such as seeking revenge, playing inferior, being powerful, or controlling. They can learn to anticipate and then practice avoiding situations that provoke their undesirable behaviors. This technique requires the partner's ability to laugh at their own behavior rather than to become discouraged when they don't catch themselves (Dinkmeyer, Pew, & Dinkmeyer, 1979).

Sue: *Honey, could you please give me a hand with fixing the television?*
Bob: *Oh Sue, you know I . . . (stops and laughs). Well, let me take a look and see if there is anything that I can do.*

The Hidden Reason

Searching for a hidden reason for behavior is a technique used to help the individual look at the thinking process used when deciding on activities. When the therapist asks the wife, for example, why she is acting in a certain way, the answer may be an honest "I don't know." Both the therapist and the husband may then offer guesses as to the reason behind the behavior. After several guesses, the person is asked, "Could it be one of these ideas makes any sense?" At this point the person will begin to understand and recognize the hidden reason. This technique enables both partners to gain a greater understanding of the purposiveness of their own and their partner's behavior (Dinkmeyer, Pew & Dinkmeyer, 1979).

Therapist: *Carol, why do you accuse David of having an affair when you say that you believe that he couldn't be having one?*
Carol: *I don't know. I really just don't know.*
Therapist: *Would it be okay if David and I came up with some guesses at what reasons you have for accusing him?*
Carol: *I guess so . . . sure, go ahead.*
Therapist: *Why do you think she accuses you, David?*
David (to Carol): *Well, I think you don't trust me anymore and you enjoy trying to get me to fight or argue with you.*
Therapist (to Carol): *Or is it possible that by accusing David you feel he will try extra hard to show how much he cares for you? Are either one of these ideas that David and I offered possible?*
Carol: *Well, I really don't like fighting. I guess maybe I would like David to show me how much he loves me because I'm not always sure that he does.*

Switching Roles is an effective technique when the couple is in conflict and both partners are taking a firm stand. Each partner is asked to take the opposing position on an issue and to discuss it as if it were their own viewpoint. This must be done seriously and not sarcastically. Each spouse is encouraged to share as many reasons as possible to try to convince their partner that this viewpoint—in reality the partner's own—is correct. This technique provides insight into the other person's beliefs and encourages more open-mindedness in resolving conflicts.

Paradoxical Intention

Adlerians believe that in order to maintain any symptom one has to fight it. By encouraging the couple to develop and maintain a symptom even in exaggerated form, the therapist is instructing them to stop fighting the symptom. Then the couple becomes more aware of the reality of the situation and sees that the consequence of the behavior must be accepted. The paradoxical recommendation is given as an experiment: "See what you can learn" (Dinkmeyer, Pew, & Dinkmeyer, 1979). Often the couples do not follow through with the recommendation. They feel the task is ridiculous. However, it soon becomes apparent to them that maintaining their symptom is equally ridiculous.

> **Example**. Mary and Tony would fight every day over finances and end up screaming at each other. They were instructed to schedule two 10-minute fights, one in the morning and one in the evening, fighting in the same manner as they did before. After the first week, they realized how silly it was to fight about the same thing over and over; so they decided to stop fighting.

SUMMARY

Adlerian marriage therapy is a collaboration between the couple and the therapist. The purpose of the therapy is to assess current beliefs and behaviors while educating the couple in new procedures that can help the couple establish new goals.

REFERENCES

Dinkmeyer, D. C., Pew, W. L., & Dinkmeyer, Jr., D. C. *Adlerian counseling and psychotherapy*. Monterey, Calif.: Brooks/Cole, 1979.

Dinkmeyer, D. C. *The basics of self-acceptance*. Coral Springs, Fl.: CMTI Press, 1977.

Dreikurs, R. *The challenge of marriage*. New York: Duell, Sloan & Pearce, 1946.

Dreikurs, R. *Psychodynamics, psychotherapy, and counseling*. Chicago: Alfred Adler Institute of Chicago, 1967.

O'Connell, W. *Action therapy and Adlerian theory*. Chicago: Alfred Adler Institute of Chicago, 1975.

Pew, M. L., & Pew, W. L. Adlerian marriage counseling. *Journal of Individual Psychology*, 1972, *28*(2), 192–202.

EQUALITY IN MALE/FEMALE RELATIONSHIPS

Ann H. Tuites and Donald E. Tuites
Nationally certified clinical mental health counselors, are currently in private practice in Wilmington, Delaware with Adlerian Counseling Associates. They have been in private practice for 12 years.

In *Social Equality: The Challenge of Today*, Dreikurs (1971) states, "Perhaps in no other area of social living is the rapid progress toward equality as obvious as in the relationship between the sexes" (p. 129).

Society has been predominantly patriarchal during most of civilization's history. Men were dominant and thought to be superior and women subordinate and thought to be inferior. However, there have been examples of societies in which women were awarded many privileges denied to men. In some primitive societies, women continue to exercise dominant rights. Dominance may have changed from one sex to another, but history reveals little evidence of equality between the sexes.

Just one generation ago, the male was thought to be the aggressor, the provider, and the protector who did the "important" work, while the female was thought to be weak, dependent, the protected housewife whose job it was to nurture the family. As women progress toward a freedom to speak out on issues, to make money, to be independent, active, and athletic, to do similar work to men, and even to be the initiator in intimate areas, many men no longer know how to feel significant. They were "supposed" to be the boss, the head of household. Moving from a position of submissiveness toward one of equality may be exciting for women, but moving from a position of power to one of equality can be frightening for men.

Individual Psychology, 42(2), June, 1986, **pp. 191–200**

The authors will explore what characterizes relationships of equality: What they are and are *not*, and how to work toward them.

The greatest enemy of an equal relationship is the desire for power or superiority. Every time a person attempts to make his or her partner act as he or she desires, the foundation of the relationship is eroded. These attempts are not always direct or obvious. They can be as subtle as being ill when it's time to go to a partner's favorite restaurant. Whenever either or both partners' main goal is power, superiority, or winning, the equilibrium is upset, and with it, the equality of the relationship.

An unequal relationship is destructive not only for the person who finds himself or herself in the subordinate position. The partner who is dominant receives his or her feeling of belonging or significance from power and superiority instead of from cooperation and contribution.

Dreikurs (1971) adds further, "The present degree of equality between the sexes on the American scene corresponds to the growing tendency toward equality in all other areas of personal and group relationships. As in other areas, the process is still going on and the ensuing friction is the source of many of our most urgent domestic problems" (p. 130).

While women are saying, "I must be equal," men are saying, "What am I supposed to do now?" and "Who am I?" It was easier to be the boss or the slave. The boss decided and the slave obeyed. Equality requires mutual respect and involves negotiating, brainstorming, decision-making, cooperating, and agreeing on mutual goals.

LIFE-STYLE AND EQUALITY

A concept central to Adlerian psychology is the Life-Style. The Life-Style of a person has several components. These include: (1) convictions concerning life, the world, other people, and him or herself, (2) ideal convictions about what life, the world, other people, and he or she should be, and (3) conclusions about behaviors he or she should exhibit in order to have a place of significance. Adler believed that the goal of all human beings is to find a place of belonging, of feeling significant. If a person does this in a positive, contributing, useful manner, he or she is in harmony with the community and finds satisfaction. If not, he or she turns to useless and negative antisocial behavior.

One of the most important influences in the development of the Life-Style is the family and, more specifically, the male and female role models presented by father and mother. Our role models, family values, interactions with our siblings, and family atmosphere are important influences in the development of our private, "logical" convictions about life, others, and ourselves.

Three case outlines are presented below to illustrate the movement in unequal relationships and the concurrent convictions or "biased apperceptions" of each individual Life-Style. In each case, the couple sought marriage counseling. The wives initiated the request, and the husbands came, although with little enthusiasm. Life-Style Assessments were conducted for each person.

Couple I

The wife always nurtured others, gave more than she received, played rescuer. When she no longer felt needed, she tried to create guilt in members of her family. She was convinced she should always be good, sacrifice, be nice, be morally superior, always let others dominate. The husband was always immersed in responsibilities, bringing in money, planning for the family, preventing his children and wife from getting into trouble. He was convinced he must be right, take care of everyone, not admit any weakness, be the boss, control the family, show his superiority by making money.

Couple II

The wife in this relationship was not only a professional rescuer but also "read minds" and assumed she knew what was best for everyone at home. She expected others to do the same and when they didn't, she turned to power and retaliation. In order to feel significant, she felt she must take care of others, never ask for what she wanted, work hard, keep everything "fair," or get revenge. The husband in this relationship spent hours in competitive sports. Much effort was spent toward building a handsome, strong body. He was friendly, enjoyed groups and spent many hours drinking with "the boys." He was convinced he must never take things seriously, must compete, and must be "macho" and attractive.

Couple III

This wife put all of her talent and energy into supporting her husband. She gave all credit to him, did ghost writing, praised him when she was with friends or business associates. She felt that she must help him achieve and must never take any credit. She must stand behind him even if it meant being dominated and not having any identity of her own. This husband always played the role of the genius of the partnership. He believed she was more competent but promoted the sham of her secondary position. He was convinced that he must be the star, the driving force, a success, first.

In all of these case outlines, the goal of each partner appeared to be superiority, being best, in control, the dominant one. Yet each couple pursued this goal in different ways. Couple I fought bitterly, loudly, and threatened divorce in each partner's drive toward power. Couple II played "enabler" and "alcoholic" year after year. The woman proved her superiority through her suffering and martyrdom and the man proved his through his being the handsome sportsman and also by proving that his wife could never control him or improve conditions. Those in Couple III lived in quiet anger with the woman feeling depressed and alone and with the man appearing to be the model husband and father. This facade slipped only when he had to look at the truth. He exploded violently when he recognized his imperfections.

In each of these cases the treatment plan included many hours of practice in the techniques of communication (discussed below). Transactions changed gradually from "Who will win?" to "What can we do to improve the situation?"

EQUALITY

No couple ever attains a perfect, equal relationship. To achieve this would be: (1) never letting their "irrational shoulds" get in the way, (2) never trying to win even when each has a big stake in the situation, and (3) never using negative emotion or anger to solve problems. To do this would be to be perfect, a state not accessible to human beings. The couples followed the dictum, "First you do and then you become." The answer, we believe, is to work toward equality, every day of your life.

Equality in interpersonal relationships does not mean sameness. Equality is *not*:

Being the same
Doing the same things
Sharing every chore
Dividing money exactly equally

Having to balance each favor, paying back exactly, "settling the score"
Winning out
Proving who's best or right

Rather, equality refers to the intrinsic worthwhileness of each human being and the equal value of personhood for both men and women expressed in equality of responsibility for the self, and equality of consideration, concern, and care for the other. An equal relationship is comprised of two self-sufficient persons who stay with each other out of choice rather than need. Self-sufficiency means having the self-confidence and skills to manage one's own life in an effective manner.

WORKING TOWARD EQUALITY

In moving and working toward equality, four skills are particularly helpful for individuals both to learn and to practice. These include: (1) level rather than vertical communication, (2) giving and receiving criticism in an assertive manner, (3) conflict resolution through problem solving, and (4) encouragement.

In each of these techniques, one person approaches the other on a cooperative, supportive plane with a joint effort in mind. The person's goal is teamwork, that is, finding a workable solution for both parties.

(1) Level Communication

In his book *How to Strengthen Your Marriage and Family*, Hugh Allred (1974) describes two styles of communication: level and vertical. The goals of vertical communication are dominance, superiority, and control. This is accomplished through: (1) soliciting attention by monopolizing conversations, interrupting, bragging, or name dropping, (2) bossing or punishing by lecturing, preaching, ordering, belittling, or using sarcasm, (3) creating or maintaining distance by talking in an aloof, disinterested manner, wandering, or avoiding closeness, and (4) surrendering by giving in or abandoning one's own wants. The following "skit" demonstrates a typical vertical communication between husband and wife. The goals of vertical communication are indicated by the number in parentheses following each sentence, corresponding to the numbers above.

Vertical

Husband: *(working on paper)*
Wife: *Will you stop doing that and listen to me! What I have to say is* really *important (1). I always make delicious dinners and plan just for the two of us. You bring that so-called friend of yours home without even calling—what consideration (2)! You are really brilliant (2)!*
Husband: *I certainly don't see the harm in having a third for dinner. There is always sufficient food for three people. Americans are noted for their overeating (3).*
Wife: *Whenever you start one of those speeches of yours, I get such a sick headache. You don't realize how bad you make me feel (2).*
Husband: *(Looking at paper) (3) Yeah, you do get sick a lot (3).*
Wife: *Well, what are you going to do? You'd better call him right now and tell him we don't want him to come any more (2).*
Husband: *Oh, all right, (sigh), I'll call him, but I really think it'll hurt his feelings (4).*
Wife: *You never care about my hurt feelings (4).*
Husband: *What do you mean, I don't care? You are always belittling me. You should try to control yourself. If you were a good person, you would be kind and loving. You always get so emotional and hysterical (2).*
Wife: *That did it! You're always calling me a "sickie" (2).*

The goals of level communication are openness, honesty, consideration, and mutual respect. These are accomplished by: (1) voicing observations, revealing ideas about oneself or the other person, giving facts or opinions, giving feedback, (2) seeking to understand by asking questions, guessing about meanings, (3) negotiating by discussing alternatives, making requests, and committing to a decision, (4) encouraging by making empathic statements, accepting the other person's feelings, and (5) disclosing one's own feelings.

The following conversation demonstrates level communication between husband and wife. (The goals of level communication are indicated by the number in parentheses following each sentence, corresponding to the numbers above.)

Level

Husband: *(working on paper)*
Wife: *Could we talk for a minute? Or, if you're busy, when would it be convenient (3)?*
Husband: *It's okay. I need a break anyway (1).*

Wife: *I've noticed that you seem to bring Bill home for dinner more and more often (1). I get really angry when I have something made for just the two of us (5).*
Husband: *I didn't think it was so often (1).*
Wife: *Well, he was here last Saturday and then again Tuesday and Friday of this week (1).*
Husband: *I don't understand, he's a nice guy (2).*
Wife: *Well, when you have so much paperwork, we hardly have any time together. When he's here so often we don't get a chance to talk much (1).*
Husband: *I see how you feel. But we rarely entertain. I'd like to have our friends over just to have a good time when we both work so hard at our jobs (1).*
Wife: *I'd like that too. You've really been getting a lot of sales. You must be proud of that (4).*
Husband: *And your new business is really growing (4)! We deserve a break (3)!*
Wife: *Well, how could we do it (3)?*
Husband: *How about planning something in advance so I wouldn't just surprise you when you don't expect it (3)?*
Wife: *Yes, and if you wanted Bill to come over, you could let me know the day before (3).*
Husband: *Well, you know how I feel about cooking, but I could do some of the cleaning or go to the store when we entertain (3). We can plan together so it won't be all on you (3, 4).*
Wife: *I feel a lot better now that we've got some new ways to handle this (5).*

Phrases that are helpful in level communication:

Voicing Observations	"This is what happened . . ."
	"I saw," "I heard," "I observed . . ."
Seeking to understand	"Let me see if I understand."
	"Is this how you feel?"
Negotiating	"What possibilities are there?"
	"What else could we do?"
Committing	"I would be willing to . . ."
	"Let's try this . . ."
	"I would like to . . ."
Encouraging	"That would really help."
	"I really felt good about that."
Disclosing feelings	"I feel sad, angry, hurt, afraid when _____ happens."

(2) Assertive Criticism

Equality is also learning how to give and receive criticism in an assertive manner. A clear, concise model described by Bower and Bower (1976) involves what is called a D.E.S.C. Script. In giving criticism, we want to tell another person that we don't like something he or she is doing. Mentally outlining the four steps before confronting the other person helps your own clarity and effectiveness.

D = *Describe*	What it is, specifically, that the other person is doing that bothers you? This should be nonjudgmental and avoid impugning motives.
E = *Express*	What does the other person's behavior do to you? How do you feel when it happens?
S = *Specify*	What do you want the other person to do? Be specific.
C = *Consequences*	What do you believe might happen if the other person does or does not decide to do what you have suggested?

A similar script is used in receiving criticism.

D = *Doing*	What am I doing that bothers you?
E = *Effect*	What effect does it have on you when I do this?
S = *Specify*	What do you want me to do instead?
C = *Consequences*	What do you believe might happen if I do this?

(3) Conflict Resolution

Equality also relates to a willingness to try to resolve conflicts by using problem solving strategies. Our emotions may signal that:

1. Something is not going according to my expectations.
2. It would help to stop using my old ineffective patterns.
3. I will count to 10 right now and try to figure out what's gone wrong.
4. I will consider problem solving instead of doing what I usually do.

The steps of the "No lose method" presented by Thomas Gordon (1970) are outlined below (p. 237):

1. We have a problem.
2. Would you be willing to discuss it?

3. When would it be convenient? (Make sure there is enough time, privacy, and a comfortable place.)
4. State the problem as you see it.
5. Both partners brainstorm ideas. Look at all alternative solutions, even if they may sound "way out" when suggested. List on paper.
6. Strike out those which are completely unacceptable to one partner or the other.
7. Find one solution agreeable to both for a trial period. (This period should be short enough to be realistic.)
8. Decide on how to implement (Who, When, How Long, Where, How).
9. Reevaluate after time allotted.
10. If it is not working, go back to No. 5.

(4) Encouragement

In his book, *Turning People on—How to be an Encouraging Person*, Lew Losoncy (1977) discusses the encouragement process and six ways to be a more encouraging person. The ideal equal relationship is created by the following elements of encouragement:

Having an attitude of complete acceptance of the other person;
Having a nonblaming attitude;
Having confidence in the other person;
Being enthusiastic about the other person's interests;
Being a nonevaluative listener;
Being empathetic.

SUMMARY

The authors have attempted, first, to define equality in male/female relationships.

Equality is Mutual Respect

The respectful partner is saying, "I may not agree with you but I respect your right to your thoughts and feelings."

Equality is Shared Responsibility

This can be done outside the boundaries of sex roles or within them. The important element is the sharing. Equality is neither walking before or behind but at my side as a friend. It is neither being a doormat nor a "muddy shoe."

Equality is Interdependence but not Leaning

If I rescue you, or allow you to "lean," I am the dominant one. There is no equality. In interdependence, I may do something with greater skill or ease but I will still encourage you to grow in that area, to become the most self-sufficient person you can be. Equality is "we" working to address the needs of the situation, each doing the best he or she can do with acceptance and understanding. Equality is each partner giving 100% toward cooperation and usefulness in the relationship rather than worrying about who is doing the most, being right, or being best.

Second, a number of specific strategies have been discussed for use in working toward this type of a relationship. Over a period of time, all may be presented to the client. The client will then choose the ones most comfortable for him or for her. There are obvious similarities. All advise approaching the partner as a person of worth and dignity. None puts one's head higher than the other's.

1. Focus on working together toward mutually acceptable solutions.
2. Avoid striving for power and superiority.
3. Become aware of your, and your partner's, biased apperceptions.
4. Aim at self-sufficiency in both partners and interdependence (not "leaning").
5. Use level communication: Voice your observations, seek understanding, negotiate, commit, encourage, and disclose your feelings.
6. Learn to be assertive—Use D.E.S.C. script for giving and receiving criticism.
7. Resolve conflict through problem solving.
8. Use emotions as a signal, not a solution to problems.
9. Be encouraging: Use acceptance, a nonblaming attitude, non-evaluative listening, empathy, enthusiasm, and confidence.
10. Practice mutual respect.

REFERENCES

Allred, G. H. (1974). *How to strengthen your marriage and family*. Provo: Brigham Young University Press.

Bower, S. A., & Bower, G. H. (1976). *Asserting yourself*. Boston: Addison-Wesley.

Dreikurs, R. (1971). *Social equality: The challenge of today*. Chicago: Henry Regnery.

Gordon, T. (1970). *Parent effectiveness training*. New York: Peter H. Wyden.

Losoncy, L. E. (1977). *Turning people on: How to be an encouraging person*. Englewood Cliffs, N.J.: Prentice Hall.

MARITAL ISSUES OF INTIMACY AND TECHNIQUES FOR CHANGE: AN ADLERIAN SYSTEMS PERSPECTIVE

Robert Sherman
Professor emeritus, School of Education, Queens College. He is also in private practice.

INTRODUCTION

Intimacy is presumed to be the height of mutual social feeling and sharing. One must be able both to put forth the self and to care about the other. Such connectedness is the opposite of alienation and its ills. Yet even in intimate relationships, which coupling and marriage are purported to be, there are many issues that arise in therapy. As we work with couples, it would be well to be alert to and understand the variety of problems and issues among couples which inhibit, confuse, or impair intimacy.

This article will discuss some of the major issues that therapists encounter in treating couples in relation to the life tasks of love and intimacy in relationships. Some major techniques for bringing about change will be briefly described.

Although not detailed in this article, the underlying theory is an Adlerian systems approach as developed by Sherman and Dinkmeyer (1987). This approach integrates common Adlerian thinking about individual motivation and social interactions with common concepts of general systems theories.

Individual Psychology, 49(3 & 4), September/December, 1993, **pp. 318–329**

Adler (Ansbacher & Ansbacher, 1956) described coupling as a process requiring mutual interest and equality.

> Each partner must be more interested in the other than himself. This is the only basis on which love and marriage can be successful. If there is to be so intimate a devotion, neither partner can feel subdued or overshadowed. Equality is only possible if both partners have this attitude . . . The fundamental guarantee of marriage, the meaning of marital happiness, is in the feeling that you are worthwhile, that you cannot be replaced, that your partner needs you, that you are acting well, and that you are a fellow man and true friend. (p. 266)

Dreikurs (1946) asserted that out of our private logic we choose a partner to meet our needs and expectations and train the person to do so. Dinkmeyer, Pew, and Dinkmeyer (1979, p. 239) incorporated a Dreikurs (1946) quotation and put it as:

> We accept someone as an intimate other not on the basis of common sense but on the basis of our private logic—as a person who offers us an opportunity to realize our personal patterns, who responds to our outlook and conception of life, who permits us to continue or to revue plans which we have carried since childhood. We even play a very important part in evoking and stimulating in the other precisely the behavior which we expect and need. (pp. 68–69)

It is clear from both quotations that one's approach to love and intimacy is a function of private logic and life-style. Systems theories further enlarge the ideas inherent in these quotes by stressing that couples engage in a complementary and reciprocal relationship in which each elicits and reinforces the behavior of the other in a continuous circle.

When a couple is formed, the two individuals must learn to accept one another's languages of love and intimacy and expand their personal vocabularies to understand and practice both languages for love and intimacy to be expressed and received as intended. The languages evolve from the private logic, personal needs, and priorities of the individuals largely based on what was most negative or missing while growing up and what was most favorable and rewarding growing up. To understand a person's unique idiosyncratic language, we have to go beyond philosophy to operational definitions—what the person does and wants done. A few examples of the language of intimacy are: being with, doing with, talking personally to and being understood, doing for or being done for, giving or receiving presents, being approved, being appreciated, being touched, being heard, being seen or noticed, being needed, being number 1. The languages also incorporate myths, beliefs, expectations, values, rules, customs, traditions, and habits.

DEFINITIONS OF INTIMACY

The American Heritage Dictionary (1970) defines *intimacy* as:

1. Marked by close acquaintance, association, or familiarity.
2. Pertaining to or indicative or one's deepest nature.
3. Essential, innermost.
4. Characterized by informality and privacy; secret . . . a close friend or confidant.
5. Very personal; private; secret. Intimate comes from the Latin "intimare" meaning "to put in." (p. 686)

Waring (1988) states: "The behavioral aspect of intimacy is predictability; the emotional aspect is a feeling of closeness; the cognitive aspect is understanding through self-disclosure; and the attitudinal aspect is commitment" (p. 38–39).

For intimacy to occur, it is typically necessary to create an atmosphere of safety and a willingness to risk one's self by sharing. To develop an ongoing pattern of intimate behavior, there is usually an expectation that the intimate sharing will be reciprocal. However, this is not always necessary. The therapist does not often share personal secrets. Sometimes in other complementary relationships one will take the role of sharer and the other the role of the good sympathetic listener. Adlerians would consider it to be a more equal and satisfying relationship if both members of a couple could feel safe to entrust the self to the other. The belief that it is best not to do so is probably based on the need to protect one's self image by being "superstrong" or to protect from expected harm were vulnerabilities to be revealed. There are those among us who are allowed to give but who are not deserving of taking from others.

Intimacy involves a process of being sufficiently interested to pay attention to one another, to care what the other is experiencing, to trust one another, and to be willing to entrust the self to the other. Intimacy requires the ability to communicate one's thoughts and feelings, the willingness and ability to listen empathically, and the skills and willingness to negotiate differences when what is shared is believed by the listener to be a threat or a put-down or a detriment to her or his interests. *Love is not a precondition for intimacy, but intimacy greatly enriches a love relationship.* Sometimes a person may prefer to share intimate confidences with a total stranger not expected to be seen again and who is regarded as safer than one's spouse.

ISSUES OF INTIMACY IN TREATING COUPLES

Differences are inevitable even among people who love each other. Conflicts emerging from differences may greatly affect the levels of intimacy that a couple enjoys. Some of the most common issues are defined here with examples of how to treat each of them. The examples are merely illustrative and not intended to be read as "the way."

1. *Being versus Doing and Other Gender Differences.* Men and women in our society are reared differently and tend to behave differently with respect to intimacy. Women tend to define intimacy as deep personal talk and connection experienced as being together. They learn to socialize early in sharing emotionally expressive relationships. Men are socialized more toward competition and achievement. They are therefore less willing to entrust themselves to another by sharing, especially vulnerabilities that could be used against them in the competition. Men express intimacy more in terms of doing things together, physical presence, and sexual intercourse. This is an increasingly researched subject. For fuller discussions see De Angelis (1989), Gilligan (1982), and Pogrebin (1987), among many others.

It is helpful to depersonalize the issue by pointing out that these are gender issues and the couple is caught in a cultural bind not of their making. For example: "Wouldn't it be wonderful if you could double your pleasure by adopting both kinds of intimacy? You could teach each other the joys of being together and doing together as ways of sharing. Men really miss out on the kind of intimacy that women enjoy. Once you try it you'll really like it." Then the couple is encouraged to share intimately now in session and then go home and practice. The assignment of the couple conference is also useful.

2. *Wanting to Change the Other.* The belief that I must change my partner is the most common source of conflict. It is often quipped that women marry men to change them and men marry women to keep them the same, each thereby stifling growth by creating an atmosphere of attack and defensiveness. This behavior goes against the wish to be accepted and respected, especially by the chosen partner.

However, in a well-functioning relationship, each spouse will automatically learn a great deal from the other as a result of their sharing together rather than being bullied or manipulated.

Declaring a truce because neither is powerful enough to overcome the other, as demonstrated by the history of the fight, is an effective way to begin to disengage any conflict. Then the therapist can teach the value of differences, negotiating skills, and appropriate communication skills.

3. *Territoriality.* The sense of boundaries around physical and emotional space varies from person to person and culture to culture. One partner's idea of a comfortable closeness may either be much too suffocating or much too distant. The result is a dance in which the person demanding more space takes on the role of pursuer/victim who is neglected by the spouse. The spouse takes on the role of a distancer/victim who is constantly being criticized and not allowed to breathe. The more the spouse pulls away, the more needy and rejected the pursuer feels and pushes harder, triggering further distance.

To break this pattern, the pursuer needs to outdistance the distancer. In most cases, the distancer will then move closer. At that point, the pursuer will want to resume the old pattern and needs help in restraining from doing so. Where separation-individuation and boundaries are weak or underdeveloped, the therapist needs to stress the uniqueness and strength of each individual, clarify and specify their different roles in the relationship, and set and reinforce appropriate rules.

4. *Intensity.* Some people are very passionate and emotive in their expression, while others are very restrained. To the first kind the second is cold, colorless, withdrawn, passive, completely out of touch with emotions. To the second kind the first is hysterical, crazy, overdramatic, out of control, and not to be taken seriously. Again, the more dramatic the first, the more cool the second, further stimulating the first to ever greater drama, including possible depression.

The hot person needs to learn to recognize that on a scale of 1–10 with 10 the highest, every event in life is not a 10. The cool person needs to learn that being more expressive of emotions can feel good and be rewarding. One technique for doing this is the use of role reversal in which the first commits to being super cool, while the other commits to being very hot with the prescription to have fun with the role. Another technique is to use some form of the antinegative or paradox. An example might be a compliance/defiance paradox in which the cool one is asked if she or he wants to solve this problem and have some fun doing it. Then suggest playing much more emotional than the other who will become angry and tell the cool person to cut it out, probably becoming more cool as the cool one becomes more emotional, eventually arriving at a better balance.

5. *Differences in Styles.* It is an axiom that some people are more comfortable when the temperature is warmer and others when cooler. There are similar differences with respect to light and dark, degrees of cleanliness and order, conceptions of time and timeliness, the choices of metaphors to express life experiences, and a host of others. Adlerians tend to be particularly sensitive to the concept of favored sense modality wherein some people prefer communications appealing more to vision, hearing, taste, smell, or touch. Failure to impact one another in the favored sense modality may create a large gap in communication and intimacy by engendering the belief that the other doesn't care. Here the therapist explains the inevitability of differences in styles as normal, engenders mutual respect for the differences, and teaches the couple negotiating skills to resolve the differences constructively. The Experiencing and Expressing Love Exercise is useful in helping the couple to become aware of their different languages of loving and intimacy.

6. *Differences in Rules, Customs and Traditions.* Coming from somewhat or greatly different backgrounds and having absorbed different assumptive values, there are bound to be disputes about how we do things. Examples are: Do we open Christmas presents on Christmas Eve or Christmas Day? If children curse at their parents, do we discuss it with them or wash their mouths out with soap? Are we allowed to vent our anger or must we be gentle and keep the peace at any price? Is Father to be undisturbed to rest when he returns from a hard day at work or does he pitch in and do his share? Can we only go out together as a couple or can we engage in separate activities? There is an important difference in impact between the conflicts in this category of issues and those in differences in styles. A strong moral component is often attached to the rules and customs that we advocate as *right* making others less good, wrong, and sometimes evil, requiring severe criticism of the person as well as the deed. Therefore, it is more difficult for the therapist to obtain mutual respect and negotiation of differences.

First, the therapist normalizes the existence of the differences. Then, sufficient communal feeling needs to be engendered to develop tolerance for each other's ways as derivative of from whence they individually came. Work on the family constellation may be used for this purpose. Then the key Adlerian question of "whither shall we go as a couple" sets the stage for negotiation. The invention and commitment to new customs and traditions is particularly useful in working with step-family couples.

7. *Being of Several Minds*. Some people feel a great need for closeness and demand it. However, if it is offered they become very frightened and push off. They bounce between the extreme fears of being abandoned or being taken over or deprived of their selfhood. Others signal strongly that they want to maintain a clear aloofness, probably to protect themselves from rejection. Nevertheless, when a partner comes close they welcome it, but may soon push off for fear that they will lose that closeness and feel the sharp pain of rejection again. Those who were physically, sexually, or emotionally abused or neglected will often also give confusing double messages about distance and closeness because they have learned that those closest to them are not to be trusted and are the most likely to inflict the greatest pain.

This situation is more complex than many of the others and does not lend itself to simple solutions. It is useful to work with the family of origin in person or through use of imagery, sculpting, the empty chair, writing mailed or unmailed letters, venting hurt and anger in session with the therapist alone, encouragement, and ego-building tactics. The therapist can point out that the partner is not and does not represent figures from the past. The partner can be alerted to behaviors and situations that elicit the spouse's fears and distrust and commit to avoid such behavior as much as possible.

8. *Symbiotic Attunement*. In its highest form, the partners pay exquisite empathic attention to one another and are able to discern what is going on with the other at any given moment without being intentionally informed. This is somewhat similar to a parent and infant interaction in which very often the parent just knows the infant's need. However, in its more garden-variety form, symbiotic attunement is likely to be the whining demand of a needy, narcissistic person whose priority is to receive the kind of intense attention and sensitivity either missed as an infant or resulting from being very much pampered and the center of attention. This person cannot communicate what she or he feels or wants because that would spoil it since that is proof that the partner doesn't care enough to attend fully to who she or he is. The partner concludes early on that she or he can never attend enough and always will be nagged and criticized. The partner then withdraws, attending even less, thus increasing the anxiety and need for the first one to get more attention. The nagging becomes a convenient excuse for the partner to maintain a safe distance. This becomes another pursuer/distancer relationship.

The therapist can help the person through encouragement and empowerment techniques to be proactive instead of being a miserable, dependent waiter. On the other end of the spectrum, the therapist can assist the person to get in touch with inner feelings of anguish and anger, and correct the mistaken ideas that flow from those feelings and early life experiences. The couple may examine the anxiety evoked by too much or too little attention.

9. *Additional Common Blocks to Intimacy.*

A. Fears such as loss of face, integrity, control of self; becoming dependent; or having to take responsibility for oneself.
B. Misunderstanding and miscommunication such as lying, withholding information, giving incomplete information, projecting one's own ideas and meanings unto another, double messages, and double binds.
C. Negative interactions such as assuming the role of pessimist, helpless one, or victim (everyone realistically experiences negative events in life. Being victimized does not mean that one's continuing role in life is to be a victim); being critical, especially by putting down the person rather than by correcting the behavior (taking on the role of inspector general or the critical parent engaging the partner in the role of rebellious child); always being right, thus leaving only the role of the wrong or incompetent one to the partner; demanding most of the time to be the boss, which leaves the roles of underling or rebel to the partner; expressing no interest in others, leaving the jobs of giving and connecting to the partner. For the most part women are expected to assume responsibility for the well-being of the relationship which places an unequal, often unappreciated, burden upon them.
D. Controlling interactions such as: withholding oneself to establish distance (leaving the role of pursuer to the partner) or as a hostile passive-aggressive act to control the conflict (which puts the partner in the position of being the overtly aggressive one); parents sharing little but questioning their children much (thus creating superior/inferior positions); doing all the talking to keep a "safe" focus on the self (thus relegating the partner to the role of good listener/caretaker); and being perfectly reasonable and calm, which translates into being right and cooperative while the partner is wrong, emotional, and unreasonable.

10. *Sexual Intimacy.* Sexual intercourse may or may not include sexual intimacy. Intercourse may involve only physical expression or be the result of rape. There are some individuals who use intercourse as a tension reduction device, a sleeping pill, or a proof of manhood or womanhood without any real interest in the partner as a person. Those are not intimate relations. Sexual interactions, with or without intercourse, that bring the couple a sense of mutual warmth, closeness, and unity may be defined as intimate. Women usually prefer much personal sharing of talk and touch as well as the union of intercourse. Men often experience their greatest sense of closeness and lovingness in the union of intercourse with a loved partner who desires to be with them sexually.

Blocks to sexual intimacy include: fear of inadequate performance; fear of loss of power, control, or self (being made smaller or absorbed); anger toward or distrust of the partner; feelings attached to earlier sexual, physical, or emotional abuse; beliefs that sex is dirty or that members of the opposite sex are in some way bad or hurtful; and differences in sexual appetites and styles of satisfaction. Problems can be created by such seemingly simple differences as he is a morning person and she a night person. One of them cannot enjoy sex if there is *any* possibility that the children or anyone else might hear them.

Clients in difficulty often ask if it is possible that sexual attraction can be restored once it has severely eroded. The answer is that most typically, if the relationship is improved, attraction may also increase again. Attraction is based on many psychological as well as physical factors.

There is, of course, a huge literature on human sexuality and sex counseling. Gender issues are considered by Carr (1988), Kantor and Okun (1989), and Walters, Carter, Papp, and Silverstein (1989). Gilligan (1982) and Pogrebin (1987) deal specifically with gender issues in intimacy.

TECHNIQUES AND TACTICS

The issues presented revolve around power, closeness and distance, boundaries, and similarities and complementarities between the couple. In dealing therapeutically with the issues, we need to attend to changing their beliefs and expectations, relative roles and places, skills and knowledge, social feeling, and patterns of communication. For discussion of these matters see Dinkmeyer and Sherman (1989), Sherman and Dinkmeyer (1987), and Sherman, Oresky, and Rountree (1991). The same sources plus Sherman and Fredman (1986) provide more detailed discussions of the theory, procedures, uses, and case examples of the techniques which follow and information on earlier additional sources of those techniques borrowed from others.

1. *The Experiencing and Expressing Love Exercise* permits the therapist to assess the languages of couple's loving and intimacy and to help them observe their individual needs, modes of expression, similarities, and differences that flow from their private logic. The exercise is based on answering and analyzing the answers to these four questions phrased in appropriate language for the clients:

A. "What does the other person actually have to do for you to feel that you are being loved?"
B. "What do you concretely do to show the other person that you are being loving?"

C. "What do you recall as the most pleasing thing about the way people related together in your family growing up?"
D. "What do you recall were the most upsetting ways that people related together in your family growing up, and what was the most missing for you in the way people related to you?"

Clients are asked to rank order their responses to each question, examine the themes that cut across the responses to all four, compare their respective answers, and indicate if there were any surprises. They can then work on the process of accommodating each other by acquiring the other's language.

The same exercise lends itself to many other tasks merely by substituting the words "emotions," "appreciation," "anger," or many others for the word "love" in the questions posed.

2. *The Intimacy Genogram.* Adlerians typically get a description of the family constellation. Most couple and family therapists now chart the family constellation as a genogram showing where each person fits into the overall multigenerational family pattern. The genogram can be designed to emphasize any specific family relationship pertaining to the problems at hand such as vocational patterns, male/female guiding lines, sexuality, nodal events, and many more. Similarly, a genogram can be constructed to reveal patterns of intimacy in both families multigenerationally by asking questions stemming from the many issues discussed earlier in this article such as intensity, territoriality, and symbiosis. Doing the genograms together helps the couple learn much more about each other and thus increases intimacy.

3. *Enhancing Attending Behavior.* The core of all intimate behavior is paying close attention to one another and sharing within the framework of that attentiveness. The major obstacle to empathic attending is placing one's self in the way for whatever defensive, offensive, or narcissistic reasons so that even when observing you I am thinking really only of me and the consequences for me. Several techniques to increase empathic attending are:

A. Therapists can prescribe the Sherlock Holmes (or the name of any other currently famous detective) Exercise. Clients are challenged to figure out their partners by being a good detective. Clients agree to observe each other very carefully from dress to bodily expressions to the timing of specific and other behaviors appropriate to the presenting problem. They are to carefully record their observations factually. In session they check out their facts and conclusions with one another.
B. Check out intentionality by having the partners inquire what they hoped would occur as a result of what they just did. Thereby, they get beyond

their own subjective perceptions and below the surface of what the partner is saying or doing. In carrying out the exercise they are already talking at a more intimate level and getting beyond the self.

C. Obtain agreement from the couple for each to acknowledge sympathetically what the other is saying or feeling. The other at least feels attended to and hopefully understood. Acknowledgment does not necessarily mean agreement. But being heard is comforting in itself and opens the door to a safer environment wherein intimacy becomes more possible.

D. A favorite Adlerian method is to suggest to the couple that they seek to catch or discover the partner doing something desirable and to count and record the number of things they observed. Who can discover the greater number? This focuses attention, and focuses it on positives rather than negatives.

4. *Sculpting*. Sculpting is another very versatile technique with a host of adaptations. These exercises get beyond typical verbal defenses and are simultaneously both metaphoric and concrete.

A. The therapist can have the couple create an intimacy sculpture in which they each can place themselves physically in relation to how they think they generally function in terms of distance and closeness and how ideally they would like to place themselves. The therapist demonstrates a few possible sculptures to convey the idea—standing apart holding hands, holding each other tightly face to face, or arms around waists facing partly toward one another and partly forward. Their sculptures are examined carefully and compared and contrasted.

B. The "what does it feel like in that place" sculpture is used for each partner to describe how the relationship seems to her or him. One person sculpts their relative positions and distance from each other. Then each is asked to describe what it feels like to be in that position. The second person sculpts and the process is repeated. Then each is asked to construct an ideal sculpture that they would enjoy better. They plan things to do to bring their ideal about. The therapist questions the risks and obstacles to doing what is planned. This will reveal additional beliefs and vulnerabilities to be examined as the plans go forward simultaneously.

C. The animal/object sculpture is more complex and versatile. Each person is asked to think of the partner as an animal or object in relation to the presenting problems and then think of self as an animal or object in relation to the partner around the same problem. The person then sculpts the relationship. An added dimension is to have them enact the situation in their animal/object roles. Some questions might be: "How does a small scared rabbit (you) make it with a big angry clawing bear (the image of the partner)?" "Is there something helpful about this situation?" "How might you do something different?" "What would be the risk of doing it differently?" "Are you surprised by how your partner depicts you and the situation?" Each person's fantasy is explored.

5. *The Couple Conference*. This is another common Adlerian technique to structure intimate behavior in a society in which the average amount of intimate time per week for a couple is 17 minutes and models for intimate behavior are scarce. The procedures are flexible and vary with the therapeutic purpose. Couples are asked to commit to one hour per week of exclusive uninterrupted time together as a ritual "same time same place" each week. One will speak for 30 minutes uninterrupted and the other will listen carefully and at the end briefly acknowledge what was heard without comment, agreement, or defense. Then the second person will speak uninterrupted for 30 minutes. This is to be neither a complaint nor a problem-solving session. It is designed only to make the self fully heard and to experience being carefully attended to.

SUMMARY

This article stressed the importance of mutual feeling, trust, sharing, and equality in couple intimacy. The importance of the individual's private logic based on early family experiences in evolving a unique individual language of intimacy and loving was briefly described. Ten categories of issues of intimacy that arise in couples therapy including intensity, style, sexuality, and gender differences were discussed and several techniques were suggested for dealing with each. Finally, five major exercises for improving intimate relations were reported: Experiencing and Expressing Love, the Intimacy Genogram, Enhancing Attending Behaviors, Sculpting, and the Couple Conference. The article is based on an Adlerian Systems approach developed by Sherman and Dinkmeyer (1987) which integrates individual motivation with systemic processes for both assessment and treatment.

REFERENCES

Ansbacher, H. L., & Ansbacher, R. R. (Eds.). (1956). *The Individual Psychology of Alfred Adler: A systematic presentation in selections from his writings*. New York: Basic Books.

Carr, J. B. (1988). *Crises in intimacy when expectations don't meet reality.* Pacific Grove, CA: Brooks/Cole.

De Angelis, T. (1989, November). Men's interaction style can be tough on women. *APA Monitor*, p. 12.

Dinkmeyer, D. C., Pew, W. L., & Dinkmeyer, D. C., Jr. (1979). *Adlerian counseling and psychotherapy*. Monterey, CA: Brooks/Cole.

Dinkmeyer, D., & Sherman, R. (1989). Brief Adlerian family therapy. *Individual Psychology, 43*(1&2), 148–158.

Dreikurs, R. (1946). *The challenge of marriage*. New York: Hawthorne.

Gilligan, C. (1982). *In a different voice*. Cambridge, MA: Harvard University Press.

Kantor, D., & Okun, B. F. (Eds.). (1989). *Intimate environments: Sex, intimacy, and gender in families*. New York: Guilford.

Pogrebin, L. C. (1987). *Among friends*. New York: McGraw-Hill.

Sherman, R., & Dinkmeyer, D. (1987). *Systems of family therapy: An Adlerian integration*. New York: Brunner/Mazel.

Sherman, R., & Fredman, N. (1986). *Handbook of structured techniques in marriage and family therapy*. New York: Brunner/Mazel.

Sherman, R., Oresky, P., & Rountree, Y. B. (1991). *Solving problems in couples and family therapy*. New York: Brunner/Mazel.

Walters, M., Carter, B., Papp, P., & Silverstein, D. (1989). *The invisible web: Gender patterns in family relationship*. New York: Guilford.

Waring, E. M. (1988). *Enhancing marital intimacy through facilitating cognitive self-disclosure*. New York: Brunner/Mazel.

HELPING ADULTS CHANGE DISJUNCTIVE EMOTIONAL RESPONSES TO CHILDREN'S MISBEHAVIOR

Gary D. McKay
A counselor in private practice and an educational and psychological consultant. He is an adjunct instructor with the Department of Counseling and Guidance, University of Arizona.

Oscar C. Christensen
A Professor in the Department of Counseling and Guidance at the University of Arizona. He has lectured on family counseling at colleges and universities throughout the United States and Canada and has been a faculty member of ICASSI in Vienna and Amsterdam.

Counselors who work with children, parents, families and teachers know how difficult it is for adults to alter their behavioral responses to children's misbehavior. It is even more difficult for adults to change their emotional responses. While we Adlerians have many effective alternative behaviors for adults who deal with children, we seldom have specific suggestions for changing feelings. We know that in order to be effective in redirecting a child's mistaken goal adults must not only alter their behavior, but must also refrain from, as Dreikurs called it, "shouting with their mouths shut." In other words, adults must cease feeling annoyance, anger, hurt or despair.

Many adults learn to stop emoting in these disjunctive ways through avoiding their first impulse and practicing the application of behavioral methods—that is, after practicing new behaviors, the feelings, underlying attitudes, and/or beliefs

Journal of Individual Psychology, 34(1), May, 1978, **pp. 70–84**

change in the direction of the new behavior. However, some adults need additional help in working on changing their feelings as well as their behavior. Because of their own faulty beliefs, adults find changing these feelings extremely difficult. This article will discuss the purposes of adults' emotional responses to children's mistaken goals and will propose methods for helping adults change these responses. It is hoped that counselors will find these suggestions useful as they work with adults who deal with children and youth.

THE FUNCTION OF EMOTIONS

To Adlerians, emotions are purposive, as are other aspects of human endeavor (Adler, 1954). Emotions provide the energy to move an individual to action (Allen, 1971; Dreikurs, 1967).

Albert Ellis' A-B-C- theory of the nature of humans (Ellis & Harper, 1975) blends well with the Adlerian concept of emotions and is helpful in learning to change feelings. Ellis contends that most people assume that A—the *Activating* event—a behavior a person fails to perform which (s)he thinks (s)he *should* perform, or a behavior occurrence in a person's life which (s)he thinks *should not* happen, causes C—the emotional *Consequence*. Ellis says that people are not aware that the cause of C is not A, but B—one's *Belief* about A, or what one tells oneself about the Activating event.

Ellis believes that individuals disturb themselves by irrational beliefs in statements they tell themselves about negative things that happen. He says that strong upset feelings arise because people translate strong desires and preferences into needs. Words, either spoken or implied, which denote absolutes such as *should, ought, need, have to, must, always, never*, indicate that persons view their preferences as needs and therefore are going to be very distraught when things don't turn out as they believe they *must*.

Furthermore, irrational beliefs contain statements about one's own worth or another's worth as a human being. Persons blame themselves and sometimes others for what happens, rather than looking for a solution.

Ellis contends people will not overly distress themselves if they learn to recognize their irrational beliefs and change them to more rational beliefs. Most of the things that happen in life are *not catastrophic*, but are merely *frustrating, inconvenient*, and *unfortunate*. If people think in terms of preferences instead of needs, they will learn to rate only behavior and *not human worth*, and although they may feel annoyed, sad or frustrated, they will not view things as *catastrophic* and therefore will not feel dreadfully unhappy. They will thus be able to lead reasonably happy lives.

There is one exception to the use of absolutes. It is appropriate to believe a "must" or a "have to" if it is a *conditional* statement. For example, "If I'm going to pass the test, I *must* study." The "conditional must" does not produce unduly upset feelings *unless* persons view the event as a *need*, tie up their worth with the event, and are distraught about not achieving their goal.

Mosak and Dreikurs (1973) point out that both Adler and Ellis believe "emotions are actually a form of thinking, that people control their emotions through controlling their thinking" (p. 45). Thus, in our Adlerian stance, there is credence for utilizing Ellis' ideas. In the section on procedures for changing emotional responses to children's misbehavior, we will discuss how adults can directly challenge and dispute the beliefs and purposes which create their disjunctive emotions.

BELIEFS AND PURPOSES ASSOCIATED WITH ADULT EMOTIONAL RESPONSES TO CHILDREN'S FOUR GOALS

In light of the preceding discussion, we notice that the negative or disjunctive emotions adults experience when children pursue the four goals serve purposes for the adult. Generally, the emotional responses give the adult energy to move into action. In addition, we can see that these emotions arise from irrational beliefs, which we call disjunctive beliefs because they separate the adult and child, thus blocking a more effective relationship.

Disjunctive beliefs contain absolutes. Adults cannot create disjunctive emotions unless their beliefs contain absolutes—either stated or implied. Furthermore, with the exception of the adult's disjunctive belief concerning a child's attention-seeking behavior—which is really a mild discomfort—the absolute statement leads to overexaggeration and blame. Adults blame themselves and/or the child when their beliefs are violated—they tend to equate their own or others' behavior with the worth of the total person. While disjunctive beliefs always reflect immediate adult goals, they may also be life style statements for some adults.

The opposite of the disjunctive belief is the conjunctive belief. This type of belief creates conjunctive or positive emotions which serve to facilitate cooperation and mutual respect. Conjunctive beliefs focus on *preferences* instead of *absolutes*. Adults realize that while they *do not like* the behavior, it is *not catastrophic*, only *inconvenient, unfortunate* and *frustrating*. While they would like the child to change, it is *not absolutely essential*, but merely *better* for them and the child if the child changes. This thought process makes it possible for adults to influence the child to change, not by demanding change, but by recognizing that the child behaves this way because (s)he is discouraged, and will probably change the behavior and goal when given the responsibility to do so. The adult can then stop blaming him/herself or the child.

It is important to caution adults not to "should about shoulding." In other words, if adults have difficulty making changes and start to tell *themselves* absolutes about the fact that *they* aren't changing, they will become even more discouraged. It is important to help adults focus on the advantages of changing rather than that they should or must change (McKay, 1976).

Below are four flowcharts which describe disjunctive responses associated with each of the four goals of children's misbehavior. Appropriate alternative conjunctive responses are also given. Each chart describes the disjunctive and conjunctive beliefs, the purposes arising from the beliefs, the emotions generated to move the adult to action, and the behaviors chosen to carry out the adult's purpose. To facilitate understanding, we will comment on each chart separately.

Chart 1

When a child makes an inappropriate bid for attention, the behavior may interfere with adults' pursuing tasks which they consider important. The adults may feel annoyed, and their annoyance is generated from disjunctive beliefs. Looking at Chart 1, the reader will notice that the first part of the belief—"I have a right to continue what I'm doing without interruption"—is true, and telling oneself this part of the belief will not produce annoyance or the tendency to remind and coax the child. The second part of the belief is what produces difficulty in the relationship, for it contains an *absolute* and therefore *demands* that the child change. Why *should* the child stop interrupting? After all, from the child's point of view (s)he is only trying to belong in the best way (s)he knows how—employing a method that works. The adults' reactions assure the child of a compensatory feeling of belonging.

If adults concentrate on the conjunctive sentences they will not feel annoyed, but will feel determined not to reinforce the child's behavior and will look for

Chart 1

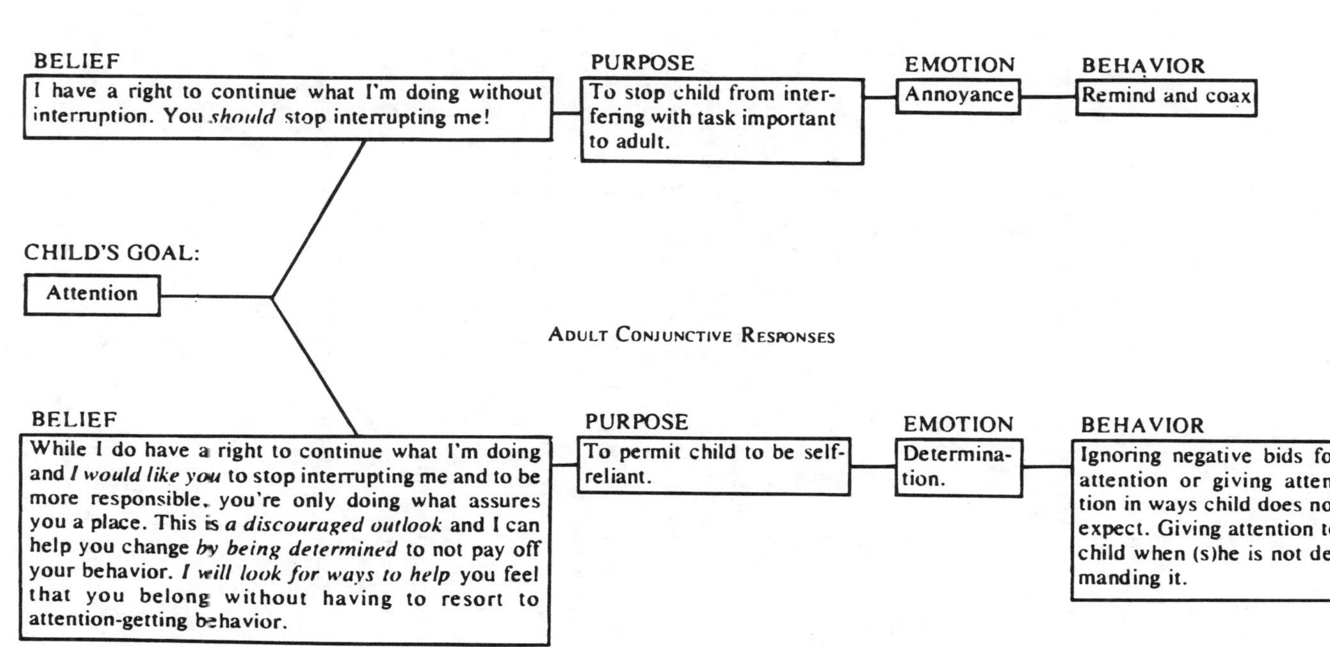
ADULT DISJUNCTIVE RESPONSES
BELIEF
I have a right to continue what I'm doing without interruption. You *should* stop interrupting me!
PURPOSE
To stop child from interfering with task important to adult.
EMOTION
Annoyance
BEHAVIOR
Remind and coax
CHILD'S GOAL:
Attention
ADULT CONJUNCTIVE RESPONSES
BELIEF
While I do have a right to continue what I'm doing and *I would like you* to stop interrupting me and to be more responsible, you're only doing what assures you a place. This is *a discouraged outlook* and I can help you change *by being determined* to not pay off your behavior. *I will look for ways to help* you feel that you belong without having to resort to attention-getting behavior.
PURPOSE
To permit child to be self-reliant.
EMOTION
Determination.
BEHAVIOR
Ignoring negative bids for attention or giving attention in ways child does not expect. Giving attention to child when (s)he is not demanding it.

alternative behaviors to help the child become self-reliant. This belief will lead adults to problem solving.

Chart 2

When a child pursues power, adults may feel angry if they view the child's behavior as a threat to their personal prestige and authority. If adults decide to fight the child to prove who's boss, the anger serves the purpose of establishing control. If the adult gives in, the anger serves the purpose of getting even for losing ground. When adults decide to neither fight nor give in, but to win the child's cooperation, determination will result.

Chart 3

Revengeful behavior proves very difficult for adults to handle because they may believe the child does not love them or has wounded their pride and diminished their worth. Adults generate hurt feelings to give themselves permission to get even with the child. Then anger is created to carry out the retaliation. Ellis (1976) points out that hurt is generated from self-depreciating statements. In other words, when adults receive revengeful behavior, they blame themselves for the child's attack. The first part of the disjunctive belief on Chart 3—"How *horrible*. You attacked me," etc., illustrates this point. Then, Ellis states, we immediately cover up the hurt feelings and make ourselves angry and blame the other to excuse our self-blaming. It is more comfortable to blame the child than to blame ourselves. The second part of the belief—"How dare you. You're unfair," etc. shows how adults cover up the hurt with anger towards the child.

Once adults realize that the attack they receive comes from the child's own deep discouragement—retaliation for real or imagined wrongs—they are in a position to develop more conjunctive beliefs and as a result will find themselves first experiencing regret that the relationship has deteriorated to this point, then feeling empathy for the child's own hurt, and finally, determination to not further discourage the child, but to concentrate on improving the relationship.

Chart 4

A feeling of despair is experienced by adults when a child displays inadequacy—if adults believe the child is inadequate. These feelings are generated to give adults permission to give up—to disown any responsibility for helping the

Chart 2

Adult Disjunctive Responses

BELIEF	PURPOSE	EMOTION	BEHAVIOR
It is *terrible* when you don't do what I want you to because I *must* be in control in order to be a good parent (teacher), and you *must* do what I say or *I'm not a worthwhile person!*	To control child. (If adult gives in—to get even).	Anger	Fight or give in.

CHILD'S GOAL: Power

Adult Conjunctive Responses

BELIEF	PURPOSE	EMOTION	BEHAVIOR
While I find it *frustrating and inconvenient* when you don't do what I say, it's *not terrible*, and although *I would like* to control you, *I am still a good parent (teacher)* and a *worthwhile person* despite my inability to control you. In fact, *trying to control you* will not help you *develop self-discipline* so I will *not continue to contribute* to your discouragement by fighting or giving in. I'll *maintain mutual respect*. It's really *too bad* you choose to learn the hard way!	To win child's cooperation.	Determination and regret	Withdrawing from conflict and letting child experience consequences. Finding ways for child to use power constructively and enlisting cooperation.

CHART 3

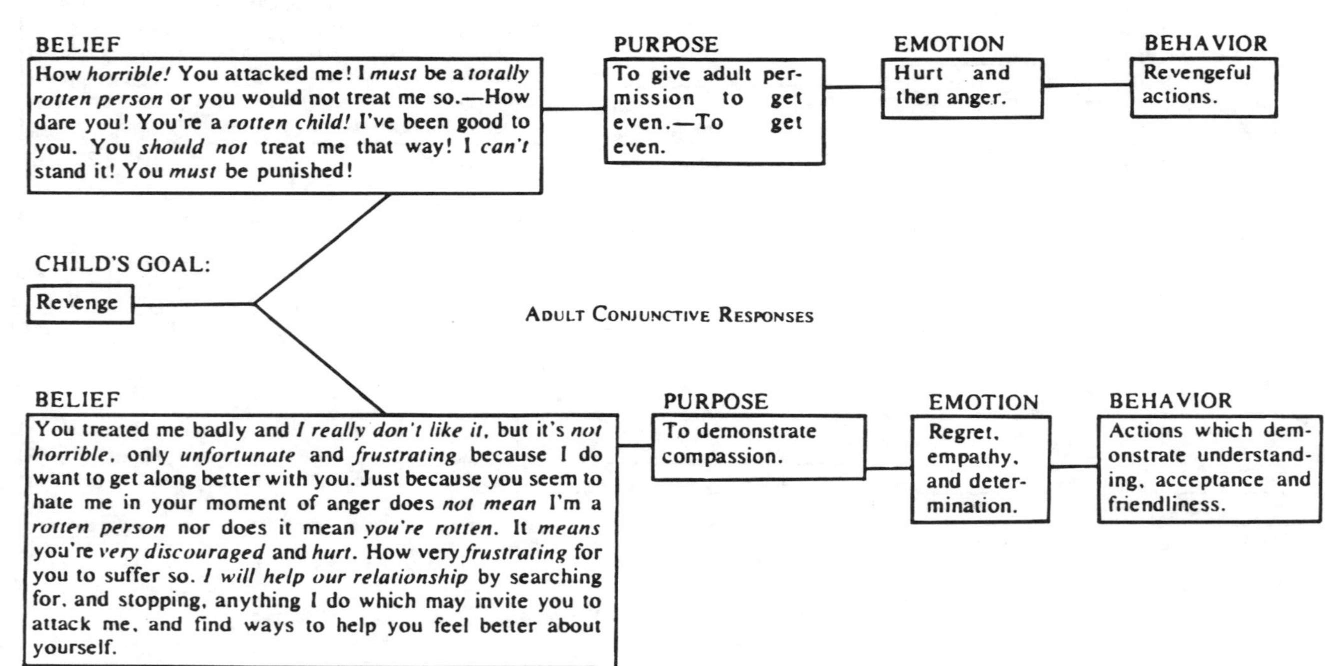
ADULT DISJUNCTIVE RESPONSES
BELIEF
How *horrible!* You attacked me! I *must* be a *totally rotten person* or you would not treat me so.—How dare you! You're a *rotten child!* I've been good to you. You *should not* treat me that way! I *can't* stand it! You *must* be punished!
PURPOSE
To give adult permission to get even.—To get even.
EMOTION
Hurt and then anger.
BEHAVIOR
Revengeful actions.
CHILD'S GOAL:
Revenge
ADULT CONJUNCTIVE RESPONSES
BELIEF
You treated me badly and *I really don't like it*, but it's *not horrible*, only *unfortunate* and *frustrating* because I do want to get along better with you. Just because you seem to hate me in your moment of anger does *not mean* I'm a *rotten person* nor does it mean *you're rotten*. It *means* you're *very discouraged* and *hurt*. How very *frustrating* for you to suffer so. *I will help our relationship* by searching for, and stopping, anything I do which may invite you to attack me, and find ways to help you feel better about yourself.
PURPOSE
To demonstrate compassion.
EMOTION
Regret, empathy, and determination.
BEHAVIOR
Actions which demonstrate understanding, acceptance and friendliness.

Chart 4

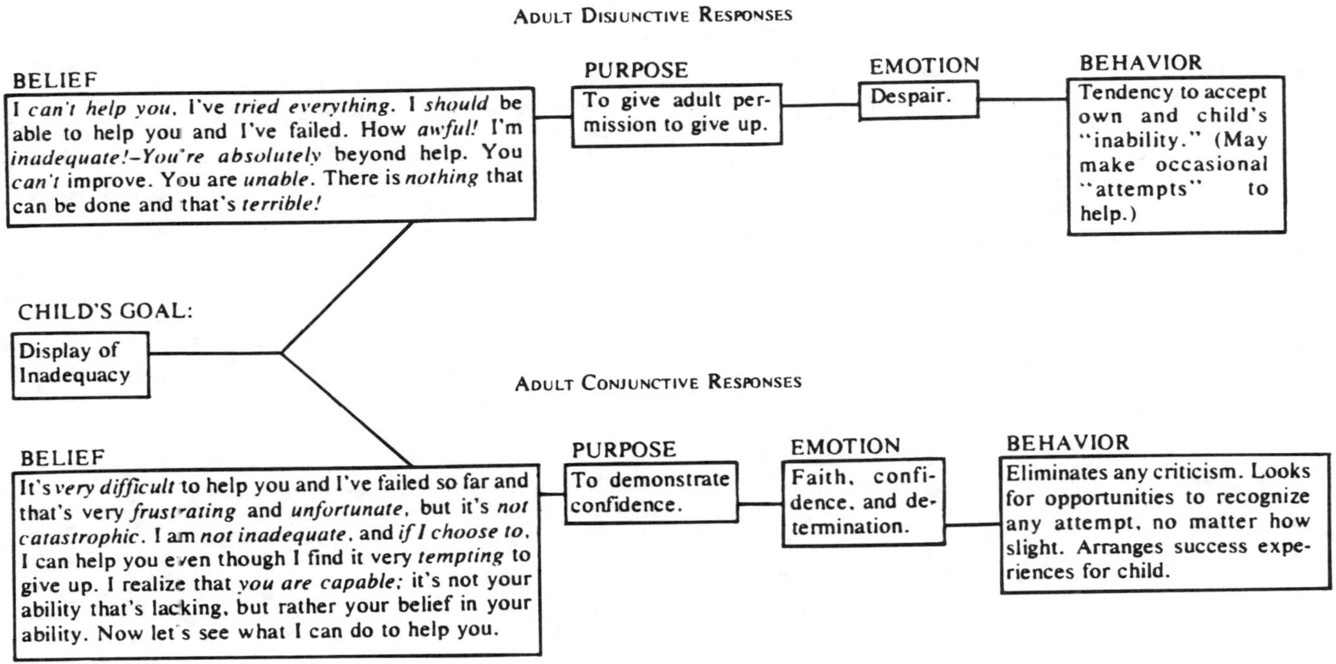

Adult Disjunctive Responses

BELIEF	PURPOSE	EMOTION	BEHAVIOR
I *can't help you*. I've *tried everything*. I *should* be able to help you and I've failed. How *awful!* I'm *inadequate!–You're absolutely* beyond help. You *can't* improve. You are *unable*. There is *nothing* that can be done and that's *terrible!*	To give adult permission to give up.	Despair.	Tendency to accept own and child's "inability." (May make occasional "attempts" to help.)

CHILD'S GOAL:

Display of Inadequacy

Adult Conjunctive Responses

BELIEF	PURPOSE	EMOTION	BEHAVIOR
It's *very difficult* to help you and I've failed so far and that's very *frustrating* and *unfortunate*, but it's *not catastrophic*. I am *not inadequate*, and *if I choose to*, I can help you even though I find it very *tempting* to give up. I realize that *you are capable;* it's not your ability that's lacking, but rather your belief in your ability. Now let's see what I can do to help you.	To demonstrate confidence.	Faith, confidence, and determination.	Eliminates any criticism. Looks for opportunities to recognize any attempt, no matter how slight. Arranges success experiences for child.

child. This phenomenon is similar to the generation of hurt feelings in that adults first believe they are unable to help the child—"I can't help you," etc.—then cover up these inadequacy feelings by believing the child is inadequate—"You're *absolutely* beyond help," etc. To counteract these feelings of inadequacy, adults must first develop feelings of faith and confidence which are conveyed to the child, and, again, become determined not to give up.

PROCEDURES FOR CHANGING DISJUNCTIVE EMOTIONAL RESPONSES

Below are several procedures for changing feelings and beliefs. Some of these procedures are behavioral in nature. Some Adlerians may object to using behavioral approaches. The justification for dealing with emotions through behavioral methods is that behavior change generates emotions appropriate to the new behavior. Similarly, attitudes or beliefs appropriate to the new behaviors and emotions are also potentially created. The basis for this reasoning is the holistic nature of the human and the implicit interaction among behavior, emotion and attitude. By changing any one of these, the others may also be modified.

Avoiding the First Impulse and Careful Attention to Tones

Dreikurs cautioned us to avoid our first impulse and to do the unexpected. He said that when a child misbehaves, the adult must refuse to be bothered by the deed, become a friendly bystander, and then apply the appropriate procedure (Dreikurs & Grey, 1970; Dreikurs & Soltz, 1964). The question becomes how does one "refuse to be bothered."

Dreikurs told us that tone of voice is the best indicator of attitude and feelings. He also said that attitudes or beliefs change as adults discover they can influence the child through applying democratic procedures (Dreikurs & Soltz, 1964). Therefore, through careful attention to tone, one can change one's feelings. If adults *deliberately* concentrate on offering a choice with a friendly but firm tone, and work at expressing regret when the child makes a decision which indicates (s)he has chosen negative consequences, adults will not feel annoyed or angry. Therefore, when action requires talking, careful attention to tone is an effective way to change disjunctive feelings—at least in that moment. As adults begin to experience success at winning the child's cooperation, they often find that their feelings and attitudes or beliefs change as a result of this success.

In addition to careful attention to tone of voice, it is important that the adult also carefully attend to the nonverbal "tones" such as facial expression, gestures and body posture, as these are also indications of attitudes and feelings. Adults can develop appropriate verbal and nonverbal tones through behavioral rehearsal in the pare.nt study group, at home, or in front of a mirror in order to develop conjunctive responses.

Many adults manage to be firm and friendly when verbally giving a choice, but if the child makes the "wrong" decision by choosing to experience the consequence, the adult becomes angry. If adults are to be effective, they have to be willing to accept the child's decision and simply allow the child to learn from experience. (Dinkmeyer & McKay, 1976). Adults can prepare themselves during their behavioral rehearsals for the possibility of the child accepting the consequence.

Using Diversionary Tactics

In some instances no talking is indicated and the problem becomes how to maintain silence without emoting disjunctive feelings. Some situations require adults to remain in the room with children; others involve removing a child without words; and still other situations call for adults to withdraw from the scene of conflict. In these situations diversionary tactics can be employed.

Diversionary tactics basically involve *forcing* oneself to focus on another thought or activity—*something which has nothing to do with what the child is doing*. It is usually not helpful to try to force oneself not to feel a certain emotion because this sets up an internal battle which is usually lost. So the tactic is to divert or distract one's thinking. Behavioral rehearsal helps adults train themselves to do this. Again, it is important to attend to nonverbal communication.

Below are some suggestions for diverting oneself.

Focusing on Another Thought or Activity. One can focus on a pleasant scene, TV, reading, shopping list, what one is going to teach next, other children in the class—anything that will divert one's thought.

Talking Out Loud About Something Else. With some situations, such as dealing with tattling or other attention-seeking behaviors, when a child persists in an argument, or tries to force one to pay attention to his/her demands, it is effective to talk about another subject such as, "Oh, my feet hurt, my back aches . . .!" Or, "Let's see, next I have to . . ." Teachers find it helpful to keep moving in the room and talk to the class or another child about another subject.

Planning a Time to Feel Bad. This is a form of paradoxical intention. The adults plan a specific time to feel annoyed, angry, etc., and to really tell the child what they are feeling. The catch is, the child is not around to hear it! In this way adults are giving themselves permission to "mis-emote," but only at a specific time and in a specific way. The adults choose a certain time each day when the child is not present and spend a specific amount of time—say 10 minutes—mis-emoting. They spend that time talking out loud about all the things they are upset about concerning the child's behavior. For example, if a father finds himself frequently angry with his daughter, he spends his mis-emoting time really telling her off—as if she were present. He can put her picture on a mirror to aid in his attack. He must spend the full time mis-emoting or he will not experience the full effect of the exercise. When adults catch themselves mis-emoting at times other than the planned time, they check the emotion by saying to themselves "Save it!" This procedure works for the following reasons: First, the adults do not fight the feeling but merely delay it by giving themselves permission to feel this way at a specific time. Secondly, adults soon discover that they have an extremely difficult time mis-emoting for the full 10 minutes. They usually begin to see the humor in the situation and find themselves feeling less angered when the child misbehaves. To be effective, the procedure must be used until the adults notice a significant reduction in the disjunctive feelings.

With any of the above procedures, adults usually discover that their feelings change shortly after applying the procedure. They can then think more clearly and decide how to improve the situation. After frequent applications adults begin to experience success in taking charge of their feelings. As a result the child's behavior changes and adults generally begin to feel disjunctive emotions less frequently.

Disputing Disjunctive Beliefs

With some adults, the above techniques are not enough. In such cases, the counselor can teach adults how to dispute their disjunctive beliefs. There are several disputing methods. The first step in using any of these methods is to recognize the purpose of the emotion one wants to change and then to search for the sentences one needs to tell oneself to create the emotion. It will be helpful to use the statements we have provided to give adults an idea of what to look for. While the adults' statements will be in their own words, the statements will be in context to our examples. Adults will also need conjunctive beliefs to counter their disjunctive ones. Again the counselor can give adults our examples as counters to get them started.

Two disputing methods are explained below. They were adapted from Schmidt (1976). Readers will find other procedures in Ellis and Harper's *New Guide to Rational Living*.

Screaming Internally and Countering. This process involves aggressively attacking disjunctive beliefs by silently screaming them out. The adults locate their disjunctive belief and silently shout "Get out!" This is not a "control yourself" technique but rather a "take charge" method—adults take charge of their own thoughts. The internal scream is repeated until adults succeed in driving out the unwanted thought. Then, they immediately counter with the appropriate conjunctive belief. It is important to instruct adults to take note of the different feelings they experience once a disjunctive belief has been successfully blasted out and replaced by a new sentence. Adults can practice this method whenever they catch themselves feeling negatively about a child, and, of course, when the adults are not in actual contact with the child. During the actual negative encounter with the child, adults can employ tonal or diversionary tactics.

Exploring the Consequences Through Fantasy. This procedure involves fantasizing a frequent problem with a child, then exploring the negative consequences of continuing to believe a disjunctive belief and the positive consequences of changing to a conjunctive belief. Adults contract with themselves to spend three specific periods a day disputing their disjunctive beliefs. The process is repeated three times at each sitting. The following steps are essential to the process.

1. The adults imagine themselves in a frequently occurring scene with a child which invites them to feel and act negatively.
2. They then locate and say the usual disjunctive belief to themselves and experience the resulting feelings.
3. Next the adults begin to think of all the ultimate negative consequences that can occur if they continue to believe their disjunctive beliefs and emote and behave in line with the beliefs. For example: "If I continue to believe I have to get even with Dave.—I will continue to become hurt and angry and punish him.—He will probably continue to rebel and get even.—Our relationship will most likely deteriorate further.—I won't enjoy him.—He may do something to increase his retaliation such as stealing or drugs." The adults continue to list the negative consequences for about a minute, then stop and repeat the entire process two more times during each period. It is important to encourage adults to fantasize the worst possible results of continuing to believe their disjunctive beliefs which lead to disjunctive emotions and behaviors.

After adults practice this process for a specific time period, such as a week, a second component is added. During the disputing sessions, after imagining the negative scenes, telling themselves the disjunctive beliefs and stating the negative consequences, the adults follow the steps below.

1. They take charge and scream internally "Get out!" or "Stop!"
2. Then the adults imagine the scene again, only this time they respond with the appropriate conjunctive belief and take note of the new feelings and behaviors. The adults picture their nonverbal behavior as well.
3. Next, the adults fantasize about all the positive things that can happen as a consequence of the new belief and resulting emotions and behaviors. Taking our example from point 3 above to this step: "If I decide I don't have to get even with Dave.—I'll be unimpressed with his provocations, let him experience the consequences and talk with him about friendly things.—Eventually he'll probably become more cooperative.—Our relationship will probably become more pleasant.—I'll really enjoy having him around."

This process is repeated in its entirety three times at each of the three sittings. Each disputing session takes about 10 minutes.

The above disputing methods are designed to be used when adults are not actually in contact with a child. These disputing methods will be more effective if paired with one of the methods listed for use when in actual contact with the child.

Reminders and Signals

Adults can devise reminders and signals which will alert them to appropriate responses. Notes on a mirror such as "Watch your tone of voice" help remind adults to attend to how they talk with a child. Ellis suggests persons carry note cards with rational statements (conjunctive beliefs) and make certain they look at them. Cartoons which illustrate one's particular "quirk" are often effective, as they help the adult develop a sense of humor about otherwise serious situations (McKay, 1976).

Selecting the Appropriate Emotional Change Procedure

The approach depends, of course, on one's knowledge of one's client. Counselors can begin with diversionary tactics and then, if needed, add the disputing techniques. A combination of procedures may be helpful. Another approach is to share this article with adults and ask them to experiment with the procedures that seem most feasible for them.

If none of the suggested procedures are effective, a life style work-up may be advisable.

SUMMARY

In this article we have discussed the purpose of adults' emotional responses to children's goals of misbehavior and specific procedures for helping adults change these emotional responses. We have suggested that disjunctive emotions are the result of the adults' disjunctive purposes and beliefs and that we can help them change to conjunctive purposes and beliefs through one or a combination of the following procedures: avoiding the first impulse, careful attention to tones, using diversionary tactics, disputing disjunctive beliefs, and using reminders and signals.

REFERENCES

Adler, A. *Understanding human nature*. Greenwich, CT: Fawcett, 1954.

Allen, T. W. Major contributions: The Individual Psychology of Alfred Adler: An item of history and a promise of a revolution. *The Counseling Psychologist*, 1971, *3*(1), 3–23.

Ansbacher, H. L., & Ansbacher, R. R. (Eds.). *Superiority and social interest: Alfred Adler: A collection of later writings*. New York: Viking Press, 1973.

Dinkmeyer, D., & McKay, G. D. *Systematic training for effective parenting*. Circle Pines, MN: American Guidance Service, 1976.

Dreikurs, R. R. *Psychodynamics, psychotherapy and counseling*. Chicago: Alfred Adler Institute, 1967.

Dreikurs, R., & Grey, L. *A parents' guide to child discipline*. New York: Hawthorn Books, 1970.

Dreikurs, R., & Soltz, V. *Children: The challenge*. New York: Duell, Sloan & Pearce, 1964.

Ellis, A. Techniques of handling anger in marriage. *Journal of Marriage and Family Counseling*, 1976, *2*, 305–315.

Ellis, A., & Harper, R. A. *A new guide to rational living*. N. Hollywood, CA: Wilshire Book Co., 1975.

McKay, G. *The basics of encouragement.* Coral Springs, FL: CMTI Press, 1976. (Booklet)

Mosak, H. H., & Dreikurs, R. Adlerian psychotherapy. In R. Corsini (Ed.), *Current psychotherapies.* Itasca, IL: F. E. Peacock, 1973.

Schmidt, J. A. Cognitive restructuring: The art of talking to yourself. *Personnel and Guidance Journal*, 1976, *55*, 71–74.

CONSEQUENCES: AN ALTERNATIVE TO PUNISHMENT

Floy C. Pepper
Coordinator of the Emotionally Handicapped Program for Multnomah County Education Service District and an instructor in special education at Portland State University.

Mildred Roberson
An instructional consultant in the Emotionally Handicapped Program for Multnomah County Education Service District in Portland, Oregon. Mrs. Roberson is coauthor of several articles dealing with Adlerian techniques in the school and in the home involving troublesome children. Mrs. Roberson is cofounder, along with Floy Pepper, of the Rudolf Dreikurs Institute of Oregon, which is a nonprofit organization dealing with family and marriage counseling. She also acts as a consultant to school personnel concerning educational and behavioral matters.

The social order presents rules for living that all human beings must learn in order to function effectively. These rules can be valuable to the adult in getting children to see the relationship between their own acts and the result of their actions. The social order consists of a body of rules that operates on an impersonal level and must be learned and followed in order for the child and adult to function adequately.

We need to realize that today the adult can no longer "make" children behave, work, or do what is demanded of them (even for their own good). We cannot control our children; instead we need to guide them into becoming

Individual Psychology, 38(4), December, 1982, **pp. 387–397**

responsible individuals (Dinkmeyer & McKay, 1973). We cannot "teach" responsibility; we must give it to children and let them learn how to handle it. We must allow children to choose and then to accept the responsibility for their choice.

We need to realize that we can no longer impose our will on our children or control them, but need to guide them. Adults need to realize that old-fashioned punishments (spanking, slapping, etc.) are not nearly as effective as they seem to think they are or as they used to be in an authoritarian social order. Children believe that this type of punishment gives them the right to hit and slap others also. Usually adults become angry and the child is quick to sense the adult's frustration. The child responds negatively and then the adult is not successful in getting the child to change the behavior. Therefore, we need to use different techniques to motivate the child toward cooperation and more acceptable behavior. We need to win the child's cooperation.

The use of *logical consequences* is one of the most important techniques for improving the behavior of youngsters, insuring their cooperation, and having good relationships with them. The concept of consequences—natural, logical, punishment, and otherwise—has been a source of misunderstanding for both teachers and parents. This paper proposes to clarify the issues concerning consequences and will attempt to put the concept of consequences into a more workable framework.

NATURAL CONSEQUENCES

Natural consequences represent the natural flow of events without the interference of the adult. This concept was presented over a 100 years ago by Herbert Spencer. The principle states that no person will willingly do what he believes is harmful to himself. For example, if a child bumps his or her head or touches a hot stove, the natural response is to avoid that action the next time. Natural consequences, such as the discomfort of going without a coat in cold weather, provide a method for the adult to allow the child to learn from the natural order of events. Only in moments of real danger, such as a life-threatening or maiming situation, is it necessary to protect the child from the natural consequences of disturbing behavior. The adult does not threaten the child, argue, or concede, but rather permits the child to discover on his or her own the advantages of respect for order. Stimulation from without is replaced with stimulation from within. By experiencing consequences the child develops a sense of self-discipline, responsibility, and internal motivation.

> **Example.** Ward received a gift from his grandfather that he prized very much—a saw that had been used by him in his work of carpentry. Ward spent $2.50 of his own money to have it sharpened. Still after repeated warnings, he left it outside after a hard day of building his cabin in the backyard. The next day he found his prized saw all pitted with rust. Despite many tears and much rust remover, he now knows it will never be the same.

In the above example, the child learned to respect the order not because he was punished, but because he learned that order was necessary for effective functioning.

APPLIED CONSEQUENCES

An applied consequence is the application of imposition of a consequence by an adult for a misbehavior. The consequence is logical in that it relates to the behavior, but there have been no prior discussions or agreements, and the situation is taken care of on the spot.

> **Example.** Joe tracks mud into the kitchen. Mother tells him to mop it up. (Mother reacts quickly without prior discussion.)

> **Example.** Drexel has a habit of changing channels on the TV at the class "TV time" without class consent. The teacher decides that if Drexel can not let the other people watch the program of the group's choice, he will have to find another TV or get group consent. Without these two options available, Drexel is asked to leave the room if he does not want to watch the program that is on.

An applied consequence is what happens the first time a child misbehaves. Then later, the adult and child discuss the situation and agree on the consequences. Thereafter, the result is a logical consequence.

> **Example.** Joe and mother discuss Joe's tracking in mud. They agree that Joe is to leave his muddy shoes on the back porch thereafter, or he will have to mop the kitchen.

It requires perceptivity and skill to arrange effective consequences. There is a fine line of distinction between logical consequences and applied consequences. The successful application of logical consequences presupposes that the adult is a friendly bystander. An adult who feels threatened or defeated is in no position to use logical consequences because he or she is too involved personally.

The techniques of using logical consequences and personal disengagement depend on each other: One can not take place without the other.

> **Example.** It began some time ago as an applied consequence: One of the boys who had just washed but not dried his hair came down the hall dripping water all the way. He was asked to take a rag and clean it up. In a subsequent group discussion it was agreed upon by the group that this was a fitting consequence for such a behavior.
>
> I left Debby in the kitchen to finish rinsing her hair. When she appeared in the living room, hair dripping wet, I had her look back down the hall at the trail of water. "Do you remember when we discussed this in a meeting a couple of weeks ago?" I asked.
>
> "I forgot. I'll clean it up."
>
> "Thank you," I responded.

LOGICAL CONSEQUENCES

Logical consequences are guided. A logical consequence must be discussed with, understood, and accepted by the child; otherwise the child may consider it punishment. Children can quickly see the connection between their behavior and consequences if it is correctly presented. Most logical consequences can be turned into punishment if incorrectly applied.

If adults will use the following rules, they will usually have good results (Grey, 1972):

1. The consequences must be related to the misbehavior.
2. A choice must be given as often as possible. (It must be emphasized that if the consequence is used as often as possible, only one choice can be given: the choice between what children want to do and what they should do. Should the child refuse to make a decision, then the adult can say, "You are putting me in a position to make a decision for you!"

   > **Example.** Jim had a habit of being late to catch the bus. In fact, he liked to play games and have the bus driver look for him. The teacher, the bus driver, the parents, and Jim discussed the situation and decided that Jim could choose to be at the bus stop at the proper time or he could choose to walk home. The emphasis was on Jim's decision; the choice was Jim's.

3. If the voice is friendly, the consequences are more effective.

4. Don't say "I told you so." The quickest way to nullify the result of a consequence is to crow about it or to warn the child about it.
5. Don't use logical consequences where you can't—where danger is involved, or when the child is in a power conflict, is seeking revenge, or is assuming disability.
6. Understand the goal of the child. Logical consequences work best with the goal of attention getting. When children are seeking power or revenge, they are often so busy asserting their superiority over an adult or getting even with an adult that they do not care what results their actions incur. (Changing the relationship is more important in this case than having the child do the task.)

Consistent use of logical consequences is extremely effective and usually results in a decrease in friction and an increase in harmony, whether used in the classroom or in the home, with one person or with a group.

> **Example.** Running in the halls was against the school rules. Several of the children were seen running in the halls by teachers and other children in the class. The class discussed this problem and decided that anyone who was seen running in the halls would have to remain in class under supervision or would have to walk from place to place with an assigned person.

In many group situations, the other children will use logical consequences among themselves.

> **Example.** The children and the teacher agreed after a discussion that persons who splashed other children at the water table would have to leave that particular activity. Two days later, Tony splashed water at Steve while at the water table. Steve reminded him of the previous discussion. Two children joined Steve in the discussion, telling Tony he'd have to leave and go to another area. Tony put the water toys down and left.

Logical consequences are guided by an adult, but must be experienced by the child as logical in nature. The adult trusts the child to choose and to accept responsibility for his or her choice. Adults remove themselves from the position of authority by refusing to fight or to give in. Instead they let children experience the results of their misbehavior and assume responsibility for their actions. Sometimes children must experience the inconvenience of disorder before they can recognize order and the restrictions it imposes as beneficial and vital.

The best consequence can be turned into punishment through misapplication or too much talking. Most of our disciplining is done by coaxing, reminding, threatening, and punishing—which may destroy the effect of consequences—rather than by simply allowing children to experience the unpleasantness of their actions.

PUNISHMENT

I would like to digress from Dreikurs' concept of consequences and take a look at punishment. Webster defines *punish* as imposing a penalty on for a fault, offense, or violation or in retribution or retaliation; dealing with roughly or harshly. *Punishment* is defined as retributive suffering, pain, or loss; severe, rough, or disastrous treatment.

Punishment then, as viewed by most adults, is imposed by adults, and the consequence has no direct relationship with the misbehavior. The consequence may or may not involve physical punishment. (Sally spilled her milk: Mother slapped her. Joe tracked in mud: Mother isolated him in his room for two hours. John used his pocket knife to carve a deep slash in his desk: The teacher yelled at him, shook him, and sent him to the principal.)

The following example illustrates the type of an interaction that frequently takes place. The adult in such a situation usually doesn't understand why the child becomes resentful or defiant.

> **Example.** The newly repainted bathroom walls showed evidence of shoe marks belonging to two fifth-grade boys. When questioned about the matter, the boys admitted to marking the walls intentionally with their waffle-stompers. Their retribution was to work for the janitor during recess, cleaning the walls and toilets.

The cleaning of the walls where the boys made the footprints seems like a logical consequence to the adult, and he or she sees nothing wrong in adding an extra task so that the boys will learn a lesson. In reality, the cleaning of the walls is an applied consequence, while the cleaning of the toilets is punishment.

Adults must show children that they are interested in helping them, not in making them "pay for their crimes." We have no guarantee of how children perceive our actions; we have a much better chance of success if we make them aware that we do not enjoy their sufferings. When the adult continues to be friendly, the child senses that he or she is valued, even though the behavior is not.

Logical consequences must be used with no strings attached. If adults use logical consequences with the intention of forcing children to give in to their wishes, if they are unwilling to accept children's own choices, or if they attempt to manipulate through the use of logical consequences, children will perceive this. Instead of positive change in behavior and lasting results, the child will respond with fortified resistance. Perhaps an easier way to see the differences in these three types of consequences and punishment is in chart form (see Table 1).

Since logical consequences only work on the attention level and since we get into sticky situations with applied consequences and punishment, we need to examine other methods of solving conflict situations between children and adults.

SOLVING CONFLICT

In "Techniques of Conflict Solving," a chapter in *Maintaining Sanity in the Classroom* (Dreikurs, Grunwald, & Pepper, 1971), the authors stated:

> Whenever a child disturbs, actively or passively, a conflict arises. This tests the teacher's ability to resolve it. Without such skill, the conflicts continue even if a temporary peace has been established. The principles of problem solving in a democratic transaction are so important that each teacher should, almost automatically, be able to apply them.

TABLE 1
Consequences Versus Punishment

	Consequences			
	Natural	**Applied**	**Logical**	**Punishment**
Consequences	Flow naturally from child's action	Logical result of child's behavior	Logical result of child's behavior	Illogical result of child's behavior
Adult's Role	No interference	Imposes the results on the child	Guide the child into 2 options	Imposed the results on the child
Child's role	Has no choice	Has an implied choice	Has a choice	Has no choice and no alternative

Conflicts are inevitable whenever people live together. In the autocratic past, conflicts could only be resolved through a contest; the stronger won out, and decided the outcome, and the weaker had to accept it. This is no longer possible in a democratic setting. Recognizing the child's goals and helping him to change them is an integral part of problem solving. When we outline the basic principles of resolving conflicts, we will see that some of them have already been discussed, while others need further clarification. What are the principles?

1. One can no longer resolve any conflict by either fighting or giving in. Fighting or imposition violates respect for the child; and giving in, or permissiveness, violates the respect for the adult. In a democratic setting, conflicts have to be resolved by *mutual respect*. If a teacher does not know how to do that, she will find it difficult to deal effectively with conflict situations.
2. To resolve a conflict requires *pinpointing the issue*. Regardless of its content, it always implies a disturbed relationship. While the opponents may argue about a specific issue, they use the content of the conflict only to fight each other. It is always a question of who gives in or wins out, of status and prestige, or personal advantage or abuse. To be more specific: the real issue behind any conflict with a child is one of the four goals of his disturbin g behavior. Unless the teacher realizes this, she cannot understand the conflict. If she believes in various causes which are assumed to be behind his behavior, she cannot understand him nor the nature of the conflict.
3. All transactions between any two people are based on "agreement." True, this agreement is not necessarily a conscious one or one spelled out in any form, but it is an agreement nevertheless. If two people get into a fight, for whatever reason, it is so because both decided to fight. After all, they wouldn't have to fight if they were to decide not to. In this sense, what they do or don't do is by an unspoken agreement. In this sense, one can say that there is never any lack of communication or cooperation as is widely assumed. Whatever goes on between any two people, be it positive or negative, it requires full *agreement and cooperation.* If one doesn't agree, then the specific form of transaction which exists between them cannot continue. Therefore, any conflict solution requires a change in agreement. A new form of agreement and cooperation is needed if the transaction should be changed. The change of agreement requires the realization that one can only change oneself. One cannot expect a change from the other as long as one continues his own behavior.
4. Any new transaction requires establishing *mutual responsibility* and *participation in decision making*. In a democratic set-

> ting, nobody has the power to impose his will on the other and remain democratic. Nobody is willing to submit to demands and everybody feels entitled to decide what to do and to participate in decisions which affect him.

> Points 2, 3, and 4 require a clear understanding of how to deal with the four goals of children's misbehavior. In evaluating a teacher's effort to cope with a conflict situation, the points made above can serve as a yardstick. They indicate effective approaches and explain failures which are due to violation of the basic principles of conflict solving.

Natural consequences require no intervention, as has been noted above. Therefore, there is no methodology to their application on the part of the adult; the consequences just happen. The principles guiding the application of logical consequences have also been outlined. It is in the area of applied consequences, especially when there is not a harmonious relationship between child and adult, that a methodology needs to be defined.

In resolving conflict it is sometimes necessary to use three methods commonly used in business negotiations: agreements, arrangements, and contracts.

Agreement: An informal point of harmony intended to facilitate cooperation toward a given end. The time required to reach an agreement is usually brief; the method is verbal; the process is consensus. An agreement is readily reached when the atmosphere is healthy, feelings are mutually supportive, and goals are similar.

> **Example.** It took very little for Mike to get angry or upset. One day in group discussion, Mike related that he didn't like himself when he lost control and wanted to do something about it. The teacher asked Mike, "Could it be that you want your own way and want to control everyone and everything?"
>
> Mike responded with a sly grin and mumbled, "Yeah."
>
> The teacher then asked Mike, "When you get angry, is there anything that you can do that will help you work off your anger?"
>
> Together they came up with an agreement. Mike was going to try and catch himself getting angry and say to himself, "Aha, I caught myself." It wasn't long before the next incident occurred. Mike caught himself and was very surprised and pleased and let the teacher and the class know that he did it.

The above agreement implies that Mike can handle this behavior and shows a unique relationship between Mike and his teacher. Mike was therefore able to find a better way to handle his anger and frustration.

Arrangement: A formal statement, usually verbal, intended to delineate an agreement carefully. It requires a considerable effort, some compromise, and constant review. It is usually required when trust has yet to be freely exchanged and when goals have been divergent.

> **Example.** Jeff's report card this quarter showed several bad marks. Jeff's teacher discussed this with Jeff to determine why his grades were so low, especially in reading and math. It was determined that the reason was that he had not been turning in his assignments. The teacher explained that she had to follow certain rules and there were certain rules Jeff had to follow, "During this grading period the class had to turn in six written assignments. How many did you turn in?"
>
> "One!"
>
> "I will have to give other written assignments. What do you want to do about it? What are your intentions? Perhaps we could make some sort of arrangement which would help you. Can you think of anything?"
>
> Jeff replied, "I think if you would check my notebook each day I would keep my work up."
>
> The teacher replied, "I am willing to make that kind of an arrangement." This arrangement has worked well.

In the example above, the child experiences the consequences of his own behavior as well as the reality of having to make a decision and an effort to bring his behavior into the expected and acceptable limits of social living. The relationship between the adult and child may or may not be strained, but there may be a feeling of lack of trust.

Contract: A negotiated written document intended to specify, very clearly, the conditions involved and in which certain goals will be pursued. It is highly formal and is frequently used as a way for initiating the beginning of improving a poor relationship. It is not unusual to call upon a third party to assist in its pursuit.

Behavior Contract

Name:________________________
School:_______________________
Grade:________________________

It is agreed by all concerned that the following conditions will be met in an effort to help Randy improve his school behavior. We feel it is very important to Randy to be in school and we want him to attend class as long as his behavior contributes to a positive school experience for himself and his classmates. Randy will have two behaviors to bring under control:

1. Randy will raise his hand and gain permission before talking.
2. Randy will not engage in kicking or hitting other children.

To help Randy achieve these goals, the teacher will verbally reinforce Randy for producing the desired behavior. When Randy feels himself beginning to want to hit or strike out at others, he will remove himself to the "cooling off" corner (which is isolated from the rest of the room) until he feels he can return to his desk and continue with his task.

____________________	____________________
Date	Randy
____________________	____________________
Parent	Teacher
	____________________
	Principal

Quite often after the signing of a contract, it is helpful to shake hands in a businesslike manner. The use of arrangements and contracts are necessary in direct proportion to the degree of cooperation and trust in working relationships.

Many times a child will agree to a logical consequence because at that moment he or she is seeking attention (Goal 1) and feels cooperative and friendly. At other times, the child may be in a power conflict (Goal 2) and refuse to honor a previous decision of logical consequences. The adult needs to withdraw at the moment of conflict and then to set up negotiations *later* when the child and the adult have calmed down and the probability of reaching a workable solution is increased.

Most people who have a basic knowledge of Dreikurs' concept of consequences are in reality using applied consequences when they think they are using logical consequences; they find that it breaks down when the child goes beyond Goal 1. Goals 2 and 3 place the adult in a leadership role in the adult-child relationship. The adult has to be the leader of "what to do?" Otherwise the child will continue to use tactics of tyranny and what adults seem to fear most, disrespect.

We have discussed various possibilities for children to experience consequences that are closely related to their behavior, and that they usually accept without reservations and without considering themselves maltreated. Children will respond to logical consequences and they will usually abide by applied consequences, but they will fight back when punished.

REFERENCES

Dinkmeyer, D., & McKay, G. *Raising a responsible child*. New York: Simon & Schuster, 1973.

Dreikurs, R., Grunwald, B., & Pepper, F. C. *Maintaining sanity in the classroom*. New York: Harper & Row, 1971.

Grey, L. *Discipline without tyranny*. New York: Hawthorn Books, 1972.

FAMILY LIFESTYLE ASSESSMENT: THE ROLE OF FAMILY MYTHS AND VALUES IN THE CLIENT'S PRESENTING ISSUES

William G. Nicoll
Assistant professor in the counselor education program at the University of Cincinnati.

E. Clair Hawes
A counseling psychologist in private practice in Vancouver, British Columbia.

One of the family's basic developmental tasks is the socialization of children to fulfill roles both within the nuclear family and in outside social groups (Aldous, 1978). The family serves as the primary source from which the individual develops a sense of personal identity in relation to the world (Adler, 1958; Bowen, 1970; Minuchin, 1974). This socialization process involves the transmission of family values, attitudes, myths, and apperceptions regarding how one should best approach social, marital, and occupational roles. Personal growth in counseling, therefore, may be facilitated by assisting the client(s) in obtaining insight into dysfunctional myths and values derived from his/her family-of-origin and its effect upon present life adjustment. The client can then be assisted in making new decisions or developing new perspectives regarding his/her approach to life problems.

This article is the result of a project to develop a systematic counseling technique for assessing the impact of the Family Lifestyle on the client's present life

Individual Psychology, 41(2), June, 1985, **pp. 147–160**

difficulties. In particular, this technique is designed to elucidate specific values, attitudes, myths, and mistaken apperceptions developed within the family-of-origin which are adversely affecting the client's present functioning in social, occupational, and/or marital roles. The counseling technique developed combines aspects of the Adlerian individual lifestyle assessment technique (Eckstein, Baruth, & Maher, 1975) with the family genogram technique (Barnard & Corrales, 1979). The authors have found this approach to be useful in both individual and group counseling settings and to be applicable to marital and family counseling as well. Following a review of the principal concepts involved, lifestyle and genograms, the counseling technique will be described and a brief, illustrative case study presented.

THE FAMILY LIFESTYLE

Through the familial socialization process, each individual develops his/her own unique system of beliefs, values, and attitudes regarding him- or herself, others and his/her relationship to the world; that is, an Individual Lifestyle (Adler, 1956). Adler defined his concept of the Individual Lifestyle, or style of living, as based upon the individual's "law of movement"; that is, his/her particular set of attitudes, values, and apperceptions regarding life, goals in life, and how best to set about attaining these goals. The individual's Lifestyle is viewed by Adlerian counselors as a cognitive framework by which behaviors are selected, generally at a level of unawareness, that will move the individual toward his/her goals in life while avoiding behaviors or actions that would endanger his/her sense of value and belonging (Papenek, 1972).

Adler's development of the Individual Lifestyle concept was in part influenced by the earlier works of the sociologist Max Weber and his work on the Collective Lifestyles of groups (Ansbacher, 1967). Weber (1946) noted that members of different groups, subcultures, and cultures tended to share similar values, attitudes, and patterns of living that differentiated them from other groups or cultures. As an intermediate step between the development of the Individual Lifestyle as noted by Adler and the Collective Lifestyle of the cultural group(s) to which the individual belongs as noted by Weber, Deutsch (1967) has suggested the concept of the Family Lifestyle. This concept reflects the family's unique "biased apperceptions" (Dreikurs, 1967) of the outside world or society and the family's prescribed, as well as proscribed, approaches toward coping with and having a significant place in this world. The Family Lifestyle, then, represents the family's own shared values, myths, and attitudes regarding appropriate goals and behaviors for its members.

The concepts of Collective Lifestyle, Family Lifestyle, and Individual Lifestyle are interrelated. The individual's unique Lifestyle—or personality style—will of necessity reflect, to some extent, the Family Lifestyle within which it developed. Moreover, the Family Lifestyle will, in turn, reflect the particular Collective Lifestyle of the subculture(s) and culture to which it belongs. In partial support of this concept of the Family Lifestyle, one notes the large number of authors in the field of family therapy who have made similar observations. That is, when one analyzes a family system over several generations, one becomes aware of both functional and dysfunctional values, myths, and interactional patterns which have been transmitted from one generation to the next (Boszormenyi-Nagy & Sparks, 1973; Bowen, 1976; Ehrenwald, 1963; Framo, 1970; Trotzer, 1981; Whitaker & Keith, 1981).

Rhodes and Wilson (1981) have noted that from the day we are born until the day we die, families remain powerful influences whether the family members continue to be involved with one another or remain completely aloof. This is true even though the family is no longer a structured social unit with well defined roles. The structure of any family's shared identity or value system—i.e., Family Lifestyle—will be influenced by its history, myths, and the cohesive quality of the inter-relationships. The particular lifestyle or personality of individual members will, in turn, be affected by their perceptions of personal value within the family constellation, the justice of the family environment, and their sense of encouragement or discouragement as a family member.

The Family Lifestyle, as noted by Deutsch (1967), begins to develop in the early years of marriage in much the same manner as Adler noted that the Individual Lifestyle, or personality, begins to develop in early childhood. Each marriage joins a man and woman plus their respective family systems and Family Lifestyles. Often partners come to the marriage expecting to recreate, albeit with some improvements, their own family of origin's style of living. Each spouse may then strive, overtly or covertly, to gain preeminence for his or her particular family lifestyle. The successful resolution of this sometimes stormy and difficult period is the emergence of a unique couple or family identity. This new family identity, or Family Lifestyle, will reflect a synthesis of values, attitudes, and myths from each spouse's family of origin. Thus, the characteristic values and interaction patterns of past generations will have a significant impact upon the myths, values, and interaction patterns of present and future generations (Barnard & Corrales, 1979). As family relationships continue through the generations, the life of the family is extended almost infinitely (Rhodes & Wilson, 1981).

Family Myths and Values

The Family Lifestyle may be viewed as being comprised primarily of the shared values and myths of the family system. Boszormenyi-Nagy and Sparks

(1973) have discussed the importance of family values in terms of loyalty issues. Membership in a group, such as the family, requires that one, to some extent, internalize its value system. Each individual member develops a set of values and attitudes that comply with its internalized injunctions or rebel directly against them (i.e., the "black sheep"). Through such loyalty commitments, a sense of belonging or cohesion and having a significant place or role within the family system is provided. This process can be observed at a variety of levels, from the national or societal to the subcultural or ethnic group to the familial level. Viewed systemically, each level serves as a subsystem of the preceding larger subsystem and therefore reflects or incorporates in some way its value system as well. Thus, one important element of the Family Lifestyle is the shared value system of the family group.

The second major aspect of the Family Lifestyle is the "family myths" (Ferriera, 1963). Ferriera has defined family myths as "well integrated beliefs shared by all family members concerning each other and their mutual position in the family life" (p. 457). These myths tend to go unchallenged in spite of the distortions in reality which they typically incorporate. Thus, family myths specify the particular roles, attributes, and value of family members in their transactions with one another. Byng-Hall (1973) has suggested that such myths are of three types: (1) "ideal self-images," which are behaviors all members are pressured to adopt; (2) "consensus role images," which are the roles all agree each individual actually occupies; and (3) "repudiated role-images," which are proscribed behaviors and attitudes of the family. Dysfunctional family myths maintained by the client often serve to lock him/her into rigid roles and behavioral patterns throughout his/her life. It is important for counselors to assist such clients in reexamining these myths and adopting more functional or growth-oriented attitudes.

The importance of identifying significant family values and myths and their impact on a client's presenting issues is further indicated in Trotzer's (1981) observation that conflicts typically revolve around value/belief issues. While presenting problems may be defined in terms of role, behavioral, or individual dimensions, there is always an ultimate relationship with the value system of the individual or family (Trotzer, 1981). This view is also reflected in Adlerian psychology, which maintains that deviant, ineffectual, or conflict-creating behavior stems ultimately from dysfunctional or mistaken attitudes and values (Manaster & Corsini, 1982).

Contextual Family Therapy, as developed by Boszormenyi-Nagy, & Ulrich (1981), also recognizes the need to organize interventions around identifying and resolving conflict issues emanating from the transgenerational and cultural heritage of the family of origin. Boszormenyi-Nagy and Sparks (1973) note that members develop a sense of loyalty to the groups to which they belong and particularly to their family of origin. Since the family is the initial and primary source for meeting one's need to belong (Dreikurs, 1964), any behavior which then contradicts familial expectations or family myths and/or values might be viewed as threatening to one's sense of familial belongingness. Thus, the family value system and family myths tend to continue throughout life; that is, to influence, usually at a level of unawareness, each individual member's perceptions of self and his/her relationships to others and society.

FAMILY LIFESTYLE ASSESSMENT

Family myths and the family value system are the two primary components of the Family Lifestyle. One means by which these myths and values appear to be transmitted in the family socialization process is through family stories and descriptions of ancestors, siblings, and/or relatives. This process is similar to the transmission of culturally shared values and beliefs—i.e., the Collective Lifestyle—through folktales and children's stories. One example is "The Three Little Pigs," which substantiates the Protestant work ethic so dominant in our culture. In investigating the role of family myths and values in the client's presenting issues, it is therefore useful to focus upon these family stories and descriptions of extended family members.

Genograms

One method which has proven productive for focusing the counseling session on the influences of the Family Lifestyle—i.e., family myths and values—is the genogram. When combined with the conceptual approach of the Individual Lifestyle assessment (Eckstein, Baruth, & Naher, 1975; Mosak, 1977), the genogram provides the counselor with a logical and useful extension of the Adlerian counseling technique. Guerin and Pendagast (1976) have aptly referred to the genogram as a "roadmap of the family relationship system" (p. 452). It has been utilized in counseling to identify such problematic family issues as finances, sex, parenting, and affection (Guerin & Pendagast, 1976) as well as to give the counselor insight into attitudes regarding sex roles, occupational injunctions, divorce, family relationships, and the power and communication processes in families. For further information on the genogram one may refer to Barnard and Corrales (1979), Carter and McGoldrick (1980), and Paul and Paul (1982).

A further benefit of the genogram has been suggested by Orfandis (1979), who noted that clients frequently become interested in their genograms and are able to begin work themselves to obtain insight into their particular problem(s). Furthermore, the genogram technique has the benefit of appearing less "psychological" and mysterious to the client(s) than many other insight-oriented techniques such as projective testing. Reluctant clients, group members, or family members can therefore often be more readily "won over" to entering into the counseling process by being invited to share seemingly more factual information regarding their families of origin. This can be particularly beneficial in marital or family therapy with reluctant fathers. Shapiro and Budman's (1973) research has pointed out that the father's attitude toward and investment in counseling is the critical factor for both continuation and positive outcome in family counseling. Guerin and Pendagast (1976) have noted further that the genogram technique transforms the initial evaluation process into "an emotionally validating experience for the family and as such fosters the process of engagement" (p. 457).

The Family Lifestyle assessment technique utilizes the genogram along with the conceptual strategy of the Individual Lifestyle assessment technique to identify those dysfunctional aspects of the Family Lifestyle—i.e., shared values and myths—which adversely affect the client's present life adjustment. During an Adlerian lifestyle assessment, the counselor looks at the relationships within the family-of-origin to better understand the values, beliefs, role expectations, and biased apperceptions of the individual. Further, the counselor looks at early recollections, or early memories, as symbolically representing themes directly related to the client's current attitudes and approach to life and relationships (Adler, 1956; Mosak, 1958). Similarly, in assessing the Family Lifestyle the counselor and client utilize the family genogram to look at both relationship patterns and characteristics of extended family members, defined within the family-of-origin as being essentially positive or negative, to identify family values and family myths. Also, often repeated family stories regarding members and ancestors are interpreted much like early memories to identify themes which embody highly salient family values. The Family Lifestyle assessment, therefore, extends the Individual Lifestyle investigation vertically through several past generations and horizontally in terms of the extended family. This provides a greater understanding of the origins and, more important, the relative strength of family values and myths and the meaning they hold for the client.

The client(s) is first presented with a large sheet of newsprint and provided with instructions in developing a family genogram. After completing the genogram for three to four generations, the client(s) is instructed to go back over the data and, for each person represented, recall from his/her perspective as a child how the family tended to view that person and whether he/she was defined as a positive or negative model. The counselor then requests that the client provide recollections about stories told within the family regarding extended family members or ancestors. Often the client never met, or remembers little of, a particular relative or ancestor about whom family stories have been passed down through the generations. Embodied in such family stories, however, are strong family values regarding who or what they should or should not be in order to obtain a position of status, value, or significance within their family system. The descriptions of extended family members, on the other hand, tend to reveal myths regarding relationships and role prescriptions and injunctions. Thus, these family stories, as well as the client's personal recollections regarding family members, are found to reveal powerful family myths and values which the client has, in some manner, internalized and which continue to influence decisions and behavior in his/her current life situation.

Application in the Counseling Process

Upon completion of the genogram data, the client(s) is invited to share the information in the genogram with the counselor as follows: "Begin with yourself and tell us about each person you have put on the genogram." As the individual discusses the family, he or she often begins to see emerging patterns or to discover new insights. If not, the counselor may ask questions to lead the client toward significant themes: "Do you see any trends forming?" or "How do you feel about that information?" The degree to which each client has a pattern of similar issues, attitudes, or values across several generations is scrutinized. This knowledge provides the counselor and client with a better understanding of the impact these conclusions have on present functioning in occupational and interpersonal roles.

It has been the authors' experience that it is best to allow the client to lead, as much as possible, in exploring his/her genogram and the family stories. This allows the counseling session to become a mutual process between counselor and client(s). Moreover, it removes the counselor from the role of "omnipotent healer" expected to "cure my problems" and invites the client(s) to become an equal partner in counseling with equal responsibility for outcome. Having the graphic product of the genogram to view and reflect upon has also been found to increase the level of involvement and understanding for the client. Clients typically take the genogram home between sessions and spend considerable time reviewing and gaining new insights from their genograms and the descriptions and stories they have provided. The counselor intervenes when it becomes evident that the client is avoiding or overlooking significant value messages and myths appearing in the genogram and gently redirects the client to confront these issues.

The technique has proven particularly useful in group counseling and personal growth group work. The counselor can utilize input from the group to assist the client-on-focus in identifying messages regarding appropriate roles, behaviors, values, myths, and so forth. Further, in a group setting, clients find it growth-inducing to observe the broad range of family values and myths which occur. They are confronted, in a sense, with the undeniable subjectivity of their conclusions and approach to life. The Family Lifestyle assessment technique appears particularly amenable to several counseling/therapy situations for assisting clients to understand and reconsider the values and myths derived from their family of origin which may be affecting their current life situation. Some potential uses of this technique would be:

1. Individual counseling when unresolved issues with one's family of origin are apparent.
2. Premarital counseling to identify the rules, values, and myths that each spouse is bringing to the relationship. Thus, assistance might be given in assessing strengths while also noting potential problem areas which might be discussed on a preventive basis.
3. Marriage and family counseling to assist members to gain a better understanding of how and why problems are experienced as they are. Such knowledge can provide a sense of optimism that there is a positive direction yet to move in.
4. Sexual dysfunction often involves family of origin issues around sex which need to be explored (Kaplan, 1974, 1979; Masters & Johnson, 1970).
5. Enrichment or personal growth groups with individuals or couples to focus and redirect decisions around past messages, myths, and value systems that influence present personal and relationship satisfaction.
6. Couple enrichment where a more intense understanding of the meshing of family dynamics provides a sense of the accomplishments within the relationship that the couple has attained.
7. Divorce support groups where individuals can observe patterns they may have been following which result in difficulties in intimate relationships.

CASE STUDY

Marilyn was a thirty-six-year-old female, never married, who came to a personal growth group with specific concerns regarding her difficulty in developing satisfactory intimate relationships with men. After completing the genogram as instructed, Marilyn began the interpretive process. Pointing to each person on her genogram (figure 1) as she described them, she stated:

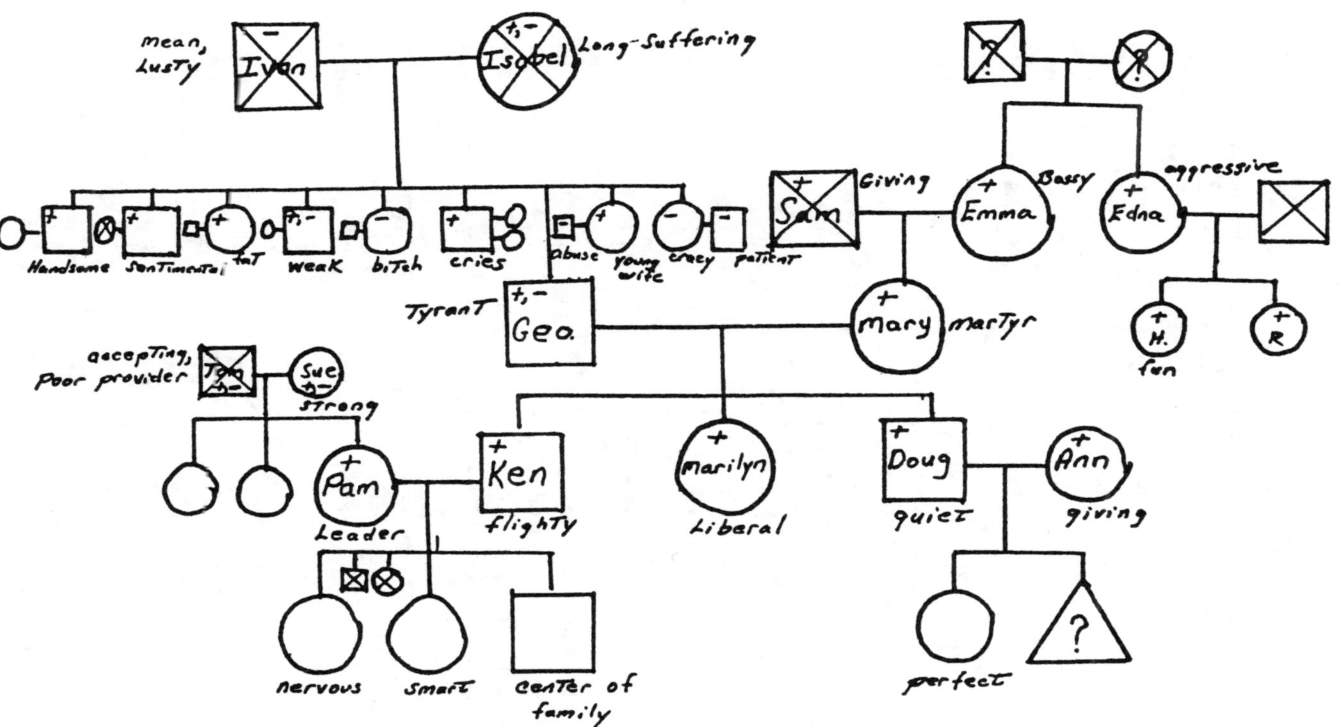

Figure 1. Marilyn's Genogram

"I'm 36; my older brother Ken is four years my senior and my brother Doug is eight years my junior, and we are the three siblings of Mary and George . . . Ken, first born, flighty, nervous, loving, preoccupied, successful. He is an officer going on twenty years in the army. I came next, four years later. The stories about me were always that Mom held her breath before I spoke, that I was before my time, that I was too liberal for the fifties when people wanted women to shut up and I wasn't shutting up . . . Doug came eight years later . . . The stories about him in the family revolve around his tremendous need for privacy. He is very quiet, he is very resourceful . . ."

Marilyn apparently began at an early age to express her goal in life of declaring her independence and resisting the possibility of being squeezed out or controlled by others, e.g., her two brothers. As she began describing the significant males on her genogram, a pattern emerged in which she regarded males as typically tyrannical, not particularly dependable or good providers, the source of family problems, and tending to be guided by their emotions. She particularly focused on her father and paternal grandfather as prototypical male figures especially in terms of their roles in intimate relationships with women. This was reflected in Marilyn's perception of her father and other men as being bigger than they are: "After a couple of years in therapy, the therapist said to me, 'How tall is your father?' and I said, 'Oh, about 6′1″; and he is shorter than I am [5′4″]. Amazing!"

Women, as Marilyn described them, generally were other-oriented and "fun" individuals. However, of central importance for her were two models, her mother and paternal grandmother, whom she viewed as long-suffering, used by men, and "martyrs" due to their marital relationships. This then was the family myth; women lose their independence and sacrifice their potential in intimate relationships because men tend to be tyrannical and domineering.

Reinforcing the strength of these family myths as perceived by Marilyn was a family story which conveyed an important family value for her. During her monologue the family story about Sam, her maternal grandfather, emerged as highly significant in her life.

"The story about him which breaks my heart is that apparently I was his favorite, and it seems I never walked until I was 18 months old. I would walk, but I wouldn't let go of his one finger. Then he died, and a week later I walked by myself. My mom always said, 'Your Grandpa wanted to see you walk.' That was a very dear story because even though I didn't know him, I knew that he loved me, and knew that I was always accepted by Sam. He was a homebody. Emma would go out and get into her political thing, and travel like crazy, and party and everything, while Sam was home, making the bread. A very giving man."

Fifteen minutes into her monologue, Marilyn stopped suddenly. As with most clients, she spontaneously began to make her own interpretations with minimal guidance. This high level of involvement of the counselee in the discovery/insight and redecision process is one of the unique strengths of the technique.

> **Counselor:** *What are you noticing, Marilyn?*
> **Marilyn:** *For years, I have thought that the man was the strong one, and I'm seeing a lot of strong women. They may be behind the scenes . . . I see a lot of aggressiveness, I mean, I have always loved Emma, and when I was growing up in the fifties, I wasn't supposed to be like Emma, I was supposed to keep my mouth shut and not talk about civil rights and not talk about sex. There was a whole list of things I wasn't allowed to talk about and that's why I got beat. But Emma, in my mind, was dynamic and had the fullest life of anybody. And I admired her. I also admired Sam, because he was where he wanted to be. He loved being home; he loved my mom. Emma had a hard time with Mom when she was born . . . she was really sad as she was not to have any more children. Sam said, "I don't ever want to lose my wife, I can't stand the possibility that you might die."*
> **C:** *I cannot live without my wife.*
> **M:** *Which is amazing because I thought I was the only one that wasn't married for other reasons. [Long reflective pause] For a long time I thought that men used women as victims, in similar ways that my dad used my mom. God knows, Emma was a survivor, she was such a stable person, as I am . . . I can't believe the strength of all of these women. I've never seen them all in front of me like this!*

The counselor's role was to then assist the client in focusing upon the issues that emerged as central messages. In Marilyn's case, a strong family value appeared to be conveyed in her story about Sam.

> **C:** *Going back to Sam and Emma. Not only was Emma somehow the epitome of the female, or what you are striving to be, but Sam was the one about whom the story gave the message, at a level of unawareness, "For Grandpa's love, let go of the finger. Once I let go of the finger, I am independent, walking alone, and I am finally being what Grandpa wants—to be more like Emma." I'm wondering if there is some concern with relationships with men in that you are afraid to grab hold of the finger again?*
> **M:** *Please say that again. [The counselor was close to the central point but needed to restate it more clearly in the client's language.]*
> **C:** *There is a sense of, "If I get into a close relationship with a man, I am holding on to his finger again." Going back to the story up here, you are afraid of losing something . . .*

M: *Oh, yes!!*

C: *It seems you are starting to recognize now that sometimes men are holding on to your finger more than you are holding on to their's.*

M: *That's funny. Oh, Lordy! But I always felt like I was the weak one, like I needed them, and I was damned if I was going to do that because when I have, I've gotten stepped on. I didn't realize my own strengths . . . Oh, I'm so glad this is on tape, I don't want to lose this. That is interesting you should say that about Sam and letting go of his finger.*

C: *Your whole life is trying to somehow show him, "I'm walking alone."*

M: *Wow!! Oh, Sammy baby! [recognition laughter] I've never seen this before. You know, when your dad beats the hell out of you and tells you to keep your mouth shut, that is pretty powerful.*

C: *Why did your dad have to beat you?*

M: *Because I wouldn't keep my mouth shut.*

C: *You were not going to let some man tell you to keep your mouth shut.*

M: *Yeah! And Ken, Kenny would stand over there in back of Dad as Dad was coming at me, and Kenny, my God, he is the biggest peace maker . . . he would whisper, "Mar, cool it."*

C: *So here was another man you weren't going to have tell you what to do.*

M: *Very good! And I've done anger work regarding Ken too. My God, isn't that something!!*

Marilyn had recognized that in spite of much individual therapy in previous years she still had little insight into the myths derived within her family-of-origin regarding male and female roles and her strong family value on independence which, in combination, had led her to avoid intimate relationships. Since this Family Lifestyle assessment was done in a time-limited personal growth group experience, there was not opportunity for Marilyn to work further on redirecting her perceptions and intimate relationships with men. However, like many other participants in these groups, she later sought out further counseling to work on issues which surfaced during the investigation into family myths and values.

As illustrated in the above case study summary, a powerful counseling technique results when the family genogram is approached from the perspective of the Adlerian Individual Lifestyle assessment. Specifically, clients are assisted in working with the therapist to obtain insight into the influence of family myths and family values, as perceived by the individual, on their current perceptions of self and functioning in social, occupational, and marital roles. The technique can be highly beneficial to counselors and therapists in assessing, with the client, current mistaken apperceptions, attitudes, and values as they relate to presenting issues. The counselor or therapist can then assist in helping to redirect the client in more positive and useful directions. Often the models for this more productive view of self and relationships exist in the client's genogram itself. The most powerful aspect of the technique may well be the client's ability to become actively involved through a tangible object, i.e., the genogram, in discovering new insights into dysfunctional familial influences. Clients can then make new decisions about and use new behaviors in their lives.

REFERENCES

Adler, A. (1956). *The Individual Psychology of Alfred Adler*. H. Ansbacher & R. Ansbacher (eds.). New York: Basic Books.

Adler, A. (1958). *What life should mean to you*. New York: G. P. Putnam's Sons. (Original work published 1931).

Aldous, J. (1978). *Family careers: Developmental change in families*. New York: J. Wiley & Sons.

Ansbacher, H. (1967). Life style: A historical and systemic review. *Journal of Individual Psychology, 23*(2), 191–211.

Barnard, C. P., & Corrales, R. G. (1979). *The theory and technique of family therapy*. Springfield, Ill.: Charles C. Thomas.

Boszormenyi-Nagy, I., & Sparks, G. M. (1973). *Invisible loyalties*. New York: Harper & Row.

Boszormenyi-Nagy, I., & Ulrich, D. (1981). Contextual Family Therapy. In G. S. Gurman & D. P. Kniskern (eds.), *Handbook of family therapy*. New York: Brunner/Mazel, 187–225.

Bowen, M. (1976). Theory in the practice of psychotherapy. In P. Guerin (ed.), *Family therapy*. New York: Gardner Press.

Bowen, M. (1970). Toward the differentiation of a self in one's own family. In J. Framo (ed.), *Family interaction: A dialogue between family researchers and family therapists*. New York: Springer.

Byng-Hall, J. (1973). Family myths used as defence in conjoint family therapy. *British Journal of Medical Psychology, 46*, 239–250.

Carter, E. A., & McGoldrick, M. (1980). *The family life cycle: A framework for family therapy*. New York: Gardner Press.

Deutsch, D. (1967). Family therapy and lifestyle. *Journal of Individual Psychology, 23*, 217–223.

Dreikurs, R. (1967). *Psychodynamics, psychotherapy and counseling*. Chicago: Alfred Adler Institute.

Dreikurs, R. (1964). *Children: The challenge*. New York: Hawthorn Books.

Eckstein, D., Baruth, L., & Maher, D. (1975). *Lifestyle: What it is and how to do it*. Chicago: Alfred Adler Institute.

Ehrenwald, J. (1963). *Neurosis in the family and patterns of psychosocial defense*. New York: Harper & Row.

Ferriera, A. (1963). Family myth and homeostasis. *Archives of General Psychiatry, 9*, 457–463.

Framo, J. L. (1970). Symptoms from a family transactional viewpoint. In N. W. Ackerman, J. Lieb, & L. K. Pearce (eds.), *Family therapy in transition*. Boston: Little Brown.

Guerin, P. T., & Pendagast, M. A. (1976). Evaluation of a family system and genograms. In P. Guerin (ed.), *Family therapy*. New York: Gardner Press.

Kaplan, H. S. (1974). *The new sex therapy*. New York: Brunner/Mazel.

Kaplan, H. S. (1979). *Disorders of sexual desire*. New York: Brunner/Mazel.

Manaster, G. J. & Corsini, R. J. (1982). *Individual Psychology: Theory and practice*. Itasca, Ill.: F. E. Peacock.

Masters, W. H. & Johnson, V. E. (1970). *Human sexual inadequacy*. Boston: Little, Brown and Company.

Minuchin, S. (1974). *Families and family therapy*. Cambridge, Mass.: Harvard University Press.

Mosak, H. H. (1958). Early recollections as a projective technique. *Journal of Projective Techniques, 22*, 302–311.

Mosak, H. H. (1977). *On purpose*. Chicago: Alfred Adler Institute.

Orfandis, M. M. (1979). Problems with family genograms. *American Journal of Family Therapy, 7*, 74–76.

Papenek, H. (1972). The use of early recollections in psychotherapy. *Journal of Individual Psychology, 28*, 192–202.

Paul, N., & Paul, B. (1982). Death and changes in sexual behavior. In F. Walsh (ed.), *Normal family processes*. New York: Guilford Press.

Rhodes, S., & Wilson, J. (1981). *Surviving family life*. New York: G. P. Putnam's Sons.

Shapiro, R. & Budman, S. (1973). Defection, termination, and continuation of family and individual therapy. *Family Process, 12*, 55–56.

Trotzer, J. P. (1981). The centrality of values in families and family therapy. *International Journal of Family Therapy, 3*, 42–55.

Weber, M. *Essays in sociology*. (1946). Trans. & ed. by H. Gerth & C. Mills, New York: Oxford University Press.

Whitaker, C. A. & Keith, D. V. (1981). Symbolic-experiential family therapy. In A. Gurman & D. Kniskern (eds.), *Handbook of family therapy*, New York: Brunner/Mazel.

ADLERIAN FAMILY THERAPY: AN INTEGRATIVE THERAPY

Don Dinkmeyer
President of Communication and Motivation Training Institute,
Coral Springs, Florida.

Adlerian family therapy is based upon a theory of human behavior originally developed by Alfred Adler and later expanded by Rudolf Dreikurs. Adler recognized that most individual problems were social in nature.

The central theme of Adlerian psychology is based upon the beliefs that people are indivisible, social, creative, and decision-making beings whose beliefs and behavior have a purpose. Thus, the individual is best understood holistically. Thoughts, feelings, and beliefs unfold in a consistent and unified pattern of action.

Adlerian psychological principles particularly applicable to family therapy include the following:

1. Social interaction. All behavior has social meaning. Each of us is socially embedded in an interactive social system. We are a continuous influence upon each other. Any movement by the individual or the family creates movement in all other components of the system.

Satisfying human relationships require effective interpersonal skills. Social interaction is not an option, it is a requirement. Family therapy can teach family members practical procedures for relating within the family, and then into the larger systems of school, work, and society. Adlerian family therapy is a process

Individual Psychology, 42(4), December, 1986, **pp. 471–479**

that provides opportunities to learn or relearn. The family therapist often prescribes a regular family meeting as a process for increasing the opportunities for positive interactions between members of the family (Dinkmeyer & McKay, 1976).

Humans are social beings and their behavior is always best understood within a specific social context. They seek to find their place in the group, to "belong."

2. Purposive behavior. Purposiveness is the basic tenet of Adlerian psychology. Behavior is teleological movement toward a goal. Movement and actions of the individual reveal the individual's purpose or intentions. Thus, behavior that at first appears to be confusing becomes understandable once the goal is known.

The therapist observes transactions and involvement, and offers tentative hypotheses. As we influence the family member's goals and beliefs, we begin to influence his or her behavior. The therapist attempts to influence subjective goals and mistaken perceptions of each family member and the family unit. If the goal is valued and useful but methods are lacking, the next step is to examine the methods and find a more satisfactory way of moving toward the goal. For example, the goal of family fun may be resented when the father autocratically decides the "fun" activity. The family meeting is an alternate way of discussing possible activities.

This approach is differentiated from a causal orientation. Adlerians believe that the goal itself, because it gives direction and meaning, can be regarded as the final cause.

Understanding each family member's beliefs and goals has a strong effect on understanding the family dynamics. As beliefs and goals that direct behavior are identified, it is possible to predict behavior in a given social setting.

3. Unity, pattern, holism. The individual cannot be understood except as a unified whole. We need to understand all aspects of a person's beliefs and perceptions as they relate to unique goals. Isolated events are understood in relationship to the total pattern and movement toward the goal. Adlerians believe that our movement is intentional, and that we are responsible for our behavior.

4. Striving for significance. The purpose of behavior is to overcome feelings of inferiority and to attain feelings of superiority. As humans we have inferiority feelings that emerge in childhood. As we develop, we become aware that we are truly insignificant when compared to the universe. This brings about our continuous striving to overcome the challenges of life: work, social, sexual, self, and spiritual. Our motivation is a continuous desire to overcome feelings of inferiority,

to compensate through striving to achieve. We continuously work from a minus to a plus.

A person's behavior, perceptions, attitudes, and ways of relating clarify how that person believes he or she fits into the social system. How each of us seeks to achieve significance is clearly reflected by how we seek to be known. We are creative beings. Our actions are based upon our subjective perceptions. We do not merely react.

5. Subjective perceptions. Behavior is a result of our subjective perceptions. The therapist understands the perceptions of the family members, which are responsible for their subjective views of life and give all their experiences meaning. Thus, as one sees the world so does one act in it, and the subjective beliefs guide the movement of the individual. For example, a marital separation is an event that has a different, self-created meaning for each family member.

The Adlerian system places great emphasis upon the family atmosphere. It is primarily during childhood that the family becomes an influence on the development of the personality. A person's sense of self, human relationships, and how he or she relates to the world is influenced by the family atmosphere.

6. Family constellation. The family constellation refers to the birth order of each child. The child's position in the constellation provides a unique perspective on social relationships. Adlerians recognize that the meaning a person gives to position in the family is of greater importance than the ordinal position. The family constellation position may be influenced by factors such as emotional ties between family members, age differences, sex of siblings, characteristics of each sibling, alliances of the parents and the relationship between the parents.

7. The life-style. Life-style refers to the person's basic orientation to life, the pattern of perceptions unique to the individual. Life-style is first influenced by family constellation and family atmosphere. The central goal of life-style is termed the fictional goal. This goal influences and organizes our experiences and behavior.

Family therapists must be aware of the life-style. As life-styles become evident, it is important to see how they mesh and interrelate with other life-styles to form a family life-style.

8. Social interest. Adler believed that social interest was the measure of mental health insofar as it reflected the individual's capacity to give and take, the willingness to participate and cooperate for the common benefit of the group. In the

family it is important to understand the family members' willingness to work with each other and give up their personal preferences for the family good. Social interest thus is a measure of the individual's sense of belonging.

STRUCTURE OF ADLERIAN FAMILY THERAPY

Adlerian family therapy establishes a plan or goal for each session. This plan is based on the therapist's understanding of the goals, intentions, and beliefs of each family member. The therapist then focuses on transactions between the members of the family to help them move toward more active-constructive behavior.

A major task in family therapy is goal alignment between family members as well as the therapist. Family therapy becomes an opportunity for the family to become involved in cooperation, building self-esteem, to enable themselves to see conflicts, to develop a sense of humor, and to increase their social interest.

Adlerian family therapists emphasize trusting psychological movement and its meaning. For example, a family member says one thing and does the opposite. The person's behavior is in line with his goals, even though he might not be aware of it at the moment or may deny the goal.

THE INITIAL INTERVIEW

The initial interview establishes the nature of the relationship and what family members can expect. The therapist deals with various members of the family to get some ideas about their priorities, attitudes, and beliefs. It is important from the very start to make some kind of contact or connection with each member of the family system. This is done by asking them to tell a little bit about their perception of the problem and by understanding their meanings, feelings, and beliefs.

Even though young children may not understand the purpose for being there, it is important from the start to respect them and to get some idea about how they see relationships.

In this initial phase the therapist is seeking answers to the following questions, even though they usually are not presented formally.

1. What does each person want to happen in the family relationship?
2. What does each family member see as the main challenge or issue faced by the family?
3. Are family members aware that the purpose of the session is to focus on change, not merely complaining?
4. What does it feel like for each person to live in this family?
5. Identify the family atmosphere. Is it autocratic, democratic, or permissive?

At this point the therapist also collects family constellation information. It is important to identify the position of both father and mother in their original families and how they perceive their positions. It is interesting to note that parents often have the most conflict with children who are in the same position that they were in as children. For example, the father was an oldest child; is he having problems with the oldest child in this family?

The therapist begins to identify the roles that various members play in the family. Do the family members have restricted roles or do they function in a variety of tasks? Are there boundaries that have been set up? How confined do they feel to their roles?

Adlerian family therapy observes and notes certain family faults and weaknesses. However, even more important is the diagnosis and identification of the assets of the family. From the very first contact the therapist is asking: What are the general assets of the family as a unit? What are the assets of each family member? How can these assets blend into the family system?

DIAGNOSIS IN FAMILY THERAPY

The therapist is interested in identifying goals of the family and the transactions that are the result of the goals and beliefs. There is also an investigation of the priorities and how they influence certain characteristic patterns. Adlerians investigate the private logic and goals with tentative hypotheses. The therapist suggests to an individual or the family as a whole some hunches in a tentative manner, "Could be . . ." or "Is it possible . . ." and alludes to the goal and pattern of behavior.

In the diagnostic procedure the therapist identifies who is seeking change. More important, is he or she willing to change? What is the type of change he or she desires for the family or individuals in the family and the change he or she wants in him- or herself? Resistance is understood as purposeful behavior. What does the person get from the resistance?

Encouragement is the most important technique to promote change. Most interpersonal problems are the result of discouragement. Encouragement is the process of building the individual's self-esteem, enabling him or her to be more able to cooperate with other members of the family. The encouraging family therapist plays a significant role during the diagnostic phase of therapy. Instead of focusing only on the pathology, liabilities, and weaknesses, the therapist is equally interested in strengths, assets, and resources. The therapist becomes a "talent scout," identifying assets that will enable family members to deal more effectively with the challenges of living.

The therapist learns to look for and affirm any positive movement or involvement. He or she is able to see the positive side in anything that first appears to be negative.

TEACHING FAMILY SKILLS

Adlerian family therapists often put an emphasis on helping the family solve problems by acquiring skills. The traditional Adlerian method is the family meeting. This is an opportunity for the family to make decisions together in a regularly scheduled meeting of all family members. The purpose is to make plans, provide encouragement, and solve problems. Family meetings insure that all family members will have a weekly forum in which to be heard and listen to each other.

In other instances, the family therapist will help with family conflict resolution procedures. The steps suggested in the conflict resolution process (Dinkmeyer & Carlson, 1984) include:

1. Show mutual respect by listening carefully and acknowledging that the other person has a point.
2. Pinpoint the real issue. Identify the priority that seems to be dominant, whether it be status, prestige, or the need to control.
3. Seek areas of agreement by concentrating on what you're willing to do, making no demands that other members of the family change and agreeing to cooperate rather than fight.
4. Mutually participate in decisions where all feel they are a part of the decision-making process.

Nicoll and Hawes (1985) have recently suggested a process for Family Life-Style Assessment. This concept deals with the family life-style, which is the family's unique and biased perceptions. The family life-style represents the family's own shared values, myths, and attitudes regarding appropriate goals and behavior for its members.

According to Nicoll and Hawes (1985), the family life-style may be understood through noting shared values and myths of the family system.

A method that has proven productive for focusing on the influences of family lifestyle, i.e. family myths and values, is the genogram. Combined with the life-style assessment, the genogram provides a logical, helpful extension for Adlerian family therapists. A genogram then becomes a road map to the family relationship system.

In assessing the family life-style, the genogram helps the members look at both the relationship patterns and characteristics of family members defined within the family of origin. It also seeks to identify family values and family myths. Family stories are interpreted often like early memories to identify things that embody basic family values. The family life-style assessment therefore extends into the life-style investigation. This provides a greater understanding of the origins and, more important, the role of the strength of family values and myths and the meaning they hold for the client (Nicoll & Hawes, 1985).

TECHNIQUES IN ADLERIAN FAMILY THERAPY

This section will provide a brief overview of technique.

1. There is a focus on understanding and influencing psychological movement. The therapist is concerned not only with what is said but specifically with what people do and their nonverbal communication. Transactions between people help us to understand their goals, priorities, and beliefs.

2. There is intensive work with the methods that the family members currently use to communicate with each other. Often a therapist will note that communication seems to be from superior to inferior positions. Families are encouraged in their communication to focus on what is positive and encouraging. Therapists make some simple communication rules:

a. Each person speaks for himself.
b. Speak directly to each other, not through the therapist or some other person in the family.

c. Listen and be empathic to the feelings and beliefs of other members of the family.
d. Do not look for someone to blame.

3. Focus on the real issue. Therapists observe transactions and interactions to identify the purpose of what is being communicated. At the same time they identify how these patterns and beliefs influence the behavior of the family. It is essential to identify the real issue, not the symptom. The real issue may often align itself with priorities such as being in control, being superior, getting even, or showing power.

4. Encouragement. Encouragement is demonstrated early by the therapist's interest in identifying assets and strengths, not just weaknesses and problems. The therapist often encourages by being empathic to all members of the family. Family therapy itself is encouraging insofar as it includes some of the following characteristics:

a. Each person now feels he or she is listened to.
b. Members of the family are intentionally empathic and understanding.
c. There is a focus on the strengths, assets, and resources of relationships.
d. Perceptual alternatives are developed, first by the therapist and then by members of the family. Members learn to recognize there are positive ways to look at any negative situation.

5. Confrontation of the private logic. The private logic includes the goals, ideas, and attitudes. In a sensitive and perceptive manner, the therapist enables members of the family to be aware of the discrepancies between their behavior and their intentions, their feelings and the feelings they reveal, their insights and their actions. Confrontation thus is used to stimulate therapeutic movement by mirroring to the family members their mistaken goals.

6. Paradoxical intention. Paradoxical intention or antisuggestion persuades the person to produce the symptom he or she appears to be complaining about. The symptom is actually prescribed and the person is encouraged to become even more "symptomatic." The paradox helps to reframe the system. It changes the entire meaning given to a situation.

7. Role reversal. Many family members do not understand how their behavior is perceived by others. In role reversal each person is asked to act as if he or she were the person he or she is in conflict with. Then he or she is asked to express as clearly and honestly as possible how he or she believes that person perceives the relationship between themselves, the family, and how people are working

together. The person who is having a role reversed then has an opportunity to react by indicating which parts of the role reversal were accurate and which parts were not in line with his or her thinking.

8. Resistance and goal alignment. Resistance in family therapy is usually best understood as a lack of common goals between therapist and family. Aligning goals so that they are all moving toward the same purpose is basic to bringing about change. Family therapy is complicated when one parent is concerned about the children's academic achievements while the other pushes athletics and the son or daughter is mainly interested in social life. In such a set of confused purposes, the therapist helps the family find areas of agreement to compromise so that they can live together more cooperatively.

9. Setting tasks and getting commitments. The therapist works with the family to establish certain tasks and commitments to specific changes that the family and individual members indicate they desire. Task setting begins in the first session, where each member is asked to state his or her goals and what he or she would like to see changed. The more specific the task, the more readily it can be accomplished. Family members make specific contracts and are expected to share progress made at the next meeting.

10. Summarizing. Summarizing is a way of verbalizing the perceptions of members of the family and looking at the theme of the session. The therapist may decide to have a summary at the close of the session in which family members summarize what they have learned. The therapist also summarizes and clarifies commitments and tasks.

SUMMARY

Adlerian family therapy is unique in the following:

1. There is a continuous focus on promoting active, constructive behavior, and on watching closely for any progress or movement that can be encouraged.

2. Family members learn that they must change themselves before there is any attempt to change other members of the family. Self change always facilitates relationship change.

3. The therapist helps the family learn effective problem-solving techniques. Family therapy has an educational component.

REFERENCES

Dinkmeyer, D., & Carlson, J. (1984). *Time for a better marriage.* Circle Pines, MN: American Guidance Service.

Dinkmeyer, D. C., & McKay, G. D. (1976). *Systematic training for effective parenting.* Circle Pines, MN: American Guidance Service.

Nicoll, W. G., & Hawes, E. C. (1985). Family lifestyle assessment: The role of family myths and values in the client's presenting issues. *Journal of Individual Psychology, 41*, 147–160.

FAMILY COUNSELING: A DEMONSTRATION[1]

Rudolf Dreikurs
Emeritus professor of psychiatry, Chicago Medical School, and founder of the Alfred Adler Institutes in Chicago and Tel-Aviv, the Community Child Guidance Centers of Chicago, as well as the *Individual Psychology Bulletin* which he also edited and which was the forerunner of the present Journal. He devoted his life to the propagation of Adlerian thought through teaching and demonstrations throughout the world. He was the author of numerous books and articles translated into many languages.

The participants are: the father (Mr. F.), the mother (Mrs. F.), the 17-year-old daughter (Sally), the 11-year-old son (Mike), and the co-counselor, Mr. Robert L. Powers (Mr. P.).

We often have 2 counselors in our guidance centers. It was the original development in Vienna where we usually had a physician and a psychologist co-counseling. The whole method of co-counseling began in Vienna under Adler in the 20's, and we do it very often here too. Today Bob Powers is helping me out as much as might be necessary. We have limited time, and we have to go pretty fast.

Dr. D.: *Now I should like to ask you, Sally, with whom should we talk first, with your parents or with you?*
Sally: *With my parents.*
Dr. D.: *Is this all right?* (General nodding. The children leave the room.

---

[1]Demonstration at the Fourth Brief Psychotherapy Conference, Chicago Medical School, Chicago, March 24–25, 1972.

Journal of Individual Psychology, 28(2), November, 1972, **pp. 207–222**

Dr. D. turning to the parents.) *Will you tell us please what your problems are and why you came?*
Mr. F.: *Why we came here today? Well, actually we didn't know what we were coming into when we came here today.*
Dr. D: *Huh! Didn't people tell you anything?*
Mr. F.: *We were told we were coming to a family counseling service. We did not know we were going to be a demonstration group. It's a little bit of a disappointment in that respect.*
Mr. D.: *So would you like to go home?* (Mrs. F. whispers, "Yes.")
Mr. F.: *For myself I can take it, for my wife and my family, I don't know.*
Dr. D.: *If you don't want to be here you can go home.*
Mrs. F.: *We felt that if this could help our son we would be glad to participate.*
Dr. D.: *Ah, you see, this is a demonstration. It's a class. Most of the counseling which I do is a demonstration. You learn something, and they learn. So if you don't mind, I shall explain what goes on to the audience, and have a discussion with them, while I talk with you. Is this alright?*

You see there are a number of these little things which are very effective and in which we train our students. Here you have something which is characteristic of this new technology of which I spoke earlier. In our child-guidance work with parents we bring a new psychology, a new technology, into the family. And its main point is to replace the traditional form of argument, of pressuring and so on, with stimulation from within.

I just did something which is extremely important. I don't know whether any of you realize the significance of what I did. I told Mrs. F. she could go home. Instead of saying to yourself, "I have to calm her or pressure her," you must give her a chance to leave. Hardly ever will a mother leave, once she has come, because she realizes there is something that might benefit her family. I have seen it time and again. In one particular case there was a large hall of 500 people. The mother didn't want to come, but she didn't want to let the father go alone either. So she came with him and sat there quietly. And after about ten minutes she began to talk—and couldn't be shut up. (*Some laughter.*) These are the kinds of arrangements where you achieve stimulation from within, instead of pressure from without.

Dr. D.: *Now what is the problem? Are you ready to discuss the problem with me?*
Mrs. F.: (Not audible.)
Dr. D.: *Yes, but you must talk loud enough that one can hear you.*

What is the problem?

Mrs. F.: (Whispering) . . . *I guess.*

Mr. F.: *Well, our son has a behavior problem in school, although that's just a small part of it. The behavior problem developed into a situation where he would go into a rage, and he would be uncontrollable. This has never happened in my presence so I haven't really seen. . . .*

Dr. D.: *Well where is he uncontrollable? At school?*

Mr. F.: *At home mostly, although at school he has been so disruptive in class for the past three years that he has been in what is called an ERA class, an Early Remedial Assistance class. This year for the first time he has been put into a regular class. I don't know if it's the pressure from the regular class or pressures at home or what.*

Dr. D.: *I'm interested in that you said, you yourself have never seen him in a rage.*

Mr. F.: *Well I've seen him wild, but never in these actual rages where he has in one or two instances threatened to take pills . . .*

Mrs. F.: *. . . and kill himself. He's also threatened to kill himself by drowning.*

Dr. D.: *Did he tell you so? And what is your answer?*

Mrs. F.: *Well, at first I used to fight him and then I told him to go ahead and do it.*

Dr. D.: *Has he diminished his threat?*

Mrs. F.: *Well, when he first started threatening, there was a point when I didn't know what to do. The first time he did it, he took most of his clothes off—we have an upstairs and down—threw them down the stairs at me, and said, "I don't want anything you gave me, and I'm going to kill myself." And I told him not to be funny. But he locked himself in the bathroom and said he's going to drown himself. So he filled the sink with water and stuck his head in it. But he couldn't because he happens to be a terrific swimmer. And he came out and laughed and said: "I couldn't do it if I wanted to, because I couldn't keep my head under the water." And I said okay.*

Dr. D.: *Good.*

Mrs. F.: *I hope he can't hear me. The door is open. But he came out soaking wet, and finally when I did get him calmed down, he had taken . . . I don't remember if this was the same time he took his bottle of medication, which then was Ritalin, and threatened to take the whole thing. I chased him all over the house to take it away from him. But after a while I realized that I would just stop chasing him and tell him to go ahead and take it and I'll take him to the hospital and have his stomach pumped out. So he quit doing that.*

Now, here you have the whole situation. We are always accused of improper procedure because we immediately jump to conclusions. When I see a patient or a client, after the first few sentences I know what goes on. This is only possible when you accept that behavior is purposive. Whatever a child does is for a purpose. We described the four goals of the disturbing behavior of a child. The child wants to belong, but gets the wrong idea about how he can belong, and then he switches from the useful way of belonging to the useless side and disturbs. Without knowing the four goals, neither parents nor teachers are a match for him. They don't know what goes on. They fall for him. They do exactly what he wants them to do. And so the child manages the parents and the teachers.

The first goal is, he wants special attention. He prefers the attention in a nice way but if he can't get it, he disturbs. He would rather be scolded, threatened, and punished than be ignored.

When the fight becomes more intensive, the child moves to Goal 2, power. He will show you, "If you don't let me do what I want, you don't love me. I will see to it that you do what I want, but I don't do what you want." We are raising in America a whole generation of tyrants. Tell them what to do and they don't do it. Tell them what not to do and they feel honor-bound to do it.

When the fight becomes more intense, the child is no longer interested merely in attention and power. He wants revenge, Goal 3. He thinks he can have a place only when he can hurt you back as much as he believes he was hurt.

And then we find Goal 4, where the child is so discouraged that he wants to be left alone because he doesn't think anything can be done.

Now one of the ways by which we train parents and teachers to recognize the goal of the child, is by showing them that not merely by observing what the child does can they see in which direction he moves, but also by their responses to his actions. This is actually the best way to recognize the child's goal, namely to watch your immediate reaction to his provocation. When you get annoyed, the chances are he wanted attention. When you feel defeated, he wanted power. When you feel humiliated, hurt, he wanted revenge. And when you feel like throwing up your hands and saying, "I don't know what to do with you," you do exactly what the child wants you to do—"Leave me alone, you can't do anything with me." And thus most adults trying to correct the child's behavior do in their immediate reaction the worst possible thing: They reinforce the mistaken goal of the child.

It is quite obvious from the description we heard that this boy has the power over his mother. "I will show you, you either do what I want, or else." So my first impression is that the mother and the one who does it most often, the teacher, get into a power conflict with the child. Whenever you fight with a child you have lost before you even start. The child is a much better fighter, he can do all kinds of things, endangering himself and so on, to force you to give in.

The new technology means, there is no sense in fighting, there is no sense in forcing. You have to learn to stimulate from within. No temper tantrum has any meaning if there is no audience. And it is the teacher and the parent who provide the audience for such "uncontrollable" behavior. But it is uncontrollable only for them. It is not uncontrollable for him; he can stop any tantrum immediately. You see this in adults. They suffer from a temper tantrum to make people do what they want. But in the midst of the worst tantrum, as soon as the door opens and the neighbor comes in, they are completely quiet—only to continue the temper after the neighbor leaves. You must realize that all this is not conscious, yet well designed. You are dealing here with a tyrant.

Dr. D.: *You and so many parents and teachers must learn how to cope with a tyrant. You can cope with him neither by fighting nor by giving in. But there are various things you can do and which we recommend. One of them you apparently found out for yourself. Right? The moment you said, "Go ahead kill yourself," he lost the power over you. The moment you stop being frightened by a tyrant, there is no sense any more in being a tyrant. What do you think about this?*
Mr. F.: *Well I guess I don't know what to say really. It's just because he's never done this to me. I guess I'm the mean old dad and I . . .*
Dr. D.: *You know why he has not done it to you? Because you don't fall for it.*
Mr. F.: *Well, I tell him. I'm not asking him what to do, I'm telling him and insist that he does what I tell him. If he goes too far . . .*
Dr. D.: *In general we don't believe in any overpowering and so on. But with this power of children, to show them that they won't get anywhere and that you can cope with them, deprives them of their methods. Do you beat him up?*
Mr. F.: *I've hit him, not very often. I mean it's a rare occasion if I will hit him. But . . .*
Dr. D.: *Does it have any good effect?*
Mr. F.: *Well, I think it helps a little.*
Dr. D.: *But not for very long.*
Mr. F.: *Well, for very long? I mean if you achieve your objective then I would say it helps.*
Dr. D.: *You don't achieve your objective if the same thing happens afterwards again. Your objective would be to help him to stop it alto-*

gether. But if he only heeds at the moment you punish him, then you only teach him the lesson that power is all that counts. You play right into his hands. He tries to overpower others and you try to overpower him. But we have to help the children to learn that overpowering is not the best way of finding one's place in life.

Now let's perhaps go through a typical day to see what the problems are. Very often when one goes through a day, one runs into all kinds of situations which the parents didn't realize were problems about which they can do something.

Now is there anything further that you want to tell us about him in general that upsets you, before we go through the average day?

Mrs. F.: *He doesn't like to do his homework.*

Dr. D.: *Please, here is a technique which we use. From the assumption that everything the child does has a purpose we come to the conclusion that the crucial question is, what does mother or father do about it? When I train counselors, they have to learn this first lesson. Whenever the mother says what the child does, you come with the question, "And what did you do about it?" Because what you did about it reveals the purpose of what the child had done. Everything a child does is well designed, well calculated to get results, although the child is not aware of this. No child will continue any misbehavior if he doesn't get results. That is already present in infants when they size up the situation. Whatever gets results, they will continue. In our present situation parents and teachers are unable to help children because they do not know techniques of a democratic type. They therefore make it all the worse by actually satisfying the child's intentions. So, is the temper still going on?*

Mrs. F.: *Oh yes. It's still going on.*

Dr. D.: *Can you give us a recent example? Everything has to be concrete.*

Mr. F.: *Well the most recent example I would say happened—unfortunately my wife lost her father just recently. Her parents lived in Florida, and she had been down there for three weeks. Then they brought him back here, put him in a hospital, and he passed away a couple of days later. After the funeral and everything, the following day, I had gone back to work and my wife's mother was with us.*

Grandmother. In our families you must always look for the grandmother. The influence of the grandmother is in many cases pernicious. She stands up for the child's right, because the grandparents and the child have a common enemy. (*Laughter.*) This is not necessarily so, but always watch for it. For instance even in juvenile delinquents, who are understood as being neglected; having a tyrannical father, and all kinds of bad living conditions, you find that the real culprit is the one who felt sorry for them and encouraged them in their desire, "I can do whatever I want." The grandparents have a tendency to spoil children. And spoiling means to teach them, "I can do what I want, and I don't care what you or society want." It isn't in all cases like that, but you always watch for it.

Dr. D.: *Now what happened?*
Mr. F.: *Well, I'd gone back to school with him that day, because the day that my father-in-law passed away there had been a note from the teacher that she wanted to see one of the parents.*
Dr. D.: *Let's stop here, because I like always to discuss everything as it comes up; it clarifies the situation. Why does the teacher want to talk with the parents?*
Mr. F.: *Well, because he was disturbing the class.*
Dr. D.: *Right. And do you know what I advise parents to do? When the teacher asks them to come and tells them what the child is doing wrong, I advise the parents to ask the teacher what she proposes to do. Because it is her job, and only if she does not know how to do her job does she blame the parents. How many of you are teachers? I can tell you a secret about teachers. Teachers send "love letters" home, because the child is tardy, does not study, and so on. Why? Do they really expect the parents can do something? It is the teachers' way of getting even with the child. They feel defeated by him in class and want to make it out on him at home, in which they usually succeed.*
Mr. F.: *Except that in this case he is so disruptive that he keeps the whole class from learning.*
Dr. D.: *That is the job of the teacher. The teacher has to learn how to deal with a class with a disruptive child. And the teacher who knows how to do it can actually succeed. The teacher has a group to work with. She has a whole room of children to help her. But the teachers are not prepared to deal with any child who doesn't want to learn, who doesn't want to behave.*
Mr. F.: *What the teacher . . .*
Dr. D.: *But wait. So she called you.*
Mr. F.: *She called me. So I went in and talked to the teacher. Mike wasn't doing his work, and is always trying to get the whole attention of the teacher. As long as he's the center of attention, that's fine. But once the teacher has to pay attention to the other 30 some children in the class that creates a problem.*
Dr. D.: *No, only if the teacher doesn't know what to do about it.*
Mrs. F.: *I used to get a call from the school a couple of times a week—to take him, and keep him home at lunchtime, because he was creating problems and they couldn't handle him. And I would be keeping him*

home until I went to see the principal. I told him I felt he belonged in school. And he told me that if he was going to continue to create problems, I would have to keep him home.

Dr. D.: *You must keep in mind that at the start of this pathology of our situation is that we did not learn the new ways of coping with each other. We have a law according to which everybody who prevents a child from going to school is punishable. And this law is mostly violated by principals and teachers.* (Laughter.) *But that is a sad situation and we have to cope with it. Now I want an example of a temper tantrum.*

Mr. F.: *Well as I started to say before, I had gone to school with him on the morning and then I went on to work and I got a call that there was a problem at home, and I should come home immediately. He was sent home from school. The school psychologist had been at school that morning and said that she felt that he was on the verge of a nervous breakdown.*

Dr. D.: *Who, the psychologist?* (Laughter.)

Mr. F.: *He was quite disruptive in class. The principal sent the boy home, and he refused to go. So he called my wife. Considering the circumstances, she having just buried her father the day before, this created quite a turmoil between my wife, my mother-in-law, and my son. I didn't know who was worst off at the moment.*

Dr. D.: *Here we have to come to a first important suggestion. If you want to learn how to cope with your child, you have to let the school and him fight it out with each other. You can't do anything about it.*

Mrs. F.: *But the school doesn't want to be bothered fighting it out, and they keep constantly telling me I have to keep him home. They cannot keep him in school because he created too much of a disturbance.*

Mr. F.: *There is a feeling among many of the parents in our school that our school is interested in the above average and the achieving child, and takes much less interest in the child that's average and below. And this has created a problem. In fact the fourth grade he was in, had two classes and he was in the class in which the principal double-promoted all the children except three.*

Dr. D.: *Let's stop right now because we don't get anywhere. I can not help you in dealing with the school. I have to help you to deal with him at home; so let's forget about the school because there's nothing you and I can do about it at the present moment. Right? But you can learn to cope with him at home. And mother is beginning already to extricate herself from the affects of his tyranny. Now what are the problems at home?*

Mrs. F.: *Well, they put him on a new medication, and so far I don't know if it's having the effect that it should have or not, because he hasn't* *been in school since he started. He was out of school three weeks this past time because of the problem. He just went back the other day. I took him to school Wednesday, no, Tuesday, and the principal was out.*

Dr. D.: *Please, do me one favor, let's leave the school out. We can not do anything about the school right now. You have to learn to cope with the problems which you have with him at home. That's the only thing that we can do now.*

Mr. F.: *Well since he has been going back to school now, at the moment, there has not been any problem; but he is getting medication and tranquilizers.*[2]

Dr. D.: *That's all right, there's a whole history about that; but we can't go into this at this point. When we started our guidance centers we were accused by social workers that in this superficial form of counseling we could only deal with very mildly disturbed children. And my answer was, they are wrong. When a child is brain-damaged, or has anything else wrong, the parents still have to learn how to cope with him. And that is what we are trying to do, regardless of how difficult the situation may be, to see how we can improve the situation and have a different relationship at home. This is what I would like to discuss with you. What bothers you at home?*

Mrs. F.: *Nothing at the moment, really.*

Dr. D.: *You mean as long as it's outside it doesn't bother you?*

Mrs. F.: *No, I don't mean that at all.*

Dr. D.: *Now let's start with this morning. How does the morning begin?*

Mrs. F.: *Well, I get him up for school.*

Dr. D.: *You are upset right now. Did I upset you?*

Mrs. F.: *No, I have a slight migraine that I got yesterday and I still have it. So that's what is upsetting me.*

Dr. D.: *Boy, school, migraine, what can we do with all this? Do you know that the whole relationship between child and parents is decided in the morning? That is usually the crucial mistake and the first improvement: How do you wake him up?*

Mrs. F.: *I usually go up and sort of shake the bed a little bit.*

Dr. D.: *How many times do you have to wake him up?*

Mrs. F.: *Well, he usually gets up pretty good when he's in the mood.*

Dr. D.: *And if he is not?*

Mrs. F.: *Well, then it takes a little longer, but he gets up far easier than my daughter does.*

Dr. D.: *They both have the same idea, to put mother in their service.*

[2]The case record shows that in a recent EEG examination Mike had 6 per second spike discharges. He has been taking medication for dysrhythmia.

Mrs. F.: *Well, Mike doesn't bother me as much getting up in the morning as Sally does.*

Dr. D.: *That's right. She has you in her service.*

Mrs. F.: *Don't they both?*

Dr. D.: *They both do. Would you like to improve the situation?*

Mrs. F.: *I'd love it.*

Dr. D.: *The first step is to help the parents to extricate themselves from the demands and tyranny of the children. If you really want to have a new relationship you have to start in the morning. Whose responsibility is this to get up? Whose responsibility?*

Mrs. F.: *Well, I would say theirs, because they have things that have to be done.*

Dr. D.: *Yes, but who is taking on the responsibility?*

Mrs. F.: *I guess I am.*

Dr. D.: *That's right. And you cannot teach children responsibility, you can only give it to them. I will make a number of recommendations. We have a limited amount of time and I want to talk with the boy too. The first thing is that you declare your independence in the morning. You tell them: "Whether you get up or not is your problem; it has nothing to do with me." Could you do that?*

Mrs. F.: *I'll try.*

Dr. D.: *First, you have to be sure that you want to extricate yourself. What else happens? How about eating?*

Mrs. F.: *No problem, Mike is a big eater. Sally doesn't eat any breakfast.*

Dr. D.: *How do you feel about your daughter not eating any breakfast.*

Mrs. F.: *It used to bother me but I told her if she doesn't want to, it's her stomach.*

Dr. D.: *But you see, it bothered you a great deal.*

Mrs. F.: *At first. But it doesn't any more.*

Dr. D.: *When the parents are bothered, it is an invitation for the child to do it. The children are very adept to find out what the parents can't stand, and then they do it.*

Mrs. F.: *I guess we were the same when we were kids.*

Dr. D.: *Yes. Do they fight with each other?*

Mr. F.: *Yes.*

Dr. D.: *What do you do about that?*

Mrs. F.: *What do I do? I try to stop it, but it doesn't always work, and the rest of the time I let them fight until Frank comes home, and stops them.*

Dr. D.: *When father comes home what do they do then?*

Mrs. F.: *They usually go to their own corner.*

Dr. D.: *You see we have such a tremendous amount of ground to cover in a very limited time. So I have to make this very short and* *merely indicate in which direction you will have to move. The fighting of the children is for the benefit of the parents. The one who provokes is usually the one who wants mother to come to his rescue. One tries to get special attention by fighting, the other tries to fight this. And the parents have to stand it. Now I will give you some ideas of the direction in which you can operate eventually, so that you have an idea of what can be done. Do you have somebody to work with, a counselor or somebody?*

Mrs. F.: *Well, we are going to the doctor.*

Dr. D.: *Well then he has to work it out with you. The first thing is, whenever mother gets upset, which means the children go after her, she has to retreat, and the best place to retreat is the bathroom.*

Mrs. F.: *That's exactly what Dr. Rosenberg says.*[3]

Dr. D.: *That's right. One has to understand the purpose of behavior or otherwise people think you give in to the child, when you go to the bathroom. In the bathroom the mother can find her independence.* (Laughter.) *But she has to know how to do it. If you don't do it properly it doesn't work. You have to know how to use the bathroom. Essential is a transistor radio, so that you can't hear what goes on outside. And you will be surprised how the family stops fighting and how much harmony you can have in a family from this one step of mother going to the bathroom. But you must be willing to extricate yourself. What prevents mother from being effective, is her tremendous sense of responsibility—"I have to see that they don't hurt each other; I have to see that they get up on time, I have to do it." The mother takes on the responsibility and the children have none.*

The next important thing is the so-called family council. Once a week you get together to discuss everything that goes on, not dictating to them, but listening to them. In the family council everybody has the right to say what he thinks and the obligation to listen to what the other one thinks. We are right now writing a textbook on this, because so many parents do not know how to be democratic. We have to train parents to be democratic leaders and to become effective in this way. Instead of the personal battles which go on, all problems are brought up on one day of the week, and we will see what can we do to understand each other and to help each other. There is something for you to develop. Right? Now what is your reaction to this?

Mr. F.: *Well, it should work out. But it is not that easy.*

Dr. D.: *The difficult step is only one: to be determined, "I want to do it." When you do it halfway, the child will call your bluff. These things*

[3]Dr. Bina Rosenberg is an associate of Dr. Dreikurs. Mike had been brought to her by his parents five weeks prior to the present demonstration.

are effective only when you really sincerely say, this is their job, they have to take care of it.

Mr. F.: *Well I'm all for giving him responsibility.*

Dr. D.: *Do you agree in general with what I have suggested?*

Mr. F.: *Well, how can I disagree?*

Dr. D.: *You can, you are the boss.*

Mr. F.: *Well, you are the expert.*

Dr. D.: (Turning to Mrs. F.) *What is your reaction?*

Mrs. F.: *Well I've tried this bathroom bit once, because I had one occasion to try it since I had spoken to the doctor. I went in, locked the door, and started to read a book, and Mike stood there pounding on the door, and I just ignored it as long as I could.*

Dr. D.: *And after you could no longer endure it, what did you do?*

Mrs. F.: *I went out and scrubbed the bathroom floor, I scrubbed the basement.*

Dr. D.: *But you must keep in mind that most parents make one mistake with the bathroom; the bathroom technique works only when you have the radio in the bathroom.*

Mrs. F.: *I can see where it would.*

Dr. D.: *You see, no recommendation will have any effect unless you do it properly, and these are things to discuss and to learn. I can only make this broad outline today. Regardless of how disturbed the child is, you can learn to cope with him.*

Mr. P.: *May I make a comment on that, Dr. Dreikurs?*

Dr. D.: *Yes, please.*

Mr. P.: *A lot of people have read about Dr. Dreikurs and the "bathroom technique" because it was reported in the daily papers. One of the questions that comes up about it very often is whether it is not just one more tactic for mothers to use in fighting with their children. And if, after she has gotten into a conflict with a child, mother suddenly withdraws to the bathroom, it is a fighting tactic, and probably an unfair one. Once you are in a fight, it is very difficult to withdraw and then to expect not to be part of the fight.*

It is when the fighting starts, when the children begin provoking her, that mother must decide to go to the bathroom, instead of fighting. "Excuse me, I have to go to the bathroom," is an unarguable declaration. This is a substitute for fighting, not a better way of fighting.

If this recommendation is followed, the mother is not nearly as likely to have the child pounding on the door. But when, as a form of fighting, mother's part is to go into the bathroom, then the child's part is, understandably, to pound on the door. Do you agree with me, Dr. Dreikurs?

Dr. D.: *Yes, fully.*

Mr. F.: *But this is not both children fighting with each other.*

Mr. P.: *No, I mean with you.*

Mr. F.: *It is just the one fighting with me.*

Dr. D.: *It doesn't make any difference with whom he fights. You can not succeed in fighting with the child. You see for 8000 years in our civilization we have had a technology of relationships, where one had to be the boss and have the power for drastic punishment, and one could subdue people. Today one can't anymore. Try to subdue a child and you will see what will happen. He subdues you.*

Now how is the relationship between the children? How is the girl? Do you have any problems with her?

Mr. F.: *Well, her big problem is that she's not the least bit interested in school, which has us quite worried. She puts no effort out at all. If she graduates I feel it's a major miracle.*

Dr. D.: *And what do you do about it?*

Mr. F.: *I don't feel there is anything we can do about it.*

Dr. D.: *Do you do anything about homework and so on?*

Mr. F.: *I try and talk to her about the importance of getting an education, that she'll be able to do something when she grows up. But it just doesn't seem to . . .*

Dr. D.: *You see, neither parents nor teachers know the psychodynamics. Our children lose more and more interest in school thanks to the work of the teachers who don't know how to stimulate learning and only know how to fight and to discourage. I guess from what you said that she is probably overambitious, and overambition leads to underachievement. "If I can't be on top, then I don't want to be anything else."*

Mr. F.: *She's never been that good a student really.*

Dr. D.: *That is a consequence of never having been interested in studying. Is there anything in life that she can do well?*

Mrs. F.: *She likes animals, she loves animals. If she didn't have to go to school any longer to become a vet, she would have done it, because she loves to be with animals.*

Dr. D.: *And why? You see every one of these statements is fraught with meaning, which one has to explore. Very often when people like animals it is because they can control them. They have the situation under control. But with people it doesn't go.*

Mr. F.: *But she has liked animals since she has been an infant, really.*

Mrs. F.: *She would walk out the door and chase the dogs down the street. She was this type.*

Dr. D.: *Yes. We can't go into all of these aspects, there is a lot of material to cover. But apparently she's not interested in doing the average thing. She wants to do something special. Does she have friends?*

Mr. F.: *Yes.*

Dr. D.: *What kind of friends does she have?*
Mr. F.: *Well, I think she's a sensible girl, she has sensible friends. To my knowledge she has never experimented with drugs, which I have to give her a lot of credit for, because in high school today drugs can be a serious problem. And I feel she hasn't experimented with sex, which can also be a serious problem.*
Dr. D.: *I would be careful not to let her know that you would count it as a serious problem, because then she might be stimulated to do it. So be careful. Anyhow I can see that there is no deeper problem. I don't know whether we should go into any more today. But I would suggest to you the same as what I said about your boy. The problem of learning is a problem of the school. And it's up to her how she wants to deal with the school and what to learn. And since she has the motivation to become a veterinarian she will have enough motivation to just pass. But she's not interested in school. Is there another problem which bothers you about her?*
Mrs. F.: *Not really.*
Mr. F.: *One problem that bothers me quite a bit is the matter of religion. I came from a very religious family; we are of the Jewish faith. I was brought up in the orthodox tradition, although I'm not quite orthodox right now.*
Dr. D.: *Now please, time is very short.*
Mr. F.: *The problem there is, that I feel that she doesn't hang around with children of the same faith and I'm quite concerned about the possibility of intermarriage in the future.*
Dr. D.: *Of course the problem is that we lose influence over our children. We have our own ideas and are not willing to give in. But did you so far get much out of our discussion?*
Mr. F.: *Definitely.*
Dr. D.: *I would like to talk with the children.* (The children are called in.)

You can see from what even the limited circumstances permit that we are really working on brief therapy. From the first moment of diagnosis we show people what they can do differently. I maintain, and that is what I try to imbue in my students, if a client comes to me and leaves my office the same as when he came in, I have failed him. In every interview I try to explore all posibilities. A very important man in Israel pointed out, "Professor Dreikurs talks with each client as if it were the last time he had a chance to talk with him, not wasting time with relationship investigations, and immediately starting with the therapeutic, corrective effort." And I think that came out pretty well in our discussion.

Dr. D.: (To the boy, who in the meanwhile had taken his seat next to him.) *Now would you mind to be open with me and to talk with me?*

Mike: *No.*
Dr. D.: *Good. Now, why are you here?*
Mike: *I don't know.*
Dr. D.: *Do you want me to believe that you don't know?*
Mike: *I don't.*
Dr. D.: *How many of you believe that he doesn't know why he is here?* (Laughter.) *Now why don't you tell me what you think why you are?*

This is what we do. We confront the child with his goal in a very well defined technique. You ask: "Do you do that? Is it true?" Yes. "Why do you do it?" The child never knows. He will either say, "I don't know," or he will give you a rationalization. Then comes the next important question, "Would you mind if I tell you why you are doing it"? And then you come with the confrontation, always introduced with the words: "Could it be that . . ." "Could it be that you want to keep mother busy?" "Could it be that you want to show your power?" I think I am traveling internationally quite a bit, and it has come about that at various conferences in various places, people recognized immediately who were my students by these words "Could it be"? You don't reproach anybody. You don't accuse them. You try to reveal.

Dr. D.: *So you think you don't know why you are here?*
Mike: *Right.*
Dr. D.: *And that is the reason you don't want to tell me?*
Mike: *Yes.*
Dr. D.: *Now could I tell you what I think is the reason why you don't want to tell me?*
Mike: *Yes.*
Dr. D.: *Could it be you don't want to do what people tell you?*
Mike: *I guess so.*

Recognition reflex. (*Laughter.*) When you guess what he does, he begins to see.

Dr. D.: *I think that is part of your troubles. Your mother and your father don't know what to do with you. Am I right?*
Mike: *Right.*
Dr. D.: *Do you know what to do with them? Honest.*
Mike: *I don't know.*
Dr. D.: *Do you think he knows what to do with father and mother?*
Mrs. F.: *No.*
Mike: *Yes, he does.*
Dr. D.: *Now into what kind of troubles do you get? Do you get into troubles?*

Mike: (Inaudible.)
Dr. D.: *Can you hear him? Now into what kind of troubles do you get? Why did you not take your microphone when I told you to take it? Your first reaction is, "No." When I tell you to speak in the microphone, you don't want to. Am I right?*
Mike: *Right.*
Dr. D.: *Now I can imagine what kind of troubles you get into in this way. With whom do you get into troubles?*
Mike: *My teacher.*
Dr. D.: *Now what kind of troubles do you have with your teacher?*
Mike: *Well, I want to do my work.*
Dr. D.: *Yes, and she doesn't let you do your work? Now what kind of troubles do you have with the teacher?*
Mike: *Well, like one time she wanted me to do my spelling during a different class, and I wasn't there that day, so I refused.*
Dr. D.: *Did you refuse at other times too when the teacher told you to do something.*
Mike: *No.*
Dr. D.: *Come on.*
Mike: *Not all the time.*
Dr. D.: *Not all the time, but most of the time?*
Mike: *About half.*
Dr. D.: *And do you know why you are doing this?*
Mike: *To get at the teacher.*
Dr. D.: *No. May I tell you what I think?*
Mike: *What?*
Dr. D.: *Could it be that you want to show the teacher that you are strong enough and she can't make you do anything?*
Mike: *Yes.*
Dr. D.: *You see, you have the power. You know how to manage mother, you threaten her with doing things, to kill yourself, whatever it is, apparently because you want everyone to do what you want.* (Very slowly:) *And what do you do if people don't do what you want?*
Mike: *I try to get my way.*
Dr. D.: *And you get mad.*
Mike: *Uh huh.*
Dr. D.: *Do you have temper tantrums?*
Mike: *Yes.*
Dr. D.: *Why do you think you have temper tantrums?*
Mike: *I don't know.*
Dr. D.: *Could it be the same, you want to show your power?*
Mike: *Yes.*

Dr. D.: *What would happen if you would have a temper tantrum in the classroom and the teacher would have stopped screaming?*

It is very effective to let the child have his temper tantrum and to tell the class we can not do anything we have to wait until he's through and he doesn't go on with the temper tantrum very long. But our teachers do the reverse: "Stop it," and then they become completely defeated.

Dr. D.: *Could it be that you wanted to show everybody "I can do what I want?"*
Mike: *Yes.*
Dr. D.: *You think that is a good idea?*
Mike: *No.*
Dr. D.: *Ah yes, you think it's a wonderful idea, you enjoy it.* (Laughter.) *You see, every child knows what he should do, he just decides not to do it. Now I hope you will work with somebody to help you. You see you are a nice boy if you want to, but if you don't want, you're a tiger. The principal doesn't know what to do with you, the teacher doesn't know what to do with you, nobody knows what to do with you. Isn't that wonderful?*
Mike: *No.*
Dr. D.: *How can you say no? It's an achievement. You should get an A on how to defeat grown-ups. Shouldn't you?*
Mike: *No.*
Dr. D.: *Well anyhow* (turning to Sally), *do you have any problems with your parents?*
Sally: *No.*
Dr. D.: *No?*
Sally: *Well, yes at times.*
Dr. D.: *Like what?*
Sally: *At times I want to go out and they won't let me.*
Dr. D.: *You want to go out. Do you have any other problems with them?*
Sally: *The car.*
Dr. D.: *The car. That is a typical juvenile problem. The war between the generations, the gap: the car, and dates. All the way through, until the poor parents are really thrown in every direction, the kids support each other, and each family tries for itself to solve the problem, which they can't. How about getting up in the morning?*
Sally: *Well, I can't do it.*
Dr. D.: *You can't do it. Why not?*
Sally: *I just can't wake up.*

Dr. D.: *You can't wake up?*

Sally: *Too tired.*

Dr. D.: *Too tired? You see that is a typical rationalization. May I tell you what I think is why you don't get up?*

Sally: *Yes.*

Dr. D.: *Could it be that you want your mother to come to your service and get you up?*

Sally: *No, I get up when I'm not tired.*

Dr. D.: *At times. Couldn't you get up every time?*

Sally: *Not if I'm too tired.*

Dr. D.: *You will be surprised how you could get up, once you realize why you don't get up. It is your way of putting your mother in your service. If mother would declare her independence and refuse to be an alarm clock, do you think you could get up by yourself?*

Sally: *Oh, I get up all right, she doesn't wake me up.*

Dr. D.: *She doesn't wake you up?*

Sally: *No.*

Dr. D.: *But she says she does because you don't get up unless she comes several times.*

Sally: *She comes up and tells me to get up, and if I get up, I get up.*

Dr. D.: *And if you don't get up, what does she do?*

Sally: *I wait a few minutes and then I get up.*

Dr. D.: *And doesn't she come afterwards again to remind you?*

Sally: *No.*

Dr. D.: *I might be wrong, but I have the feeling that you use her very much as a servant for you to get up. I might be wrong about that.*

Sally: *Sometimes.*

Dr. D.: *And sometimes you are fighting also for your rights that you can do what you want? Right?*

Sally: *Yes.*

Dr. D.: *This is part of the generation problem. Now we can only briefly outline what I feel that the problems are. And I would like to help mother to become independent. For instance, do you fight with each other?*

Sally: *Sometimes.*

Dr. D.: *Why?*

Sally: *He gives my mother a hard time.*

Dr. D.: *Now why are you saying that?*

Sally: *Because of the tantrums.*

Dr. D.: *Now may I explain to you? He wants to show mother and the rest of the world, "I can do what I want, and when I want to fight, I will fight." This is his way of defeating her. Mother can not stand it. So I have* *suggested to mother to become independent. About your getting up, that is your problem, about fighting; about many other things which you could not talk about. And I told her whenever she gets upset with anyone of you, to go to the bathroom, and to wait there until it's over. What do you think about that? Do you like that?*

Mike: *She always does that.*

Dr. D.: *Do you like it?*

Mike: *No. Well I don't mind.*

Dr. D.: *You don't mind. You try to get her out of the bathroom as quickly as possible. Don't you?*

Mike: *Yes.*

Dr. D.: *Because she hasn't used the radio yet, you see? When she has the radio, she will learn to become independent and then you will have to take care of yourself. What do you think about it? Is it a good idea?*

Mike: *Yes.*

Dr. D.: *Now do you want to say something? Not a word.*

So I think and hope you have gotten at least some idea about our technique. I don't maintain that we really have solved the problem but we indicated the way in which it can be solved. Thank you very much.[4]

[4]The week following the demonstration Mike and his parents were seen by Mr. Sherwood Perman, psychologist and associate of Dr. Rosenberg. He reports: "Mrs. F. felt that she had learned a great deal and attempted to put what she learned into practice during subsequent weeks. Mike felt that the session was not useful to him but that Dr. Dreikurs had understood him. Mr. F. stated that he did not learn anything at the session."

In reference to this comment by Mr. F., it is interesting that Dr. Garner singled out the remark by Mr. F., "You are the expert" as an example of a response which is merely compliant, wanting to please the therapist, rather than problem-solving.—Ed. note.

INDEX

A-B-C theory, 414
Academic achievement, 46–47, 71
Achievement. *See* Academic achievement
Ad lib humor, 169
Adlerian psychology
  assumptions of, 3–4, 35, 57
  explanation of, ix
  principles of, ix–xi
  schools and training centers offering courses in, xi
Adlerian techniques. *See also* Therapeutic techniques
  confrontation techniques, 27–28
  encouragement techniques, 27
  in marriage/couple therapy, 385–386
  placing responsibility, 28
  pushbutton technique, 27
  task-setting technique, 26
Agreements, to solve conflict, 437
Alcohol use
  alcoholism vs., 237–238
  among married couples, 256–262
Alcoholism. *See also* Chemical dependency; Chemically dependent clients; Substance abuse
  contemporary Adlerian views of, 235–236
  as disease, 234
  extent of, 244
  life style and, 232–233
  in married couples, 256–262
  problem drinking vs., 237–238
  treatment recommendations for, 236–240, 257
Allusions, religious, 143–148
Alternatives, confrontation used to present, 118, 126
Anger, 9, 424. *See also* Temper
Antabuse (disulfiram), 258
Applied consequences, 431–432
Arrangements, to solve conflict, 438
"As if" technique
  explanation of, 153–154
  fantasy and daydreaming as, 155
  function of, 37, 154
  imagery as, 155
  Implosion and flooding as, 155–156
  metaphor as, 156
  non-strategic task assignment as, 158–159
  paradoxical prescriptions as, 157–158

reframing as, 158
role playing as, 154–155
Attention
adult responses to child's pursuit of, 416–418
mutual storytelling for children seeking, 340–341
play techniques for children seeking, 289–290
sickness to gain, 84–85
Autonomy, 29, 30

Behavior. *See also* Children's misbehavior; Client behavior
confronting immediate, 124–125
disruptive, 312–322
encouraging patient to adopt new, 74–75
personal responsibility for, 24. *See also* Client responsibility
Beliefs
conjunctive, 416
disjunctive, 415, 424–426
Bereavement, following abstinence from chemical
dependency, 248–249
Biased apperception, 123
Birth order. *See also* Firstborns
adopting new behavior and, 74–75
case study illustrating use of, 75–76
human development and personality and, 70–72
importance of, 36, 69
patient cooperation in therapeutic process and, 72–73
patient life style hypotheses and, 73–74
as personality determinant, 57–58
research on, 69–70
Bossy children, 288–290
Buber, Martin, 11

Cartoons, 170
Chemical dependency. *See also* Alcoholism; Smoking cessation programs; Substance abuse
components of, 245
as emotional disorder, 244–245
Chemically dependent clients
avoiding pitfalls with, 249–250
bereavement and panic in, 248–249
confrontation of, 248
critical time factor for, 246
denial system in, 245–246
holistic treatment program for, 251–253
medication for, 247–248, 258
Children
attention-getting, 289–290
bossy, 288–290
example of counseling, 275–284
feedback about relationships with adults by, 331–332
misbehavior in. *See* Children's misbehavior
mistaken ideas in, 293
mutual storytelling technique used for, 339–345
play in, 285–288. *See also* Play; Play therapy
stories for psychological self-understanding used for, 312–322
use of early recollection with, 273–274, 305–310
withdrawn, 290–291
Children's misbehavior
disjunctive emotional responses to, 413–427. *See also* Disjunctive emotional responses
mistaken goals of, 339, 469
mutual storytelling technique to address, 339–345
play therapy to address, 285–288, 323–335. *See also* Play therapy

Circular questions, 108
Client behavior. *See also* Behavior; Children's misbehavior
  birth order and, 72–73
  elements entering into interpretation of, 18–20
  feelings as component of, 16–17
  goal-directed component of, 13–16
  situational context of, 17–18
Client resistance
  case example of, 198–200
  as conflict between therapist and client, 195–196
  confronting, 117, 193
  denial system and, 245–250
  to family therapy, 464
  holistic treatment programs for, 251–253
  model to understanding and solving, 194–198
  symptoms and, 194
Client responsibility
  Adlerian techniques to encourage, 26–28
  Adlerian therapist's attitude toward, 25–26
  conclusions regarding, 32–33
  to finding meaning of life, 138–139
  overview of, 24–25
  techniques used by other schools of psychotherapy to encourage, 29–32
Clients, religious, 143–148
Commitments
  in family therapy, 464
  pointing out meaning of, 146
Communication
  in couples, 260–261
  level, 393–395
  in play therapy, 325–326
Competition, between siblings, 42–44, 59
Conflict resolution
  agreements for, 437
  arrangements for, 438
  contracts for, 438–439
  equality and, 396–397
  in families, 461
  principles of, 354–355, 435–437
Confrontation
  of biased apperception and private logic, 123
  characteristics of, 112–113
  of chemically dependent clients, 248
  of existing alternatives, 126
  explanation of, 27–28, 37, 111–112
  of hidden reasons, 123
  of immediate behavior, 124–125
  interpretation vs., 112, 122
  of mistaken goals, 480
  of mood states and feelings, 123
  of mottoes, 124
  of private goals, 124
  of private logic, 115–116, 123, 463
  purpose of, 111, 113, 121–122
  of responsibility for change, 126–127
  of responsibility of responses of others, 125
  of self-defeating behavior, 125–126
  of time factors, 127
Confrontation techniques
  for destructive behavior, 116–118
  main issues for use of, 127–128
  for subjective views, 113–116
  use of, 122
Consequences
  applied, 431–432
  conflict and, 435–439
  fantasy used to explore, 425–426
  logical, 432–434
  natural, 430–431, 437

Content error, 15
Contextual Family Therapy, 444–445
Contracts, to solve conflict, 438–439
Couple Conference, 411
Couple therapy. *See* Marriage/couple therapy
Courage
  case example of patient lacking, 85–87
  as healthy attitude, 356, 357
Criticism, assertive, 396

Daydreaming, 155
Denial, 245–246
Depressed clients
  interruption techniques for, 268–271
  recurring themes recited by, 267–268
Destructive behavior, 116–118
Discouragement, 135–136
Disease, alcoholism as, 234
Disjunctive beliefs
  disputing, 424–426
  explanation of, 415
Disjunctive emotional responses
  beliefs and purposes associated with adult, 415–422
  need to change, 413–414
  procedures for changing, 422–426
Dissociative techniques, 208
Disulfiram (Antabuse), 258
Diversionary tactics, to change disjunctive emotional responses to children, 423–424
Dream interpretation
  Adlerian, 95
  example of, 99–102
  function of, 37
  procedures for, 98–99
Dreams
  function of, 96–97, 102–103
  mechanisms used in, 97
  symbolism in, 96

Early recollections (ERs)
  Adlerian use of, 81–83
  advantages of using, 87–90, 305
  examples of, 84–87
  explanation of, 305
  first encounters of married couples used as, 362–378. *See also* First-Encounter-of-a-Close Kind (FECK)
  gathered during play therapy, 329
  interpretation of, 36
  for marriage/couple counseling, 352
  used with children, 273–274, 305–310, 329
Emotional bridge technique, 207–208
Emotional responses. *See* Disjunctive emotional responses
Emotions
  as component of patient behavior, 16–17
  explanation of, 16
  function of, 414–415
Empathy, birth order and, 71
Encouragement
  in marriage/couple counseling, 356, 397
  in play therapy, 325, 334
Encouragement techniques
  explanation of, 27
  humor used in, 168–169
Enhancing Attending Behavior, 409–410
Equality
  explanation of, 392–393, 397–398
  life style and, 390–392

in male-female relationships, 389–390
working toward, 393–397
Existential psychotherapy, 31
Experiencing and Expressing Love Exercise, 408–409

Fables
explanation of, 131–132
helping cope with disappointment, 140–141
illustrating excessive pleasing, 134–135
illustrating self-defeating behavior, 137–138
therapeutic use of, 132–133
Families
functions of, 441
personality development and dynamics in, 59–60
problem children and working with, 275–276
treatment of alcoholics and, 239, 257
Family constellation
explanation of, 40, 56, 458
importance of, 36
life style assessment focused on, 40–55, 196
for marriage/couple counseling, 352
in personality diagnosis, 56–68
play therapy to gain information about, 328–329
Family constellation interview
case description following guide for, 64–65
guide for, 60–64
interpretation of, 65–68
Family council, 476
Family groups, for chemically dependent clients, 252
Family life-style assessment. *See also* Life-style assessment
case study in, 448–453
genograms and, 445–449
Family therapy. *See also* Marriage/couple therapy
demonstration of, 466–484
diagnosis in, 460–461
elements of Adlerian, 456–459
initial interview in, 459–460
relapse technique used in, 175–176, 181
teaching family skills in, 461–462
techniques in, 462–464
Family values
client telling about, 52
explanation of, 42–43
Fantasy
to explore consequences, 425–426
use of, 155
Feelings. *See* Emotions
Fictional goals, 153–154
Firstborns, 71–72. *See also* Birth order
First-Encounter-of-a-Close Kind (FECK)
application of, 377–378
as assessment tool, 366–368
examples and discussions of, 369–377
explanation of, 362–363
requests for, 368–369
Flooding technique, 155–156

Gender differences
relationships and, 389–390
in views of intimacy, 403
Genograms
application of, 446–448
benefits of, 445–446
explanation of, 445
Gestalt therapy, 30–31
Goal-directed behavior, 13–16

Goals. *See also* Mistaken goals
  adult emotional responses to children's, 415–422
  confrontation of private, 124
  disclosure in play therapy of, 330
  fictional, 153–154
  that aren't one's own, 136–137
Grandmothers, 471–472
Group play, 287. *See also* Play; Play therapy
Guilt, 143, 144

"Happy hour" homework, 170
"Here and now" confrontations, 116–117
Hidden reason technique
  confrontation using, 123
  used in marriage/couple therapy, 386
Hillel, 146
Humor
  to interrupt depression, 268
  positive uses of, 167–169
  psychology of, 164–166
  as therapeutic technique, 37, 132
  used to strengthen marriages, 169–170
Hypnosis
  reorientation through, 213–220. *See also* Reorientation
  traditional views of, 205–206
Hypnotherapeutic approaches
  dissociative technique, 208
  emotional bridge, 207–208
  explanation of, 38
  for habit change programs, 221–227
  overview of, 205–206
  reframing, 209–211
  somatic bridge, 206–207
  storytelling, 208–209

Imagery, 155
Implosion technique, 155, 156
Inadequacy
  adult responses to child's pursuit of, 418, 421, 422
  mutual storytelling for children with goal of, 344–345
Increasing Please Behaviors exercise, 259
Inference sharing, 330–331
Inferiority, 139
Interaction, during play therapy, 326–327
Interpretation, confrontation vs., 112, 122
Interruption techniques, 268–271
Interventive interviews
  circular questions in, 108
  explanation of, 107
  reflexive questions in, 108–109
  strategic questions in, 109
Interviews
  diagnostic and therapeutic, 107
  initial family, 459–460
  interventive, 107–110
Intimacy
  approaches to, 401–402
  in couples, 403–408
  explanation of, 400, 402–403
  techniques for, 408–411
Intimacy Genogram, 409
I-Thou relationship, 4, 9–11

Jesus Wept, 144
Jokes, 170

Laterborns, 71–72
Laughing Game, 31–32
Laughter, 164. *See also* Humor
Life style
  of alcoholics, 232–233
  developing hypotheses concerning patient, 73–74
  early recollections to illustrate, 82, 83, 195

elements of family, 442–444
enabling patient to understand his or her, 74
equality and, 390–392
explanation of, 39, 194, 293, 458
fictions supported by, 154
myths and values comprising, 444–445
reorientation of, 213–214

Life-style assessment
in chemically dependent clients, 249–250
elements of, 25–26
family, 445–453. *See also* Family life-style assessment
focused on family constellation, 39–55
function of, 36, 39–40
in marriage/couple counseling, 352
in play therapy, 327–329

Limit-setting, 327
Lithium carbonate, 247
Logical consequences
explanation of, 432–434
use of, 434–435

Lot's Wife, 144
Loyalty dilemmas
case examples of, 298–302
conclusions regarding, 302–304
explanation of, 294–295
methods for meeting, 297–298
as private logic, 295–297
types of, 295
use of, 273

Male-female relationships
changes in, 389–390
life style and, 390–392
working toward equality in, 393–397

Manipulation
nature and effects of, 8–9
through technique, 4

Marriage education centers
advantages and disadvantages of, 359–360
function and organization of, 358–359

Marriage/couple therapy
Adlerian techniques in, 385–386
for alcohol-affected couples, 256–262
assessment and interpretation in, 352–354
establishing and maintaining relationship in, 351, 381–382
four-way, 357–358
general improvement strategies for, 259–261
humor used in, 163–170
intimacy issues and, 403–411. *See also* Intimacy
marriage education centers used in, 358–360
providing insight in, 383–384
purpose of, 347, 380, 381
relapse technique used in, 176–178, 181
reorientation and re-education in, 354–357, 384–385
understanding couple in, 382–383
using First-Encounter-of-a-Close Kind, 362–378. *See also* First-Encounter-of-a-Close Kind (FECK)

Marriages
assessment of, 363–366
as system, 380
as tasks, 365

Mathematics, 46–47
Medication
for chemically dependent clients, 247–248, 258
for depressed clients, 268

Metaphors
as "as if" technique, 156
explanation of, 156

as hypnotherapeutic approach, 208–209
Misbehavior. *See* Children's misbehavior
Mistaken beliefs
confrontation techniques for, 115–116
early recollection visualization to reconsider, 92–94
explanation of, 90
Mistaken goals. *See also* Goals
addressed in mutual storytelling, 339–345
adult emotional responses to children's, 415–422
of children, 339, 469
confronting, 480
Motivation
focus on presently ongoing, 14–15
identification of patient's, 15–16
Motivational cues, analysis of, 15
Mottoes, confrontation using, 124
The Mount of Temptation, 145
Multimodal treatment, 221–227
Mutual storytelling. *See also* Storytelling
to address goal of attention, 340–341
to address goal of inadequacy, 344–345
to address goal of power, 341–343
to address goal of revenge, 343–344
explanation of, 339–340
function of, 340, 345
Myths, family, 444, 445

Natural consequences, 430–431, 437

Optimism, 356
Overgeneralizations, 26

Parables
explanation of, 131
as hypnotherapeutic approach, 208–209
illustrating imitation, 137
illustrating inferiority feelings, 139
illustrating social isolation, 133–134
therapeutic use of, 132–133
Paradox
relapse technique and, 178, 180
used in therapy, 38, 186
Paradoxical prescriptions
"as if," 157–158
background of, 182
client cooperation and, 197–198
developing rationale for, 184–185
disqualifying significant other and prescribing, 186–188
explanation of, 157, 182
following up, 188–189
principles of, 183
steps in delivering, 183–184
used in marriage/couple therapy, 387
Parents
honoring unworthy, 147
influence of, 58–59
loyalty dilemmas in dealing with, 294–295
as participants in play therapy, 334–335
Partners, rating one's, 353–354
Patients. *See* Clients
People pleasers, 134–135
Personality
Adlerian assumptions regarding, 57
birth order and, 70–72
family dynamics and, 59–60

Placing responsibility technique, 28, 50. *See also* Client responsibility
Plato, 285–286
Play
  Adler's view of, 286–288
  participation in group, 287
  techniques to understand, 273
  various views of, 285–286
Play therapy
  exploring life style of child during, 327–329
  illustrations of, 288–291
  insight phase of, 329–333
  relationship establishment phase of, 324–327
  reorientation phase of, 333–335
  techniques used in, 323–324
  use of, 274, 323
Positive interpretation. *See* Reframing
Power
  adult responses to child's pursuit of, 418, 419
  mutual storytelling for children seeking, 341–343
Powerlessness, 233–234
Presenting existing alternatives technique, 28
Private logic
  confrontation of, 115–116, 123, 463
  fictions supported by, 154
  loyalty dilemma as, 295–297
  understanding client, 5–6
Psychological self-understanding, 312–322
Punishment
  consequences vs., 429–435. *See also* Consequences
  explanation of, 434
  logical consequences as, 432, 433
  physical, 430, 434
Puppets, 288
Pushbutton technique
  for depressed clients, 268–271
  effectiveness of, 271
  explanation of, 27
Put-down humor, 165, 166. *See also* Humor

Questions
  changed into statements, 30–31
  circular, 108
  during play therapy, 326
  reflexive, 108–109
  strategic, 109

Rabbi Ellijah, the Goan of Vilna, 145–146
Rabbi Tarfon's Admonition, 145
Rebuttal, in loyalty dilemmas, 297, 302, 304
Recollections. *See* Early recollections
Reflexive questions, 108–109
Reframing
  explanation of, 158
  as hypnotherapeutic approach, 209–211
Relapse, in chemically dependent clients, 250, 261–262
Relapse technique
  conditions for use of, 180–181
  explanation of, 38
  in family counseling, 175–176
  in marriage counseling, 176–178
  theory of, 178–179
Relationships. *See also* Marriage/couple therapy
  adult-child, 331–332
  equality in male-female, 389–398. *See also* Male-female relationships
  establishment of therapeutic, 82, 83

intimacy in marital, 400–411. *See also* Intimacy
I-thou, 4, 9–11
in marriage/couple therapy, 351, 381–382
therapist-child, 324–327
Religious allusions
illustrations of, 144–147
use of, 143, 147–148
Reminders, for appropriate responses, 426
Reorientation
case example dealing with, 216–219
explanation of, 214–215, 384
hypnotherapeutic process for, 215–216, 220
in marriage/couple therapy, 354–357, 384–385
in play therapy, 333–335
as step in counseling process, 213–214
Repentance, 143
Resistance. *See* Client resistance
Responsibility, 125–126. *See also* Client responsibility
Responsibility for change technique, 28
Responsibility for responses to others technique, 28
"Revealing the hidden reason" technique, 115–116
Revenge
adult responses to child's pursuit of, 418, 420
mutual storytelling for children seeking, 343–344
Rogers, Carl, 10
Role playing
as "as if" technique, 154–155
with children, 273
explanation of, 154
Screaming internally, 425
Sculpting technique, 410–411
Self
presentation in dreams of, 98
rating, 353–354
Self-defeating behavior
confrontation of, 117–118, 125–126
fable illustrating, 137–138
play therapy to teach children to contain, 324
Self-determination, 233–234, 237
Self-esteem
safeguarding, 294
safeguards of, 194, 196
Self-hypnosis, 224–226
Selfishness, 146
Self-responsibility, 5
Serenity, 147
Sexual relations, 407–408
Siblings
birth order of, 57–58. *See also* Birth order
competition between, 42–44
dynamics between, 59–60
Signals, for appropriate responses, 426
Smoking cessation programs, 221–227
Social interest
development in children of, 287–288
explanation of, 458–459
Social isolation, 133–134
Somatic bridge technique, 206–207
Spiritual needs groups, 252
Statements, questions changed into, 30–31
Storytelling
humorous, 170
as hypnotherapeutic approach, 208–209

mutual, 339–345. *See also* Mutual storytelling
for psychological self-understanding, 312–322
Strategic questions, 109
Stress, 163–164
Subgroups, in families, 41
Subjective feelings, 113–115
Substance abuse. *See also* Alcoholism; Chemical dependency; Chemically dependent clients; Smoking cessation programs
Adlerian approach to, 38
extent of, 244
Support groups, 251–252
Switching roles technique, 386
Symbols
in dreams, 97, 101
sociocultural origins of, 96
Symptom prescription, 157

Task assignments
"as if," 158–159
in marriage/couple counseling, 355–356
Task setting
explanation of, 26
in family therapy, 464
Temper, 47–48. *See also* Anger
Temptation, 145
Tension-releasing humor, 165–166. *See also* Humor
Therapeutic relationship, 82, 83
Therapeutic techniques. *See also* Adlerian techniques; *specific techniques*
to encourage client responsibility, 26–32. *See also* Client responsibility
overview of, 36–38
pitfalls of, 1
stressing direct application of Adlerian theory, 3–6
Therapists
attitude toward client of, 25–26
function of, 1–2
impact of therapy on, 9
patients who look for magic answers from, 138–139
Therapy
attitudes brought to, 356–357
client participation in decisions regarding, 27
four-way, 357–358
impact on therapist of, 9
need for situation-oriented, 4
purpose of, 1
Time for a Better Marriage, 261
Topic groups, 251
Transactional analysis, 29–30
Traps and Escapes model
being stuck phase of, 196
case example of, 198–200
escape phase of, 196–198
explanation of, 194
setting the trap phase of, 194–195
springing the trap phase of, 195
Triangles, 294. *See also* Loyalty dilemmas
Two-track humor, 166. *See also* Humor

Valium, 247
Values
family, 444, 445
identification of faulty, 26
Visualization
of early recollections, 91–94
guiding clients toward, 91, 92

Withdrawn children, 290–291

LIST OF CONTRIBUTORS

Sharon Arkin, Psy.D., is an Assistant Research Scientist and Principal Investigator on a 5-year National Institute on Aging Alzheimer's rehabilitation research and student training program, and a clinical psychologist in the Department of Speech and Hearing Sciences, University of Arizona, Tucson, Arizona.

P. Lawrence Belove, Ed.D., is a licensed psychologist and lecturer at Keene State College.

Barbara L. Borden, Ed.D., is a school psychologist in Highland Park, Illinois.

Mark S. Carich, Ph.D., is a psychologist with the Department of Corrections in Collinsville, Illinois.

Jon Carlson, Psy.D., Ed.D., is a psychologist in Lake Geneva, Wisconsin, and a professor at Governors State University, University Park, Illinois.

Oscar C. Christensen, Ed.D., is a professor emeritus at the University of Arizona, Tucson.

Helen K. Cooley, M.A., is a counselor and consultant in Evergreen Park, Illinois.

Raymond J. Corsini, Ph.D., is a psychologist in Honolulu, Hawaii.

Linda K. Dann was a counselor at an elementary school in the East Baton Rouge Parish school systems.*

---

*No current information available.

Don Dinkmeyer, Ph.D., is a psychologist with Communication and Motivation Training Institute in Coral Springs, Florida.

James Dinkmeyer, M.A., is a mental health counselor in Coral Springs, Florida.

Rudolf Dreikurs, M.D., was a psychiatrist in Chicago, Illinois, and a founder of the Alfred Adler Institute.

Barbara Fairfield, M.Ed., is a counselor in Lanham, Maryland.

Lucille K. Forer, Ph.D., retired in 1997 from private practice in clinical psychology, Malibu, California.

Merna D. Galassi, Ed.D., is an elementary school counselor at Seawell Elementary School, Chapel Hill, North Carolina.

Marie Hartwell-Walker, Ed.D., is Director of Adult Outpatient Services, ServiceNet, Northampton, MA.

E. Clair Hawes, Ph.D., is a psychologist in Vancouver, British Columbia.

Sidney M. Jourard, M.D., was a professor of psychology at the University of Florida, Gainesville.

Carol Kivel was a writer, secretary for the Adlerian Society of Arizona, and a volunteer with the Pima County CASA program.*

Richard Royal Kopp, Ph.D., is a psychologist and professor at the California School of Professional Psychology in Lost Angeles California.

Terry Kottman, Ph.D., is an associate professor of counseling at the University of Northern Iowa, Cedar Falls, Iowa.

Judith A. Lewis, Ph.D., is a professor at Governors State University, University Park, Illinois.

MaryAnn Lingg, Ph.D., is an assistant professor in Chesterfield, Missouri.

Robert J. McBrien, Ph.D., is Director of Student Counseling Services, Salisbury State University, Salisbury, Maryland.

*No current information available.

Gary D. McKay, Ph.D., is a psychologist with CMTI West in Tucson, Arizona.

Alvin R. Mahrer, Ph.D., is a professor, School of Psychology, University of Ottawa, Ottawa, Canada.

Frank O. Main, Ph.D., is a professor and department chair at the University of South Dakota, Vermillion, South Dakota.

Harold H. Mosak, Ph.D., is a psychologist and faculty member of the Adler School of Professional Psychology in Chicago, Illinois.

Thomas J. Murphy is a psychologist with the Veterans Administration and a faculty member at the Adler School of Professional Psychology in Chicago, Illinois.

William G. Nicoll is an associate professor at Florida Atlantic University in Boca Raton, Florida.

Kristin R. Pancner, Ph.D., is a psychologist in Fort Wayne, Indiana.

Helene Papanek, M.D., was a therapist based in New York City.*

Floy C. Pepper, M.S., is a consultant in classroom management and Indian education for Oklahoma State University, Stillwater, Oklahoma.

Miriam L. Pew, M.S.W., is a psychotherapist and educator in Edina, Minnesota.

W. L. (Bill) Pew, M.D., was a psychologist in Minneapolis, Minnesota.

Joseph (Yosi) Prinz, Psy.D., is a clinical psychologist and Head of the Parent Education Department, Ministry of Education, Jerusalem, Israel; and is a clinical psychologist, Mental Health Clinic for Children and Adolescents, Ministry of Health, Jerusalem, Israel.

Mildred Roberson, M.A., is a retired teacher.

Robert Sherman, Ed.D., is a professor emeritus at Queens College, New York.

Bernard H. Shulman, M.D., is a psychiatrist in Deerfield, Illinois, and a faculty member at the Adler School of Professional Psychology, Chicago, Illinois.

*No current information available.

Steven Slavik, M.A., is a counselor/therapist in Victoria, British Columbia.

Len Sperry, M.D., Ph.D., is a psychiatrist and professor at the Medical College of Wisconsin, Milwaukee, Wisconsin.

Kathy Stiles, Ph.D., is in private practice in Lewisville, Texas.

Ann H. Tuites was a nationally certified clinical mental health counselor in private practice in Wilmington, Delaware.*

Donald E. Tuites, Ph.D., is a family counselor in Wilmington, Delaware.

Jayne Gardner (Warlick), Ph.D., is in private practice (Family Works Inc.), Arlington, Texas.

John D. West, Ed.D., is a professor at Kent State University, Kent, Ohio.

Michael T. Yura, Ph.D., is Professor in the Department of Counseling, Counseling Psychology, and Rehabilitation at West Virginia University, Morgantown, West Virginia.

John J. Zarski, Ph.D., is Director, Clinic for Child Study and Family Therapy, University of Akron, Akron, Ohio.

*No current information available.

ABOUT THE EDITORS

Jon Carlson, Psy.D. Ed.D. is a Distinguished Professor at Governors State University and psychologist at the Lake Geneva Wellness Clinic. Dr. Carlson was the first doctoral graduate in clinical psychology from the Adler School of Professional Psychology, where he also holds the certificate of psychotherapy. He has served as the editor of both *Individual Psychology: The Journal of Adlerian Theory, Research, and Practice* and *The International Journal of Individual Psychology*. He is the author of 25 books and over 100 professional journal articles. He has received service awards from American Psychological Association, American Counseling Association, International Association of Marriage and Family Counselors, American Board of Professional Psychology, and the North American Society of Adlerian Psychology.

Steve Slavik, has an M. A. from the Adler School of Professional Psychology, Chicago. Currently he is a counselor with an Employee and Family Assistance Program in Port Alberni, British Columbia. Previously, he has worked for other community agencies in British Columbia and has been self-employed in a private practice in counseling and therapy. He has a number of publications in professional journals and is the editor of *The Canadian Journal of Adlerian Psychology.*

He was born in Texas and attended various universities and graduate schools, studying philosophy, literature, mathematics, and oceanography before settling in Canada and discovering Adlerian psychology. He is interested in learning to become more flexible and client-centered in his approach to counseling within the Adlerian framework.